NO PARALLEL

THE WOORAYL SHIRE

1888   1988

To Mariètje en Harry
with love from Riky
Inverloch 20-3-99.

'The direct course which necessity obliged us to pursue led us during 22 days of almost complete starvation, through a scrubby land, and, for exhausted men, a trying country, which, however, for its valuable timber of blue gum and blackbutt has no parallel in the colony.'

Extract from report of Count Paul Strzelecki to Sir George Gipps, Governor of NSW, on his 'Journey from the Yass Plains by the Australian Alps and Gipps Land to Port Phillip', 1840.

NO PARALLEL

THE WOORAYL SHIRE
1888   1988

JOHN MURPHY

THE SHIRE OF WOORAYL

in conjunction with

HARGREEN PUBLISHING COMPANY

First published 1988
Hargreen Publishing Company
(A Division of M. & M.A.H. Nominees Pty Ltd)
144 Chetwynd Street, North Melbourne, Victoria 3051, Australia

National Library of Australia
Cataloguing-in-publication entry

Murphy, John, 1924- .
No parallel, the Woorayl Shire.

Bibliography.
Includes Index.
ISBN 0 949905 37 2 (Hargreen).
ISBN 0 7316 2335 (Shire of Woorayl).
1. Woorayl (Vic.) — History. I.
Woorayl (Vic.) II. Title.

994.5′6

Typeset in 11 on 11½ Goudy Oldstyle by Town & Country Typesetters Pty Ltd,
Abbotsford, Victoria.

Printed by Brown Prior Anderson Pty Ltd,
Burwood, Victoria.

Australia
1788-1988

This publication has been partially funded by the
Australian Bicentennial Authority to celebrate Australia's Bicentenary in 1988.

CONTENTS

PREFACE

The first centenary of Woorayl Shire in 1988 is an appropriate time to record the events which led to its formation and the progress made since its inception. In terms of history one century is not a large segment. Yet the transformation that has taken place in this area of South Gippsland in that time has been phenomenal. When first formed in 1888, Woorayl Shire comprised 240 square miles, or half its present size. The coastal region comprising Inverloch, Tarwin Lower and the Waratah Bay area was not included and yet figures prominently in the early chapters of this book. This was done so that readers might get a balanced view of the overall development of the area.

Within the constraints of time and space I have endeavoured to portray a true and accurate picture of the factors which led to the growth of present community organisations. The people mentioned in this history are representative of the whole — men and women, leaders and led, with their successes and failures, their hopes and disappointments that are the lot of us all. It has not been possible to include the names of every prominent councillor, citizen or family during the course of a century, so it is hoped readers will generalise in forming a mental picture of the society and way of life of our forbears.

Over a lifetime I have spoken to many of the sons and daughters of the original pioneers. Where possible, I have allowed these people to speak for themselves so that their actual words may be recorded for history. I am deeply indebted to the proprietors of *The Great Southern Star, The Leongatha Sun* and *The Leongatha Echo* for their coverage of events. Although minute books of Woorayl Shire and other institutions authenticate events, it was the local newspapers which added the personal touch to the narrative of day-to-day life that makes history. All residents will greatly appreciate the wisdom of former lawmakers in stipulating that copies of newspapers must be filed with the State Library of Victoria. It was only through access to these papers that a comprehensive picture of the formation and development of Woorayl Shire could be obtained.

John Murphy

ACKNOWLEDGEMENTS

Many people have helped in the production of this book, and I wish to express my thanks for their assistance. To members of Woorayl Shire Council who entrusted me with this most important work I am deeply grateful. The sub-committee appointed by Council to assist in its preparation, Mr R.G. Stanley, Shire Secretary, Miss Rosemary Abbey, Librarian, and Councillors B.T. Cusack and Reverend T.G. Williams have been most kind and considerate in allowing me control over selection of subject matter. Councillors E.J. Fisher, J.E. Hoy and H.G. Vagg have been ever-ready to help when occasion demanded. Council staff have given me every assistance with Neil Breeden of the Engineering Staff performing valuable work in the compilation of maps.

To my wife, Kathleen, and fellow members of Woorayl Shire Historical Society, I owe a deep debt of gratitude. Without their unselfish support and encouragement over eighteen months, this work would not have been completed. Mrs Daisy Bacon, O.A., archivist of the society, provided innumerable photographs and information. Mrs Ellen Lyndon read the manuscript in its early stages and made many constructive suggestions. Mr and Mrs Don Clarke, Mr and Mrs Oswald Brewster, Mr and Mrs Don Williams, Mr and Mrs James Haw, Mrs Lyn Skillern, Mrs Audrey Hall, Mrs Margaret Stokes, Mrs Jenny Chitty, Wally Cayzer, Gordon Watson, Stan Roberts, Laurie Trotman, Ron Christoffersen and Rodney Emmerson have all provided invaluable information and assistance. Gordon West and Al Vaughan read parts of the manuscript, and their comments were much appreciated. Alan Box was a great stand-by when any query on military history needed to be researched. Doug Dodd with his wonderful photographic record of Dumbalk, Wilson Coulter of Mardan, Rupert Sage of Ruby, Arthur Ashenden of Dumbalk North, Mr and Mrs H.S. Voake of Inverloch and Mr and Mrs F. Helms of Stony Creek have been most generous in the sharing of information and photographs.

Patrick Morgan from the Gippsland Institute of Advanced Education made valuable suggestions about source material, while the staff of the Royal Historical Society of Victoria Library, the La Trobe Library and the Public Records Office rendered all possible assistance in locating material. All published and unpublished sources of information are listed in the references at the end of the book. The Giles family was most helpful in allowing me access to past issues of *The Great Southern Star*, and finally, I wish to thank Tim Morfesse, my editor, for straightening out some of my convoluted English.

ILLUSTRATIONS

WOORAYL SHIRE BOUNDARIES AND SUB-DIVISIONS

Formed as a result of the severance of the South Riding of the Narracan Shire on 25 May 1888, Woorayl Shire's 240 square miles comprised the upper reaches of the Tarwin Basin. Subsequent alterations included the severance of the South Riding from Alberton Shire and annexation to Woorayl on 11 March 1890 with the Mirboo Riding severed from Traralgon Shire and annexed to Woorayl Shire on 1 May 1891. Portion of West Riding was severed and annexed to Poowong and Jeetho Shire on 30 May 1893. The East Riding was severed and constituted Mirboo Shire on 15 April 1894 with portion of Narracan Shire severed and annexed to Woorayl Shire on 28 December 1894. Portion of Woorayl Shire was severed and annexed to Poowong and Jeetho Shire on 31 May 1895, leaving Woorayl Shire with an area of 475 square miles. Only minor alterations have since been made with the area being 481 square miles, (124,579 ha.) in 1987. Stony Creek township, which is actually on the surveyed site for the town of Dumbalk, is built on the boundary between Woorayl and South Gippsland Shires.

CONVERSIONS

1 mile	1.61 kilometres
1 acre	0.4 hectares
1 foot	0.3 metres
1 yard	0.9 metres
1 chain	20 metres
1 lb	450 grams
1 ton	1.02 tonnes
1 gallon	4.55 litres
£1 (pound)	$2 (as at 1966)
1s (shilling)	10 cents (as at 1966)
1d (penny)	0.83 cents (as at 1966)

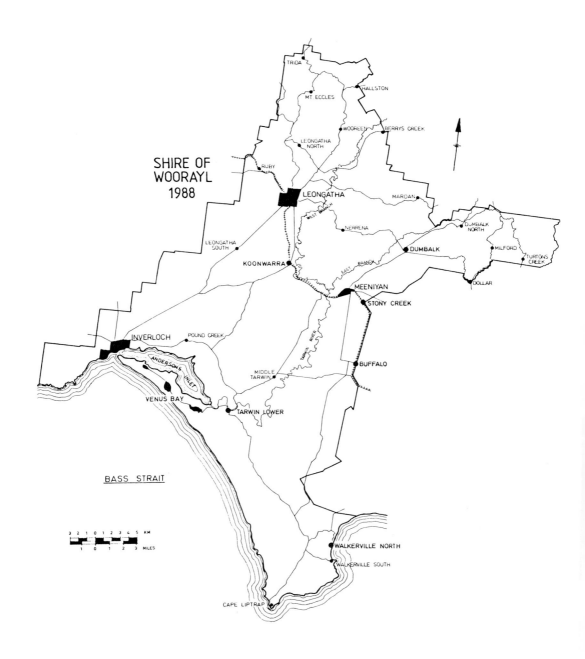

Map of the Shire of Woorayl, 1988.

1. DISCOVERY

Three months after the settlement on the River Yarra by Batman and Fawkner in June 1835, Samuel Anderson arrived from Launceston to settle on the banks of the Bass River at Western Port. Anderson was a thirty-two-year-old Scottish migrant who had spent the previous five years gaining farming and business experience as an employee of the Van Diemen's Land Company in Tasmania. With the assistance of two or three hired workers whom he had persuaded to cross to the mainland with him, Anderson set about clearing and ploughing the land in readiness for the sowing of wheat. He had no need to run cattle, as he and his men were well provided with beef from the cattle that had been set free from the military settlement at Western Port of 1826-8.

Established at Settlement Point (Corinella) under instructions from Governor Darling, as a result of the intrusions of French vessels into the area, this settlement was abandoned fifteen months after formation. The small herd of cattle left behind increased and multiplied and were virtually free for the shooting; being mainly found on the flats bordering the Powlett River to the south of the Bass River. After growing his first crop of wheat successfully and selling it at a good profit, Anderson wrote to his friend and former workmate of the Van Diemen's Land Company, Robert Massie at Circular Head, offering him a share in the new venture on the mainland. He must have described it in glowing terms as Massie soon left his reasonably well paid and secure position with the company and joined up with Anderson on the Bass Station in August 1837.

It was a very lonely life for these two men and their employees; their solitude interrupted only by the occasional visit of a trading vessel. These vessels disembarked working parties to cut wattle bark, later to be picked up and used as back cargo to London where it was in good demand for tanning. Other visitors to Western Port during these years were the occasional sealing vessels from Bass Strait sheltering from one of the frequent storms, or the few escaped convicts who had made their way across the Strait from Tasmania. Samuel Anderson was later joined by his brother, Hugh, who had studied medicine at Kirkcudbright, Scotland, before emigrating to Australia. Samuel himself had studied accountancy whilst his partner, Robert Massie, had been the mechanic

1

in charge of the mill when employed by the Van Diemen's Land Company. A visitor in 1840, Samuel Rawson, admiringly described the farm in his journal.

> Massie and Anderson have about 150 acres under the plough — they sold their wheat at 23s. a bushel, and cleared altogether by the farm upwards of £1400. The climate here being so superior to Sydney that there is seldom a failure in the crop; they keep no sheep or cattle.[1]

It was to this station, after reaching Western Port, that two members of Strzelecki's party came on 12 May 1840. The party had travelled from the Yass Plains, across the Australian Alps where Strzelecki had scaled and named Mount Kosciusko, and then descended the southern slopes to Lake Omeo. Taking advantage of earlier journeys by Angus McMillan, Strzelecki's party made good progress southwards until they encountered heavily timbered country after crossing the La Trobe River. Abandoning their horses and other equipment, the party pursued a direct course westward to Western Port. The dense, damp undergrowth through which they struggled at the rate of two to three miles a day exhausted the six members of the party who were reduced to living on raw koala meat caught by Charlie Tarra, an Aboriginal member of the group.

On arrival at Western Port, Strzelecki and three others stayed at the old military settlement a few miles north of Anderson's Station where some escaped convicts were sheltering in the old huts. These men shared their food with the starving members of the exploring party whilst directing Macarthur and Riley towards Anderson's Station. After recuperating for five days, the explorers prevailed on the convicts to take them by boat to Yallock Station at the head of the bay, and from there they proceeded on foot to Melbourne.

Stimulated by the visit of Strzelecki and the account of his journey through 'Gipps Land', Samuel Anderson decided to embark on some of his own exploratory work. Accompanied by his friend, John Thom, he proceeded in a north-easterly direction towards the present site of Korumburra. Blocked by the same forest through which Strzelecki's party had struggled, the pair veered southwards and soon came upon the Inlet marked on Flinders's chart as 'Shallow Lagoon'. Continuing their journey eastwards along the Inlet, they reached the mouth of a river fifty yards wide and very deep. In his description of the area forwarded to Superintendent La Trobe on his return from the Inlet, Anderson wrote:

> The Inlet, the mouth of which is marked in Flinders' chart, extends parallel with the coast to the South East about twelve miles till it comes within a few miles of Cape Liptrap — the river, which falls into the extreme head of it, was fresh at low water two miles from its mouth, from 50 to 70 yards wide, and evidently very deep, and had the adjoining country been such as I hoped it would prove, would have been a valuable discovery. The view from the neighbouring hills however, was most unattractive — nothing to be seen for more than twenty miles in every direction but extensive heathy plains and hills, and all the low country along the banks of the river covered with impenetrable scrub of tea tree and prickly mimosa — the tops of the ranges seen about 30 miles off appearing as thickly wooded as those which turned us to the North East — altogether I have never seen a more worthless tract of country,

there not being I believe in a span of 5 to 600 square miles grass enough to feed even a single bullock.

As I believe the river I have described to be hitherto unknown to Europeans, I think myself entitled, as the discoverer, to give it a name, and as I know no one more entitled than your Honor to give such a distinction, I, with your permission will call it La Trobe. Trusting that your Honor will excuse my troubling you at such length.

    I have the honor to remain,
        Your Most Obed' — Hble Servant,
        Sam Anderson.[2]

Anderson's suggestion that the river be named La Trobe was not feasible, as Strzelecki had already given that name to one of the rivers in central Gippsland he had discovered several months earlier. Instead it was given a more appropriate name of Aboriginal origin, Tarwin, as it had been for centuries a natural boundary and meeting place between different tribes for bartering purposes. The word 'Tarwin' was derived from the Aboriginal word 'darwhin', meaning 'thirsty', or 'fruit of creeper'.[3] Anderson's journey was a minor feat of exploration, and it is only fitting, therefore, that the Inlet was named after this young Scottish migrant.

Following receipt of Anderson's letter describing his discovery, La Trobe instructed Assistant Surveyor, Mr T.S. Townsend, to make a more detailed inspection of the Inlet. Sailing from Geelong in the Revenue Cutter, *Prince George*, it was found on arrival at the Inlet that the sand bar across its entrance precluded entry, so the cutter anchored for five days outside the bar. Townsend and Captain Moore came through the bar in a row boat oared by several convicts, landed on the beach near the present site of the Inverloch township and thoroughly explored the area around the Inlet during the next five days. Townsend subsequently reported:

> We continued along the northern shore of the Inlet where we found the water so shallow that at low water the men having to drag the boat across the flats nearly 1 mi. before we could get water to float her. About 8 mi. up the river the water becomes fresh . . . After having reached a point about 11 mi. up we were completely stopped by the fallen timber which lay across the bed of the river . . . When returning we walked along the beach in the direction of Seven Cliff Point and searched the country in that neighbourhood for coal. There are many specimens of petrified wood amongst the cliffs and one vein of coal about ½ in thick embedded in the sand stone cliff. This is marked on the map as Specimen Point. On returning to the cutter we encountered three very heavy rollers, the first of which capsized two of the crew. At 10.15 we reached the cutter which had been laying to in 5 fathoms of water distant about half a mile from the breaker. Mr. Woodward the mate of the cutter informed me that in his visit to Western Port he met Mr. Anderson who considered the entrance to the lagoon quite impracticable for vessels and that the Inlet was not more than 10 mi. long.[4]

The prediction that the entrance was 'quite impracticable for vessels' has been only partially borne out by subsequent events. Although dangerous, it has proved to be negotiable with shallow draft vessels. Nevertheless, it has exacted a considerable toll in lives since the first entry of Europeans. The bluff overlooking the Inlet is still known as Townsend's Bluff after this first government surveyor to enter the Inlet.

Further survey work on this section of the Victorian coast was carried out in 1842 by Lieutenant John L. Stokes, RN, in H.M.S. Beagle, who mapped the coast from the northern shore of Western Port to within sixteen miles of Corner Inlet. It was left to the Smythe brothers to make the full and detailed survey of the coast including the creeks, ranges, swamps, lakes and marshes within one day's walk of the seashore. Henry William Hutchinson Smythe had been appointed to the Surveyor General's staff in 1837, and after considerable experience in survey work, he and his brother George Douglas Smythe were commissioned to thoroughly survey the Victorian coastline. This work was done between 1841 and 1856, and many of the names given by these brothers to features along the coast are still in use, such as Eagle's Nest and Petrel Rock on the east side of Cape Paterson, whilst Point Smythe commemorates the detailed work of these two men.[5]

The publication of Strzelecki's report of his journey from the Monaro to Western Port aroused great interest in the new colony. To would-be squatters and established graziers, it appeared that here was land available for occupation, and the sooner it was filled with flocks and herds the better. Squatters from the Monaro followed McMillan's tracks southwards towards Corner Inlet almost immediately. In Melbourne another group formed a new company, The Gippsland Company, with the intention of obtaining a segment of 'Caledonia Australis', the name McMillan had chosen for the new lands that he had discovered on his journeys south of the Monaro. The Gippsland Company chartered the 300 ton ship Singapore, and after searching the coastline from Western Port southwards, found a suitable port at Port Albert in February 1841.

Other vessels soon followed, and by 1842 cattle were being shipped from Port Albert to Tasmania. McMillan is reported to have shipped 900 head of cattle out of the port in the first twelve months of its opening. Some went to New Zealand, but the majority were shipped to Hobart in a small ship, the Water-witch.[6] Odell Raymond, a NSW grazier and magistrate who had taken up a run on the Avon River, in a letter to C.J. Tyers in 1842, stated that:

> there were already in Gippsland about 7,000 head of cattle . . . thirtyfive thousand sheep . . . and about 100 horses. At Port Albert there were 144 free men, 33 bond, 26 free women and 17 children — most of them in service, the remainder living God knows how on the beach, where they have erected huts for themselves waiting they say for the town allotments to be put up for sale.[7]

The lack of a passable land route for livestock between Port Albert and Port Phillip, together with the difficulties of arranging shipping, led to attempts by different parties to proceed along the coast via Massie's and Anderson's Station at Western Port. In August 1842 Odell Raymond left Port Albert for Melbourne with three companions on good horses but had to abandon the horses after fourteen miles of travel owing to the dense scrub. Continuing their journey on foot, they soon ran out of provisions and were forced to subsist on the birds and koalas that the Aboriginal members of their party captured. Fortunately, they were rescued from their plight on the eighteenth day of their journey by Mr

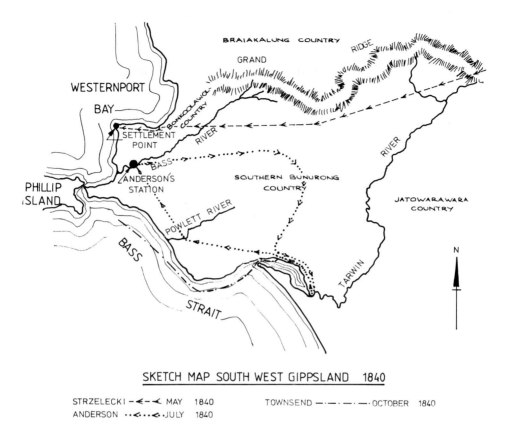

SKETCH MAP SOUTH WEST GIPPSLAND   1840

STRZELECKI -◄- -◄ MAY 1840   TOWNSEND —·—·—·—·OCTOBER 1840
ANDERSON ··◄···◄·JULY 1840

Smythe who was then surveying the coast between Western Port and Anderson's Inlet.[8]

Following an unsuccessful attempt in 1843 to find a route through Central Gippsland to Port Albert, Crown Commissioner C.J. Tyers decided to equip a government party of twelve men under the leadership of Mr G.A. Robinson, chief Protector of Aborigines, to find a suitable land route along the coast to the new port. Included in the party were six native police under Sergeant Major Windridge and three convicts, one to ride ahead on horseback to point out the best track through the scrub, one driving the bullock dray carrying the stores and the other to be the handyman and cook for the party.

The other member of the party, G.H. Haydon, a newly-arrived Englishman, left an interesting account of this journey in his narrative *Five Years in Australia Felix*. After making quite good progress past Western Port, the party arrived at the mouth of the Tarwin on 29 April 1844 where they were held up for several days negotiating a safe crossing for their dray and stock. Haydon observed that:

> To cross the stream logs had to be laid in corduroy fashion on either side of the chosen crossing place . . . some weak animals were hauled across by rope and the

remainder were swum across using as a lead animal a horse hauled by a rope. The dray was floated across on empty casks but in mid stream it sank and attached itself to a sunken tree so that it could not be pulled free until the next day it was floated off on high tide. No stock was lost and in the next remaining five miles we crossed good grass land and on the sandy hills surrounding them saw great quantities of feldspar near the surface and numerous creeks of good water.[9]

After a further three-week journey southwards, their provisions were so depleted that one of their working bullocks had to be killed and eaten. However, a relief party had been sent out from the settlement of Victoria, the official name of the surveyed township adjoining the port, to meet them, and they arrived satisfactorily without any more losses. By this time another party arranged by Edward Hobson was bringing a large mob of cattle down from Western Port to the Port Albert District, following the tracks made by the Government party. Twenty men on horses, together with an adequate supply of oats, left Western Port in charge of several hundred cattle, but not all of the cattle arrived at their destination. Many were drowned in crossing the Tarwin, while others were lost in the scrub. By the time the party eventually reached Port Albert, some two months after setting out, a total of 240 head of cattle and two horses had been lost. Included in this party were William Bennett, his wife Lavinia Hasell Bennett and their five children. Fortunately, Mrs Bennett kept a written record of day-to-day events associated with this early journey to Gippsland. It gives a graphic account of the difficulties encountered in the crossing, and it serves to illustrate the hardships encountered by the pioneering women of that era in accompanying their husbands to the new lands being opened up for settlement.

6.5.1844   We reached within one mile of the Tarwin but not till an hour after dark. The children and I had to walk for some miles, the scrub was so fearfully bad. This was very fatiguing; the wheel track of the dray was our only path. We had the greatest trouble to force our way.

9.5.1844   We moved down to the Tarwin with the intention of crossing. A fence was made to keep the cattle up and at low tide the cattle were brought to the river side, but to each one's disappointment, they refused to go into the water. Mr. Hobson had them forced and drowned 11 without getting one to go over.

10.5.1844   Mr. Hobson and Mr. Reoch went up the river to find another crossing place.

11.5.1844   In the evening the two gentlemen came back. They had found a good place 13 miles further up. We started for the new place but did not get more than three miles as they had to make bridges.

15.5.1844   We got over the river and had to walk nearly up to our knees in water for a mile, over a reedy swamp. The poor children had great trouble in getting along. I had to carry one some of the way and Bennett another all of the way. The gents and men were employed in dragging with ropes the horses and cattle out of the bog. Most of the cattle were got out and all the horses except one which died in the bog.

16.5.1844   Wet the whole day with occasional hail showers and bitter cold. We were obliged to put ourselves on short allowance of bread.

17.5.1844   With much joy bid farewell to the Tarwin. Did not make more than three miles over several cold, wet swamps.

19.5.1844 Wet all day with the wind S.W. We camped early. The cattle knocked up for want of food . . . our bedding quite wet . . . great fears of our flour running out.

21.5.1844 The poor bullocks were more than once thrown down. The drayman got into such passions at times that I thought he would have killed his bullocks. His wife did not escape his rages. He threatened to knock her down as well as the bullocks. A good many of the cattle were left behind, they were too weak to travel.[10]

Undeterred by their hazardous entrance to Gippsland, William and Lavinia Bennett, in partnership with Lavinia's brother, Albert Brodribb, successfully established themselves on a fine property south of Morwell called 'Hasellwood'. The district subsequently became known as 'Hazelwood' which was later changed to 'Churchill'.

Notwithstanding these losses, other parties with stock were soon using the coastal route, although not without difficulty. On his arrival at Victoria (township of Alberton), John Gellion wrote to his partner in Melbourne, Rickards, describing his experiences:

1 Aug 1844 . . . Dear Rickards,
We were just seven weeks on the road from the time we left home, and during the whole journey we suffered great hardships and losses of cattle from the badness of the weather and lack of roads . . . We got on pretty well to the 'Tarwine' or Big River. Here the weather commenced to rain, which continued for eight days without intermission. The following morning we made an attempt to cross the cattle at Hobson's crossing place, but either from the cold water or the width of the water not one of them would look at it.

We then resolved to make a yard and after three days in completing that we got them over, losing three head. All that time the cattle and horses were standing nearly up to their bellies in water and without anything of consequence to eat. We next started on our journey resolving to stop at the first place we could find feed for them, which we were fortunate to come to the next day. Every day the cattle were dropping and by the time we came to within a week of the end of the journey we lost nearly all the old cattle and the young weak ones.
Kind regards to all,
John Gellion.[11]

Gellion's subsequent ventures were not fraught with such difficulties and losses, and he became a successful grazier in the area adjacent to the new port. The district of Gelliondale commemorates this early Gippsland pioneer.

Little mention is made of the Aborigines in the early records of travel along the coastal region. During preceding centuries, the Tarwin River had been the meeting place of the two tribes between whose respective tribal territories it had formed the boundary. The southern Bunurong tribe held the land that stretched from the Tarwin to the Bass River, while the Jatowarawarra clan of the warlike Kurnai tribe ranged from the Tarwin to East Gippsland. Notwithstanding their traditional animosity, these two branches of their respective tribes traded with each other — the Bunurong clan being the axemakers of the region. Their axeheads of diorite were obtained from several small quarries that were found on the western side of the Tarwin at Pound Creek, Ruttle's quarry near Inverloch and at Leongatha South.[12]

Trading between the tribes was interrupted by sporadic raids into each other's

territory, either as a result of long-standing feuds or in search of wives for the
young men. Evidence of this deep-seated animosity is provided by G.H. Haydon
in his description of contact between the two tribes. Included in Haydon's party
were some native police, members of the Port Phillip tribe, and he noted their
reaction after crossing the Tarwin River.

> We suddenly came upon a deserted camp of the aborigines; it contained upwards of a
> hundred huts; observing this, the blacks who were with me, i.e. the Native police,
> worked themselves into a violent passion and commenced throwing their tomahawks
> and knocking down the huts in every direction. They said, this had been a camping
> ground of the Gipps Land natives, who were their enemies.[13]

The wide estuary of the Tarwin with its many swamps and backwaters
provided a natural habitat for all manner of duck and waterfowl that the
Aborigines were skilful at catching. Swimming underwater, they simply pulled
the birds down quickly and silently until their hands were full. During winter,
swan eggs provided a handy source of food — one swan egg being equal to five
hen's eggs. On the edge of the swamps, there was an abundance of animal life
easily caught by the Aborigines: native rats, bandicoots, pademelons, wallabies,
echidnas and possums, while in the late summer there was a great variety of
native fruits such as kangaroo apples, native cherries and raspberries. Between
the mouth of the Tarwin and the Ten Mile Creek, the high sand dunes that
fringe the coast shelter a series of dried-up swamps that provided ideal camp sites
for the Aborigines over the centuries. Evidence of this occupation is provided
by the large number of middens that occur along this strip of low-lying land.
Middens are composed of shells, blackened hearth stones, charcoal and sand
that have accumulated into large mounds over a long period of time — the word
'midden' is derived from the Scandinavian word 'mødding', meaning a rubbish
or manure heap. Such middens have proved a rewarding searching ground for
anthropologists. S.R. Mitchell, author of *Stone-Age Craftsmen*, relates that he
collected some 800 stone chip-knives from a camp site near the Ten Mile Creek
south of the Tarwin.[14] These chip-knives were flakes knapped from larger stones
known as 'cores'. The cores were carried around by Aboriginal women in dilly
bags and a flake taken off whenever a sharp knife was needed for killing or
skinning purposes. Within their own territory, each clan or sub-group, comprising between twenty and thirty people, would have a regular pattern of
movement in order to take advantage of seasonal supplies of food. Only
estimates are available of their total number with William Thomas, former
Protector or Guardian of the Aborigines for more than a quarter of a century,
reckoning the Bunurong at not less than 500.[15]

In winter months they moved inland from the coast away from the cold sea
winds to the less open reaches of the forest where wind did not penetrate.
Evidence of their migration into the hill country at some time is provided by the
occasional finding of axeheads at scattered places up to thirty miles inland, even
as far north as Mount Worth in the Strzelecki Ranges. Here early settlers found
several small stone quarries had been opened up, and many axeheads and
sharpening stones were found in this vicinity. The dense, and in most cases
impenetrable, scrub and undergrowth that covered the hill country of South

Gippsland precluded the Aborigines from travelling through this region, and it is only logical that they frequented the coastal plains area.

The arrival of European settlers destroyed their centuries-old way of life. Decimated by disease, racked by inter-tribal warfare because of being forced off their traditional hunting grounds, the remnants of the Bunurong tribe, estimated by William Thomas as a mere 87 in 1838, gradually drifted into tribal reservations established for them by the Government. In these they were at least provided with food and shelter, albeit not of the kind suited to their constitution. George Dunderdale summed up the effects of this treatment when he stated that:

> It had been the Commissioner's duty to give one blanket annually to each live native, and thus that garment became to him the Queen's livery, and an emblem of civilization; it raised the savage in the scale of humanity, and encouraged him to take the first step in the march of progress. His second step was into the grave. The result of the gift of the blankets was, that the natives who received them ceased to clothe themselves with the skins of the kangaroo, the bear, or possum. The rugs which they had been used to make for themselves would keep out the rain, and in them they could pass the wettest night or day in their mia-mias, warm and dry.
>
> But the blankets we kindly gave them by way of saving our souls were manufactured for the colonial market, and would no more resist the rain than an old clothes-basket. The consequence was that when the weather was cold and wet, the blackfellow and his blanket were also cold and wet, and he began to shiver; inflammation attacked his lungs, and rheumatism his limbs, and he soon went to that land where neither blankets nor rugs are required. Mr. Tyers was of the opinion that more blacks were killed by the blankets than by rum or bullets.[16]

When George Black arrived at the Tarwin in 1852 to take possession of the Tarwin Meadows run, he found only six Aborigines left. They told him that their enemies had killed many of them, but Black does not say to which tribe they belonged — by that time the tribal organisation had broken down. Some had been employed as Native Police by the Government, while others had drifted towards cattle stations such as Anderson's or on to Government reserves.[17] Little physical evidence is left of their centuries of occupation of the area, with the exception of the occasional midden in the sand dunes which is exposed by the wind.

It has been estimated that at the onset of European settlement, there were twenty-six different tribes inhabiting what is now the State of Victoria. Although certain words in their language were common to most of the tribes, nevertheless, each tribe developed its own peculiar dialect. In Gippsland it is estimated that six or seven different dialects were spoken.[18]

By far the greater percentage of Aboriginal place names given to the South Gippsland area are taken from the dialect of the Yarra Yarra and coastal tribes that frequented the Port Phillip area. This vocabulary was compiled by Daniel Bunce, who made a detailed and conscientious record of their dialect and the English translation of their words. In Bunce's translation of the dialect, there are several words with the suffix 'gatha': myrnongatha meaning 'finger'; thirrongatha meaning 'elbow, haunch, thigh, leg'.

Another factor to be considered when translating Aboriginal place names into English is that there was not one word for some singular objects; for example, the Tarwin River as a whole, but rather there was a different name for each bend and landmark along its course.

Prominent Aboriginal place names of the South Gippsland area and their meanings are:

Allambee	to recline, seated, sitting, to sit on a seat, to sojourn, to remain a while
Buln Buln	lyre bird
Drumdlemara	bottle, a flask
Dumbalk	bleak, chilly, frosty, ice, freeze, hail, frozen
Gunyah Gunyah	huts or shelters
Jeetho	depart, detach, send away, dismiss, exit, fly
Jumbunna	colloquy, conference, discourse, to tell, repeat
Kardella	possum, or 'I don't remember' (Queensland word)
Kirrak	kick
Koonwarra	swan
Koorooman	kangaroo, or cattle
Kongwak	catch, to stop
Korumburra	maggot, blowfly
Leongatha	cheek-tooth, dental, relating to the teeth, tooth
Mardan	bewail, cry, weep, doleful, pain, gloomy sullen grief, groan, lament, unhappy, moan, sob, wail
Meeniyan	moon, lunar, relating to the moon
Mirboo	kidneys, reins
Nerrena	name
Tarwin	(from darwhin) thirsty, or fruit of creeper
Wonthaggi	borne, drag, to pull along, get, bring, haul
Woorayl	lyre bird
Wooreen	lips.[19]

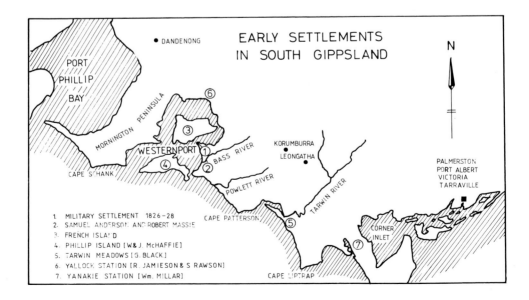

EARLY SETTLEMENTS IN SOUTH GIPPSLAND

1. MILITARY SETTLEMENT 1826–28
2. SAMUEL ANDERSON AND ROBERT MASSIE
3. FRENCH ISLAND
4. PHILLIP ISLAND [W & J. McHAFFIE]
5. TARWIN MEADOWS [G. BLACK]
6. YALLOCK STATION [R. JAMIESON & S RAWSON]
7. YANAKIE STATION [Wm. MILLAR]

2. EXPLORATION

In geological terms, the river flats and sand dunes at the mouth of the Tarwin are of comparatively recent origin. The coast line was originally several miles inland, with sea waters covering most of the land around the inlet and the lower reaches of the Tarwin River. With the passage of centuries, enormous quantities of mud and silt washed off the soft Jurassic mudstones that constituted the Tarwin watershed. These were subsequently deposited at its mouth, forming what is now known as the famous 'Tarwin Meadows'. The original outlet of the river directly into the sea was blocked by the formation of a sandbar. This caused the diversion of the river channel almost ten miles westward to discharge through Anderson's Inlet. Because of its inherent fertility, the Tarwin Meadows area was the most valuable grassland on the route between Western Port and Port Albert, and it was natural that it should be taken up quickly. This was done by George Raff in 1842. His nearest run holder was Alexander Chisholm whose run was centred on the Powlett River and the Cape Paterson area.

This area was later to become known as the 'Wild Cattle Run'; the largest cattle run in South Gippsland. Its name was derived from the progeny of the cattle that had been abandoned by the military settlement on Western Port in 1826. Its area was estimated at 256,000 acres, having a carrying capacity of 640 head of cattle — roughly a beast to 400 acres. The rental for this run amounted to £10 annually plus a levy of threepence per head on the number of cattle being carried. Its boundaries were defined in the *Government Gazette* as 'Bounded on N. by the Strzelecki Range; on W. by Powlett River; on the E. by the Tarwin River; on the S. by the sea or coast line'.[1]

George Raff held the Tarwin Meadows run for a short time, then sold it in 1843 to Edward Hobson, nephew of Captain W. Hobson who surveyed Port Phillip. Hobson's principal intention was to use the Meadows as a resting place for stock en route from Western Port to Port Albert. After two years, the run was transferred in January 1845 to Alexander M. Hunter in partnership with Messrs Bourne and Raff. None of the partners spent much time at the Meadows during their short period of occupancy. Like Hobson, they preferred to use it as a staging camp. The Meadows did not appear to have a great monetary value as it was later claimed that Hunter sold his interest in it for a saddle and bridle![2] In

1852 the run was purchased by Mr George Black for the sum of £60. Its boundaries at that time were from Cape Paterson on the north where it included Chisholm's run, and almost to Cape Liptrap on the south. The improvements erected by Hobson and Hunter during their years of tenure consisted of a small wattle and daub hut of two rooms. Split lengths of tea-tree were used for the walls which were then laced with laths to hold the plaster. Originally roofed with silver tussocks, this was to be Mr Black's home for many years.

George Black was no stranger to farming. Unlike other squatters who were more interested in dealing in stock for a quick profit, Black took the long view and invested his limited capital in permanent improvements so as to increase its subsequent productivity. Arriving in Australia from Scotland in 1840 at the age of twenty-seven, he quickly found employment as manager of Boneo Station at Cape Schanck and subsequently at Pericootta Station on the Murray River.[3] The ten years that he spent managing these stations gave him a good insight into the conditions confronting pastoralists in Australia and no doubt assisted him in developing the Tarwin Meadows Run as a profitable enterprise. His purchase of the run in 1852 was fortuitous as it coincided with the discovery of gold at Ballarat and Bendigo. The subsequent inrush of population inflated the price of all produce, particularly livestock. Cattle and horses, especially draught horses, were in great demand during the 1850s. E.M. Curr, in *Recollections of Squatting in Victoria*, states that the price of a good riding horse in the 1840s exceeded the year's wage that he paid to one of his shepherds. In the gold rush of the 1850s, the price of a draught horse was three times that of a saddle horse. No doubt the sale of stock during these years enabled Black to push ahead with the clearing and improvements to his run.

It was a very lonely life at the Meadows in the 1850s and '60s, particularly during the winter months when water covered vast stretches of the flats and the cattle were often belly deep in the marshes. Being of literary tastes with some training in medicine and law, Black no doubt spent quite some time during these months reading the journals and books that he purchased on his annual trip by bullock dray to Melbourne. In 1853, while resting in a hut on the Bass River on his return journey from Melbourne with stores, he was accosted by six men. Two were armed convicts from Tasmania who had forced the other four, woodcutters, to row them across Bass Strait in a stolen boat. After Black supplied them with food, the convicts emptied the contents of a stolen mail bag on to the floor. In it were gold watches, Tasmanian notes, gold coins and other jewellery. They told him to take what he wished if he would show them the way to Melbourne. Black refused as he was on his way back to the Tarwin, but on the arrival of his bullock team and dray at the hut, he allowed the driver to guide the party back to Melbourne. Shortly afterwards the driver left Black's employment, so possibly he was rewarded with some of the contents of the mail bag. The two convicts were James Dalton and Andrew Kelly, both of whom were apprehended in Melbourne. Extradited to Tasmania, they were hanged for the murder of a policeman.

This encounter with escaped convicts from Tasmania was to be the forerunner of several more during the 1850s and '60s, but fortunately no harm befell Black.[4] One party of convicts arrived in a sixty foot sailing boat that they beached at Venus Bay. Their aim was to replenish their stores at the Meadows and continue their journey elsewhere. Black outwitted them by setting them on their way to Melbourne and then burning the boat, the remains of which were visible on the beach for many decades.

Before the construction of the lighthouse on Wilson's Promontory, shipwrecks were not uncommon on the stretch of beach from Anderson's Inlet to Cape Liptrap. Many of the buildings erected at the Meadows in the early decades were fashioned from timber salvaged from these wrecks. Most of the wrecks occurred during storms, but on one occasion, on 2 April 1853, the *Duke of Wellington* of 387 tons drifted ashore on a calm night with a heavy swell from the west at the Ten Mile Beach. No lives were lost, but the vessel was totally wrecked.[5] Venus Bay was a particularly dangerous stretch of coastline for sailing ships, as there is a very strong pull towards the shore with an incoming tide that sailing ships found hard to overcome in a strong westerly.

Visitors to the Meadows in the early years of settlement were few and far between, but when they did arrive, they were greeted with a warm welcome. As the river presented a formidable barrier to new arrivals, Black kept a small row boat moored on the homestead side so that it might be rowed across to fetch the occasional guest. His friends were instructed to light a fire on the ridge across the river known as 'Black's Bluff', and then to wait on the bank until the boat was rowed across. On Christmas Eve, 1861, John Simpson of Hurdy Gurdy and Westaway Stations at Western Port arrived at the Tarwin to spend Christmas at the Meadows. Not wishing to put Black to the bother of rowing the boat across, he decided to swim his horse over the river. This was a dangerous exercise at low tide as the banks were very muddy and almost impossible to climb unless on corduroy; that is, logs, either split or round, laid in the mud to form a temporary roadway. In crossing, Simpson was drowned and his body washed up the following day. The horse was found with one stirrup missing, and it is possible that Simpson may have been kicked by the horse in its struggle up the muddy bank. Simpson's body was buried on the bank in a line with the tombstone that is now erected adjacent to the roadway.[6]

By 1869 Black's leasehold runs, comprising Tarwin West, the Toluncan Run from the Tarwin to Morgan's Creek, the East Tarwin Run from Venus Bay to Morgan's Creek, the Shallow Inlet Run and the Cape Liptrap Run, amounted to 75,900 acres. As the leases expired, they were not always renewed, as Black found that sometimes the stock losses that he experienced on these runs did not justify the effort and expenditure necessary. The North Tarwin Run was the first to be given up for that reason.

In 1871 Black married Isabella Emily Watson of Walwa Station on the Murray. The homestead that he erected for his new bride at the Meadows included material salvaged from the wrecks on the nearby beaches. The cost and difficulty of bringing any building material from Melbourne at that time was enormous. The Tarwin could be crossed with safety only on two or three days a month at the highest tide to avoid the mud on the banks. The drays were floated across with barrels lashed underneath them. If a wagonette were used, it was lowered into two boats on long planks and then dragged through the water to the opposite bank. Any building material that could be salvaged from wrecks was, therefore, invaluable. Some of the material from the *Duke of Wellington* was used in the construction of the first homestead at the Meadows.

The end of the 1860s marked the beginning of the slow decline of the gold-fields of Ballarat and Bendigo. The quickly won surface gold was exhausted, and mining developed into leads that required considerable capital to exploit. This led to the formation of mining companies, and the self-employed miners of former years became wage-earners of the new firms. Many cast their eyes south-wards to the newly-opened territory of Gippsland where large areas of Crown land were becoming available for selection. Although the more open parts of East Gippsland were quickly taken up by squatters within a decade or two of discovery, the forest area that had been traversed by Strzelecki had remained dormant during the mad rush to the goldfields of the 1850s and 1860s.

Strzelecki had left for England in 1843, three years after his exploratory trip through Gippsland. There he supervised the publishing of his manuscript, *The Physical Description of New South Wales and Van Diemen's Land*. This book was well received in London and brought him to the notice of government and literary circles. The British Government appointed him to act as agent in the administration of the British Relief Association set up to alleviate the distress in Ireland caused by the famine of 1846-48. His work in this field was highly regarded, and coupled with his literary success, he was awarded the Companionship of The Bath by the Queen and elected a Fellow of the Royal Society. At this time, he joined the committee organised by Caroline Chisholm to promote the emigration of young women and girls to the Australian colonies.[7] It is highly probable that some of these young women were to spend part of their lives in the areas discovered by Strzelecki during his short stay in Australia.

In 1873 this Polish explorer, scientist and philanthropist, whose name is perpetuated by the Strzelecki Ranges, died in London. He had outlived his co-discoverer of Gippsland, Angus McMillan, by eight years. McMillan died at Iguana Creek in 1865 as a result of injuries received when his pack horse slipped and rolled on him.[8] Neither of these explorers could have foreseen the extent of the development that was to take place in Gippsland during the next century, and neither of them reaped any great financial reward for their discovery of this fertile province.

In 1862 Surveyor G.T. McDonald, with a party of axemen, cut and surveyed a track through the Gippsland forest from the Lang Lang River, through what is now known as Poowong to Morwell. This track, portion of which is still in use more than a century later, provided an entrance into the South Gippsland hill country for selectors. As in other parts of Australia where mining provided the initial stimulus to development of an area, the same pattern prevailed on a minor scale in South Gippsland. When gold was discovered at Stockyard Creek, later renamed Foster, in 1870, a track was cut from the main Gippsland coach road near Moe through Delburn, Darlimurla, Mirboo North and then to Foster. With the discovery of black coal at Korumburra, a track was opened between that district and Anderson's Inlet by a mining surveyor named Turner in 1873. Three years later, in 1876, Surveyor Whitelaw cut a pack horse track from Foster northwards through the present site of Korumburra towards Poowong. Once these surveyed tracks had been made through the forest, it was only a matter of time before settlers followed in search of good agricultural land.

During the 1850s and 1860s, several Land Acts were passed by the Victorian Government making provision for selection before survey on certain defined

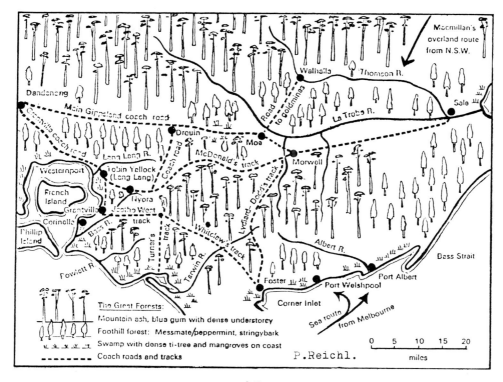

Sketch map of Gippsland, 1870 (from P. Reichl).

Crown lands and also on leasehold land held by squatters when the leases expired. *The Land Act* 1869 authorised selection before survey of areas up to a maximum of 320 acres at a nominal purchase price of £1 per acre, subject to the following conditions:

> The Licensee must not transfer his right, title or interest to any other person. Within a period of three years he must enclose the land with a substantial fence, and cultivate one acre in ten of the total area. A rental of two shillings an acre per year would be payable for the period of the three year lease. At the end of this time the selector could purchase his block by paying the outstanding fourteen shillings per acre outright or by taking a further seven year lease at two shillings per acre per year.

At the time of passing this Act, these conditions seemed liberal enough, but events proved otherwise. Most of the selectors were unable to meet their repayments. The Government was obliged to pass an amending Act in 1878 whereby the period of licence and lease was increased to twenty years, whilst the rent was halved to one shilling per acre per year. Any person over the age of eighteen years was entitled to make a selection provided that he or she could fulfil these conditions — the only exception was that of a married woman living with her spouse. It followed that often families selected several blocks adjacent to each other, and in some cases this proved a wise move. In others it proved to be an impossible task to clear the forest and bring even a portion of the selection into production, so that a vast number of leases were forfeited.

The first selections on land bordering Anderson's Inlet were made in the mid-1870s. The Henderson brothers from Portarlington selected at Pound Creek, Allotments 7 and 8, in August 1876, while around the mouth of the Tarwin, Robert Fisher took up a selection shortly afterwards.[9] Employed as a coach driver with Cobb and Co., Fisher had lived and worked in the Lilydale district, but he was so impressed by the Tarwin area that he persuaded others to follow him to the Inlet. William Cashin and Thomas Lees from Lilydale and Coldstream heeded his advice, and both of these gentlemen played a prominent part in the early development of the community in the Tarwin Lower district. Communication was still by the coast road pioneered in 1844 by the Government party under Mr G.A. Robinson.

The tide of selectors flowing southwards from the goldfields of northern Victoria in the 1860s and the 1870s encroached on the holdings of other squatters besides Black. John D. McHaffie, another Scot, settled on Phillip Island in 1842. He had built up his flocks until by 1868 he was running 25,000 sheep on the island. Selection soon reduced his land to 500 acres, so McHaffie purchased the lease of Yanakie Station in 1869. He appointed his young book-keeper from the island, William Millar, to manage the station for him.

William Millar was born in the parish of Auchterderran in the County of Fife, Scotland, on 21 February 1846. Having received a reasonable education, he was employed as a school teacher and later served with the Black Watch Regiment, a famous Scottish Infantry Regiment of the British Army. Millar developed the Yanakie Station successfully for McHaffie, and subsequently acquired the lease for himself. Regular visitors to the Yanakie Station were members of the Musgrave family whose father, Captain Thomas Musgrave, was keeper of the lighthouse on Wilson's Promontory. Once a fortnight one of the two Musgrave boys, Thomas Malcolm or John Bailey Musgrave, rode in from the lighthouse to pick up mail and mutton.

It was an isolated life for the family at the lighthouse, and the only education the children received was that given by their parents. Captain Musgrave was not unused to isolation, as he had been shipwrecked and marooned on an island off the coast of New Zealand for eighteen months. Before managing the Wilson's Promontory lighthouse, he was in charge of a similar one at Cape Schanck. William Millar must have taken a liking to the Musgrave boys because he offered them a job on the station, even though at the time they were only in their early teens. Thomas Musgrave recalled how he first crossed the Tarwin River at the age of fifteen, whilst in Millar's employ, bringing sheep down from Phillip Island to the Yanakie station.

> We took delivery at the Bass of 4,000 sheep and travelled them to Yanakie by the Coast road. We crossed Bowen Creek, near Kilcunda, on the beach, and had a job to cross on account of quick sands. Our next trouble was crossing Screw Creek. We tackled that at low tide and got half the sheep across, and had to wait for a rise of the tide so that we could swim them on to hard ground. Our next creek to cross was Pound Creek but we succeeded in fording that without a mishap. Our next trouble was the Tarwin, which we crossed without much trouble. We built a yard on the bank of the river, making the river one boundary. Then we filled a flat bottomed

boat with sheep and rowed across in front of the penned sheep. In five minutes the whole 4,000 sheep were in the water following the boat, and landed without a single loss.[10]

Millar shipped his first wool from Yanakie Station in 1873. At that time there was a considerable traffic in sailing vessels along the Victorian coast, and small coastal ships were in the habit of calling into Anderson's Inlet with supplies. Another port of call on the southern coast was Waratah Bay, named after the S.S. *Waratah* that sheltered there after being damaged by a storm en route from Sydney to Melbourne in 1854. On arrival at Melbourne, the Captain, William Bell, made his report to the shipping authorities of the existence of a good, safe anchorage. It then became known as 'Waratah Bay', with Bell Point being named after Captain Bell.

In his management of Yanakie Station, William Millar kept an observant eye out for traces of minerals. In 1874 his name appears on a mining lease taken out on 200 acres on the Yanakie side of Shady Creek, in the parish of Welshpool. The purpose of the lease was the extraction of tin. The following year, he discovered the limestone deposits fronting Waratah Bay. T.M. Musgrave recalled the occasion:

> I accompanied my father and the late Wm Millar when they discovered Marble Cliffs afterwards known as Waratah Bay Lime Kilns. The three outcrops or bluffs as we called them were named Ellrick's Bluff (the first bluff coming from Sandy Point) a distance of nine miles; the next was Millar's and the third was Murray's bluff.[11]

At that time lime was being obtained from deposits situated in the Geelong and Mornington districts where the limestone was burnt in kilns to produce quicklime. Large quantities were required for the rapidly growing metropolis of Melbourne where it was used in mortar for brickwork, for plaster and for white-wash purposes. Millar, who had lived for some time in the Geelong area, was quick to realise the potential of the find and immediately contacted shipping agents Bright Brothers of Melbourne, with a view to developing the deposits commercially. After inspection of the area, Bright Brothers were sufficiently impressed with the value of the discovery that a decision was made to construct kilns adjacent to the deposits. A suitable wharf was planned for the bay along which the quicklime could be railed for loading on to coastal ships to be transported to Melbourne.[12]

Construction of the jetty presented the first problem, as no materials could be landed from the sea until it was completed. The site selected for its construction had several small reefs running through it so that it had to be built with several curves in its total length of 350 yards. The timber adjacent to the bay was not considered to be of sufficient quality to warrant using as piles. Bullock teams were used to haul the logs from the Ten Mile district some seven or eight miles towards Anderson's Inlet. Considerable difficulty was experienced by the bullock drivers in turning their teams in the narrow confines of the beach, but the jetty was eventually completed. The Ten Mile timber proved its durability, as remains of the original piles were still visible almost a century later.

Kilns were constructed to the standard pattern used at other deposits — between forty to sixty foot in height of burnt brick. It is probable that these bricks were brought in by ship as back loading, although some doubt exists as to their origin. The absence of suitable clay deposits nearby would tend to rule out local manufacture. But some bricks have been salvaged from the kilns with the markings 'W B' embossed on them, possibly denoting that they were made at a small kiln at Waratah Bay.[13]

The initial shipment of quicklime arranged by Bright Brothers to be taken by the ship *Blackboy* was completely destroyed by fire, although the ship was saved. The demand for quicklime was quite strong in Melbourne, so further shipments were made successfully with the result that the whole enterprise entered a reasonably long period of profitability. In all six kilns were built, five in close proximity to the main jetty and the sixth a mile further to the south at Bell Point. After being blasted from the face of the cliff, the limestone was carted in horse-drawn drays to the head of the kiln, where it was tipped into the kiln between layers of firewood and 'breeze', a term used for coke. The kilns were kept full and allowed to burn for years, the material slowly sinking at the rate of two feet six inches per night. In the process the fuel entirely disappeared, the burnt limestone or quicklime collecting in the eye of the kiln which was shaped like a wine glass. This was removed with shovels when sufficiently cooled, then stored in jute bags for shipment to the metropolis.[14] At sixteen bags to the ton, a

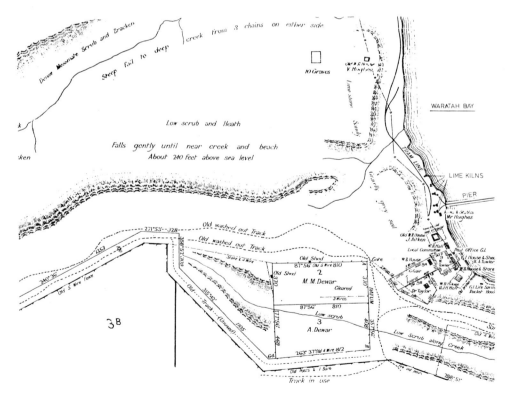

Waratah Bay and lime kilns.

large quantity of bags was needed, and one man was kept in constant employment repairing them after use. A narrow gauge tramline was laid from the head
of the kilns to the Bluff, a distance of approximately 500 yards. This was used for
hauling the limestone, and an extension of this line for upwards of a mile was
used for obtaining firewood for the kilns. Early photographs of the hills surrounding the settlement at the turn of the century show them as completely denuded
of trees as a result of the continual cutting for use as firewood in the kilns.

Bright Brothers operated the kilns successfully for some time and then sold
their interests to the partnership of William Wischer and William Walker, the
latter being Commissioner of Customs at Melbourne in 1880. It is most likely
through Walker's influence that the name of the settlement gradually changed
to Walkerville. Several of the small coastal ships that called for the quicklime
were wrecked in storms in and around the Bay before a lighthouse was established on a rocky headland above Bird Rocks. Originally, this was a kerosene
lantern that was lit daily by an employee of the Department of Ports and
Harbours, yet it was greatly appreciated by mariners and no doubt instrumental
in the saving of many lives. Between seventy and eighty men were employed at
the kilns or at wood cutting during the 1880s and '90s.[15] Their cottages were
clustered at the foot of the cliffs, most made of corrugated iron and appearing to
be built one on top of the other. Although the bulk of the output from the kilns
was shipped to Melbourne, some quicklime as well as limestone was sent to
Lakes Entrance and Sydney.

As the township grew in size, the residents soon felt the need for civic
amenities. The first priority was the provision of a school for the children. A
petition was forwarded to the Education Department on 30 August 1882 listing
ten parents with forty-three children, twenty-five of whom were of school age. A
visit of District Inspector Hepburn to the settlement in March 1883 revealed
that an annual attendance of eighteen was estimated. In the meantime, a room
fourteen foot by twelve foot in one of the cottages belonging to Mr G. Warner
was being used as a classroom. The teacher was Mrs Dewar, wife of James
Dewar, the works manager. This room was leased to the Education Department
at £12 per annum, and Waratah Bay, S.S.2514 officially opened on 23 May 1883
with Margaret Compton as headteacher.[16] Miss Compton and other visitors to
the township travelled on the regular steamship route from Port Melbourne, a ·
trip of from twelve to sixteen hours in coastal vessels *Rubicon*, *Gazelle* or
Maitland, prior to the opening of the railway to Foster in 1891.

Following the erection of a community hall that was used to serve the social,
religious and recreational needs of the residents, the school was transferred to
the new building and was within a stone's throw of the sea. S.S.2514, situated
'on a sideland a few yards from the beach', was reputed to be the closest of any
school to the tide line, as former students recalled that in heavy seas spray
would cover the schoolroom windows. Indeed, almost all the activities of the
township were concentrated in the narrow confines of the area between the
cliffs and the sea. A blacksmith's forge, stables for the horses and storage sheds
for the lime were situated adjacent to the kilns. A general store and a coffee
palace catered for the needs of the local residents and the occasional visitor.
Church services were held regularly in the hall together with dances and other
parties. Like all isolated communities, the people had to provide their own

entertainment. Music for dances usually consisted of a piano, violin and a wallaby-hide drum. For outdoor sport a paddock at the top of the cliff was used for 'that most ancient and most noble of English games — cricket' — and the Waratah Bay Eleven played many a game between teams from Fish Creek and Tarwin Lower. On a hillside just north of the township, a small cemetery was established where burials took place as the occasion arose.

In 1885 Waratah Bay was the setting of the last chapter in the saga of Martin Wiberg, the ship's carpenter who had allegedly absconded with 5,000 gold sovereigns from the steamship *Avoca* in 1877. The sovereigns, the property of the Oriental Bank, were loaded on board at Sydney in a sealed bullion box and placed in the ship's strongroom under the supervision of bank officers. Upon arrival at Williamstown, the bullion box, still taped and sealed, was transferred to the P & O Liner *China*, its destination being Colombo. On reaching its destination, bank officials were astounded when they opened the sealed box and found the sovereigns gone and the box jammed with sawdust. Suspicion fell upon those members of the crew of the *Avoca* who had recently left the ship, amongst whom was a twenty-six-year-old Norwegian, Martin Wiberg, who had been employed as ship's carpenter. On 2 March 1878 Wiberg had selected a block in the Tarwin Valley, eighteen miles up the river from Laycock's selection near Townsend's Bluff.[17] The police, after combing the area for a considerable time, eventually arrested him at a camp on the Powlett River. On raiding his camp they recovered approximately 200 sovereigns that were identified as those from the *Avoca*. It appears that the Oriental Bank had ordered these sovereigns for use in Colombo with a distinctive wreath on them in lieu of St George and the Dragon, as it offended certain religious sects in Ceylon.

After being transferred to Melbourne for further questioning, Wiberg promised to show police the place where the rest of the sovereigns were hidden. He was taken back to the Tarwin by Inspector Secretan, together with Detectives Duncan and Mahony. Proceeding to the spot on the river bank where he stated the gold was hidden, Wiberg managed to elude the police and escaped into the scrub.[18] Upon returning to Melbourne without their prisoner, the police faced a barrage of criticism from the Melbourne press over their conduct of the affair. A reward of £500 was offered for Wiberg's arrest, and three search parties, which included black trackers, were despatched to Gippsland. Frank Dodd recalled the arrival of one search party at his camp on the banks of the Tarwin.

> Early in the year 1879 we were surprised one Sunday morning to see two blackfellows and a white man, who soon made their mission known. They were in search of Wiberg, the ship's carpenter from the SS 'Avoca'. Their intention was to follow the river down and come upon Wiberg from the rear as it was known that he was living about the mouth of the River Tarwin, at Anderson's Inlet.[19]

After intensive searching, the police parties eventually arrested Wiberg in his camp at the spot now known as 'Eagle's Nest'. Following a trial before a judge and jury, Wiberg was found not guilty on the count of larceny, but guilty on the second count of receiving, and was sentenced to five years gaol with hard labour. After serving out his sentence, Wiberg returned to his wife who had been staying with relations at Waratah Bay. There are many accounts of his subsequent disappearance from the Bay, but the most reliable appeared as a letter in *The Great Southern Star* of 4 June 1897, written by an eye-witness, James Dewar Junior, whose father was works manager of the lime kilns.

Martin Wiberg left here in a small boat 10 ft × 8 ft — a thing that I could lift single-handed — to cross from Waratah township to the Glennie Island, a distance of 15 to 16 miles, when it was blowing a gale from the south west, and, to make it worse, he was under the influence of liquor. Several of the inhabitants tried to persuade him that he was going to his death but he was a very determined man, and more so when anybody tried to point out that he was not in a fit state to undertake the task before him. So he started and we watched him till he got perhaps a mile out, where the sea was much more broken; he was then sitting very low in the boat and we could only catch occasional glimpses of her as she rose and fell with the waves. After a short while we could not make out which was the boat and which was the broken water, so we had to give it up and await further developments. Some time later the dinghy was picked up on Yanakie beach, also the oars, his coat and hat and several other small things, but Martin Wiberg was never seen again. Mr. J. Brown joined Matthew Olsen in the yacht on the ninth day and cruised about the bay for two or three days in the hope of picking up the body, but without success. Under the circumstances I think that I am justified in stating and believing that Martin Wiberg is dead, although some believe that he got on board some steamer and got away. That, to my mind, is out of the question, because if he had got in the fairway of the coasting or intercolonial boats his dinghy would have drifted outside Wilson's Promontory, and not on to Yanakie Beach. I maintain that Martin Wiberg was drowned in Waratah Bay, knowing what I do regarding small boats in a seaway and seeing what I saw on the day of his departure for the Glennie Island. Yours faithfully,
Jas Dewar, Junr.
Waratah Bay. May 20 1897.[20]

Above: Lardner's survey camp, Leongatha, 1888, below the railway bridge (from Woorayl Shire Historical Society).

Left: Tree felling, Dumbalk, c. 1890 (from D. Dodd).

3. SELECTION

In his efforts to get the Waratah Bay lime deposits into production, William Millar made several trips to Melbourne from Yanakie Station. Prior to 1876, Millar's route took him along the coast road past the Meadows and the Inlet. With the opening of Surveyor Whitelaw's track in 1876, Millar used this new route on his journeys to Melbourne. The new track ran from Stockyard Creek through Jeetho West to Grantville on Western Port. On these journeys Millar deviated at times in search of good agricultural land or mineral bearing deposits. Twenty-five miles from Stockyard Creek and six miles north of the Tarwin River, Millar found an area of rich, volcanic, red soil that impressed him greatly. It bore a striking resemblance in type and structure to soils around Tower Hill in the Western District. Realising that it would soon be snapped up by other selectors, Millar obtained the services of a surveyor as quickly as possible so that he might register his claim.

The whole process of selection and settlement was dependant on surveying teams that were active throughout Gippsland in these decades. During the period 1850-1890, practically the whole of Victoria was surveyed and large portions of it released for settlement under the different Land Acts that were passed by the Victorian Parliament. All of these Acts needed the skills and fortitude of surveying teams to map and sub-divide these areas into allotments of either 640 acres in the drier parts of the State or of 320 acres in higher rainfall areas such as Gippsland. It called for considerable skill on the part of the surveyors in planning for water rights to each block, access roads and provision for townships where necessary.

The actual surveying work was done by parties of from eight to twelve men. These were usually made up of six to eight competent axemen to clear a visible sight line between reference points, one or two chain men for measuring distances, the head surveyor and his assistant. Creeks and rivers were traced to their source and every bend shown on the surveyor's charts. Mountain ranges, often clothed to the summit with dense timber, had to be crossed. In low-lying areas such as the Koo-Wee-Rup swamp and the Tarwin River flats, survey parties worked knee deep in water during much of the year. In summertime many areas were teeming with snakes. But the survey parties continued with their work of measuring and mapping blocks for the army of land-hungry selectors anxious to obtain a foothold in the new areas.

Land was made available for selection after being surveyed by registered government surveyors, such as John T. Lardner who was responsible for the survey of large areas of Central and South Gippsland. Born in County Galway, Ireland, in 1839, Lardner went to New Zealand in 1863, and after three years of surveying in that dominion, he crossed to Victoria in 1866 and joined the Lands Department. In 1874 he surveyed 11,000 acres of the Koo-Wee-Rup swamp, and subsequently laid out the townships between Pakenham and Warragul. In 1878, when William Millar found top quality land adjacent to Whitelaw's Track, Lardner was busy on the Central Gippsland Line, so Millar obtained the services of another authorised surveyor, Mr A.H. Burbank.

William Millar pegged his block on Whitelaw's Track early in 1878 and succeeded in getting Mr Burbank on to the area shortly afterwards. It was in uncharted territory, so Burbank had to make his own reference points from the sun and stars. He filed the following report to his superiors:

> Survey Camp,
> Leongatha,
> 28 May 1878.

> M. Callanan,
> District Surveyor,
> Melbourne.

> Sir . . . I have the honor to forward you plan, copy of field notes and computation sheet of survey made for Wm Millar in the Parish of (unnamed.) I have based the work on a meridian line taken by the sun (which I tested.) I was unable to see the stars on account of the cloudy sky — otherwise I would have checked it by them. I am camped on Gwyther's Creek about six miles North West from the Tarwin River on Whitelaw's pack track — 28 miles from Stockyard Creek from where all stores must come. I have the honor to be Sir — Your most obedient servant,

> A.H. Burbank,
> Authorised Surveyor.[1]

Word of the discovery of new areas of good land soon spread, and Burbank surveyed fifteen blocks that had been pegged out by other selectors before being called away elsewhere. The law at that time stated that whoever put their pegs in first got the land, but it could not be pegged before 9 a.m. or after 4 p.m. It meant that whenever a new area of suitable land was discovered, there was keen competition for blocks. The two Musgrave brothers, John and Thomas, aged twenty and eighteen respectively, who were working for Millar at the time on Yanakie Station, pegged out blocks adjoining Millar's. According to Thomas Musgrave, they obtained horses from Mr Millar and rode by way of the coast road, with the intention of crossing the Tarwin in a boat. This had to be done at high tide.

> But alas, when we arrived at the crossing the tide was out, and there was nothing for it but to walk, to make sure of getting to our country before another party who we knew were making for the same country by way of Whitelaw's track from Foster. These gentlemen were the late Mr. Jas. Gwyther and the late Mr. R. Stephenson.

However, we arrived at our destination first, and our rivals arrived some hours after we had got our pegs in. But we all joined as neighbours and explored the several areas of our choice and parted good friends, our neighbours going back to Foster to join the steamboat for Melbourne (via Port Albert).[2]

The applications by Millar, Musgrave and others were heard and considered by the Land Board at Cranbourne on 18 July 1878 and granted subject to the provision of roads. Burbank made no provision for roads between these new selections other than allowing access to Whitelaw's Track. No doubt he was waiting until the main survey party under J.T. Lardner could complete the official plotting of the area. It was not until five years later that Lardner arrived at that particular spot. In a letter to Mr Callanan, Surveyor General, dated 23 August 1883 he stated:

I enclose plan of an allotment applied for by Jane Nation, parish of Leongatha. The survey was partly made by Mr. Burbank before he left the district but he furnished no plan. I have completed the survey in connection with road work in the locality and I suppose the survey fees can now be placed to revenue and the application proceeded with.

John Lardner.[3]

The survey parties provided gainful employment for young men who were waiting on a block to be allocated. It was not easy work as George Cross, who later selected at Leongatha South, testified:

In 1884 I joined a gang of scrub-cutters, as the land was all closed against selection till it had been surveyed into blocks. I put in two years with the surveyors with this work. Many a time we went for a whole day without water. Then we would cut down a wattle tree, cut it into lengths and stand it up on end, and catch the sap to get a drink. We were obliged to get all our provisions from Mirboo; a distance of about 25 miles, and pack horses were used as a means of conveyance. On one occasion I set out for Mirboo with seven pack horses for provisions. I arrived there and it started to rain, and we had what is now known as one of the old "Gippsland floods" of early days. As soon as the rain ceased, I started on my return journey with the loaded horses — 2 cwt. on each horse. When I arrived at the Tarwin River my mate said to me, "We will have to turn back; the river is too high." I said, "No; the men in the camp will be hungry. We must swim through."
He said he could not swim, so I told him if he stuck to his horse it would take him over safely. After a while he agreed to face it, and we lined the horses up in single file, and coupled each horse's head to the tail of the one in front of him. I took the leading horse and we set out. We had to swim three quarters of a mile and then landed safely on the other side. My mate had high top boots on, and they filled with water. He was terribly cold and could not do anything for himself. I tried to get his boots off and, with great difficulty, managed it. I then got a fire going and prepared a meal, and attended to the horses. We rested for an hour, then travelled on and reached the camp (now Wilson's property), about 9 p.m. having left at 5 a.m.[4]

Burbank listed the spot where he camped as Gwyther's Creek — a name confirmed by Lardner in his final official plan. The fact that the district was officially unnamed was the least of the troubles for the dozen new settlers clustered around the creek. Once a fortnight one or two settlers went to Foster with a pack horse, a trip of twenty-five miles that took from early morning until late in the evening. If no horse was available, they walked to this small mining township and persuaded the storekeeper to pack out two horse loads of 'tucker', including one horse load of beef. The storekeeper would not come unless there was an order for two horse loads. The meat was shared out amongst different settlers who usually boiled it and ate it cold for the next week or two. This monotonous diet was relieved by the blackfish that abounded in the streams. Easily caught and weighing up to four pounds, these fish were a great standby for the first settlers in the forest. If camped near a stream, the settler would cast a line before breakfast and catch sufficient for the day in a couple of minutes. Some spent an hour or so on a Saturday evening, caught enough for the week, then cured and smoked them.

Camped on their blocks, the settlers did not have to spend time travelling to work — the work surrounded them. Tents were reasonably satisfactory in the summer months but damp and cold in the long winter months. The first task was the cutting of a section of the forest and scrub so that a hut could be built in the cleared area that would be safe from falling limbs. The Musgrave boys set to work.

> We managed to cut about five acres which we thought was quite a stroke of work. We completed it about Christmas time, then our next job was to go at splitting posts and shingles for a hut — a work of art indeed for novices to tackle. However, we accomplished that feat very creditably, splitting about 200 five-foot palings and enough shingles to roof a hut 10ft × 15 ft. We dug a hole and buried our camping outfit, building timber, tools etc., covered the lot with about a foot of earth, then took our departure for Yanakie station where we put in about six weeks waiting for the burning-off of the cut scrub. The burning season was then from the 1st March (although I might say that very few waited for the lawful date) so the first good day we let it go, together with several other new selectors who pegged out land at the same time as we did.[5]

On the southern side of Millar's and the Musgraves' selections, Jacob Thomas selected two blocks of fertile red soil that he named 'Lyre Bird Mound'. Thomas, a mining engineer from Ballarat, brought considerable capital with him to Gippsland. This enabled him to employ men to assist him in the development of his property. At the end of the first year of occupation, Millar had cleared 100 acres, Thomas 50, and Gwyther, the Musgrave brothers and Stephenson 20 acres each. The land to the north-west of Millar's was selected under a non-residential clause by James, Walter and Jane Nation of Melbourne. James Nation listed his occupation as 'gentleman', resident at Kew, while his brother, Walter, is listed as a soap and candle manufacturer of Melbourne with Jane Nation listed as 'gentlewoman'. Having access to other sources of income, they were able to employ gangs of scrub cutters to speedily develop their property that later became known as 'Springdale'.

Many of these scrub cutters were ex-sailors who soon developed the necessary skills required for bush work. Among Nation's cutters was Oscar Tamlander, a native of Finland, who blended in well with the pioneering Australians. Thomas Musgrave recalled:

> Oscar Tamlander was then among Mr. Nation's employees, and often with a party of

other sailors of foreign nationality, would visit us on a Sunday, that being the only day in the week work was suspended. Their wages were 25 shillings a week and found, and these sailor lads were the happiest lot of chaps I ever met. We quite enjoyed a visit from them especially Oscar; he was the most enlightened having had about a year's experience with Australian farmers, and he was the very life of the party.[6]

There were few women on these early selections. Mrs Mary Gwyther from Dunkeld was there only three years when she died in 1887. Her husband, anxious to have her buried at Dunkeld, sent word to the Thomas family on Lyre Bird Mound asking if they would assist in taking Mary's remains to San Remo to catch the steam ship en route to Williamstown. As Mr W.C. Thomas described:

When the body arrived it was encased in the rough timber of the bush, which the husband had made after laying his wife out, as there were no other women out there. All through that night I walked, with one hand holding the horse and the other the lamp, over plains, through scrub and ti-tree flats. Hour after hour passed until the 35 miles had been traversed, and we arrived at San Remo just in time to see the steamer move off. The husband had followed behind during that dreary night. The constable at San Remo was in a difficulty; he said we had no right to move a body without a doctor's certificate. Of course, we had acted in ignorance. The husband was anxious to have her buried in the family grave at Dunkeld, but after numerous telegrams to the coroner at Dandenong permission was given for burial at San Remo. One of the

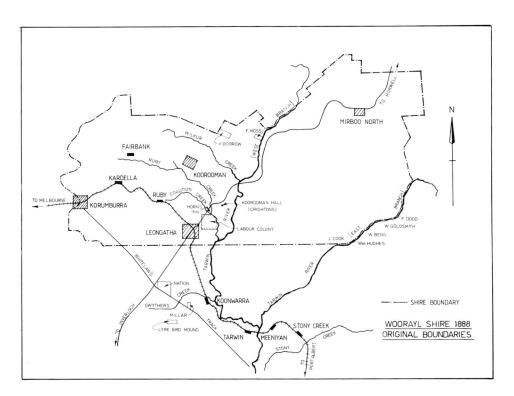

most affecting sights was the school children gathered round that lonely grave. Evidently the school mistress had passed through trouble herself, and she had let the children gather the wild flowers, and at a signal they threw them into the open grave and almost filled it.[7]

Periodically, the Thomas family took a bullock wagon from Lyre Bird Mound to San Remo for stores or paid a carrier to bring them in at the rate of £50 per ton cartage. If the weather broke and the wagons became bogged, the non-perishable goods were covered with bark and left on the side of the track till the next summer. With the arrival of the Thomas family at Lyre Bird Mound, it became the centre for gatherings on a Sunday when Mr Thomas conducted a religious service that was often attended by his fellow selectors. As settlement increased, Mrs Thomas was keen to see a church started in the district. Mr Thomas donated the necessary site, and with the enthusiasm of fellow adherents of the Wesleyan congregation, arrangements were made for a church to be built on Lyre Bird Mound. This was to be the first public structure erected to serve the new community growing up around Gwyther's Creek.

At the same time as new settlers were pushing into the forested area of South Gippsland from the south via Whitelaw's Track, two other streams were coming in from the north. With the completion of the central Gippsland railway in 1877, eager land seekers were penetrating southwards into the great forest that clothed the Strzelecki Ranges. A party under the charge of Surveyor Liddiard cut a track from Moe to Foster in 1872 that joined up with the one from Morwell at Delburn. This junction of the tracks in the forest was the starting point for many of the selectors moving down the valley of the Tarwin into the rich Mirboo, Dumbalk and Koorooman districts. To assist these men in their search for suitable blocks, guides were necessary to take them through the uncharted forest. Most notable of these was John Gallagher who set up camp at Mirboo North. He possessed an extraordinary skill in finding his way through the bush and returning to his starting point. For almost a decade, 1877 to 1887, he made a good living showing people the land available for selection. He charged £10 for his 'guided tours' — the full amount if a block was selected or £1 a day otherwise. During this time, upwards of two hundred selectors were guided through the forest by this unusual bushman.[8]

Two of the first selectors in the Tarwin Valley were Peter Carmichael and Frank Dodd. In December 1877 Carmichael inspected the area and was so impressed with the quality of the chocolate soil that he took a box full of it back with him to his home town in the Western District as evidence of its fertility. There it aroused considerable interest and led to others trying their luck in this newly-discovered portion of Victoria. Frank Dodd made the journey from Melbourne in Christmas week of 1877, accompanied by his nine-year-old son and a companion, George Goldsmith. One of the main reasons Frank Dodd decided to come to South Gippsland was that he and his wife had already lost four children through the heat and privation of living conditions in the northern part of the State. After walking the last ten miles down the Tarwin Valley, Dodd selected his block adjacent to the river, approximately three miles north of the present township of Dumbalk. Like the other settlers on Liddiard's and Whitelaw's Tracks, the only tools available to Dodd for land clearing and building purposes were those that could be carried or brought in by pack horse. These comprised axes, mauls and wedges, crosscut saws, crowbars, shovels and the Trewhella or pump jack used for manoeuvring logs into position for burning.

Huts were usually built with round timber, but a few settlers preferred sawn framing to obtain a better quality home. A good splitting tree was selected, felled with axe and crosscut saw and then sawn into suitable billets — ten to twelve foot long for studs, longer for joists. A pit six foot long, four foot wide and seven foot deep was then dug adjacent to the fallen tree, one of the billets was manoeuvred over the top of the pit with jacks and levers and the process of pit sawing began. One man stood on top of the log drawing the long pit saw upwards on a marked line, while another in the pit pulled the saw on the downward cut — and quickly became covered with sawdust. It was a long, slow process, but there was no alternative if the huge logs were to be turned into suitable lengths of sawn scantling. Initially, roofing material was of shingles; that is, short lengths of split palings thirty inches by four inches.

These shingles were used for many years until, with improvement in transport and the financial position of the settler, they were replaced by galvanised, corrugated iron. In many cases the iron was simply nailed over the shingles. Such a roof improved the insulation properties of the house, being much warmer in winter and cooler during the summer. Owing to the high cost of transport, the only materials purchased were the nails, windows and (if finances permitted) softwood for doors. For cladding purposes, pit-sawn weatherboards were sometimes used, but many homes were clad with split slabs or palings nailed on to the framework. Most first homes were of two rooms with a gabled roof and a skillion attached to the rear. Some of these homes, with modifications, can still be seen almost a century later in and about South Gippsland. Frank Dodd's first home on the Tarwin measured sixteen foot by thirty-two foot and cost over £100. Others who selected along the valley of the Tarwin in the summer of 1878 with Frank Dodd and Carmichael were the brothers Goldsmith, Hughes and Sherar, and Messrs Jagoe and Lander. Within a comparatively short time, the blocks along the river were taken up, and contact was made with Anderson's Inlet within a year or so of first selection. At the same time as settlement was taking place along the Tarwin and on Whitelaw's Track, other settlers were struggling up over the forested hills from the township of Waterloo (Yarragon) on the Central Gippsland line. Two of the first settlers to come from this direction were Isaac Griggs and Tom Hall, Senior. A letter from a member of the Hall family stated:

> When Mr. Hall and Mr. Griggs set out from Waterloo to find their blocks . . . they had no idea where they were and had to return. They obtained the services of Mr. Wingil More, a one-armed and powerful man who had worked with surveyors, to show them where their blocks were, which he did. Mr. John O'Bryan also had to return to seek help from the original surveyors to discover his selection.[9]

As there was no grass for the horses, they were taken back to the starting point and the settler then made the return journey on foot. Carl Hamann, who selected at Fairbank in 1881 at the age of eighteen, carried a leg of beef weighing 70 lbs from Poowong to his selection along a bridle track — a distance of fifteen

Paling home at Buffalo, 1880s. Left to right: Mrs Janet Jones, Joe Murdoch and Mr R. Jones. In the enclosure are young wild pigs (from D. Mackie).

Mardan pioneer Sandy McKinnon with his sons Angus, James, Thomas, Alexander, John, Donald and Duncan, c. 1888 (from D. Bacon).

miles. On another occasion, in order to keep his axes in perfect order, he carried a grindstone the same distance. Kerosene was a precious commodity in selectors' camps, and Hamann brought back a four gallon tin to his camp on foot when required.[10] When George Cross finally got his selection at Leongatha South after his two years with the surveyors, his only means of transport was 'shank's pony'. He carried a bag of sugar (70 lbs) from Inverloch, seven miles to his selection, and the following day shouldered a bag of flour (100 lbs) the same distance.[11]

Until the opening of the Great Southern Railway line in 1891, the immense quantities of timber prevalent on all the selections was of no monetary value to the settlers. Rather, it was looked upon as a hindrance to progress, and the sooner it was cut and burnt, the quicker the land could be sown to grass. The splitting of logs for sale as barrel staves, palings for fences and sawn scantling for building purposes had to wait until rail transport was available before any financial return could be derived from this vast resource of first-class timber.

Selectors with only limited capital faced an almost insuperable task. Working on their own, clearing their land was a slow, laborious task that produced no immediate cash return. Some men brought capital with them into the forest, and these fortunate people employed contractors to fell the timber, cut scrub and sometimes burn and pick up the remaining limbs. Good axemen were common in this era, and many techniques were used to lessen the amount of work entailed in clearing. Many adopted the practice of felling all trees up to two foot in diameter and ringbarking the rest. The practice of using spring-boards in felling large trees was introduced to lessen the work of cutting through the buttresses at the base.

Another practice was called 'notching' or felling 'drives'. This method entailed cutting the trees half way through on the lower side all the way up the hill, and then when the wind was in the right direction, felling large trees at the top of the hill would start the 'drive', and the whole section fell like a pack of cards. A good method, but dangerous if the wind was choppy. In 1883 two brothers, Burnet and Joe Watt, had a fall ready to drive when the wind changed and brought it back on them. They crouched behind a log for a time, and then, thinking the danger had passed, Burnet put his head up to have a look and was struck by a falling spar and killed instantly. Joe Watt was badly injured but lived for another three years before dying of his injuries.[12]

Burnet and Joe Watt were two of eight sons of Colin Arrott Watt who migrated from Scotland in 1851 and founded a flour mill at Malmsbury, Victoria. In 1882 Mr Watt, with his large family, was able to select over 1,000 acres of the highly fertile land in the Koorooman Parish. His homestead, Arrott, on Allotment 39, was one of the first homes to be build in the area. At the time of the accident involving his two sons, the family home was still at Malmsbury. Both of the boys were carried to Mirboo North, then by coach and train back to Malmsbury.

Watt's nearest neighbour, Thomas Crighton, selected his block at the same time, the summer of 1882-83, and for the first two years lived in a tent on his selection. After clearing a section of the forest, Crighton managed to erect a log hut, and rather than roof it with shingles as was commonly done, he arranged for roofing iron to be brought to Mirboo North and then on pack horse to his selection at Koorooman. The tracks were practically non-existent, so that for the last four miles, Crighton, with the assistance of two men, carried the roofing iron, weighing somewhere near a ton, on their backs to the selection.[13]

The selections around the present township of Leongatha were taken up during 1882-83 by pioneers Watt, Crighton, Allison, Begg, Bruce, Groves, Myers, Fortescue, Groom, Leach, Shingler, Eccles, Horn, Bellingham, Russell and Johnson. As Peter Johnson recalled:

> We came in from Mirboo with a land selector's guide named Bob Stewart — a good bushman who knew the inhabited country to the westward. In one of his explorations he found good country on Wild Dog Creek and offered to show me where it was for the usual fee of five pounds per block. We were two days in reaching it through dense scrub and a towering forest of blackbutt, bluegum, blackwood, white swamp gum and messmate. Not even a pack track. We scrambled over logs, ridges and gullies with only a compass and a bushman's marvellous sense of locality. We returned to the settlement at Mirboo at the end of 5-6 days, our clothes in tatters but the pegs were in on our block. I was soon followed by other pioneers whom Stewart led singly or in groups.[14]

The forest was so dense in the Koorooman area that even at midday there was only twilight at ground level. Another settler, James Black, who was also guided in by Bob Stewart, said that the forest floor was so dense 'that only a man and a wallaby could get through'.[15] Section 19 of *The Land Act* 1869 stated that selectors were to identify their allotment by placing at each corner of the land applied for

> a conspicuous post or cairn of stones between the hours of 9 o'clock in the morning and 4 o'clock in the afternoon, with a notice affixed in writing on each post or cairn of stones, giving his name and address, the approximate extent of the land applied for, and that he is an applicant for the land.[16]

On the naturally fertile soils of the Koorooman area, the dominant species of trees were the blue gum (E. globulus) and blackbutt (E. regnans), ranging in height to 300 foot. The blackbutt tended to favour the creek and river flats with the blue gum on the higher land. Blackwood was plentiful in this forest with many specimens well over 100 foot. The main understorey was of musk, hazel, blanket wood, lomatia or wild holly, Christmas bush, silver wattle, jeal wood, austral mulberry, myrtle and pittosporum ranging up to sixty foot in height with ferns and grasses making up the ground layer. Where the soil was slightly less fertile, the blue gum and blackbutt were replaced by sapling scrub; that is, gum saplings ranging up to three foot in diameter and from 60 to 120 foot in height.

Even this scrub varied enormously. On the ridges it consisted mainly of hazels, wattles and blackwoods, while along the gullies and creeks, these species were mixed with large numbers of tree ferns, some of which were seventy foot in height and fifteen foot in circumference at three foot from the ground. The lighter grey soils, such as those found in the hills of Nerrena between the west and the east branch of the Tarwin, supported a predominantly messmate forest (E. obliqua) and peppermint (E. radiata), with an understorey of melaleucas, hazel, blanket wood, dogwood, prickly mimosa and supplejack.

The Johnson brothers, Peter and William, took up two blocks of roughly 320 acres each on the Coalition Creek (Blocks 7 and 8, Parish of Koorooman), comprising highly fertile red basalt soil with grey soil flats adjoining the creek. They spent the first two summers camped in tents while cutting a section of the forest, returning to their home at Daylesford for the winter months. Two years after selection they took up residence permanently.

> We arrived here on 2 March, 1884 having travelled from Daylesford by horse and dray. After getting all our possessions in, the first thing was to build a house. Two men and a twelve-year-old boy split the timber and built a four roomed house, each room twelve by twelve feet with eight foot walls, in three weeks. We arrived on the 6th of March and went into the new house on the 1st of April. There were two families in the district at that time, viz. J.N. Horn and Harry Leach who came in 1883. Harry Leach was a butcher and delivered meat once a week.[17]

Their neighbour, Johann Nicholas Horn, originally came from Schleswig Holstein, a province between Denmark and Germany. His selection was predominantly composed of greysoil flat of an extremely fertile nature but covered with dense timber and huge tree ferns owing to its swampy nature. Horn built his first humble dwelling adjacent to the Coalition Creek, partly, as he informed his children, so that 'he would not have far to go to catch his breakfast of blackfish'.[18] Horn had served as an ambulance man or stretcher bearer during the Franco-Prussian War and was quite competent at first aid. As accidents were not infrequent, this knowledge proved invaluable, as the nearest doctor was forty miles away through dense forest at Drouin.

With the arrival of the railway at Mirboo North in 1886, the settlers in the Koorooman district arranged for a working-bee to build a bridge over the Tarwin. Peter Johnson and his neighbour, Harry Begg, were given the task of felling the spars over the river — two from one side and one from the other to be used as main bearers. So expert were they at this task that none of the three trees had to be moved from where it fell. The decking was pegged down with wooden pegs as iron spikes were not available. The whole bridge was built in one day, and it then could be used for bullock and horse teams to bring supplies from Mirboo North.

Scrub cutting was done during the winter, spring and early summer months. A good burn during late summer would enable grass seed or other crops to be sown. Initially, there was not a great danger of fire getting away as the sections cut were relatively small and isolated from each other by the uncut, standing forest. 'Picking up' after the first fire was a heavy, laborious task calling for a great reserve of strength and stamina on the part of the settler. When accomplished, small areas adjacent to the homestead were planted with potatoes, vegetables, maize and almost invariably an orchard, so that the lack of fruit could be overcome within a few years.

Grass seed was broadcast by hand immediately after the burn in the autumn, as the residue of ashes provided an ideal seed bed rich in potash that resulted in prolific growth during the following spring. If sufficient stock was not available to keep the new grass reasonably short during the spring months, the new pasture could be attacked by caterpillars when the grass ran up to seed in December.

As soon as a limited amount of grass became available for stock, settlers commenced dairying in a small way. Sheds were roughly made from round saplings with slab floors. Cows were sometimes milked out in the yard if of a quiet temperament but were usually bailed up for this twice daily routine. The milk was set in large flat dishes for up to two days to allow the cream to set. This was then skimmed off and made into butter. After being taken by pack horse to Mirboo North to be railed to Melbourne, it realised between fourpence and sixpence per pound, depending on the market. Peter Johnson's neighbour, William Begg on Rubybank, sent his daughter Annie to Melbourne to learn the techniques of cheese-making. Cheese was also packed to Mirboo North and then railed to Melbourne where it realised sixpence per pound.

As there was no export market for butter before the introduction of refrigeration, the Melbourne market was glutted in the spring and early summer months with minimal returns to the producer. This led to some settlers heavily salting their butter and placing it in small barrels, or firkins, in which it would be kept for some months and perhaps realise a better price. Some was sent by coastal shipping via Anderson's Inlet, but the unreliability of the service soon led to the demise of this practice. One settler on the steep hills south of Korumburra, Mr W. Rainbow, tried this outlet but found

> There was no cool storage in those days, at least not at the Inlet, where the only building was of iron. Judge of our surprise about a fortnight later to learn that our butter was still in this 'cool room', and that the boat would not be there for at least a couple of days; so we took some more down and got the boat this time, and got the butter away, which arrived in Melbourne safely; but word came back that most of it was in a liquid condition; but bad and all as it was, we received 1s to 1s 1d per lb. for it. I do not think town folks were so hard to please in those days.[19]

Alive to the possibilities of providing accommodation for newcomers to the district, J.N. Horn quickly established a small lodging house and hostelry on the Coalition Creek. It gradually acquired the status of a post office for the surrounding district of Koorooman — the 'office' being a large hole in a hollow tree where any mail for the nearby settlers was left high and dry until such time as it was collected. The Koorooman Post Office was officially proclaimed in 1887 and served the district for four years until the Leongatha Post Office was opened in 1891.[20] Horn's lodging house, constructed of round timber, clad externally with split palings and lined internally with hessian, was the first to receive a roadside licence for the sale of wines and spirits in the area. In order to commence trading, Horn applied for the excision of one acre of land from his agricultural leasehold block on the Coalition Creek. A note from Surveyor General Mr M. Callanan to Surveyor Lardner on 6 January 1885 approved of this excision, which was to be the first lot of land used for business purposes in the Leongatha area.[21]

The need for a township site to serve settlers in the Koorooman area had been obvious for several years. Charles Leach, in a letter to Hon. J.H. Tucker, Minister for Lands, stated:

24 June 1883

Dear Sir,
    Can I ask you to reserve a township site in the parish of Koorooman on the Ruby

Creek. I was out there a few weeks ago looking after a business site — finding no township reserved. I took up a selection with a view of starting a business, not being well to your land laws. I find there is a great difficulty in doing so on selected land. It is only right and fair to ask for a reserve. There are now over 60 selectors and 17 miles away from the nearest store or business and the very worst roads in the colony. In fact they cannot get anything out in the winter months. Can I suggest the best site, I think would be at the junction of the Poowong, Mirboo, and Trafalgar roads which is central, level, and well watered, on the Ruby Creek near the Wild Dog Creek. However, I am quite willing to leave that to you and the surveyors.

Your obed. servant,

Chas. Leach.[22]

The choice of township sites ultimately rested on the good sense and foresight of the head government surveyor in the field at the time. In this case it was John T. Lardner who finally selected the township site of Koorooman, five miles due north of the present town of Leongatha. He chose a gravelly ridge on the track from Mirboo North to Poowong between the Wilkur and Ruby Creeks. Although reserved for township purposes in 1884, the site was not proclaimed officially until some three years later when Governor Loch gave the official approval in the *Government Gazette* of 25 March 1887. When making the choice of site, Lardner was not to know the route of the South Gippsland railway planned between Dandenong and Foster. Trial surveys for the proposed line began in 1884, but considerable difficulty was experienced in finding a suitable route over the divide between the Bass and Tarwin watersheds.

Where the final survey for the Great Southern Railway crossed the blazed track between Nation's Springdale property and Horn's Roadside Inn on the Coalition Creek, Lardner reserved several hundred acres of Crown land for the present town of Leongatha. This blazed track, described by Thomas Musgrave who carried the mail along it on a pack horse as 'a drain of mud enclosed by walls of scrub', later became known as the 'coast road'; that is, the road between Mirboo North and Anderson's Inlet. Musgrave's description of the area corresponds with that of another pioneer who, when asked of his earliest impressions of the Leongatha township area, replied 'I saw a bear where the railway crossing now is, and I followed the surveyed track through to the east'.[23]

One of the biggest hazards to newcomers to the area was that of getting lost in the forest. Just prior to the opening of the track from Springdale at Leongatha South to Horn's, a man and a woman had set out to walk from Springdale to Mirboo North. Upon taking directions, they had evidently veered too far to the right, missed reaching the track at Horn's and got lost in the bush not far from the Tarwin River. After wandering around for a few days, they eventually lay down side by side and died of exposure and starvation. Their skeletons were found several years later during clearing. When an inquest was held at Leongatha, no information was available as to their identity. As there was no indication of any foul deed, the Coroner, Major Bartrop, directed Constable Gorman 'that no inquiry was necessary and that the remains be interred in the Leongatha cemetery as meriting the respect of civilized man'.[24]

Large logs lay across the track from Horn's to Mirboo North, at intervals, often resulting in accidents. When James Mitchell of Wilkur Creek jumped his horse over a log, the animal came down into a crabhole and fell heavily on the rider's leg, causing a fracture above the knee. Horn bound up the limb as well as he was able and did all he could to ease the sufferer's pain. Mitchell then rode to Mirboo North, a distance of fifteen miles, and was taken to Melbourne by train the following day.[25]

The second section of the Great Southern Railway line between Korumburra and Toora was undertaken by contractor Mr A. O'Keefe, whose tender for this mammoth task was £322,693 17s 10d.[26] The route surveyed had to be first completely cleared of huge trees, cuttings excavated, gullies filled, bridges built — all done with horses, bullocks and men. The logistics of providing materials and provisions for the work-force were formidable. Up to 700 bullocks and 200 horses were used in the formation and laying of the line. In some cases the teams transporting fodder for use by sub-contractors working on the line used up one-third of their load before reaching their destination. A regular line of steamers deposited construction material at Inverloch where it was hauled by bullock wagon to the Leongatha, Koonwarra section. For the southern section it was deposited on a private wharf specially built by O'Keefe on the banks of the Franklin River. A section of line was laid from the wharf to a point near Bennison, and from there O'Keefe worked northwards towards Korumburra and southwards towards Toora. Engines, trucks and railway line were brought in by sea from Melbourne and Sydney, and the line slowly progressed over the Hoddle Range. This part of the contract was one of the most difficult — a creek in this area had to be crossed eleven times in two miles. Cement for culverts had to be carted in by pack horse, one cask to each horse. Landslides were a constant problem with thousands of cubic yards of earth having to be shifted by horse scoops as a result. Three bridges were necessary over the Tarwin River, the longest being over 1,000 foot while the others were approximately 500 foot.

Explosives were used to remove the large stumps of trees on the surveyed route and any rock formations encountered. Camps were situated where large cuttings had to be formed, one of the two largest being between Kardella and Ruby, adjacent to the Coalition Creek and known as 'The Brickyards'. The other major camp was at the Black Spur near Koonwarra where up to 200 men were encamped for a considerable time — this spot being still known as 'Camp Hill'.[27] During its occupation, the top of this hill was covered with tents of varying sizes and descriptions and put to many and varied uses. Some were used as boarding houses for the single men, others were used for married men with their families, while larger tents were used for blacksmith shops, stables and offices.

Mr Hugh McCartin, who later opened the Commercial Hotel at Leongatha, conducted a large store at this site to cater for the needs of the work-force. The campsite was criss-crossed with drains, but with the constant traffic of men and horses, it was a quagmire for many months of the year. As a result of the cold, wet conditions, a nine-year-old girl, Miss Hogan, daughter of one of the workmen, died in the camp in 1891 and was buried in a nearby paddock owned by Mr J. Holt. The grave was fenced off and a cypress tree planted that was a landmark in the district for many years. Due to a re-alignment of the highway in 1956 the tree was removed and the remains re-interred in the Leongatha Cemetery.[28]

O'Keefe carted ballast back from Foster as the iron rails gradually crept up the track until eventually he met up with his second team of men who were working down the line from Korumburra. These two gangs joined their respective sections of line at Ruby, and the first passenger train on the line was run on 30 October 1891 — a special run for the benefit of patrons who wished to attend the Melbourne Cup![29]

As in many construction works, accidents occurred. Not all the workers were as skilled as Peter Johnson and Harry Begg in the felling of the trees on the desired spot. On Saturday, 14 September 1889, Denis Maher and William Holm were engaged in tree felling with a group of men adjacent to the line at Leongatha. A rope and pulley was attached to the tree to stop it falling on nearby tents, but unfortunately, in the course of its descent, it brought down another tree which fell on the two men. Holm was killed instantly, while Maher sustained a compound fracture of one of his legs. Horn was immediately sent for and dressed the wounds of the injured man, while Peter Johnson set out on horseback to ride to Drouin for a doctor. Leaving at 5 p.m., he rode all night through mud often up to the horse's knees, arriving at Drouin at 5 a.m. The doctor there was not keen to embark on the journey through the forest unless Johnson guaranteed his fee, which he did. The two then returned to Leongatha, arriving at 3 p.m., by which time a doctor from Foster had arrived on the scene, but to no avail — the injured man died the next day.[30] Both men were interred in the newly-surveyed cemetery to the south of the township. So dense was the bush that the graves were inadvertently dug on the roadway and had, subsequently, to be shifted.[31]

The track leading past the Leongatha Cemetery to Inverloch was a nightmare to teamsters. On the low-lying stretches, seven miles of corduroy was laid by Messrs G. Cross and C. Simon to enable the teams to get through with their loads. Although corduroy was suitable for light vehicles, this temporary roadway did not stand up to bullock wagons laden with beer barrels. George Cross described the scene on the Inverloch track as the first wagonette was brought from Melbourne to Inverloch by boat for Mr Horn.

> It had to be brought along a bush track, and for the last eight miles to Leongatha ten men cleared sufficient scrub for the vehicle to be driven along. It had been used as one of Cobb and Co's coaches. Hugh McCartin and the late Robert Bair had the liquor for their hotels at Leongatha brought from Melbourne by boat. The early settlers had the experience of seeing 40 bullocks attached to a wagon, on which were 16 barrels of beer. The wagon was bogged to such an extent that the bullocks pulled the front portion off, and the barrels rolled into the mud.[32]

When wheeled vehicles were impossible to use, the sledge proved a ready, reliable and cheap alternative. For the first fifty years of settlement, the sledge was of incalculable value in the transport of goods and people. Simple to construct, hard wearing, versatile in its uses, impervious to the mud over which it would slide, it was the chief mode of transport during the winter months. Peter Johnson and a neighbour made a two day trip from the Coalition Creek to Poowong on a sledge before the construction of the railway. They returned later with the first plough to be brought to the district lashed to it.

The droving of stock along the pack tracks was a trial of perseverance. Johnson relates how he and his brother purchased a flock of twenty sheep, and after bringing them on to their block, there were only four alive the next morning owing to the ravages of dingoes during the night. When Phillip Bellingham commenced a butchery business on the outskirts of Leongatha to service the railway construction workers, it took him three days to bring a mob of sheep along the track from Jumbunna to Leongatha — a distance of seven miles.

Sheep raising in South Gippsland at that time was more of a hazard than cattle raising owing to the depredations of dingoes. Some settlers tried the old Scottish practice of tying bells to the sheep to frighten the dingoes away, but it was of no avail. Poison and baited gin-traps were also used to curtail their activities, but in the initial stages of settlement, it was necessary to fold the sheep each night in yards made from split slabs from five to six foot high. When a beast was to be killed, Bellingham travelled seven miles to a paddock near Korumburra, taking a cow with him to act as a coacher or decoy. This cow had a calf running with it that was left yarded at Leongatha. The purchased steer or bullock was released together with the decoy cow which would immediately head back to its calf followed by the animal to be killed.

Apart from the fish that could be readily caught in the streams, the daily diet of early settlers consisted of the basic necessities. Meat, mostly eaten cold, oatmeal for porridge, bread or damper, tea and sugar were the staple fare until vegetables could be grown or some fruit trees brought into bearing. Wallabies were eaten at times and proved a valuable standby in times of necessity. When Henry Sutherland began work for Jacob Thomas at Lyre Bird Mound, his wages were £1 per week plus keep, which was a good wage at the time, but he was not so happy about the keep.

> Food was rationed out, so much corned meat; fresh meat when it was available; so many pounds by weight of potatoes and bread. Jam and butter were not provided but a barrel of molasses stood in a corner and the workmen were permitted to each take a tin and fill it at the tap.[33]

Not that Thomas was hard on his men. Indeed, he was regarded as a good employer, a kindly man and a well-respected member of the early community in the district. He had been brought up in the old, hard, Welsh school of life and believed in working daylight to dark, six days a week with church on Sunday.

With all the difficulties associated with settlement, there were other men with capital like Jacob Thomas who could foresee the potential of this heavily forested land. Peter Shingler, a young Englishman from Shropshire, selected 320 acres near Korumburra where he farmed for six years. He named this property 'Coal Creek' because of the discovery of black coal nearby. After several years there, he decided that the land to the east was more amenable to farming, so he sold Coal Creek and re-selected adjacent to Leongatha. In a letter home to his family, he relates his experiences of life in the new colony.

> South Gippsland is an expensive place to start farming; not getting a quick return. It is a healthy climate and in my idea this is the first consideration. The soil is rich and there is plenty of rain. The land in years to come will be valuable. Just tickle the soil and the seed will grow. The selectors are mostly out of Melbourne. The tracks and roads are first cut out of the forest only wide enough for a horse to go along . . . There are dingoes, kangaroos, wallabies and small harmless bears, platypusses,

Miss D. Shingler and Mr T. Bowler, The Grange, Leongatha (from Woorayl Shire Historical Society).

parrots. The plumage of the eaglehawk is gorgeous. The native pheasant Lyre bird is common. The male bird has a splendid tail and imitates all the birds in the forest.[34]

Peter Shingler's mother and sister arrived from England to set up home in this new land bringing their furniture and possessions by sailing ship to Inverloch. As soon as the track was opened to Leongatha, Shingler hauled material by bullock wagon for the construction of his homestead on their new property, The Grange, adjacent to the Leongatha township. Like the home of Jacob Thomas on Lyre Bird Mound, it became a centre of hospitality in the newly-settled district and was the setting for the first Church of England service held in the area.

It could be said that the opening of the railway marked the end of the pioneering era of South Gippsland. Although a tremendous amount of physical work in the development of farms, homes, roads, townships etc. remained to be done, the tyranny of isolation felt by the first settlers no longer prevailed. The economic benefits were incalculable. Without the facilities provided by the iron road to the metropolis, the full potential of the fertile lands of South Gippsland could not be fulfilled. The financial gains were immediately discernible. No longer did stores have to be hauled by bullock wagon from Inverloch or Mirboo North in the summer months and left by the track during the winter. The dairy farmer no longer had to pack his butter to the railhead at Mirboo North or the wharf at Anderson's Inlet and rely on the vagaries of coastal shipping for it to be transported to Melbourne.

Cattle from drought-stricken pastures in the north of the State could be railed to the lush pastures that were being established amongst the rolling hills of South Gippsland. Potatoes and onions, for which the ground was eminently suitable, could now be grown and sold at a profit. Prior to the opening of the railway, these crops were not economic owing to the huge cost of transportation to markets.

Other less intangible benefits the railway brought to the area were an influx of new settlers and the ready access to hospital and medical facilities previously unavailable through isolation. This was the beginning of a new era. Improved access to South Gippsland brought people with new ideas, new forms of recreation, a wider breadth of vision who could sometimes more readily appreciate its natural advantages and potential than those born in the area. All of these factors influenced the next stage of development for the community living in the watershed of the Tarwin. In a geographical and cultural sense, it tied the communities living along the Great Southern line more intimately to the metropolitan area than to those living along the Central Gippsland line. The Strzelecki Ranges, even after settlement, proved a physical and mental barrier to the intermingling of the population of these two regions that even a century of development has not entirely eliminated.

4. COMMUNITY FORMATION – CHURCH, SCHOOL, SHIRE

The sense of isolation experienced by pioneering settlers in the forest must at times have been overwhelming. Not all were fortunate enough to come as members of a family group, where tasks could be shared and there was at least a modicum of conversation to lighten the day's toil. Some people, by reason of upbringing, education or spiritual reserves, were able to withstand long periods of isolation better than others. For many the intense desire to acquire land of their own, the pressing necessity to erect a home for their loved ones, and the challenge presented by the all-pervading bush, stretched their physical resources to the limit. After a day of hard manual labour swinging the axe or plying the crosscut saw, they returned to their huts to cook an evening meal by the light of a kerosene lantern.

Little energy or time remained for reading or social intercourse — the first generation of pioneers was occupied with the problems of the present. In the big timber country, up to thirty large trees had to be felled before safety could be ensured from limbs falling on to the tent or hut. On Lyre Bird Mound there were 400 to 500 saplings to the acre and bracken fern ten foot high facing the Thomas family.[1] The entrance track into the selection was often merely a tunnel of mud for nine months of the year — distance was not merely measured in miles, it was also measured in the time and effort that had to be expended to traverse it.

The majority of men and women who took up residence in the Tarwin Valley in the early decades of settlement were God-fearing people whose intense faith helped them to survive the hardships and vicissitudes of those early years. Firmly believing in the words of the Scripture that 'where two or three are gathered in My name, there am I in the midst of them', they quickly formed themselves into small congregations of their respective denominations. Services were held in private homes on the Sabbath where prayers would be said together and hymns sung. Occasionally, an itinerant clergyman would be present after enduring considerable hardship travelling along narrow packtracks often knee deep in mud. As the congregation grew, the services were held in the small halls that began to be erected in these isolated communities. The Church not only fulfilled the spiritual needs of the early settlers, it provided form and fabric to the pattern of their lives.

Along the coast a visiting clergyman from Yarram called at Waratah Bay and Tarwin Meadows once or twice a year, at which times services would be held. It was not until 1886 that the first regular church services were held in the newly-settled forest areas of the Tarwin Basin. At Koonwarra this took place under the guidance of Henry Medew, a lay reader of the Methodist Church who worked for Jacob Thomas on Lyre Bird Mound. As their congregation increased, a Mr James Smith was appointed Home Missionary for the Koonwarra district in 1886, and early in 1888 as a result of several working-bees, a small church was built on Lyre Bird Mound.

The official opening was a great success, presided over by local member, the Hon. F. Longmore, MLA, with the Reverend E.S. Bickford conducting the service. A picnic was held for the occasion followed by a sale of gifts, refreshments, singing and many speeches to mark this important event. As it was too dangerous to return along the forest tracks at night-time, the activities kept going as best they could till daylight.

Some of the ladies who were suffering from the effects of the prolonged celebrations went to bed in relays in a nearby house.[2] In August 1887 Mr Smith

Working-bee at Koonwarra, 1903. Clearing a site for the Methodist Church (from D. Bacon).

held the first Methodist service in the Dumbalk district at the home of Mr and Mrs F. Dodd, Senior. Until a suitable hall could be obtained for services, it was decided to alternate the place of service between the homes of Frank Dodd and Thomas Trease.

Other denominations quickly organised services for their members. In 1885 the home of Mr Robert Smith of Mardan West was the setting for the first Presbyterian Church service held in the Koorooman area. This was conducted by Mr Duncan, a Presbyterian missionary stationed at Mirboo North, and was to be the forerunner of many more held in the newly-settled areas.

The need for a public hall for social events and church services in the Koorooman district was evident to all. At a meeting held at the home of Mr Thomas Crighton on Saturday 15 September 1888, it was decided to erect a building to serve the needs of the growing community. This hall, the first public building to be erected in the Koorooman area, was situated on a half acre of land donated by Mr T. Crighton, roughly half a mile east of Horn's Roadside Inn. A very simple structure of pit-sawn hardwood, cut by nearby selector Jack Russell, it measured thirty foot by sixteen foot. Windows were of calico, and the problem of seating accommodation was solved by the provision of rough planks resting on blocks. It was not an architectural wonder, as the press correspondent of *The Mirboo Herald* noted on 14 January 1889.

A queer box it looked in the distance with its roof on the square and doors ajar, but a close inspection proved that distance doth not always lend charm. The energetic secretary Mr. Myers explained the usual difficulties in erecting a Mechanics' Institute.

Six months later, Mr Myers described the building in a letter in which the committee offered it to the Education Department for use as a school: 'the dimensions of the building are — length 30 ft, width 16 ft, height 12 ft. There is a fireplace in the building also spouting. There is no water tank or out offices'.[3]

This small wooden building, although crudely built, marked the beginnings of community life in the Koorooman area and served to give it an identity that it had previously lacked. For the preceding two summers, residents had gathered at Johnson's property nearby for the annual picnic held on Boxing Day. People spared no effort to attend this function, as at that time of the year the tracks had dried out sufficiently enough to make travelling by horseback or on foot less of an ordeal. One man arrived at the picnic leading a pack horse on which he had placed three young children: two small ones in a bag on one side balanced by a larger child on the other. His wife followed riding another horse and carrying a baby.[4] At the third picnic, on Boxing Day 1888, the hundred or so present adjourned to the new Koorooman Hall for a dance to celebrate the occasion.

The following year the picnic was transferred to the township of Leongatha, where the running events took place on the newly-levelled track prepared by O'Keefe in readiness for the laying of the sleepers and lines of the railway.[5] This is the first recorded athletic meeting to be held in the township of Leongatha. Between 200 and 300 people attended, the foot races being held according to Stawell rules. The main event was the 200 yards handicap with prize money of £5 for first, 7s 6d for second and 2s 6d for third. Long jump, hop, step and jump, putting the stone, tossing the caber, horse jump, chopping match and a go-as-you-please race with prize money of £2 completed the program. For those not athletically minded, a horse race was conducted on the southern side of the station, the starting point being in the vicinity of Simon's Lane.

Just as the opening of a hall for social gatherings and religious services signifies the beginning of community life, so also does the opening of a school signify growth within an area. The pattern of school openings in South Gippsland in the period 1880-1900 traces the course of the tide of settlement.

The Education Department numbered the schools consecutively as they were opened, so the official number of any school gives a reliable indication of the year in which it was opened; for example, Waratah Bay, S.S.2514 opened in 1883 was followed by Mardan, S.S.2516 in 1884.

The year 1886 saw the opening of schools at opposite ends of the Tarwin watershed. Pound Creek, S.S.2775 opened in one room of a wattle and daub cottage owned by a Mrs Love, situated near the south-western corner of block number nine. This room was leased by the Department for one shilling per week, and the school was operated half time with Inverloch, S.S.2776, which opened in August of the same year, also in a room in a private house on the site of the former Methodist Church in a'Beckett Street.[6] The settlers who had pushed their way over the hills from Yarragon in the early 1880s were provided with a school at Hallston in 1886 when S.S.2825, formerly known as 'Allambee South', opened in December of that year.

Berry's Creek, S.S.2925 on St Ellen's Road was the first of four schools to be opened in 1889, only to be burnt down in the 1898 bush fires along with several others. Dumbalk North, S.S.2945 opened in a paling-clad building, half lined with a shingle roof on Allotment 8, Parish of Dumbalk. It was leased by the Department at ten shillings a month at the same time as Cashin's Hill, S.S.2949 opened only a little over a mile from Tarwin Lower. Koorooman, S.S.2964 opened almost at the end of the school year on 29 November, with Isiah Davis as the first headteacher in the newly-built hall on Crighton's hill overlooking the site of the new township of Leongatha.[7]

As construction of the railway line progressed, the canvas camps set up along the surveyed route contained many married men who had brought their families with them. The children in these camps were virtually running wild and causing distress to their parents. A letter to the Education Department from a Mrs Cath Shanahan, requesting provision of a school, illustrated the situation.

13 August, 1889.
I am induced to write to you, asking for a teacher to be sent to this district as soon as possible, as there are forty or more children within school distance of this township. When the Inspector visited here last April, he promised us a school within a short space of time. Since then we have not heard about it. Now my husband has a building erected on a township block — which he is willing to let to the Education department for a term of six months or more at a nominal rent, providing a teacher is sent here soon. It is really a pity to see so many children actually running wild here, and no school within several miles of them while the population is increasing here weekly.[8]

This letter of Mrs Shanahan produced the required result, because the Department accepted the offer of the lease of the building and opened S.S.2981

MRS. SHANAHAN'S
DRAPERY
ESTABLISHMENT,
KOOROOMAN.

MRS SHANAHAN begs to notify to the Public of Koorooman and surrounding district that she has opened as above, and invites inspection of her first-class Stock of Useful Drapery, which will be found to contain Seasonable Goods of Every Description.

Everything sold at the Most Reasonable Prices for Cash.

KOOROOMAN HOTEL.

J. N. HORN

BEGS to notifiy to the Public that he has opened the above HOTEL, where travellers can be supplied with every comfort.

Ales, Wines and Spirits of the best quality.

GOOD STABLING.

J. N. HORN,
Proprietor.

Public Notices.

SHIRE OF WOORAYL.

APPLICATIONS, addressed to the President, will be received at the Post Office, Mirboo North, till 10 a.m. on TUESDAY, 18th SEPTEMBER, 1888, from Persons qualified to fill the under-mentioned offices :—

SECRETARY, Shire of Woorayl, at a Salary of £75 per annum.

VALUER and RATE COLLECTOR to the Shire of Woorayl, at a Salary of £75 per annum.

And ROAD OVERSEER, at a Salary of £175 per annum.

Specifications of duties may be inspected at the Post Office, Mirboo North.

GEO. F. NETHERCOTE,
Secretary, *pro. tem.*

Fruit Trees !
Fruit Trees !
FRUIT TREES
OF ALL DESCRIPTIONS.

All Apple Trees Worked on Blight-proof Stocks.

THREE VARIETIES DITTO, PERFECTLY BLIGHT-PROOF.

Early Albert & Webb's Buninyong (Giant)

RHUBARBS.

H. BORROW,
KOOROOMAN.

Advertisements from The Mirboo Herald, *1888-9.*

on 22 September 1889 under the charge of a Mr Denholm. His task was not an easy one, teaching thirty-eight pupils with little in the way of materials or equipment other than that provided by the pupils. An urgent request to the Education Department resulted in the arrival from Mirboo North, via the mailman, of thirty-six copy books and twenty-four slates, with the cost of transport being thirty shillings. The slates were of immediate benefit, but the copy books had to await the arrival of desks before being used. Within a short time Mr Denholm was replaced by Mr John Jeffrey as headteacher, who described the building in a letter to the Department as being

* 28 ft by 14 ft; two doors in it, one at each end;
* constructed of weatherboards, shingle roof;
* no spouting or tank;
* there are spaces left for two windows, which at the present time are
* half boarded up and canvas is nailed on the other half;
* only one closet, and another is badly wanted;
* a blackboard is also wanted very badly;
* there are two rough desks in the school, which will do until the roads get better, but it would be better to send three or four more.
* the building is situated on Mr. Shanahan's township allotment, just at the corner of the proposed railway station.[9]

John Jeffrey, in a letter of 20 November 1889, claimed that it was impossible to teach all the subjects under these primitive conditions. He asked the Department to expedite matters as 'the roads leading to this place from North Mirboo Railway Station and also from Anderson's Inlet are now open for traffic'.[10]

District Inspector Bothroyd supported the sentiments expressed by Jeffrey and urged the Department to build a permanent school on the two-acre site that had been reserved, noting that

Leongatha is the centre of a fertile and thickly settled district, and it will only need the completion of the railway line to make it, perhaps, the most important township of the Great Southern Line.[11]

Any building of size was very much in demand in the newly-emerging township, and no doubt Shanahan had many requests for the use of his, particularly over the weekend. On one occasion Jeffrey was asked to remove the desks on the Friday afternoon and clear the floor. On Monday morning, when teacher and pupils arrived for school, they found the floor covered with sawdust and bloodstains about the walls. It had been used the previous evening for a boxing bout between one of the local pugilists and a visiting Maori employed in the railway construction gang.

When school resumed after the Christmas holidays on 30 January 1890, Jeffrey informed the Department that the following articles of furniture or equipment had arrived safely: one Master's desk, press, and stool; two blackboards; one easel; three small forms; one closet (in six pieces); and one tank.[12]

As Michael Shanahan required the leased school building for other purposes, the Education Department was forced to relinquish tenancy of it on 1 April 1890. The new school was still in the course of construction, so Jeffrey kindly offered to teach the pupils in his own home; senior pupils in one room thirteen foot by twelve foot; the juniors in another under the care of a monitor. This make-shift arrangement continued all during the winter and spring of 1890. In addition to children from the township, some pupils walked miles along bush tracks to take advantage of Jeffrey's tuition.

The few scholars attending 'the front room' would always appear on time from different parts of the scrub, sometimes wet through from the wet bush. The Horn family from a bush track now called Horn St. The Blackmore family had a long way to walk but would get there. The Worthys came from over the hills near Ruby.[13]

It was not until 19 January 1891 that Jeffrey was able to move into the new departmental building measuring thirty foot by twenty foot, erected at a cost of approximately £300, with his enrolment by March of that year having increased to fifty-five.

The building of Shanahan's, formerly occupied by the Education Department, was the site of the first public Mass celebrated by the Catholics in the township. It had now been acquired by Edmond Hayes who continued to operate it as a general store. Some time in 1890, Father Michael Curran rode from Sale to visit members of his faith that were scattered throughout South Gippsland. He stayed at the home of Mr John Hassett, a little to the south of the new township, for several days, and then gathered together the Catholics from the area for Mass which was held in Hayes's store. Many of those present were working either on the railways or on the survey camps, and it is recorded that John Lardner, son of the surveyor, served as altar boy at this first Mass.[14] Through the action of John Hassett, Hugh McCartin and other members of their faith, an acre of land was purchased in 1890 for the site of a Catholic Church in Ogilvy Street, but it was not until another five years had elapsed that this church materialised.

In the same year, 1890, Mrs Mary Shingler wrote to the Anglican bishop requesting services to be held in the district, stating that 'she had been living in the area for eight years without having the benefit of attending divine service'. Bishop Goe replied 'that if men and means were forthcoming, this need would be attended to'. As a result of this request, the first service of the Anglican Communion was held at the Shingler homestead, The Grange, one mile to the north of the township, on 25 February 1890.[15] Over thirty people attended, some travelling twenty miles or more on horseback.

This first service of the Church of England was conducted by Archdeacon H. Langley, while other clergy from nearby districts attended. Reverend C.J. Chambers rode twenty miles from Foster over poor tracks as did Reverend H.D. Putron Hitchcock who travelled almost as far, from Mirboo North. At this service Mr W.R. Elvery, lay reader, was licensed for service, a task that he fulfilled with the utmost dedication over the next few years. Many stayed all day at Shingler's homestead and enjoyed their hospitality.

In the evening they journeyed through the scrub to the newly-built Koorooman Hall, some two miles to the east where another service was conducted. At this first meeting of the Anglican Communion in the area, plans were made to put the Church on a more substantial footing. But it was not until the following year, 1891, that tenders were called for the erection of a vicarage on land that had been purchased in Peart Street, Leongatha.[16]

During the years 1888-91 there was considerable confusion within the district over its actual name, some calling it Koorooman and some Leongatha. This was brought about as, when Government surveyors laid out an area in parishes, the usual practice was to reserve up to two square miles within each parish for a future township. This township reserve was often given the name of the parish in which it was located. Thus, the township reserve on the crest of a hill roughly five miles due north of the present site of Leongatha, but in the Parish of Koorooman, was proclaimed as the township of Koorooman. Upon completion of the railway survey in 1887, the township of Leongatha was surveyed the following year by John Lardner and named as such after the adjoining Parish of Leongatha to the south of Koorooman.[17]

In the meantime, the post office of Koorooman, officially gazetted in 1887, was located at Horn's Roadside Inn one mile to the north of the newly-planned railway station so that the address of all nearby residents was given as Koorooman. Some mail for the early settlers in the area came via Anderson's Inlet and then by pack horse to the Koorooman Post Office at Horn's. Jack Musgrave carried it as far as Nation's Springdale property, and from there it was brough to Horn's by Peter Johnson. Other mail was carried from Horn's to Mirboo North by Mr Blackmore who often experienced great difficulty in crossing the flooded Tarwin during winter months.

The growing sense of identity that was slowly surfacing led to the initial steps being taken for local government. When the Alberton Shire was inaugurated in 1864, with headquarters at Yarram, its boundaries included the Tarwin watershed area. With the creation of the Narracan Shire in 1878, the areas of Boolarra, Mirboo North, Mardan, Koorooman (Leongatha) and Korumburra became the South Riding of the Narracan Shire with its headquarters at Morwell.

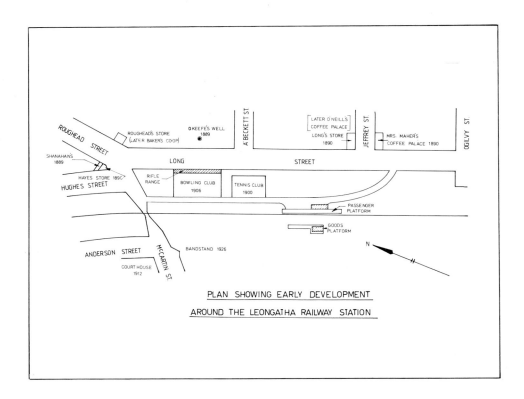

PLAN SHOWING EARLY DEVELOPMENT
AROUND THE LEONGATHA RAILWAY STATION

To the landholders of the newly-settled Tarwin Basin, this change of Shires appeared to be of little benefit, as it still seemed to be too large for any attention to be given to local needs. A public meeting called to discuss the situation was held at the Mechanics' Institute at Mirboo North on 27 September 1887, where despite some opposition, it was decided to press for a severance of the South Riding from the Narracan Shire. The meeting was addressed by Mr Charles Ogilvy, who pointed out that the South Riding provided more than one-third of the revenue but was under-represented on the Council. A severance committee was formed at this meeting comprising Messrs Ogilvy, McCartin, Inglis, Kennedy, St. Ellen and Williams. Their task was to communicate with leading members of their respective communities and seek support for the motion of severance. Only three weeks later, a further meeting of delegates from districts within the South Riding was held at the home of Mr Robert Smith of Mardan West on 17 October 1887. These delegates were Begg, Watt and Allison (Leongatha); Ogilvy, McCartin and Ridgway (Mirboo); Inglis, Elliot and St. Ellen (Mardan), and Brydon, Amiet (absent), Western (Korumburra).

Mr Inglis was voted to the chair, and considerable discussion took place as to the name of the proposed new Shire. Several Aboriginal names and their meanings were submitted by Mr Inglis that had been obtained from Mr Howitt, Police Magistrate. After discussion, a vote was taken that resulted in four votes for Woorayl, four votes for Tarwin and two votes for Sassafras.[18] On a final vote, Woorayl, meaning 'Lyre Bird', was chosen by a majority of one.

Under the rules of local government, any petition for severance had to be accompanied by a deposit of £20. The cost of obtaining the petition and the raising of the £20 was left to the delegates. In all probability, most of the amount would have been provided personally by these prominent gentlemen. The petition was duly circulated and lodged with the Department of Public Works with the £20 on Saturday, 24 March 1888 by Mr Groom, MP, accompanied by Mr Inglis and Mr Scarlett of the Mardan district. Almost two months later, on 25 May 1888, the Woorayl Shire was officially proclaimed.[19] With a total area of 240 square miles, a population of 1,500 and 610 ratepayers on the roll, it was divided into two ridings: East Riding comprising Mirboo North and the Mardan areas and the West Riding comprising Leongatha and Korumburra.

Almost immediately, a sense of rivalry developed in the West Riding over the choice of councillors to represent the different areas. The township of Korumburra had been surveyed by Lardner prior to Leongatha, and with the discovery of coal in the vicinity, it was slightly more developed. This early sense of rivalry was exacerbated by the decision of the Minister of Railways to site the changing station at Leongatha, a decision that was subsequently reversed in favour of Korumburra, much to the chagrin of Leongatha residents. Other matters added to this rivalry, but basically it stemmed from the innate feeling of residents that one or the other of these two towns was destined to become the leading centre on the South Gippsland line. This rivalry was remarked upon by 'A Rambling Correspondent' in the Korumburra *Great Southern Advocate* of 9 May 1890 when he stated 'There will be a jealous feeling between the two towns' — a statement that has been borne out on different occasions in later years. The geographical position of Korumburra meant that its natural affinity lay more towards the west at Poowong, rather than the east at Mirboo North and Leongatha. This latent discontent with being linked to communities to the east and south in local government matters led to the subsequent excision of the Korumburra area from the Woorayl Shire only three years later on 29 May 1891.

The first elections for the new Shire took place on Saturday 9 August 1888 when 592 of the 610 ratepayers voted. Three councillors from each riding were elected: Messrs Smith, Olarenshaw and Scarlett from the East Riding together with Messrs Western, Watt and Allison from the West Riding. At the inaugural meeting of the new Shire Council held at the Mechanics' Institute, Mirboo North on 29 August 1888, Cr William Scarlett was elected President with the Secretary *pro tem* being Mr G.F. Nethercote. Subsequently, Mr Charles Ogilvy was officially appointed to this position on 9 September 1888, a position he was to hold for the next twelve years. A local doctor, Dr J.P. Montgomery of Mirboo North, was appointed Health Officer, and it was decided to hold monthly meetings on the Tuesday preceding the full moon.[20] This choice of meeting time was common to all organisations and functions held in the forested areas of South Gippsland during the first few decades of settlement. The tracks along which the people had to return to their homes on horseback were dangerous enough, even in moonlight.

One of the first questions the new councillors faced was the choice of a seal or emblem for the new Shire. Fortunately, there were men and women in the district who had a sense of the importance of history and gave the matter serious thought. A lengthy letter that appeared in *The Mirboo Herald* on 21 September 1888 on the subject evidently impressed the new councillors.

> As the new seal for the above shire is one of the first of the several important factors required to complete the adjustment of this new shire, I respectfully draw the attention of those upon whose shoulders the duty and decision of choosing this climax design rests. There is little doubt that by the time the next centennial of this country swings round the forest scrub and most of the giant trees will have passed away, taking with them the beautiful flora and fauna peculiar to the present native foliage, scrub, forests, etc., never again to be seen and remembered by mankind. I would respectfully suggest that competitive designs for the said seal should be advertised for, and three or four liberal prizes should be offered. The principal flora should be represented thereon, the whole to be encircled by that beautiful Supple Jack creeper in full blossom.
>
> The main feature, of course to be a representation of that beautiful whistling song bird, the Woorayl, in company with the black-fellow, kangaroo, wallaby, emu, etc. whilst perched amongst the branches might be the possum, bear, eagle, etc. Should the foregoing suggestions be deemed worthy of notice, there is little doubt but that the grotesqueness thereof would be equally interesting and admired in time to come by posterity.
>
> Yours, etc.,
> One of the Shire Severance Delegates,
> St. Ellen's. Berry's Creek. 17 Sept. 1888.

Councillors, conscious of the Shire's lack of income, did not furnish any funds or prize money for a competition to choose the seal or emblem. They did, however, adopt the lyre bird as the emblem and approved the prototype design submitted by Messrs Stokes and Martin with the exception 'that the body of the bird is considered too small in proportion to the tail'.[21] Following this slight

Meeting of Woorayl Shire Council, August 1891. Back row: Messrs C.S. Ogilvy (Shire Secretary), Young (press), Brown (press), Crs Allison, McCartin, Ritchie, Smith, Henderson, Benn, A. Ogilvy (Valuer and Rate Collector), G. Gray (Road Overseer). Front row: Crs Cashin, Higgs, Allen, Watt, Goldsmith, Cook.

Bellingham's butchery, Melbourne Road, Leongatha, c. 1890 (from Woorayl Shire Historical Society).

amendment to the design, Council minutes of the meeting on 30 October 1888 record the motion of Cr Olarenshaw and Smith:

> That this Council do now adopt as the official seal the emblem of a Lyre Bird, with bordering of 'Supple Jack', an impression of which shall be made in the minute book in connection with the record of these proceedings, and shall be henceforth the seal of the Woorayl Shire.

The question of dual names for the Koorooman-Leongatha area was still far from being settled. The railway station and the State school had been gazetted as Leongatha, but the post office, police station and the local businesses were referred to as Koorooman. When *The Great Southern Star* was launched on 13 August 1890 by W. McPherson and Co., the banner headline of the first issue proclaimed it to be 'Circulating in Koorooman, Mardan, Korumburra, Inverloch, Lower Tarwin, Black Spur, Mirboo North and surrounding districts', with no mention of Leongatha.

Of the fifteen business advertisements carried on the front page of this inaugural issue, only two are listed as being carried on at Leongatha; the other thirteen are listed as being at Koorooman. Of the two Leongatha notices, the first was of T.H. Brown, 'Coachbuilder, Wheelwright and general Blacksmith' who stated he had commenced business in Main Road (opposite the police station). The other announced that the Leongatha Cash Store, Robert Long, Proprietor, had all sorts of 'Groceries, Ironmongery, Drapery in stock'. E. and J. Hayes, Koorooman, advertised that they had large stocks of 'Mauritius Sugars — Crystals, Brown and White on hand' plus 'Old Jamaica Rum, bottle and bulk . . . Flour, oats, bran, pollard and chaff . . . Men's suits from 18s. 6d. to 55s. . . . Boots and shoes including Watertights, Gippslanders, Balmorals, Lace ups, Elastic sides, Leggings etc'.

The inaugural issue of *The Great Southern Star* also included a letter from a newcomer to the district.

> When I left another place to come here, I had Leongatha in mind, but, lo and behold, on my arrival it was nothing but Koorooman. On all sides I heard the name, and Koorooman Post Office met my enraptured gaze. Then I was told the police camp was known as Koorooman, as also were the banks, then again, the State School is called Leongatha. It appears to me that as if we are between a well-known individual and the deep sea. For my own part I do not care which it is, but we must be unanimous. Koorooman puts one in mind of Black Billy, Lubras, Mia-Mia etc. Leongatha is a decidedly prettier name. But hang the prettiness, sir, let us have the best name for business.
>
> GIVE IT A NAME.

The newly-formed Koorooman Progress Association also was concerned at the duality of names and arranged for a plebiscite of the district to be held through the medium of *The Great Southern Star*. The Association arranged for the following form to appear in the 23 August 1890 edition of that paper.

I FAVOUR THE NAME OF
NAME
ADDRESS

Looking east from Leongatha Railway Station, 1892. Long's store and Mrs Maher's Coffee Palace are in the centre (from E.W. Allison).

All residents within a five mile radius were requested to fill in the form and return it to the Association. The result of this survey was twenty-four in favour of Koorooman and only four in favour of Leongatha. This reflected the rather limited circulation of *The Great Southern Star* at that time. Before the end of the year, however, on 22 November 1890, ratepayers decided at a public meeting held at Bair's Coffee House that the name of Avondale should be adopted for the township.[22] A petition to this effect was drawn up, and signatures obtained and presented to the appropriate authorities. The controversy was finally decided by a proclamation in the *Government Gazette* of 5 December 1890 for the township to be known as 'Leongatha'. In the same issue of the *Gazette*, the original proclamation of the township of Koorooman was officially revoked. The following year the name of the post office was changed to Leongatha, together with the police station and banks. Koorooman Post Office had operated for only four years, from 1887 until 1891.[23]

For the first two years of its existence, Woorayl Shire Council met at Mirboo North. There were no public buildings in the Koorooman, Leongatha area other than the small thirty foot by sixteen foot Mechanics' Institute building on Crighton's Hill, and it was being used five days a week for school purposes. As it was becoming increasingly evident that the Leongatha area was to become the centre of the Shire, Council decided to hold their monthly meetings in the embryo township; the first taking place on 23 September 1890 in 'the building known as Bair's'.[24] Bair's Coffee House, later re-named the 'Otago' upon granting of a full hotel licence in March 1891, continued to be the venue for Council meetings until such time as the new Shire offices were completed in November 1891. These consisted of three rooms adjacent to the Leongatha Mechanics' Institute that was built about that time. The association of the Woorayl Shire Council with Bair's premises continued for over ninety years, as Council adjourned to the Bair's Otago Hotel on each meeting day for their midday lunch — surely a record for a municipal Council and a compliment to the members of the Bair family who carried on the traditional occupation of hotelkeeping since the building of their first premises in Leongatha in 1890. Owing to the increased volume of Council business, this practice was discontinued in 1985, and Woorayl Shire councillors now have refreshments served in the Shire offices.

First Woorayl Shire offices (from Woorayl Historical Society).

5. A GROWING SHIRE

Councillors of the Woorayl Shire, when confronted with the magnitude of the problems that beset their area, must often have wondered where to begin. In the 240 square miles that constituted the Shire, there were no all-weather roads for wheeled vehicles. The Shire itself was virtually dissected by the Tarwin River from north to south and by the Great Southern Railway line nearing completion from west to east. It was along these axes that development was fast taking place. The growth of any community brings associated problems from all sides, and Woorayl Shire had more than its share during the early decades of its existence. Then, as now, if councillors were not already aware of the problems, there was no shortage of people to point them out.

The Koorooman (Leongatha) Progress Association was formed at a meeting in Leongatha during August 1890, with a subscription fee of five shillings half yearly.[1] Its main objectives were to hasten the completion of civic amenities such as reliable postal communication, speedy completion of the railway and facilities at the station, improved roads in and about the township and the provision of an adequate water supply. The first elected office bearers of this organisation represented a cross-section of the most energetic and forward-looking members of the community whose names figured prominently in the many activities associated with its development over the next decade. Office bearers of the association were Messrs J. Hassett, President; Bellingham, Peart, Shingler, Long, Hayes, Begg, Hanlon, Greig, McPherson, McCay and Jeffrey.

A principal matter of concern was the absence of a resident Justice of the Peace. In matters of a formal nature, such as signing of legal documents, or the obtaining of a coroner's verdict, great inconvenience was caused to selectors and other residents in this regard. James Gwyther, in a letter to the Secretary of Lands, Melbourne, wrote:

Dunkeld, 21 Apr 1880.

Sir,

I have the honor to enclose the forms (3) for the members of my family, for to come under the Lands Act Amendments of 1880. You will please observe that only one is signed before a J.P. . . . the delay in not returning forms was that they could not get a J.P. anywhere near, and that as the river was impassable they could not cross under

55

the circumstances above. I beg to ask that the three applications be submitted together . . . and that the signing before a J.P. be dispensed with under the above to avoid any longer delays. Yours etc.,

Jas. Gwyther.[2]

During the winter months with the Tarwin River impassable at times, and in the event of a summons being required, the Clerk of Courts, resident at Rosedale, had to be contacted, causing great inconvenience to all parties concerned. By 1890 only five Justices had been appointed in the Woorayl Shire, two at Mirboo North, William Scarlett and Charles Ogilvy, two at Mardan, Robert Smith and John Inglis with Colin Arrott Watt at Koorooman four miles to the north of the embryonic Leongatha township.[3]

The shortage of public buildings for civic affairs was paralleled by a similar shortage of private accommodation, particularly for newcomers and travellers. No hotels had as yet been licensed for the township, and the only legitimate means of obtaining liquor was through roadside inns such as Horn's. Inevitably, sly grog shanties made their appearance all along the railway line to cater for the large number of navvies and fettlers engaged in its construction. The editor of *The Great Southern Star* condemned these shanties in no uncertain manner in the first issue.

> They are a contamination and an abomination to the place, and in many cases the ruination of the people who run them. Give us a good hotel or two and sweep the shanties off the ground they at present occupy and disgrace. Of benefit to nobody, a nuisance to everyone, supplying no want, but filling the drunkard with stuff sufficiently bad and vile to send him to the mad-house, we fail to see any justification whatever for their existence.[4]

The editor of *The Great Southern Star* was not the only person who could see the need for a hotel or two in the new township of Leongatha. There were two energetic Irishmen in the town at that time, who not only saw the need, but were striving to fulfil it as quickly as possible. Hugh McCartin, born in 1842 at Rostrevor in Ireland, arrived in Australia about 1860 and proceeded to Shelbourne, where he and his brother, Daniel, built a flour mill, purchasing wheat from district farmers. The two brothers virtually started the town of Shelbourne by erecting the first hotel, bakery, butchery and blacksmith's shop in that town. Active in public life, Hugh McCartin later became President of the Shire of Marong.[5] With the construction of the railway to Mirboo North, Hugh and Daniel McCartin came to South Gippsland and began contracting. One of their first jobs was as sub-contractors for O'Keefe on the Great Southern Railway. Sensing the potential of trading operations, Hugh McCartin commenced stores at the Black Spur camp at Koonwarra, Tarwin and Meeniyan. These stores not only catered for the navvies working along the line but also adjoining selectors, whom Hugh McCartin supplied with pack horses. At Meeniyan, Thomas Musgrave was glad to work for Hugh McCartin for a year or two while clearing his selection.

> I was employed by the late H. McCartin in his general store, and used to pack stores out to the selectors in the Dumbalk district. I had some rough trips, but as Lindsay Gordon said, 'the hardest day was never then too hard'. The selectors had just as

hard times as I had. Many of the tracks had ramps built over big logs that crossed them; also several bridges built on giant trees across the Tarwin river, where it was not safe to ride over, but in spite of all these ups and downs, everyone had a joke to tell over a nice cup of tea, which was never forgotten whenever a traveller turned up.[6]

Confident of the future progress of the town and district, Hugh McCartin promptly secured a select corner block at the first land sale of Leongatha township blocks held in Melbourne on 2 April 1889. He paid £525 for the site of the Commercial Hotel — a high price at the time for a small section of land in an embryonic township, but one which was subsequently vindicated by events. The Otago Hotel site was purchased by Mr R. Bair at a subsequent land sale on 18 June, and both hotels were built during the following year, 1890.

To obtain the necessary materials for their new premises, Hugh McCartin and Robert Bair arranged for them to be hauled by bullock wagon from Inverloch during the summer months. The Commercial Hotel duly opened for business on 5 February 1891 — the first licensed premises in Leongatha.[7] Liquor licences were a contentious issue amongst residents of the area at that time. In 1889 Hugh McCartin and Martin O'Grady, both of Leongatha, had applied to the Traralgon Licensing Court for a victualler's licence, but the Court declined to grant either until a local opinion of ratepayers was obtained as to whether the number of hotels should be increased. This poll was held in February 1890 but declared void by the Court as less than one-third of the ratepayers voted. A further poll on this subject was held in conjunction with the election of councillors in August. Polling day proved to be of a rather inclement nature as described by the *The Great Southern Star*:

> Thursday, the 14th inst., was election day and was also set apart for the taking of the Local Option Poll. Rain was falling the first thing in the morning, and it continued throughout the day, a steady, wetting rain that made one feel most uncomfortable. Notwithstanding this fact voters rolled up at the various polling places in full force, and even the ladies, to their credit be it said, mounted their horses, and through mud, slush, wind and rain, proceeded to vote for the best man — whoever that might be . . .[8]

The holding of elections in South Gippsland entailed arduous travelling by voters and returning officers alike. On this particular occasion, Mr W. McPherson and W. Hayes, deputy returning officer and poll clerk respectively for the East Riding, left the polling booth at Kardella at 5.20 in the evening after closure of the poll. The rain that had been falling during the day continued unabated, and with darkness overtaking them, the two men lost their way and had to return to Mr Brydon's, where the poll had been held, for the night. Next morning they set out again to return to Leongatha, but on reaching the Coalition Creek found that the heavy rains had washed the bridge away. One of their horses became stuck in the flooded stream, and it was only by the assistance of several neighbours with the aid of ropes, saplings and brute force that the animal was hauled out and the two men returned home safely.

The result of the local option poll indicated that a majority of ratepayers wished to see an increase in the number of hotels in the Shire, which led to the granting of a licence to Hugh McCartin on 10 December 1890 at a sitting of the

Licensing Court in Traralgon. The second licence was granted to Robert Bair shortly afterwards. Born in 1837 at Londonderry, Ireland, Bair as a young man migrated to Australia on the ship *Young America* during the gold rush of the 1850s. He spent some time on the Ballarat goldfields before leaving for New Zealand, where he remained for some fifteen years. During this time he followed the main gold rushes in the Otago province with success and gained valuable experience as a hotelier in catering to the needs of the public.[9]

Returning to Australia in 1874, Robert Bair farmed for a short time at Shelbourne before returning to the hotel trade at Darlimurla where he set up the Tarwin Hotel in 1877. In 1886 he opened the Commercial Hotel in Mirboo North, but realising the potential of the Leongatha district, commenced building new premises in the town at the same time as Hugh McCartin. After being unsuccessful with his first application for a victualler's licence at the Licensing Court in Traralgon, Bair engaged one of Victoria's leading barristers, Sir Bryan O'Loghlen, to appear on his behalf at this second application heard at Traralgon on Saturday, 8 March 1891. Giving sworn evidence, Bair stated that he

> had resided at Leongatha for six months. Had held a publican's licence for thirteen years at Mirboo North, but had let the hotel there to Charles Farmer his son-in-law. The building for which he now sought a licence had cost over 2,000 pounds. Had furnished it with all new furniture. He had been living in the house constantly ever since . . . The house contains 24 rooms, consisting of 17 bedrooms, 4 double bedrooms, 2 sitting rooms one up and the other downstairs, 1 dining room, accommodating from 25 to 30 at table. Have between twenty and thirty boarders at present. There is a seven stalled stable, two bath rooms and three outhouses. He was also prepared to put up additional bath and closet accommodation. The Shire of Woorayl has temporary offices at present in the witness' house. As showing the number of residents in the district when the Mechanics' Institute was opened on Wednesday there were about 400 present. There is good agricultural land all round the township, and he considered that it would be quite equal to Warragul in importance.[10]

Following Bair's evidence, Sir Bryan O'Loghlen called Charles Ogilvy, Shire Secretary, who also gave sworn evidence supporting the application of Bair.

> The Shire at present met at Mr. Bair's house. He produced a map showing the boundaries of the shire and direction of the Great Southern Railway. Leongatha has been chosen as the headquarters of the shire, as it occupies a central position. 218,000 acres of land rated, the number of ratepayers in the West Riding is 393 and in the South Riding 455 and the population in the two ridings is about 3,000 allowing for absentees . . .[11]

Further support for Bair's application was provided by evidence given on his behalf by Messrs Hayes, Ridgway, Douglas, Young, Roughead, Brown, Higgs, Simmons, Parr and A.L. Ogilvy. The application of J.N. Horn was then heard by the Court with Mr R.W. Smith appearing for the complainant. Horn stated in sworn evidence:

> Am holder of a roadside licence about one mile from Leongatha. Lived there about seven years, and held a licence during the last two years. Intended to build a brick

house to cost £3,000 and if required would spend another £1,000. Would build the house about seven chains from McCartin's . . . on the road to Anderson's Inlet. Could get the full amount to build the house. Borrowed the money before the court sat in December, and was paying six per cent. interest for it.[12]

After further argument by counsel for both parties, the Bench retired for half an hour, and when court resumed, it was announced that the second licence for Leongatha was to be granted to Robert Bair. On its opening, Bair named his hotel the 'Otago' after a province of the South Island of New Zealand where he had spent more than a decade. Bair had spared no pains to make it comfortable, a notable feature being 'a handsome mirror placed in the bar so that when quaffing the sparkling ale, Denis Mooney (whisky) or a good old drop of toddy, the drinkers could obtain a good view of themselves'.[13]

Other sections of the Shire were experiencing the same problems of growth as Leongatha, although to a lesser extent. A roadside licence was sometimes the forerunner to a full victualler's licence and was granted to a store to enable it to sell bottled wines and spirits. Accommodation could be provided at these establishments according to the preference of the owner. In 1893 one of these licences was granted to storekeeper Johann Matthies at Ruby, and another was granted to Mr and Mrs Tonkyn at Meeniyan who opened the first store in that emerging township. Under the *Licensing Act* of 1890, the law allowed one licensed house for the first 250 to 1,000 inhabitants and a further one to every 500 of the inhabitants beyond that number. The estimate of population was arrived at annually on the issue of the Shire voter's roll. For 1896 the estimate for the Tarwin district was 1,455, Woorayl 3,870 and Jeetho 3,115.[14]

At the Licensing Court held at Korumburra on 3 January 1896, there were several applications heard for additional licences for the Woorayl and Tarwin districts. Edmond Hayes of Inverloch, who had formerly conducted a general store at Leongatha adjacent to the railway, stated that his house was of fourteen rooms, eleven of which were available to the general public. He estimated that there were 250 inhabitants living around Inverloch. J.E. O'Brien also applied for a licence stating that he had resided at Inverloch for ten years and that his house contained eleven rooms, at present being operated with his brother under a wine licence. He intended to add another twenty-three rooms for use of the public if granted a full victualler's licence. This application was opposed by Superintendent Webb who stated 'that he had never seen a dirtier place in his life. It contained the accumulated filth of years'. Hugh McCartin of Leongatha, owner of the house, swore that the place had been recently renovated, this evidence being supported by Constable Gorman who said that he always found the place clean.[15]

Robert Fisher of Tarwin Lower, whose application for a licence was opposed by Mr Maddock on behalf of George Black of Tarwin Meadows, stated that his house was of fourteen rooms, eleven of which were available to the public. In a reply to Mr Maddock, Fisher stated that

the population of the district was 200 within a radius of five to six miles. Saw a constable once a week. Gave up his wine licence because he did not care about it. Wanted a publican's licence because it would pay better.[16]

Snagging of the Tarwin River, 1889-1894. Photo taken at Ross's Farm near Meeniyan (from Woorayl Shire Historical Society).

Superintendent Webb reported favourably on the house and Constable O'Shannassy gave the applicant's character as good and stated the need for a hotel at Tarwin Lower. J.T. Cashin also applied for a licence in the area, stating that his house was of nine rooms when examined by Superintendent Webb. After hearing the applications, the following licences were granted:

Edmond Hayes, Inverloch Hotel, assessment L.32
John Edward O'Brien, Esplanade Hotel, conditional upon the building being finished according to plans and specifications.
Robert Fisher, Riverview Hotel, Tarwin Lower, granted without costs against the objector.
Hector Campbell, Meeniyan Hotel, assessment L.40, granted with a warning that it would not be renewed if there were any more unfavourable reports of the premises.[17]

From the evidence tendered in these applications, it would appear that there were upwards of 500 people living in the vicinity of Anderson's Inlet at that time. Like their fellow settlers at Leongatha, they were also suffering under a duality of names for official purposes. The Anderson's Inlet Post Office was officially opened as such in 1883 but changed to Inverloch six years later.

Apart from hotels, the other facilities for travellers were coffee houses which sprang up wherever an enterprising individual or family thought there was a need for permanent or overnight accommodation. Two were erected at Leongatha, one adjacent to the railway station known as Mrs Maher's, on the south-eastern corner of the junction of Jeffrey and Long Streets opposite Long's store. Another was built to the south of the Commercial Hotel — a large, two-storey building virtually in the centre of the town shopping area. At Koonwarra, Bacon brothers established one in anticipation of future development in that area.[18] At Stony Creek, H. Crutchfield, brother of W. Crutchfield who operated the general store in the township, opened a coffee house in 1892.[19] As well as providing overnight accommodation for travellers, these coffee houses often provided a room for visiting medical practitioners, dentists and music teachers. In their regular visits to the small townships, these professional people provided a valuable service to the surrounding community.

Next to the problem of providing adequate housing space for the growing population of the Shire, both permanent and temporary, was the absence of any public buildings for meetings of residents. The usual practice to overcome this situation was the formation of a Mechanics' Institute in the area. The role of Mechanics' Institutes in the social life of the burgeoning communities of South Gippsland cannot be underestimated. Apart from the Churches, they were virtually the focal point of community life. They provided a centre in which important meetings, addresses, religious services, discussions and entertainment could be held.

Mechanics' Institutes originated in Glasgow, Scotland, in 1799 where Professor George Birkbeck conducted a series of lectures, free of charge, for the working-man of that city so that he might 'agreeably occupy his mental vacancy in the evenings'. They proved so successful that the idea quickly spread to other parts of the British Isles. Institutes were established in London in 1823 and Manchester in 1824, and were usually equipped with a reference and lending library, a reading room, museum, workshop and laboratory. Other Institutes were built throughout England during the next decade. Most did not progress beyond libraries and reading rooms, with lectures being given in literature, mathematics and the arts. By 1851 there were over 610 Institutes in England with a membership of over 600,000, and the number of students attending classes was in excess of 16,000.[20]

In 1839 the Melbourne Mechanics' Institute was founded (subsequently the Athenaeum), and over the next half century, they proliferated all over the State. Their general aim was the diffusion of scientific and other useful knowledge, and rather more appropriately, the provision of 'adequate facilities for the supply of deficiencies in early education'. By 1870 there were over 100 established in Victoria with another 300 being constructed between 1870 and 1892.[21] By that time the meaning of the word 'mechanic' had been enlarged to include anyone interested in acquiring knowledge through attendance at the lectures provided, or through perusal of the reference libraries. In Victoria, an added impetus to the erection of these Institutes was given by the action of the State Government in subsidising Institute libraries. Although only in small amounts, it was an added incentive to every district to get their community hall built, incorporate a library within it and obtain a small government grant annually in the process.

At Leongatha, even before the railway line was opened, prominent men in the community had taken the initial steps to establish this important facility in the township. A committee of interested persons met at the Bank of Australasia on 29 July 1890 at which it was moved by Mr McCay and seconded by Mr Fortescue that

> The Secretary and Mr. McPherson frame a circular, setting forth the advantage to the town and consequent enhancement of the value of property here, by having a Mechanics' Institute built, and soliciting donations from the property owners in aid of a Building fund; also that a circular be printed . . . Carried.[22]

The committee had already called tenders for the clearing of the block allocated by the Government for that purpose, as an item in the first issue of *The Great Southern Star* testified.

> A fine block of land situated in one of the best portions of the township, has been granted by the Govt and is now being cleared in an expeditious manner. The tender of G. Gerbich, for the sum of £15 17s 9d. was accepted for the clearing of the ground. The trees have gradually disappeared and burning off is now proceeding.[23]

Collectors were appointed to canvass the district for subscriptions, and the offer of the Koorooman Dramatic Club to provide 'an entertainment' in aid of the project was accepted. The committee also decided 'that a bazaar or fancy fair' in aid of the building of the Mechanics' Institute be held and that the assistance of the ladies of the district be solicited in the matter. The 'ladies of the district' evidently responded to the challenge of running a bazaar with a will, because a subsequent entry in the minutes of 1 May 1891 states 'Mr. Peart reported that a net sum of £145 5s 1d was handed to him by Mrs. M. Shingler being proceeds of the bazaar'.[24]

This amount represented almost a third of the total cost of the proposed Institute. The tender of Mr C. Chaplin for the sum of £475 (labour and material) was accepted on 20 November 1890 for the erection of a building of wooden construction eighty foot by thirty-five foot with walls sixteen foot high, pine floor, with twenty foot being allowed for the stage. Mr Chaplin lost no time in starting work on the project, because it was officially opened on 4 March 1891 at what must have been a gala event for the town and district. Over 400 people attended, and the program commenced with an overture on the piano by Miss E. Bair. This was followed by the Koorooman Dramatic Club with a performance of 'Deaf as a Post', the leading role being played by Mr E. Begg as Mr Walton, an elderly gent. Then there was a Grand Ball and Supper at 10.30 p.m., all for the price of 7s 6d a double ticket or 5s a single.[25]

Being the first and only public building in the fledgling township, it was natural that it should be in great demand both for daytime and evening use. For a short time it was used by Woorayl Shire Council for their monthly meetings until the first Shire offices were completed in the same year, 1891.[26] A perusal of the minute and cash books of the Institute give a detailed and lucid picture of the activities that took place in this first civic amenity. As always, many of these entries deal with the never-ending problem of making the expenditure match the income — the cash book listing the small amounts received in rent from the different functions that were held there regularly.

The Churches were the first to take advantage of the availability of a reasonably sized place for worship. Regular payments from the Church of England of 2s 6d monthly show that services were held there under the direction of Reverend Elvery. The Catholic community quickly used the facilities of the Institute to celebrate Mass whenever a priest was available. Prior to the erection of the Catholic Church in Ogilvy Street in 1895, a Sunday school was conducted on a weekly basis for which the Institute received one shilling on each occasion.

Representations that were made to the local Member of Parliament, A.C. Groom Esq., to obtain a subsidy from the Government, met with some success, and a letter was forwarded to him from the Secretary thanking him for obtaining a grant of £22 18s 3d on behalf of the Institute.[27]

The Lands Department used the Institute regularly for the conduct of sales of Crown lands and to hear disputes that arose over the terms and conditions imposed on selectors. On 9 October 1891 at a meeting of the Board at the Institute, it revoked the lease of Charles Baker that he held on 280 acres at Nerrena, and it was then thrown open for re-selection. This was a fairly common occurrence at that time owing to the almost complete absence of any monetary return from blocks. At the same meeting of the Land Board, William Milner, on Block 199A Nerrena, applied for six months extension in his repayments — this was allowed by the Board in view of his necessitous circumstances. The Crown Law Department rented the Institute after their request met with a favourable reply from the committee that 'the occasional use of the hall and the exclusive use of one room be given to the Law Dept for Police Court purposes for the sum of twentyfive pounds per annum'.[28]

Police Magistrate Smallman visited Leongatha regularly and was not impressed with the state of the thoroughfares. He stated that 'he could not cross the street without sinking over his boot tops in mud and that when he reaches the precincts of the Mechanics' Institute he is compelled to swim to the door'. William Young, the versatile and articulate reporter of *The Great Southern Star* who had to negotiate these streets on a daily basis, did not show the Police Magistrate much sympathy. His verdict on the situation was that

The council has not funds and it is hardly probable that a ferryman could be induced to start business even with the prospects of a monthly fare. Taking all things into consideration the P.M. will have to grin and bear the hardship, although as a safeguard against drowning accidents it might be advisable for him to suspend his boots around his neck and leave any superfluous clothing for the charge of the Clerk of Courts for conveyance.[29]

Even though it was a relatively small community with considerable distance separating selectors, friction sometimes arose that resulted in a court action. An early settler in the Tarwin Valley at Dumbalk, a Mr Benn, who was a plaintiff in a case, said that 'he only got half a horse returned' after lending it to a fellow selector. The Bench, being curious as to which half of the animal it was, interrogated the witness on the matter. 'The skin and the bones' was the reply.[30] On another occasion, Charles Myers, whose property lay only a mile and a half from the township, sued Johann Nicholas Horn and Harry Fortescue for damages done to his property through a fire that had spread from their selections on to his, thereby destroying a haystack, fencing rails etc. Although

Horn and Fortescue had followed the normal practice of notifying neighbouring selectors when commencing burning-off operations, Myers had objected to them doing it at that time. As they still went ahead with burning-off, despite the protests of Myers, the Bench awarded Myers £70 damages plus costs.[31]

The sombre and judicial atmosphere created in the Institute on the occasion of Land and Magistrate's Courts was relieved on numerous occasions by concerts, balls and other entertainments that were held there regularly. One of the first of the many functions held in the Institute by an outside group was the concert arranged by the famous 'Lynch Family Bell Ringers' for 30 January 1892. This group continued to visit Leongatha during the 1890s, so the local populace must have been appreciative of their entertainment. Perhaps because the settlers were mainly of British stock, they missed the familiar sound of bell ringing so vividly described by Ronald Blythe in *Akenfield; A Portrait of an English Village*.[32] Unlike England, with its close proximity of villages and towns, bell ringing in Australia never developed to the same degree of perfection that it reached in rural England in the closing decades of the nineteenth century.

Music and dancing provided the main indoor recreational activities for young and old. The ability to dance was a social grace as well as a social leveller, and the prospect of a night's entertainment was welcomed by the great majority of settlers and their families. The following description indicates the style of function of the times.

> The hall was nicely decorated with ferns and flags with the floor in good condition. First class music was supplied by Brian Hynes (violin), G. Greig (Piano), while Mrs. Shingler kindly played a waltz. The company separated at about 3 am. after singing 'Auld Lang Syne'.[33]

The Leongatha community was shortly to be deprived of the services of its pianist, Mr George Greig. As manager of the first bank to commence operations in the township, the Bank of Australasia, he was a popular figure who had played a prominent and useful part in community affairs, having had the honour of laying the foundation stone for the Mechanics' Institute. Unfortunately, when the auditors visited the branch in the autumn of 1891, they found a discrepancy in the accounts of £650. Mr Greig was charged with embezzlement at the Mirboo North Court and, subsequently, tried at the Sale Assizes on 22 April where he pleaded guilty and was remanded for sentence.[34]

Any occasion of note was usually celebrated with a ball or dance — the completion of the goods shed at the Leongatha Railway Station provided such an excuse. In January 1892, Mr Conway, the local station master, arranged for several carriages to be drawn alongside the new building with a marquee for the provision of supper, all to be suitably decorated with gum leaves. For some reason, this venue was changed at the last moment, possibly due to the non co-operation of the Railway authorities. The community gaily went ahead and had their celebration in the Mechanics' Institute, at which over 100 people were present, dancing to the music of piano, violin and piccolo. Proceedings started at 9 p.m. and ended at daylight, during which time William Young from *The Great Southern Star* had the opportunity to observe and reflect on the scene.

At gatherings such as these the onlooker cannot be otherwise than convinced that dancing has a fascination for young and old. When we observe a young couple gyrating in the giddy maze of a waltz it is manifest that a fascination exists which must be accounted for the opportunity of holding silent commune, while sweet music acts as an affinity to guide the steps. Conducted on a proper basis dancing must always rank amongst the foremost of indoor amusements.[35]

A regular booking of the hall was that of the Quadrille Assembly that was formed almost immediately after the hall was opened. At these nights, those present perfected their techniques in all the latest versions of the Alberts and the Lancers — a very popular form of dancing that enabled both young and old to dispose of their surplus energy to the enjoyment of music. An additional source of revenue to the hall committee was the rent paid by the various lodges for the use of facilities for meetings and functions. Lodges were part of the social fabric of the new community at which members of similar interests and persuasion could meet regularly in a suitable atmosphere for moral support and encouragement. Being Friendly Societies, they provided assistance to members in times of sickness, distress, old age and death by encouraging them to contribute small amounts weekly to meet these contingencies. Before Federation and even for many years afterwards, there were no social welfare schemes

Farm homestead of George Funnell, Wooreen, c. 1895 (from R. Funnell).

funded by the Government. There were relief schemes sponsored by the major Churches and some private agencies, but as a general rule, Friendly Societies were the main avenue through which the average working-man and his family could provide for the proverbial 'rainy day'.

Of the six lodges that rented the rooms provided by the Leongatha Mechanics' Institute during the early years, the most popular, largest and active was the Australian Natives' Association. As its name implies, it originated in Australia, being founded in Melbourne in 1871, as distinct from the other five that were connected with similar organisations overseas. Its membership was restricted to males born in Australia, and particularly during the first decades of its operation, its influence on national life in Australia was considerable. Through the activities and network of its branches, it played a notable part in bringing about an affirmative vote for Federation, particularly in Victoria and Tasmania. It kept a close watch on trends in education policy advocating the incorporation of 'physical, secondary and technical education' into the curriculum. It consistently strove to have the minimum leaving age for school children raised to fourteen years, and in 1904 the Association set out to beautify the surroundings of schools by offering a prize for the most improved school ground. It urged the Education Department to introduce the subject of Australian History into schools. Prior to 1905, this had not been so, and the ANA, after making vigorous approaches to Education and University authorities, succeeded in having this glaring omission rectified.[36]

The Leongatha branch of the ANA was formed on 1 June 1893 by Mr G. Fitzsimmons, Vice Chief President, and Mr C.A. McDowall, Director, representing the Board of Directors. The founder of the branch was the local constable, P.J. Gorman, who was later awarded the Police Valour Badge for his actions in saving lives at Leongatha during the devastating bush fires of 1898. The debates, lectures and discussions conducted at the meetings of this lodge all helped in the intellectual and social formation of members. These were drawn from all strata of society, and its influence and the indirect benefits to the community should not be underestimated.

A branch of the Manchester Unity Independent Order of Oddfellows was first formed at a meeting held in the Otago Hotel on 27 November 1896. Later meetings were transferred to the Lodge Room of the Mechanics' Institute. First Noble Grand of the Lodge was local blacksmith Brother E.T. Munro and the Secretary Brother R.A. Bazley who carried on business as a baker. Other lodges to use the Lodge Room of the Mechanics' Institute were the Independent Order of Rechabites, formed in 1894, the Lord Brassey Masonic Lodge in 1896, the Irish National Foresters in 1902 and the Loyal Orange Lodge in 1907. Minutes of the Institute record a motion moved by Hugh McCartin, seconded by J. Hassett, that 'if there are six societies requiring the use of the lodge room that the rental be £4 10s per annum with the understanding that the Committee pay for tuning and insuring the lodge room piano'.[37]

With the Leongatha Mechanics' Institute proving to be such a success in the provision of social amenities in the township, people living more than five or six miles away tended to form their own communities and Institutes. Owing to the smaller number of people involved, these buildings were not as large or well finished as at Leongatha. Nevertheless, they provided a suitable venue for

Church services, balls, concerts, dances and, in many cases, school purposes. At Ruby, four miles west of Leongatha, a Mechanics' Institute was opened and immediately leased to the Education Department for school purposes. S.S.3208 opened on 29 September 1894.[38]

The origin of the naming of the township of Ruby is subject to doubt. One version claims that the two towns on the South Gippsland line, Ruby and Agnes, were named after the two daughters of Surveyor Whitelaw. This claim conflicts with the report of Superintendent La Trobe on his return from the Port Albert district in March 1845. In it he states that he named one river the Franklin, presumably after the Governor of Van Diemen's Land, and a second, the Agnes.[39] The most reasonable account of the naming of the township is that it was derived from Ruby Creek. This was the name given by early selectors who found what looked like rubies, but were really garnets, along the bed of this creek. The township of Ruby is actually situated on the banks of the Coalition Creek, the Ruby Creek being two miles to the north, so the origin of the name will most likely remain a source of contention.

South of Meeniyan, the small township of Stony Creek is actually built on the surveyed site of the township of Dumbalk — this being done by Surveyor P.C. Hodgkinson in 1892. The initial movement for the establishment of a Mechanics' Institute there was made on 19 June 1893. A meeting of residents elected trustees Messrs N. Dike, A. Parkins, C.T. Ogilvy, D. Henderson, W. Crutchfield and H. Crutchfield with Mr A. C. Helms as Secretary. A site was immediately acquired and the first hall erected by Mr W. Benn. It was simply a large rectangular room with a raised platform at one end, but with no provision for the hot water necessary for supper on nights of entertainment. Consequently, whenever a ball or concert was held, a marquee had to be erected and a copper brought along to heat the water. However, these minor disadvantages did not detract from its appeal as a district centre for community enjoyment and recreation.[40]

Several miles to the north of Stony Creek, the rugged hill country bordering the Foster to Mirboo road was opened for selection in 1884. During the summer of 1887-88, three settlers, Herbert Salmon, John Nicholson and John Leishman, met on this road to exchange views while waiting for the arrival of Joe Perrin, the mailman. Hearing that one of their fellow selectors, R. Tyas, was forfeiting his allotment, these three men formed themselves into a Progress Association with Herbert Salmon as President and J. Leishman, Secretary. It was then moved that the Secretary inform Mr F.C. Mason, MLA, that at a meeting of the Progress Association of residents on the Foster to Mirboo road, a motion was carried unanimously that 'Mr. Mason be asked to request the Minister for Lands to reserve 50 acres of allotment 38 (R. Tyas) for a township site'.[41] Following a request from the Postal Department as to the name of the proposed new township, John Leishman proposed that it be called Dollar after the town of Dollar in Scotland, where he and his father before him had been educated.

The name of Buffalo Creek was given to the next railway station south of Stony Creek because of the great number of wild cattle that were found roaming in the scrub nearby. It is surmised that these cattle were the progeny of a small herd left behind from the temporary military settlement established at Western Port in 1826. After several years, an agreement was reached between the railway

Ticket to the ANA Annual Ball, 1901 (from Woorayl Shire Historical Society).

and postal authorities for the name to be shortened to Buffalo.[42] The Buffalo Mechanics' Institute first opened on 12 October 1894 and since then has been used by the community for a variety of functions including balls, concerts, weddings, bazaars, lending library, land auctions, school and Church etc. When the Institute was leased by the Education Department for school purposes in 1897, the school operated under the name of Meeniyan East, S.S.3240 for ten years as there was already a State school functioning near Myrtleford named Buffalo Creek.[43]

A division of opinion within the community sometimes occurred in the siting of a new hall. Such was the case at Tarwin Lower in 1888. An application by P.L.C. O'Shannassy as Secretary for the Committee of Management for a proposed Tarwin Public Hall was considered by the Land Board at Cranbourne on 18 May 1888. Proposed trustees were Messrs G. Black and Thomas Lees of Tarwin Lower. A postponement was successfully gained by Mr J. Cashin on the grounds that the site was not central and that it should be considered by a further representative meeting of residents. Mr Cashin claimed that the notice for the initial meeting was posted in the morning and the meeting held the same evening. The postponement allowed a new set of trustees to be elected in Messrs Thomas Lees, Alfred Brown and Robert Fisher. The hall was to be known as the 'Tarwin Lower Mechanics' Institute' and was built on the site recommended by Surveyor J.T. Lardner, Allotment 2 Section 1 of the township. By 6 March 1890, Secretary Samuel Henry Lemon reported that 'the land had been cleared at a cost of £6 12s 6d and a creditable building at a cost of £235 erected'.[44]

During the 1890s other Institutes were opened at Fairbank, Meeniyan, Koon-warra, Mount Eccles and Hallston. At Inverloch Mr and Mrs Wyeth organised a concert that realised £75 to finance the erection of a Mechanics' Institute. This was built in 1897 and served the needs of this seaside town as a community centre and a lending library for many decades. Unlike some of the other small Institutes opened at that time, the Inverloch Institute library was much in demand by local residents, with up to 2,000 books being in stock at one time, many on loan from the Melbourne Public Library.[45]

As a result of the financial stringency imposed on the State of Victoria by the depression of the 1890s, the Government considerably reduced its subsidy to Mechanics' Institutes with the result that few halls erected after 1900 were named as such. The Institutes may not have quite fulfilled the expressed aims and objects set out so clearly in their constitutions, but the functions that were able to be held within their precincts practically encompassed all the indoor social needs of the communities they were built to serve. Church services, schools, lodge meetings, polling booths, bazaars, elections, land courts, Courts of Petty Sessions, health services, concerts, balls, weddings, send-offs, Christmas parties, card nights and boxing tournaments were all held in Mechanics' Institute halls. The variety of activities fully justified the efforts and deter-mination of the men and women who founded these Institutes when they had little more than the forest floor for assembly points.

Arnold Clemann's team hauling logs to Jones's sawmill at Meeniyan, c. 1906 (from D. Bacon).

Settler's hut, Gunyah, c. 1914 (from D. Dodd).

6. INDUSTRY

The building of the Great Southern Railway line led to increased activity at Anderson's Inlet. There were six or seven bullock teams plus an equal number of horse teams engaged in cartage of goods from the jetty to points along the new railway line. Inverloch was quite a busy port in 1890 with a regular shipping service to Port Melbourne.[1] The short time that the tracks could be used during the summer months led to an application being made to Woorayl Shire Council by two enterprising gentlemen, Messrs Rout and Tomlins, for permission to lay down a steam tramway on Shire roads from Anderson's Inlet to Leongatha. After considering the request, Council decided to grant permission with the following proviso.

> That Rout and Tomlins shall give a guarantee of £350 to indemnify the Shire against legal or other expenses incurred. Work to be commenced within six months from Date of Delegation and the tramway to be completed within two years of commencement.[2]

Council no doubt felt that this suggestion of a steam tramway would partially solve their overwhelming problem of providing a road system in their newly-created Shire. Associated with the lack of roads was the necessity to construct innumerable bridges over the Tarwin and its tributaries that interlaced the new Shire. Indeed, one of the first public notices issued by the Council concerned bridges.

> Loaded vehicles are warned. The bridges over the Tarwin on the Coast Road and over Coalition Creek, near Horn's on the same road, are unsafe. All persons crossing same bridges will do so at their own risk, and will be held legally responsible for all loss and damage that may ensue and for all injury to the bridges that may be caused thereby.[3]

Many bridges were simply trees fallen across the streams at an appropriate spot, the topmost sides levelled with adzes and sapling decking fixed crossways with wooden spikes. The Johnson brothers on the Coalition Creek simply felled a tree across the creek and then split it lengthwise to enable them to cross with horses on their way to the township.[4] Frequent floods and the rotting of the decking made these first bridges extremely dangerous, and many accidents occurred resulting in injuries to man and beast.

Corduroy was used extensively by Woorayl Shire Council in the first decade of its existence. On 8 October 1889 tenders were called for 'the clearing and grubbing of roads about Koorooman also the supply of 2,500 pieces of corduroy'. This method, although primitive, did solve the problem until bluestone could be carted by horse and dray from nearby quarries. Sometimes the corduroy was laid 'in the round' without splitting, resulting in an extremely rough surface for the traveller. Complaint as to the use of corduroy near Clark's Bridge was evidenced by a letter to Council from Messrs Griffin and Geale of the Meeniyan Progress Association.

> Geale said he would sooner see round corduroy stacked on the side of the road than travel over it. They failed to see why it should be used when there was ample supplies of split messmate available.[5]

Shire Engineer, Mr T. Griffin, in reply said that only £5 could be spent on this job, and he had framed specifications accordingly. After discussion, the President promised the deputation that loam to the depth of nine to ten inches would be spread over the corduroy. Fortunately for Woorayl Shire Council, there was an abundance of good quality bluestone available in numerous outcrops scattered throughout the district. The first stretch of road to be metalled on the northern side of the Leongatha township was past Horn's. The stone was obtained from a small quarry nearby by contractor Mr D. Canty.[6]

The stone was blasted from the rockface by the use of explosives, broken down into manageable size by spalling hammers of 14 lbs weight wielded by strong men, loaded on to drays and hauled to the site of the stone crusher. These crushers were powered by a steam boiler fired with wood and were towed from site to site by bullock teams. Another quarry was actually opened in the township at the foot of McCartin Street in Worthy Street. Indeed, for many years this street was known as 'Quarry Street'. The main quarry to be opened and the one that lasted the longest was situated adjacent to the railway line approximately one mile to the south of the station on Simon's Lane. These quarries proved a valuable asset to the district, for they enabled all-weather roads to be built in a relatively short time. Being sited adjacent to the railway, the quarry on Simon's Lane soon became a profitable enterprise with crushed metal being loaded directly onto railway trucks for despatch to stations up and down the line. It provided a cash income to the town and district as there were upwards of forty men employed in the blasting, carting and crushing of the rock.

Other Shires were not so fortunate in possessing good quality bluestone for road-making and were forced to bring it in at considerable cost. The Poowong and Jeetho Shire in its formative years used red metal for its roads. This was actually the mud rock that lay underneath the topsoil that had been burnt to a red texture. The rock was easily obtained and the timber readily available for burning. Huge piles of logs were pulled into place by bullock teams, the mud rock would be piled on top of them and the logs set alight. After cooling, this red metal would be spread on the roadway where it provided a reasonable surface until the advent of cream wagons ruined this soft rock. In his report to the Poowong and Jeetho Council, the Engineer stated that 'he favoured use of blue metal from the Leongatha quarries'.[7]

With the opening of the railway in 1891, small sawmills were quickly established in close proximity to the line in an attempt to utilise the valuable stands of excellent timber readily available. Ted Higgs set up a mill in the town in 1890, but unfortunately a tree fell across his engine putting it out of commission soon after commencing operations.[8] Another sawmill was operated by E.P. Harden on the southern corner of McCartin and Peart Streets with logs being hauled to the mill by bullock or horse teams during the summer months. The vast amount of blackbutt, blue gum and messmate available for milling purposes at the time resulted in little profit for these sawmilling enterprises. Blackwood was used extensively in the lining of railway carriages, as well as in the furniture trade generally, being an extremely hard and versatile wood that polishes readily. It, too, had little commercial value because of oversupply, even though Harden installed a buzzer, bandsaw and morticing machine for dressing the sawn blackwood planks. Harden utilised it for coffin making as he was the undertaker for the district. A burial at Inverloch in the winter months involved him in three days work owing to the tortuous state of the roads. The horse-drawn hearse travelled to the Inlet on the first day when Harden made all arrangements for the digging of the grave and the funeral. The next day the horses were groomed and plumed for the actual funeral and then returned to Leongatha on the third day.

Blackwood was also widely used as staves for the manufacture of barrels — if well made they would last for decades. Beer, wine, spirits, butter, molasses, cement and many other commodities were preserved and transported in this manner. Such was the oversupply of this fine timber at the time that a stack of blackwood logs, thirty foot wide, fifteen foot high and twenty foot long that Harden had stacked on an adjoining block, proved unsaleable and was burnt for firewood.[9]

The good splitting timber, such as the mountain ash or blackbutt, was often used for palings. A paling knife was used for this purpose — a few taps with a mallet and the paling would split clean and free away from the billet. Up to 8,000 palings were obtained from a single blackbutt tree with some men specialising in this occupation. The palings were then transported to the nearest railway station for despatch to the metropolitan area where they were in good demand for the fencing of suburban allotments. *The Great Southern Star* of 11 September 1896 carried a notice from one paling splitter which read:

TENDERS.
Tenders are invited for carting of 25,000 palings (more or less) at per 100 to Leongatha or Mirboo North railway station from block known as Twomey's, Mardan. Lowest or any tender not necessarily accepted . . . J.R. Elliott P.O. Mardan.

South of Ruby there were some excellent stands of messmate and stringybark suitable for milling. A sawmill was begun on the property of Mr A. Cameron some two and a half miles south of the small township and a wooden tramline laid down to connect with the Ruby Station. This line passed along Sage's and Logan's road, approaching Ruby through what was later the Ruby State School grounds. On closure of the mill, the wooden tramlines were purchased by neighbouring farmers and used for construction of farm sheds. Evidence of their durability is provided by the fact that these sheds are still in use almost a century later.

Quarrying and sawmilling were extractive industries as they were an attempt to utilise the raw material readily available in order to obtain a cash return. Slowly but surely, however, the agricultural and pastoral industries developed and became the staple for the district. The dairy industry began in a primitive fashion with the first cowsheds, usually consisting of sheets of bark attached to poles along the side of a large log that served as one wall. The floors were of split slabs and herds were small, usually of eight to ten cows with yards of corduroy. In order to run any type of stock on the newly-sown pastures, fences had to be built to prevent them from straying into the uncleared forest. The first clearings were usually enclosed by large logs left lying on the ground, or by chock and log fences. These were made from logs of up to three foot in diameter with another smaller one placed above. The upper ones were held in place by support posts placed crosswise at a forty-five degree angle. Post and rail fences were built for stock yards and horse paddocks, while picket fences made from split palings were used for pig and sheep fencing.

After the initial burn, the laborious task of picking up the charred logs and branches and stacking them into heaps for reburning took place. In many cases this entailed as much work as the cutting of the scrub. Indeed, when done by contract, the price for this work often exceeded that of scrub cutting. If sown to grass, the regrowth of dogwood, hazel and musk had to be slashed with axes so often the settler would attempt to crop the land with a pioneer crop of potatoes as a means of levelling the actual ground. Stumps were invariably left for the following generation to attend to, as the extra land gained by removing them did not justify the effort involved. All of this hard physical work entailed in clearing their selections took its toll on the settlers and their health.

Typical was William Begg, formerly an employee of the Melbourne Harbour Trust, who with his son pegged out land at Koorooman on 18 December 1882, and four days later application was made to occupy under Section 19 of *The Land Act*, 1869. The licence was issued on 23 August 1883, and the family resided on the land from 1884.[10] Five years later, in August 1889, the following improvements had been made to his selection.

> 28 chains of post and three rail fence
> 117 chains of chock and log fence
> 160 acres sown to potatoes and grass (potato yield six tons per acre)
> Four roomed dwelling, 30 ft by 24 ft, of split timber and shingle
> garden and orchard, one acre
> stock yard and out-buildings.

William Begg suffered from rheumatism and was unable to travel from Koorooman to Mirboo North in August 1889 to make a declaration regarding an application for leasehold tenure. On 3 April 1899 Betsy Begg, widow, reported that a fire the previous year had destroyed fences and out-buildings and forced the family to sell their stock. This was the reason for rental arrears. William Begg had died prior to this date and the selection was transferred to his widow on 27 January 1900. The Crown grant was issued on 31 August 1903.[11] The Begg family, like others in the area, notified losses of livestock in *The Great Southern Star*. On 9 January 1891 E. Begg placed a notice offering '1 pound reward . . . Stolen or strayed. Two steers rising two years old. Branded (B — I) on milking side. If stolen £10 reward. E. Begg, Koorooman'.[12] Many farmers in the Woorayl shire a century later, particularly the younger ones who have grown up with herringbone dairies, might be mystified as to which was the 'milking' side of a two-year-old steer!

The 1890s brought about a major technological change in the dairy industry, one of several that were to take place over the next century. Until this time, butter had been made on the farm from cream skimmed from flat dishes of milk each holding one and a half gallons that had been allowed to set for thirty-six to forty-eight hours. Usually it was made in a Cherry-type churn, then washed and salted in a circular wooden tub about two feet six inches in diameter and four to five inches deep, known as a butter-worker. While rotating on a centre spindle, the salt was then mixed into the butter with a beater.

Notwithstanding this primitive method of butter manufacture, the amount produced in Victoria increased year by year until in the 1880s production exceeded demand with a resultant drop in prices received by the producer. Attempts had been made as early as 1863 to export butter to Europe without the benefit of refrigeration, but the result was disastrous — it was sold on the London market for cart grease![13]

The successful arrival in London of the refrigerated ship *Strathleven* in 1880, carrying eighty casks of butter that opened in splendid condition, heralded a new era for the dairying industry in Victoria. The advent of refrigerated shipping coincided with the perfection in Europe of separators that enabled cream to be skimmed from milk without the bother of setting it out in dishes and leaving it for two days. Initially produced in Germany in 1859, separators were developed further by Neilsen in Denmark, then brought to a reasonable degree of perfection by de Laval in Sweden in the late 1870s.

The separator was first exhibited in Victoria at the annual spring show in Melbourne of 1884. It was capable of dealing with sixty gallons of milk per hour, resulting in better cream than pan setting. It could be driven by a steam engine or horse works and cost approximately £50 without engine. These separators were initially purchased by small creameries where nearby farmers would take their milk daily, have it separated, and then return with the skimmed milk that would then be fed to the pigs and calves.

In the 1890s three creameries were established in the Mardan, Dumbalk and Tarwin Lower areas to cater for the milk produced in these districts. In February 1892 a meeting was held at the home of Mr P. O'Malley of Mardan at which there were ten farmers present for the purpose of forming a creamery. The ten farmers collectively had 213 cows with a total grassed area of 1,325 acres. Enquiries were made about forming a company, but it was found that it was necessary to have at least 300 cows in the area before private companies would be interested.[14] Within a decade farm separators had become almost universal in dairying districts throughout the State. Creameries became obsolete as the cream could be collected by wagon two or three times a week. In 1891 there were 445 separators in Victoria, one for every 887 milking cows, whereas ten years later in 1901, there were 4,131, or one for every 26 milkers.[15]

The changeover to farm separators saved the farmer the daily task of taking whole milk to the creamery and returning with the skimmed milk, but it nevertheless resulted in a decline in quality of the butter manufactured. With creameries the butter would usually be made on the same day that the milk was delivered. With the introduction of farm separators the cream would sometimes be three or four days old before it reached the factory, with a resultant decline in quality. Another contributing factor in the decline of quality was the risk of contamination to the cream from the intrusion of mice, rats and even snakes while stored on the farm.

The Government of Victoria was anxious to stimulate the dairy industry within the State, as it was a means to closer settlement and a source of revenue to the colony through the opening up of the European trade by the introduction of refrigeration on ships. The Deakin-Gillies Government of 1889 introduced a series of measures that were destined to stimulate the industry from a more or less back-yard component of general farm production activities to an industry geared to export. The measures included:

1. A bonus payment on exported produce.
2. A bonus payment on the establishment of dairy factories.
3. The purchase of the Melbourne Refrigerated Works at Newport to store produce for export.
4. The erection of suitable storage sheds at railway stations and the provision of refrigerated vans on trains to ensure rapid transit of produce from country to city.[16]

These measures led to the rapid expansion of the dairying industry during the 1890s resulting in 174 butter factories operating by 1895, while the value of butter exports to Great Britain had risen almost twenty-fold from £51,300 in 1889-90 to £1,081,243 in 1894-5.[17]

Many of these new factories were established by proprietary companies such as the Melbourne Chilled Butter and Cheese Factory, Kraft, Nestlé, Holdensen and Neilsen and other smaller firms. In the Woorayl Shire the first factory was formed on a co-operative basis in 1892 at Tarwin Lower.[18] It soon ran into financial difficulties and was sold to the Melbourne Chilled Butter and Produce Co. Ltd in 1896. The Dumbalk factory was formed on a co-operative basis in 1894 with a nominal capital of £2,000, the first directors being W.B. Hughes, M. Fitzgerald, W.J. Vance, R. Fitzgerald, A. Butterworth and W. Benn. Shortly after formation, Messrs W. Couper, W. Steele and R. Wilson from the Mardan district were added to the board. Operations began in a small way on land acquired from John Butterworth, and at the fourth meeting of suppliers held on 10 March 1896, the Chairman, Wilson Coulter, gave a summary of the half year's operations ending 1 February 1896.

166,548 gallons of milk purchased yielding
65,045 lbs. of butter.
23,856 lbs. were exported, av. price of 102s. 6d per cwt.
37,618 lbs. sold in Melbourne

1,102 lbs. sold at factory
2,469 lbs. now on Melbourne market.[19]

Mr Coulter stated that

the company could not show as great a profit as other factories in more favoured areas owing to the bad roads, the rough country and the distance required to cart cream, however he was satisfied with the half year's work.[20]

From a study of these figures, it would appear that farmers supplying the Dumbalk factory at that time were still carting their milk either to the factory or to the three creameries that serviced it and had not as yet invested in the purchase of separators for farm use.

The Tarwin Lower Butter and Cheese Factory Ltd, in their annual report, did not depict a situation as promising as that of Dumbalk. Intake for the year 1895-96 was 28,181 gallons of milk purchased yielding 11,170 lbs of butter.[21] The Manager, Mr Stanley, said

this represented 1 lb. of butter to 2½ gallons of milk which should have shown even a better result but for the working of the old bowl of the separator which had at last to be replaced with a new one, on account of the loss of cream estimated to be 1/6th of all that went through it. Butter sold in Melbourne brought £359, local sales £399 while expenses amounted to £330 leaving a profit of £68 for the season or a profit of 18 percent over expenses. The factory lost eleven days in the middle of the season owing to the separator bowl going wrong with the result that some of the shareholders and large suppliers purchased separators of their own which brought the supply down to as low as 120 gallons per day.[22]

The first tentative steps for the formation of a butter factory at Leongatha began in February 1894 when the Victorian Creamery Company circularised the district with an offer to build a factory at Leongatha if 600 shares were taken up at £1 per share.[23] The farming community was uncertain whether to take up this offer or to proceed with a co-operative venture as was being done at Dumbalk. At a public meeting held in the Mechanics' Hall at the end of June, it was moved by Mr D. Spencer 'that in the opinion of the meeting it is desirable and expedient to establish a butter factory at Leongatha forthwith'.[24] Mr A. Ogilvy (rate collector) was appointed as canvasser for shares, and was to be remunerated at the rate of one percent on all bona fide applications. By the beginning of August, Mr Ogilvy reported that

he can dispose of 620 shares but there are a great many others sympathetic to the idea. Inquiries reveal that up to 1,000 cows are being milked in the district which could quite easily support a factory.[25]

At a public meeting held in the Mechanics' Hall on 9 August 1894 to arrange the formation of the Leongatha Butter Factory, the following directors were elected: T.S. Ridgway (Chairman), F.H. Searle, W. Gostelow, John Symons, F.S. Laver and Mr C. Ogilvy was appointed Secretary, pro tem, on a salary of £12 per annum. The directors lost no time in acquiring a site for the proposed new factory on the south-east corner of Ogilvy and Hassett Streets. Tenders were called for its erection and subsequently let to T. Robinson of Spotswood for the sum of £308. A further tender was accepted from J. Reidy for the sinking of a thirty foot deep well with slabbed sides.[26] Within the space of six weeks, the general public was invited to the opening of the new factory on 19 December 1894. The directors soon realised that there was no adequate drainage for waste water and milk, as within a fortnight of opening, they were seeking offers for the disposal of waste milk from the factory.[27]

By the middle of February 1895, the thirty foot well had run dry, and the Secretary reported that he had spent £4 18s 0d on the cartage of water. Due to the hot weather there was a glut of second grade butter on the Melbourne market with the result that the factory was operating at a loss, paying out more to the suppliers than it was receiving from the sale of its butter. The factory then closed after being open only two months. After the autumn break in the weather, the factory re-opened on 8 April, the payment to suppliers being 4½d per pound to shareholders, but a farthing less to non-shareholders.[28]

The financial position of the new factory was so critical that directors had to give personal guarantees to the bank to enable it to continue. F.S. Laver retired from the board and three new members were elected. The new board comprised Messrs Ridgway (Chairman), Gostelow, Symons, Searle, McCartin, Long and Hynes. Minutes of the meeting held on 29 July 1895 contain the following motion:

> that the factory open on Tuesday 1 October, 1985, and that the price of butter be 6½d per lb. for the first fortnight; secretary to get postcards printed and sent to shareholders to that effect.

The position of Secretary for the Leongatha Butter and Cheese Factory Co. Ltd was advertised in *The Great Southern Star* on 20 September 1895 at a wage of ten shillings per week 'with the option of filling the post of assistant at the factory if required at further remuneration of fifteen shillings per week'. At the next meeting of the board on 14 October 1895, the following sixteen suppliers received a total of £56 9s 4d for the fortnight: W. Gostelow, H.B. Chalmers, M. O'Donnell, A.G. King, P. Waide, J. Symons, G. Huntingford, R. Hulls, Hynes brothers, J. Hyde, T. Gould, W. Turner, J. Hassett, J. Sullivan, F. Hulls and E.T. Munro.[29]

The Leongatha Butter and Cheese Factory Co. Ltd was not the only company facing difficulties at that time. At Meeniyan the creamery committee, having failed to make satisfactory arrangements with Dumbalk, decided to proceed with erection of one of their own. Shares had been readily taken up, and it was hoped to proceed with the erection of a building in the near future.[30] At Dumbalk the factory re-opened in September 1895 after being closed for the winter with good prospects for the current season. The company was badly in need of a cooling shed for their produce as illustrated by a report in *The Great Southern Star*:

> Accommodation is very insufficient, there being only a small open shed to which the dogs of the district have free access, and butter boxes, calves carcases, pork and all perishable goods are entirely at their mercy. The Progress Association some time ago endeavoured to procure a second roof for the shed and erection of a picket fence in front at a cost of £5 — it seems a reasonable request and rather hard on the dairymen to be refused.[31]

The first Leongatha Butter Factory, Ogilvy Street, 1895-1905 (from H. Morter).

Leongatha Butter Factory, Yarragon Road , 1905 (from Murray Goulburn).

The Dumbalk and Leongatha factories managed to survive their early struggles for existence, but the Tarwin Lower Butter and Cheese Factory Ltd formed in 1892 was sold to a private firm, the Melbourne Chilled Butter and Produce Co. in 1896 and later in 1904 to Australian Producers and Traders Co. The Ruby butter factory also had a rather erratic beginning. First started in 1897 by the Country Butter Factory Manufacturing Co. of 28 King Street, Melbourne, it was built almost on the banks of the Coalition Creek with a view to using the water for washing purposes and then disposing of the effluent downstream.[32] The small West Tarwin Co-operative Butter Factory, servicing farms in the Allambee, Hallston, Ferndale and Trida districts, operated from 1896 until 1903 but was then sold to the Korumburra Co-operative Butter Factory.

After several years of operation, the Leongatha Factory directors soon realised the limitations imposed on the company by the wrong choice of site. The well, although deepened, was insufficient for the needs of the factory. There was no town water supply to augment it, drainage was a big problem, and being on a level site, it was not possible to utilise the force of gravity. In 1901, in order to strengthen the capital base of the company, it was decided to offer shares to suppliers — not less than ten nor more than thirty on payment of an instalment of 2s 6d per share.[33] In effect this meant that the company changed from a proprietary limited company to a co-operative with the original shareholders receiving the equivalent number of shares in the new company.

The introduction of new blood on to the board of directors resulted in a commendable decision to re-locate the factory on a more suitable site. In 1904 the company purchased twenty acres of land fronting Yarragon Road, formerly known as 'The Scent Farm' — a section of the Leongatha Labour Colony. The Labour Colony had been established on 822 acres of Crown land adjacent to the township in 1893. The Scent Farm was that section of the Colony that had been used for the growing of flowers for perfume. The new location proved an admirable site for the future operations of the company. The sloping nature of the ground enabled the new factory, opened in 1905, to incorporate many advanced features of design that were to prove of great economic benefit in the years following. Built of brick from designs by Mr R. Kerr, a Melbourne architect, it was of three levels, thus utilising the force of gravity to the utmost.

The cream was received at the front of the building on the first floor, tipped over a cooler into maturing vats in a lower room and then drawn off as required into churns, situated underneath again. After being taken from the churns, the butter was conveyed into 'workers' where it was then processed into blocks of 28 lbs if destined for the export trade, or 1 lb or ½ lb pats for the local trade.

The coolroom was built into the side of the hill, new refrigeration plant was purchased, and with the installation of modern machinery, the factory opened in September 1905 with a capacity for producing thirty tons of butter per week.[34] Much of the credit for the design of the new factory, that was to serve the cream suppliers of the district for the next half century, must go to Stewart Curtis Wilson who was appointed Manager of the original factory in Ogilvy Street in 1901. The Department of Agriculture was so impressed with the design and layout that photographs were taken and forwarded to London for display to illustrate the advanced nature of the dairy industry developed in Victoria at that time. The availability of good water from the town supply that was installed in 1906 enabled the company to expand its operations with consequent benefits to the suppliers and the district ever since.

The cream was collected from farms by horse wagons that travelled certain routes on a regular basis — three times a week during the spring and summer months, twice a week during winter. On short runs only two horses would be harnessed, on the longer runs into the hills four horses would be used, and on the Mount Eccles run a fifth had to be taken to negotiate the steep gradients. Before the advent of motor transport the cream supply area was necessarily limited to a radius of from ten to twelve miles, although some factories obtained supply by rail, particularly if built in close proximity to a station.

Leongatha, Ruby, Korumburra, Loch and Stony Creek factories were thus situated, and many farmers naturally took advantage of this situation by forwarding cream to factories outside their own district in the belief, often mistaken, that they would obtain a better return by so doing. When the Loch factory opened in 1900, it is recorded that amongst its first suppliers was the Leongatha Labour Colony.

The availability of rail cartage of cream was a mixed blessing and caused quite a deal of discussion and dissension amongst farmers. In November 1896 the Leongatha Butter Factory reported that the weekly output was four tons of butter per week, with supply coming from all parts of the district and also by rail from stations between Korumburra and Dandenong. The actual percentage of cream that was traded outside the district is impossible to determine, but the majority of farmers tended to support the factory in their own area. Dumbalk, not being on the railway line, received little supply by rail but, nevertheless, continued to operate successfully with supply carted by horse-drawn wagons from the fertile farms in the valley of the Tarwin. Meeniyan farmers never rallied enough support locally to establish a butter factory in the township. The Dumbalk factory, however, was in a central position in the valley of the Tarwin, so proved quite satisfactory to the suppliers on the north side of Meeniyan, with very little supply coming from the area south of the railway line. At Stony Creek a private company, Wood and Co., established a butter factory in 1896 with buildings and machinery brought from a former factory at Yarra Glen.[35] The difficulties that confronted the factories at Leongatha, Dumbalk and Tarwin Lower also prevailed at Stony Creek, and after seven years of operation, in 1903, Wood and Co. sold the plant and buildings to the newly-formed Stony Creek Co-operative Butter Factory Co. It commenced operations with a capital of 1,000 £1 shares and functioned well for quite some time. Water was pumped from the Stony Creek, approximately three-quarters of a mile away, and stored in four 4,000 gallon tanks at the premises. Cream supply was obtained by use of horse-drawn wagons that traversed the Dollar and Grassy Spur areas — nearly all hill country and heavy going for the teams. At Dollar an eighteen acre paddock was purchased so that the driver and his team could stay overnight, collect cans of cream the following morning from surrounding farms and then return to the factory at Stony Creek.[36] Cheese-making was not favoured by these new factories. Although the technology was readily available, most factory managers believed that butter-making gave a better return on invested capital. At Koonwarra a small cheese-making enterprise was operated for several years on the Lyre Bird Mound property pioneered by Jacob Thomas. After seventeen years of pioneering and development, Thomas sold to Lindsay Inglis in 1896 who re-sold to Mr Macdonald in 1904. Cheese-making took place under the charge of Mr Bob Armstrong utilising the milk produced from this very fine property. The financial returns obtained from its manufacture, however, did not encourage directors of neighbouring dairy factories to diversify away from butter manufacture as their main activity.

Although the dairying industry quickly established itself as the major industry throughout the Shire in terms of value of output, number of people employed and area of land occupied, it was not the only form of production carried out on farms. In many cases it was the major farm enterprise; on others it was only a component part; in some cases just a sideline activity carried on by the womenfolk. By reason of climate, topography and suitability of the soil for grassland production, stock raising has always been a major activity on the farms of the area, whether in the form of dairy cattle and pigs, beef cattle or sheep. Horses were bred in small numbers, with every farm possessing some for draught, harness and riding purposes. As the area of cleared land increased each year, so also did the stock numbers with a resultant need for stock agents, yards and auctioneers to bring buyer and seller together. The first set of cattle yards for sale purposes in the Leongatha-Koorooman area was set up adjacent to Horn's Roadside Inn on the Coalition Creek by G. McCord, with the first sale being conducted in October 1890.[37]

This site proved unsuitable as the following year they were shifted into

The trucking yards, Leongatha, c. 1908 (from Woorayl Shire Historical Society).

Leongatha onto the lower side of Roughead Street, not far from the Long Street corner. Other stock agents to begin operations in the Leongatha district at that time were Wm. Hamilton and Co., H. Farrell and Co., Matthew Bros. and Plummer and Howard. Wm. Hamilton and Co. advertised the building of their sale yards at Leongatha on 20 July 1894 by inviting tenders for the 'splitting of 1,250 rails and 320 posts to be delivered on site'.[38] Hugh McCartin quickly branched out into the stock and station business by building yards in Smith Street. He later leased the land on which the post office is now situated for holding yards.

The newly-established pastures on the fertile red soils surrounding Leongatha proved eminently suitable for the fattening of store cattle, and within a relatively short time, the Leongatha district became known throughout the State as a prime cattle fattening area. During the 1902 drought that afflicted NSW and the northern part of Victoria, this new area of South Gippsland was lightly stocked. Stock agents were quick to truck vast numbers of store cattle that were practically unsaleable north of the divide to Leongatha, where in the space of six to twelve months, they were ready for market as prime ox beef. One of these stock agents was John Murray Peck who established an agency and yards in Leongatha in 1902 with the well-known Ted Begg of Rubybank as the first Manager.[39] Peck, a native of New Hampshire, USA, in association with three other Americans, Freeman Cobb, James Swanton and John Lamber, had arrived in Victoria in 1853 and, shortly afterwards, founded the famous firm of Cobb and Co. that was to play such a major role in transportation in Australia in succeeding decades. Peck left the firm in 1862 and, almost immediately, started in the stock and station business, establishing his own firm in the 1890s.[40] The stock yards built by J.M. Peck and Sons at Leongatha, although built from split rails and posts, also included a roofed sale ring rotunda through which cattle could be passed while the buyers were protected from the elements — the first in Gippsland. Over 800 store cattle were yarded at their opening sale in 1902 realising an average price of £6 10s 0d. Ted Begg quickly built up the stock business of J.M. Peck and Sons, later earning himself the sobriquet of 'five-to-twelve' Begg because of his habit of arriving in town at that time most days.[41]

Mr A.C. Groom, MLA for the district in the Victorian Parliament during the 1890s, was elected to the House of Representatives as the Member for South Gippsland after Federation. Through contacts made while in Parliament, Groom obtained the offer of the Kyogle Station in the Upper Richmond area of northern NSW. Impressed with its potential for closer settlement, Groom called a group of men together at William Hamilton's sale yards at Leongatha and urged them to inspect the property. After this was done, a syndicate of South Gippslanders was immediately formed to purchase this impressive property of 44,000 acres together with 9,000 to 10,000 cattle.[42] The price was £3 7s 6d per acre, with the cattle at the same value per head. A company was formed with directors W.C. Greaves (Chairman), A.C. Groom (Managing Director), R.N. Scott, John Cooke, John Smith, J.W. Anderson and John Western. Capital comprised 10,000 shares payable to £10 each of which 8,200 were allotted. The station was surveyed into farms of from 50 to 500 acres, bridges built, roads made and the township of Kyogle surveyed in the centre of the estate. Arrangements were made with the National Mutual Life Association for long term credit to be given to intending purchasers of the farms, with the result that they were all sold off within a year or two. The 300 blocks in the township were quickly disposed of at auction, the directors giving two allotments, one for a church and another for a manse, to any denomination that applied. The 1902 drought had broken with a resultant sharp rise in the price of all stock so that the 10,000 cattle purchased at £3 7s 6d per head doubled in value in a short time.[43] The Great Kyogle Land Deal, as it became known, proved an extremely profitable venture for those gentlemen who attended the cattle sale at William Hamilton's Leongatha yards in 1901 with the intention of buying store cattle only to end up land developers almost a thousand miles to the north. The town and district of Kyogle today reflects their vision and enterprise. Whatever profit was made by the South Gippsland developers has been multiplied a hundred-fold by the people who, on their own initiative, purchased portions of the station.

Pig raising as an adjunct to dairying soon became quite an important component of the average settler's activities. Fed on the skimmed milk, fenced in with picket fences made from split palings, the pigs thrived amongst the remnants of the forest, camping in the numerous hollow logs. These were quite warm and dry even during the wettest of winters, while the plentiful supply of charcoal available kept them healthy. Often one was killed, scalded and dressed for household use, and with the opening of the railway, farmers soon adopted the practice of killing them, letting them set overnight, then after sewing them into a hessian bag, taking them to the nearest railway station for consignment to Melbourne. Before long, sales were being held at regular intervals at Meeniyan and Leongatha to which the pigs were either walked, if from nearby farms, or brought in a dray. Drays were covered with rope or wire netting, and in the summertime farmers carried a bucket under the dray and threw water over the pigs to cool them. This water was drawn from the numerous springs that crossed the roadway. Early in 1896 Mr Carl Hamann, a pioneering selector of Fairbank, was bringing a load of pigs to the Leongatha market when he ran into difficulties.

> While driving a load of pigs down Shingler's hill on Wednesday last the animals set up a squealing match which frightened the horses to such a degree that they became unmanageable and bolted. After a short distance the dray turned completely over. Mr. John Hanley was fortunately passing by at the time and rendered valuable assistance in getting things righted, and as Mr. Hamann was considerably knocked about brought the cargo of pigs into the township and Mr. Hamann returned home on Hanley's horse.[44]

During the winter when the supply of skimmed milk was depleted, the pigs were often fed on potatoes that were boiled in a wood-fired copper. Potatoes were grown on practically all farms as a pioneer crop for two main reasons. First, the cultivation associated with the crop resulted in the levelling of the humps and hollows left from the clearing of the forest and provided a suitable seed bed for subsequent sowing to oats or pasture. Secondly, as a cash crop, potatoes some-times provided a welcome addition to the farm income. The unsaleable portion of the crop, which comprised misshapen, damaged and diseased tubers, together with the undersized 'chats', was valuable as pig feed.

Sheep grazing was carried on to a limited extent on many farms in addition to cattle raising and dairying. It proved more popular in the steeper hill country and also on the lighter coastal lands around Pound Creek. An analysis of figures supplied by the railway authorities shows that many graziers bought in considerable numbers of sheep for fattening purposes, in addition to breeding them on their own properties.[45] Although quite important, sheep farming did not achieve the dominance of the dairying and cattle raising industry within the Shire.

Intensive cropping has always played a substantial role in farming operations in the Woorayl Shire. First crops recorded grown were hops and arrowroot at Dumbalk by Frank Dodd, Senior. These were sold to nearby settlers, the hops being used for bread-making purposes. The fertile red soils around Leongatha, Mardan and Dumbalk proved admirably suited to the growing of onions. Owing to the prevalence of roots and stumps in the paddocks, this crop was only grown on a small scale, originally at Dumbalk in 1896.[46] Heavy crops were obtained without the use of fertilizer, and onion growing soon became quite an important industry, particularly around the Leongatha and Mardan areas. Being labour intensive, a plot of ten acres was sufficient to occupy one man full-time. This industry indirectly led to the early development of the Leongatha town and district by providing a cash crop that required little capital outlay.

Although all settlers in the early decades were preoccupied with the cutting down of trees, two men developed a thriving business in the growing of them. Henry Borrow, who came from Mount Clear near Ballarat in 1883 to select on the Wilkur Creek, soon established a nursery for the supply of fruit trees to the new settlers in the Mirboo-Koorooman area.[47] It was the usual practice for each settler to establish an orchard as soon as practicable in order to have fresh fruit within the space of a few years. Borrow, sensibly enough, catered for this local

Erecting a picket fence, Dumbalk North, 1910 (from D. Dodd).

Dipping potato seed, Leongatha Labour Colony, c. 1914. A. Prout and J. Willoughby (from Woorayl Shire Historical Society).

market and found a ready sale for his young trees. The difficulties of transport did not detract from his product. Because they were valuable for their weight, up to 100 young fruit trees could be carried back to a selection on a pack horse.

Francis Moss, from Buninyong near Ballarat, also realised the potential market for fruit and ornamental trees that existed amongst the new settlers of South Gippsland. He purchased a large property on the west branch of the Tarwin in 1888, only a few miles east from Borrow's selection, and immediately commenced operations with Mr J. Bruce as Manager. Moss found that it was an excellent site for his nursery — the trees and shrubs that were planted there thrived exceptionally well because of the residual potash from the burnt forest, and there was little disease. Mr D.S. Campbell, an early settler in the Mardan district, brought his pack horse fifteen miles to purchase sixty young fruit trees, together with cuttings of raspberries and currants.[48] Although most of his stock was sold locally, export orders were filled for New Zealand and South Africa. The biggest disadvantage of the Moss Vale nursery on the Tarwin was the travelling to the railhead at Mirboo North or Leongatha during the winter months. At times the roads would be flooded and impassable.

To overcome this problem, Moss set up a small nursery close to the Leongatha

Labour Colony on the Ruby Creek. It was leased from Peter Johnson, being part of his first selection and not far from Horn's Roadside Inn. Its proximity to the Labour Colony ensured a plentiful supply of casual labour. Upwards of 200 men were stationed at the Colony — the men being sent from Melbourne in batches of ten or twelve to learn the rudiments of farming. A small wage was paid, and after a few months, men were expected to leave the Colony and obtain employment elsewhere, although they could stay at the Colony and do day work on nearby farms if it were available.[49] The budding and grafting of fruit trees is highly skilled work, but no doubt, Francis Moss availed himself of manpower from the Labour Colony for any unskilled work associated with the establishment and running of the Ruby Creek nursery.

Established in 1900, the nine acre Ruby Creek nursery, under the management of Mr T. James, soon rivalled Moss Vale in production. By 1903 Mr James had 120,000 apple trees for sale, mainly of Northern Spy stock together with large stocks of pears, peaches, apricots and cherries. An area of 1½ acres had been sown to French, Canadian and Haricot beans for seed purposes. Large numbers of different varieties of gooseberries were propagated, and an estimated 250,000 fruit trees were available for market in the 1903 season. Little spraying was done for disease eradication, instead, large flocks of chickens were kept and allowed out at intervals to control insects, grubs etc.[50] Later, both nurseries were placed under the care of Mr George Gould who continued the good work of former managers in maintaining consistently high standards in the production of disease-free stock.

Commercial fruit growing was tried by Walter Turner on Wilkur Creek, five miles north of Leongatha. In evidence to the Railway Standing Committee, when hearing submissions as to the proposed Leongatha-Warragul railway line at Leongatha in June 1896, Turner said that

> he held 1,000 acres, 320 selected, remainder freehold, 30 acres cultivated. The road to Leongatha was good enough for horses, but not for vehicles, grew his own stock and it walked away. Had 500 sheep besides cattle. Two surveys had been made — one through his property and one a mile away. He would cultivate more if a railway was made — land worth 8 pounds per acre. Had 15 acres of orchard, carting fruit over the bad roads bruised it and made it unfit for market.[51]

Turner's initiative in endeavouring to establish fruit growing as a component of the general farm enterprises of the district was not marked with a great deal of success. Horticulture, although practised in a minor way, did not attain the prominence of the pastoral and agricultural industries. The biggest orchard established in the district was on the Leongatha Labour Colony where over twenty acres of fruit trees were grown. This orchard started under the care of Mr Ure from Gembrook, and subsequently, under Mr A. Prout proved quite satisfactory and operated for many years. Large quantities of apples, pears and plums were grown, together with currants, strawberries and passionfruit. Apples proved the most reliable and profitable crop on the Colony, although problems arose over marketing.

> 600 cases of apples being shipped to London in three consignments, the fruit being fair and of uniform size. The best prices were realised by Dumelow's Seedling which

brought 9s 6d per case. Jonathans bringing 8s 9d only. On the whole the shipment sold well realising as good prices as those of other exporters. The dock strike in London affected adversely the sales of the last two shipments.[52]

The Labour Colony had a decided advantage over other farms in that there was an abundance of manpower for the picking, grading and packing of the fruit. Since its establishment in 1893, the 822 acres of the Colony had been transformed from virgin forest into neat paddocks of cultivation and grassland. The original trees were cut down and sawn into suitable scantling at a sawmill on the Colony. Large numbers of bricks were made from clay pits for use in the flooring and construction of wells and farm buildings. Under the supervision of Colonel Goldstein, crops of flax, wheat, oats, maize, potatoes and onions, together with the associated activities of dairying and pig raising, enabled the Colony to become practically self-supporting. Tobacco was grown with only limited success. The dried leaf did not meet market requirements but it was, nevertheless, relished by the colonists.

A certain amount of dissension existed within the local community over the formation of the Colony. At a meeting held at Leongatha on 10 December 1893, a motion was carried stating 'the Labour Colony would be a burden upon the State . . . and that it shall not be in conflict with outside workmen who now in consequence and with difficulty get bread for themselves and family'.[53] Local chemist, a Mr Hancorne, had previously suggested that an approach be made to the Railway Department to disinfect the carriages in which the men arrived from Melbourne. This slur on the inmates prompted a reply in *The Great Southern Star*:

> Many thanks for copy of your valuable paper of the 10th inst. which was duly posted up in the Labour Colony for the perusal of 'THE GREAT UNSOAPED'. Naturally their attention was drawn to the uncalled for remarks of your obscure pill-compounder, as expressed by him at a public meeting held in Leongatha. As an advertising dodge for his disinfectants it is rather a clever stroke to frighten the people with Asiatic cholera and then dose them afterwards with his nostrums. However, this Mr. Hancorne, like many more in the Labour Colony, might yet have to taste the bitterness of adversity in which case I hope that he will meet with the reward he so richly merits. Had the world taken Shakespeare's advice to 'throw physic to the dogs', your chemist, like Othello would have found his 'occupation' gone long ago.
>
> > Scratchfully yours,
> > J.F.,
> > 'Bleak House', Labour Colony. 14.11.93.

Fortunately, Hancorne's sentiments were not shared by the rest of the Leongatha community. They realised only too well the harsh economic conditions that had brought about the formation of the Colony and tried to make amends for the slur on the Colonists. A report in *The Great Southern Star* of the following week stated:

> A very pleasing ceremony will take place at the Labour Colony tomorrow afternoon (Saturday) and will take the form of a deputation of the leading ladies and gentlemen of Leongatha headed by our respected clergyman, (Mr. North) waiting on the three hundred and odd maligned men in that Colony. They will present each man with a

bouquet of flowers accompanied by an appropriate scriptural text, as a practical protest and sympathy with the men who have suffered from the late uncalled for and ungenerous statements recently circulated. This is true Christianity.

The Labour Colony subsequently became an integral part of the Leongatha community, causing little or no disturbance to everyday life. Cricket and quoit matches were played between the Colony and the locals. Church service was conducted there on Sunday evenings by Reverend Mr North, and the colonists from time to time arranged concerts and entertainments that were well patronised. Newspapers of the day were read and re-read many times. At the August 1893 meeting of the Leongatha Mechanics' Institute, Dr Michael Carr moved 'that newspapers from the Library that are one week old be given to the Labour Colony'.[54] No doubt these literary crumbs from the rich man's table were relished by the colonists, even if they were a trifle stale.

Fullers' shingled homestead, Dumbalk North (from D. Shingler).

Playing rounders at a Church picnic at Dollar, 1901 (from D. Dodd).

7. HOME LIFE

Most of the early recorded history pertaining to the Woorayl Shire is the account of the activities of men, with little detail concerning the role that women played in those formative years. It is not an intentional emphasis, rather it is merely a reflection on the harsh, primitive conditions that prevailed during that era. The clearing of a forested selection called for the physical strength of young men prepared to live under primitive conditions for several years until adequate housing could be provided for women and children. The census of 1891 reveals a population for Woorayl Shire of 3,551, with a just greater than two to one ratio of men to women, 2,413 to 1,138, and a preponderance of young men to young women of three to one. The 1891 figures were as follows:

		Dwellings	People	Male	Female
Korumburra	Coal mining	16	65	55	10
Leongatha	Grazing, timber cutting	44	232	163	69
Mirboo Nth	Timber cutting	80	390	228	162
Inverloch	Grazing	42	191	107	84
Tarwin	Grazing	11	39	26	13

Ten years later the figures from the 1901 census show a remarkable change as a result of the opening of the coalfields at Korumburra and the subsequent influx of workmen and their families with associated commercial and service industries. Korumburra quickly became the major centre of population in South Gippsland — a dominance which was later to be challenged by Wonthaggi and Leongatha.

		Dwellings	People	Male	Female
Korumburra	Coal mining	522	2,445	1,305	1,140
Leongatha	Grazing, timber cutting	139	681	402	279
Mirboo Nth	Timber cutting	54	274	142	132
Tarwin	(not listed)				
Inverloch	Grazing	17	87	43	44
Walkerville	Lime burning	10	36	25	11

The 1891 census also lists the type of dwelling in use at that time. Woorayl Shire had the dubious distinction of having the largest number of dwellings, 595, made from canvas, linen and calico of any municipality in Victoria. Woorayl was followed by Alberton Shire with 312 and Mildura with 306.[1] Other types of dwellings in Woorayl Shire were listed as:

Brick or stone	4
Wood, iron, lath, plaster	563
Slabs, bark, mud	23
Not stated	20

Tents were replaced as quickly as possible by more substantial dwellings of wooden construction, usually a two-roomed structure with a gabled roof and a skillion at the rear. Wattle and daub was sometimes used for wall construction but was not popular for exterior walls because of the high and consistent rainfall. In this method laths or thin strips of wood were laced around or nailed onto the upright studs and then plastered with mud to which lime had been added. The first home built on P. Bellingham's selection on the Ruby Road adjacent to Leongatha was built in such a manner and served this pioneering family for many years.[2]

When men were living alone, the cooking was reduced to the bare minimum. After a hard day's work with axe and crosscut saw clearing the forest, the appetite acquired made even the most basic food tasteful. If there were two men in the camp, one would return home early, light the fire, prepare potatoes, rice or dumplings for tea. Meat would be bought in large pieces of up to 50 lbs weight from the nearest butcher who could be anything from fifteen to twenty miles away. Much of the meat was pickled in a barrel of brine or cooked and eaten cold. In the evenings bread-making had to be attended to. For amateurs this often consisted of soda bread or scones, but usually settlers became reasonably proficient in bread-making with yeast. There were several methods of making yeast: it could be made from hops, potatoes or even from flour, sugar and salt. One recipe often used was to

> Boil a pound of flour, a quarter of a pound of brown sugar and a little salt in two gallons of water for an hour. When milk warm, bottle it and cork it close. It will be fit for use in twenty-four hours and one pint is sufficient for 18 lb of bread.

Flour and yeast would be mixed and left to rise in a box overnight near the fire, then worked into loaves in the morning and baked. First ovens were circular camp ovens made of cast iron with three legs that enabled them to stand on an uneven surface. The lid was designed so that hot ashes could be placed on top when baking.

The arrival of a woman on to the selection invariably resulted in an improvement in these spartan living conditions so often experienced by the men during the initial years of settlement. Thomas Musgrave recalls the arrival of Mrs Mary Gwyther from Dunkeld at the selection on Gwyther's Creek.

> I will never forget Mrs. Gwyther when she first came to the district in 1884 to make a home at Fern Shade and she converted a log hut into a fairy palace. There is no one

can realise what she had to tackle. She was such a refined lady, who did not know what soiled hands were.[3]

Family care and the multitude of daily tasks associated with pioneering life lessened the sense of isolation to a small degree. Thomas Musgrave's own mother reared a large family while living at the Cape Schanck and Wilson's Promontory lighthouses from 1864 onwards. No doubt as a mark of respect and gratitude to her nearest neighbours, the Millars of Yanakie Station, she christened one of her daughters Dora Millar Musgrave. Many of the newly-arrived women had left homes in England, Ireland and Scotland in their youth, and the contrast with the primitive conditions must have daunted all but the stoutest heart. However, it did not always dampen their spirits or diminish their sense of humour or powers of observation. Nellie S. Clerk, a relative newcomer to the South Gippsland forest in the early 1880s, published a slim volume of verse in 1887 in which she vividly portrays the lifestyle of men before the arrival of their womenfolk.

A Game of Draughts

Four rooms beneath one shingled shed,
Four tables, water shuns,
Floors crumb bespread, and overhead
Skins, spider webs, and guns.
Four bachelors of sturdy stuff,
Four cooks who cook by turn,
Boil meat too tough, half mix the 'duff'
And let the damper burn.

Axes, saddles, muddy boots,
Four billies black with age,
Slab-stools, bag bunks, books, buckets, flutes,
Comprise 'The Hermitage'.
'Let's have a game of draughts' says Fred,
'Now tea is put away,
'Tis a relief to use one's head,
After cutting scrub all day.

Oh what a comic sight 'twould be,
If our English folks walked in,
They'd think that I, and all you three,
Looked mighty short of tin,
But they'd mistake, we're right enough,
We're squatters (when we dream)
So what care we, though we look rough,
We are not what we seem.[4]

One bachelor, despairing of finding a marriage partner through normal social contacts, resorted to the columns of *The Mirboo Herald* of 26 April 1889 to advertise his need.

WANTED . . . A WIFE — to suit a man of 45 years of age. Must be good housekeeper to suit farmer. Address. O.X. Club Hotel, Mirboo North.

Walter Turner, whose property Woorayl fronted the Wilkur Creek adjacent to the surveyed Koorooman township, arranged a dance in his newly-built storeroom. Turner decorated his storeroom with ferns and gumleaves, and after serving his guests refreshments, dancing commenced at 7.30 p.m. and continued until midnight. Refreshments were again served and the program interrupted for a short time while the musician for the evening, Mr Mitchell, displayed his clog dancing talents. Turner's Manager, Mr J. Phelan, gave a very creditable exhibition of sword dancing before dancing recommenced and continued until daylight. The tables were again laid out for breakfast to strengthen the guests for the return journey to their homes.[5]

The heavy rainfall and muddy pack tracks of South Gippsland did not deter young men and women from socialising whenever an opportunity presented itself. *The Mirboo Herald* of 5 November 1887 carried a report from its Mardan correspondent testifying to this commitment.

> I believe we have the hardiest young ladies here that ever existed. Last Thursday night four of them walked two miles along a pack track to a private party, the rain falling in torrents from the time they started till they reached their destinations. After dancing and singing for three hours in wet feet and sprained ankles they managed to arrive home at 3 a.m. having six escorts. The next day their dresses were observed hanging on a fence, very much in need of a brushing.

Events such as these tended to lighten the cares of early settlers, both men and women, and helped develop the social life of the district. A description of day to day life at Leongatha in 1892 is provided by the diary of Georgina Spencer, a student teacher at the State school at that time. The diary was written while she was living at Ashleigh, the home of her father, Mr Daniel Spencer, on Inlet Road one mile south of the township (Allotment 60B). This allotment stretched from Inlet Road back to the newly-formed railway line. During wintertime, Georgina often found it less troublesome to walk up the railway line on her way to the State school than along the unformed streets of the township. Mr John Jeffrey was the headmaster of the school at the time, while of the other towns-folk mentioned in the diary, Mr Peart was Manager of the Bank of Australasia, Mr Long kept a general store adjacent to the railway station on the northern side, while Mr Hayes kept a store at the junction of Long and Roughead Streets.

* * *

Feb 19, 1892. Very hot day — the people were burning all about. Went out to the concert at Crighton's Hall.

Feb 22. Very warm. Been up to school. Was talking to Miss Thomas. Mrs. Peart's baby is dying.

Mar 12. Lovely day. Father was at the township this morning — bought about 45 chickens. Rose, Will, Dave Chalmers and I went for a ride. Made a commotion as usual. Got a disappointment because the push did not show up to go to the Inlet.

Mar 17. Lovely day — had a holiday. Stacks of people going by to the St. Pat's day sports. Dan has gone to the township with a load of chaff. Every one of us here have been to the sports. Rose, Dad and I were at the concert. Did not feel well. I came home on Jack Burke's horse and a great push stopped to the Ball.

Mar 27. Cool day. Father has gone to the brickyards. The boys are out riding.

Apr 26. Lovely day. Father killed a pig this morning — quite a fuss. Walked up to school. The boys are pulling their stack to pieces. Was over to Dave's. — Churned tonight.

May 5. Fairly warm. Rained a little towards evening. Left my horse at Hayes's stable and walked to school. Dave C. brought it over to Mrs. Jeffrey's tonight — had tea there and went to the concert at Fairbank. Enjoyed myself. Arrived home about one. Robert lost his horse.

Jun 15. Nice day. Nev Bolton came this morning and started to build our chimney. The boys cut chaff this morning. Dad and Dave went to the township this afternoon. Rose has gone to class up at the Wesleyans. Dave C. Also.

Jul 2. Lovely day. Dan and Willie, Miss Chalmers and Mr. Gilbert came down this afternoon. Rose and I went up with them — had a try at tennis. Went to hear the Bell Ringers tonight.

Jul 27. Wet day. Went upon Dave's horse. Rose was at the sewing meeting at Mrs. Peart's — was playing tennis. Jim sent some flowers and a bogam board to Rose. Dan was sowing oats. Dave culling potatoes.

Aug 1. Lovely day. Was up very early washed this morning. The boys are finishing harrowing the crop. George sold old Connie. Dan and Willie have gone shooting. Caught me a possum.

Aug 3. Wet morning. Rode up to school. Rose rode up to church and waited for Dad. All of us were at the affair. Dave C. and his sister called at Mrs. Peart's this afternoon, stayed to the ball. Returned home about three o'clock. A good push at the ball.

Aug 8. Started to rain a little this morning. Dad has gone to the town for oats. Dave and Dan cutting some chaff. Our cow died this afternoon. Killed a pig. Mrs. Jeffrey is very sick. Johnny was down tonight.

Aug 30. Lovely day — washed this morning. Went to the P.O. and over to Mrs. Jeffrey's. Dave up splitting rails. Dan was up to the township for wheat this afternoon and has come up again tonight. Rose was over to see Mrs. Begg. Brought home a young bear. Dave C. came down for her to go to church meeting.

Sept 1. Nice day. The boys are busy putting in Dad's crop. Walked up to school. Was over to Mrs. J. The children were over at practice at the Mechanics' — arrived home about dark.

Oct 17. Wet day. Slept in till nine o'clock. Father went to the township — sold his potatoes to Long. Rode up today — was over at Mrs. J. and in to see Miss Thomas this evening.

Oct 18. Very fair day. Up early — washed all the morning. Father carted his potatoes up to Long's. Was over to Mrs. J. after school. Milner and Ferguson were down killing a pig. Dan and Jack Burke were here tonight.

Oct 25. Lovely day. Washed this morning. Rode up to school Mrs. Jeffrey took my horse for a ride. Mrs. Peart, Rose and her went down to the plains for a ride. Had a good canter through the township tonight.[6]

* * *

This diary of Georgina Spencer records the beginnings of social activities in addition to mundane events. Church services were being held regularly along with tea meetings and sewing meetings. Tennis matches were being played on the newly-formed court in the station goods yard. The Mechanics' Institute hall was being used for concerts by visiting artists such as the Lynch Family of Bell Ringers as well as the local school children. Georgina refers to 'the push' several times in her diary — a reference to the band of young men and women of her own age who were starting to have an impact on the social life of the district.

Two years later, in 1894, another young lady, Amy Griffin, arrived from Ireland to visit her brother, Tom Griffin, newly-appointed Engineer of the Woorayl Shire. Tom Griffin had played an important role in the construction of the Great Southern Railway as a surveyor, and soon after its completion, he was appointed to the Woorayl Shire Council as Engineer. It was a formidable task, entailing a great deal of travelling about on horseback supervising the various contracts let by the Council for road construction. It would take him four days to ride to Waratah Bay, inspect road works on his way and return to Leongatha by a different route. With his brother Charlie, Tom Griffin purchased a large property fronting the west branch of the Tarwin on the Leongatha-Mirboo North road. They named it 'Kilbaha' after a bay of that name on the west coast of Ireland where the family had originated. His sister Amy left a vivid description of her stay with her brother.

* * *

28 December 1894
Tom's buggy with a pair of lively young horses met me at Leongatha station. The drive to "Kilbaha" was quite as exciting as a run across country after the hounds. We plunged out of the township immediately into the bush, or what I call a forest, and the roads are mere tracks full of ruts and stumps, up hill and down dale. Away we tore over every obstacle, no consideration for springs or possibilities of upset seemed to enter into anybody's calculations.

I clung wildly to Tom's arm as we dived with one wheel into deep hollows or cleared a log of timber. There is no sympathy shown here for anything like nervousness. For my part, I was quite relieved when the horses jibbed just under "Kilbaha" hills and we were obliged to get out and walk up to the house. It is a very pretty cottage with verandah on three sides, most tastefully built with garden, farmyard and his offices. The hill slopes down to a little winding river at its foot and beyond the forest stretches everywhere; but most of the timber is doomed and in a few years the undulating slopes all around will be green pasture land. The curious birds and animals in the bush astonished me. There are tents rigged up outside to afford accommodation for Tom's constant visitors.

Sir Bryan O'Loghlen's eldest son left us only yesterday to go home for Christmas Day. To me it was strange to see the future Baronet washing up dishes with Kathleen, but no kind of work is considered menial here.

31 December 1894
The old year all but gone — dying in a blaze of sunshine. Tom, Fred, (Pilkington) Kathleen and I set off for a ride over the place which was truly enjoyable. There is no fuss about getting our horses ready here. They are just picked out of the paddock, the saddles thrown on and off you go. We saw

McCartin Street, Leongatha, c. 1895 (from I. Bruce).

wallabies hopping about. The green coolness of the spot is beautiful; every kind of fern from exquisite tree fern which is almost like a palace to the homely bracken, growing luxuriously under the shelter of trees. Numbers of parrots and cockatoos flit about amongst the trees. Our animals picked their way through the scrub with great ingenuity and it required no small amount of horsemanship to stick upon their backs. The views of wooded hill and slope are very lovely and unusual here, for Australia is in most places full of flat plains. Gippsland is acknowledged to be one of the most favoured districts. The sun was nearly setting when we got back to the little home perched on a hill in the midst of all this beauty and prodigality of Nature. Tom Griffin read part of the church service (Anglican) in his impressive voice.

We kept a Merry Watch on New Year's Eve, and at the stroke of midnight, Charlie fired off his double barrelled gun from the door — the most wonderful echoes! An answering volley seemed to reverberate from the hills and woods around. There is a curious amphibious animal called the platypus found in the rivers. Its habits have only been ascertained within the last few years by a Naturalist who visited Australia for the purpose. It has beautiful fur, webbed feet, a head like a rat and has a strong bill. It seems to be altogether an anomaly among animals for though belonging to the Mammalian species, it lays eggs like a bird. The colonials seem very proud of their lyre bird.

6 January 1895
Yesterday, Kathleen and I rode into the township. While we were strapping a supply of bread to our saddles, Tom cantered up on his way home after his tour

of inspection. He is 'Shire Engineer' and has to look after the roads, such as they are. Kathleen and I had a lovely ride this afternoon. We took a turn that was quite new to me and came upon bits of very beautiful scenery through scented woods. At one place there is a colony of bell birds, so called because their notes resemble tinkling of a bell. And had I first heard them when alone I should have fancied myself in an enchanted forest where the fairies were ringing their charms. These birds locate themselves in swamps. Here the wild bush represents a stern struggle with Nature who is loth to admit Man into her sanctuary.

Kathleen and I rode over to the Shinglers in the cool of the evening yesterday. They are some of the nicest people in this neighbourhood, and their place is a perfect oasis in the wilderness. It is refreshing to come upon evidences of such refinement in the bush, a pretty and comfortable house surrounded by a verandah. All covered with trailing plants, Banksia roses in various colours and set in the most beautiful enclosure fenced off from the adjoining forest. Within this charmed spot are green paddocks, a smooth lawn tennis court and a most delightful garden rich in bloom not only of flowers but fruit. I have never seen anything like the peach and plum trees laden. The grape vines growing over the walls of the house are beyond description. Inside everything is in accordance with surroundings and we partook of tea at a table set with snowy linen and bright old silver.

Mrs. Shingler and her daughter came from England and settled down here about eleven years so she and the boys are contemporary squatters and great friends. They proved so agreeable that it was later than we intended to stay. When we started for home we had the benefit of the full moon. I have described the roads without exaggeration but it never occurred to Kathleen not to set out at full gallop; nor would we have drawn bridle till we reached home except as a concession to me. When we arrived at "Kilbaha" our darling Charlie had waited

Tarwin River picnic, Dumbalk North, c. 1895 (from D. Dodd).

up for us and had put the kettle down to boil. Tom appeared in his dressing gown scolding us for being late.

17 January 1895

This pleasant pastoral life goes on much the same from day to day. Kathleen and I had another moonlight ride to church (Church of England) last Sunday night. There has been a big "burn" here which is the event of the year in these places, as a great deal depends on the scrub being got rid of in a satisfactory manner. Every now and then the stillness was broken by the crashing fall of some mighty tree and this noise, as loud as thunder, was heard at intervals.

Yesterday we rode through the bush to a neighbouring settler by the name of Mr. Mick O'Loughlin. He has about 60 acres and 12 cows. We had a cup of tea in the quaint house. The fire place was one after my own heart, occupying almost the entire breadth of the house, and roughly paved with stones upon which the brilliant logs reposed. We have had a number of visitors here lately — the colonials seem to come and go just as they like. I have had two or three rides lately. One was with Kathleen and Charlie and the latter took us along an old 'pack track' in the bush, which was the only way they had to Mirboo and to town, so to speak, before the roads were made.

Charlie's luggage when he first came here was months on its way from the sea coast (Inverloch) to "Kilbaha". It started on a bullock wagon along with stores for the local storekeeper here. The load had to be lightened at each point of the journey where any special difficulty, such as a swamp, presented itself, and in this way every article of luggage was gradually deposited along the track until the wagon arrived at its destination with two sacks of flour. The track is a very rough path through the forest where the light filters through the trees.

This part of Gippsland is the last that has been taken up as it is heavily timbered, that until lately, it was considered inaccessible. The forest extended for hundreds of miles. The most beautiful feature is the drooping fern tree — we measured one 11½ ft. long.

We saw an old trapper's hut on the verge of the forest. It was made of logs and there were the remains of his rude bed and the pack hanging over his deserted hearth. I could not help wondering what kind of human being he was, whose instincts drove him to a life amongst the wild dingoes of the bush. Charlie said he often caught possums for their skins. We went in the opposite direction for a long ride, 20 miles or more, with Tom. His duties as Shire Engineer obliges him to supervise the making and mending of roads all over the Shire. We left the forest region behind and got into places which stretch towards the sea. Tom told me he was wild with delight when first he got out of the bush.

27 February 1895

There was a great wedding here in Leongatha on Wednesday to which we were invited. It was the first of any importance in the township. The residents made a great fuss. No less than the local doctor taking a wife — the nicest girl he at least thought he could find in the neighbourhood. I went to see the festivities. The little church was prettily decorated and the wedding quite orthodox. There were no carriages. Tom had the privilege of driving the bride to church and afterwards to the Shire Hall. The bride and bridegroom stood awaiting the guests and received congratulations very gracefully. There were good speeches made.

Tom and I stayed at "The Grange" (Shinglers) and enjoyed a good night's rest. The french windows opened on to the verandah and the wild music of the birds in the early morning awoke me to a state of blissful semi-consciousness. I was always led to believe there were no feathered songsters in Australia and have been pleasantly surprised to find that the bush is alive with birds. We left Mrs. Shingler's on Sunday morning and on our way back to "Kilbaha" found church service at a little school house (Koorooman) about half way to home.

The "Kilbaha" house is perched on a round high hill with the river running at the foot. They get water from the river on a sledge drawn up the hill by bullocks. The road is below the house. They tell me I have travelled the thickest part of the Victorian bush. The country throughout is heavily timbered still in spite of the unremitting labour of the settlers. Coming home from Morwell we travelled along a beautiful spot called Bair's track.

20 March 1895
It was a great day in Leongatha on Monday, which was the 17th March, St. Patrick's day. It is a great holiday out here — I suppose as the Irish element is so conspicuous. The colonials seem to be very fond of holidays and festivals as they are generally hard working. On Monday there were sports at the recreation ground succeeded in the evening by a concert which was followed by a ball. Charlie went to the latter and said there was hardly any room to walk. Tom gave a recitation at the concert. Kathleen and I rode into the township and we went to the recreation grounds for a few minutes to see what was going on. It was like a gathering at the races at home.

A few hundred people in a wonderful variety of costumes, and deeply interested in the various contests of chopping and horse events. The band played at intervals. People came from surrounding parts of the country and vehicles of all descriptions were drawn up around the scene of action, while hundreds of horses were picketed about, some tied to fences and others feeding on ferns and undergrowth in the scrub. It was an interesting picture of bush life.

The Shinglers came to say goodbye to me the other day. It was curious to see the old lady (must be 80-years-old) quite at home on her side saddle. She jumped onto a stump of an old tree and mounted with the greatest ease and cantered off gaily. The daughter wielded an umbrella. Mrs. Shingler is a dear old lady.

Goodbye to Australia. I am going home and just beginning to realise how any other country but my own, which to me is my 'Fatherland', could be so dear, and it appears to me so lovely.[7]

* * *

This diary is a classic illustration of how an outside observer can often give a more comprehensive and detailed picture of a local scene than the inhabitants themselves. It is noteworthy that the diaries of Amy Griffin and Georgina Spencer are of young single girls in the prime of their youth. Neither was born in the district — Amy Griffin came from the west coast of Ireland and Georgina

In 1987 the Kilbaha property, Allotment 40, Parish of Koorooman, was owned by Messrs Young Bros. who have, however, shortened the name to Kilbar, while the Shingler property, The Grange, Allotment 102, Parish of Leongatha, on the Mount Eccles road is owned by Mr J. Van Eck.

Miss Bruhn ready to mount her horse, Berry's Creek (from D. Bacon).

Spencer came with her parents from the Ballarat district in 1887. Both had an observant eye for the different facets of life in a completely new community being established in the great forest.

The wedding of the local doctor referred to would almost certainly have been that of Dr Leslie Davies. The first resident doctor, Dr Michael Carr, left Leongatha for a short time to take on the practice of his brother, Dr Tom Carr, who had died in South Melbourne. He returned to Leongatha in 1899 and continued in practice in the town until 1913 when he bought a practice near Yass, NSW. The wedding of Dr Davies and the reception in the Shire Hall described by Amy Griffin could hardly be regarded as typical of the times. Perhaps more in keeping with community practice was the wedding of Mr and Mrs Benn of Dumbalk. Mrs Benn, formerly Gertie Thomas, came from Warrnambool to the Dumbalk Valley in 1886 at the age of thirteen to stay with her aunt, Mrs F. Denny. After growing to maturity, she became betrothed to William Benn. On the day of her marriage, she and her intended husband rode from their respective homes to Morwell, twenty-eight miles away for the marriage ceremony. They then rode back to Dumbalk and began their married life in the valley of the Tarwin.[8]

This was not exceptional in the great forest of South Gippsland in the 1880s. Rather, it was sometimes more practical for the bride and groom to ride to the officiating minister than to bring him to their homes for the wedding ceremony. George Cross retained vivid memories of his wedding.

> My bride elect was then living in Melbourne. She travelled by rail to Morwell, then by horse to Koorooman, where we were married. From Morwell to Koorooman we carried our luggage on a pack horse and it bolted. Its load consisted of a wedding cake, two geese, and various other articles for the wedding preparations. These were tumbled on to the road, and after catching the bolting horse, we loaded up again and continued on our way to my wife's parents' home.
>
> Two days later I had to meet the minister who was to marry us, and escort him to the house. We met near a large bridge built of logs, and of course, we told each other what we thought of the roads. He was mud from head to foot, likewise myself. After the wedding, I left my bride with her parents and went with the minister for about 12 miles, to see him safely on his return journey. I arrived back well past midnight, and next day was out cutting scrub. That was our honeymoon in Gippsland's early days. Ours was the first marriage in Koorooman.
>
> We lived there for about twelve months and then went to Leongatha South to our selection. I cleared a small patch of scrub and then built a paling cottage of three rooms. We brought ten foot iron from Anderson's Inlet on pack horse. I completed the shell of the house with palings and rough timber for uprights and then started to furnish it. Four pegs were driven in the ground in the centre of one room and a large sheet of gum-bark on these provided our table. King ferns, cut in lengths, supplied us with chairs. I built a fine large chimney, and usually rolled back logs into it with a crow bar. I was for two years working away from home during the week (my wife being alone for that time), and I was only able to be on the selection from Saturday night till Monday morning. Sunday was generally spent at scrub-cutting.[9]

Following the arrival of a woman on the selection, the camp oven was replaced either by the American stove, a free-standing iron cooker that did not require any brickwork or by the Colonial oven, a double-walled iron box with shelves and a hinged door. Varying in width from two foot upwards, they were usually bricked into the chimney, although if bricks were not available stones were used. Normally the fire was kept going from morning till night using vast quantities of wood — the task of keeping the woodbox full often devolved on the housewife.

Most kitchens were detached from the main house. One of the principal reasons for this was that, once farms became established, they usually employed one or more men, and the main house was then out-of-bounds to the hired hands. Farm workers were invariably housed in small wooden huts built nearby, to which they retired after meals in the kitchen.

The internal walls of the farm house were usually lined with hessian and paper — a relatively cheap method of lining but one that nevertheless could transform even the drabbest of homes into tasteful and pleasant surroundings. The great danger of this material was its flammability, and this was another reason for detached kitchens. If proper wallpaper could not be afforded, many settlers lined the hessian with pictures and illustrations from newspapers and periodicals. Where the head of the family followed the sport of kings, these were often of famous racehorses. Lighting was provided by candles made from fat saved in the kitchen and then poured into moulds with a wick of string or peeled rush in the centre. The fat in the moulds set overnight, and then the candles were removed and stored for future use.

Surplus fat was also mixed with wood ashes for the making of soap, although later caustic soda and borax replaced ashes for this purpose. The aim of most households was to utilise as much as possible of the farm produce and to purchase only what was absolutely necessary — not only from an economic viewpoint but because of the difficulties of transport. One such commodity that could not be produced on the farm, and yet was in great demand, was kerosene.

Kerosene lamps were almost universal. The outdoor type was known as the 'hurricane' lamp, while more decorative and elaborate types were used indoors. Kerosene was purchased in rectangular wooden cases each containing two four gallon tins. These cases and tins were put to a variety of uses both inside the home and on the farm. The housewife usually claimed the case to use for storing household linen, underclothing and the other numerous articles associated with the home. If enough cases were available, even a wardrobe could be readily constructed. Two tiers were set up three or four foot apart, the top layers joined with boards in which were set hanging screws, other boards across the back joining the boxes with a curtain across the front.

The tins were used as miniature coppers for boiling of meat, clothes, or purely for the heating of water on the top of the stove. Eggs were preserved in them for winter use. Cut diagonally, they were used as water troughs in the poultry yard or for feeding of calves, while they proved ideal for the cartage of skimmed milk to the pigs. In summertime when the tanks ran low, the kerosene tin was used to carry water from the well or the nearby spring if a horse sledge and barrel was not available. Kerosene was a basic ingredient for many tasks performed inside the home and on the farm. The housewife used it for cleansing purposes, it was used as a bleach, in starch for smoother ironing, and a few drops on the duster helped in polishing the furniture. On the mop it helped polish the floor, and the spoons and forks were given an added shine with kerosene and whiting. Jam jars were made from bottles with cut-off necks. This was done by part filling with water, tying a string soaked with kereosene around the water line and lighting the string. When the string burned out, the neck part of the bottle would be tapped sharply and it would fall neatly off.

Children's hair was given a good dressing of kerosene in the event of any nits being found in the comb. It was used for the relief of chilblains, sore muscles, dandruff, and for sore throats a few drops on a teaspoon of sugar was a standard cure. The men of the household used it for a variety of purposes, not the least being to coax damp wood into fire first thing in the morning. In the farm yard it was used for drenching cows for bloat, for rubbing udders affected with mastitis, and mixed with Stockholm tar, it was used on animal sores and wounds. In the fowl yard it was used as a disinfectant for perches, in the piggery it was mixed with sulphur and sump-oil for the treatment of mange, while in the garden it was mixed with boiling water and soap for the control of aphis, thrip and caterpillars. Whenever a dance or concert was arranged at the local Mechanics' Hall, the floor was spread with sawdust liberally sprinkled with kerosene, swept off, then sprinkled with grated candle grease. This was then worked into the floor with a weighted box drawn up and down the floor upon a jute bag — a chore much enjoyed by half-grown boys.

Butter-making as a skill was quickly acquired by pioneer women. If a churn was not available, the cream was beaten with a wooden spoon in a dish until it

Mrs C. Nicholas and Miss G. Trease off to Church (sidesaddle), Dumbalk North, 1900.

'turned'; that is, the fat separated from the buttermilk. Mrs Alice Davis, who reared a large family on their property fronting the Wilkur Creek, simply made it by plunging her forearm into a bucket of cream and stirring it for half an hour or more.[10] The time taken for the cream to turn into butter varied with the season of the year and the thickness and quality of the cream. When the butter had formed, it was salted to taste by washing in brine and then shaped with butter pats.

Pioneering women needed strong arms to cope with the multitude of tasks performed during the day. In addition to butter-making, they had to lift and carry innumerable buckets of water, carry and often cut the wood for the kitchen stove. In some households this was regarded as 'a woman's job'. The men had the much more physically demanding task of clearing the forest in readiness for pasture. Strength was needed to scrub floors, sweep, polish, black-lead stoves, wash and wring clothes without the aid of washing machines or wringers. The preparation of the meat for cooking was usually a joint effort on the part of the husband and wife. The man would do the killing. If a steer was killed, it would be shared out amongst the neighbours. 'Staggering Bob'; that is, a calf under three months of age, was eaten only as a last resort. Quite a lot of the meat went through the mincer for use in meat pies or potted meat, while most households killed a bacon pig once a year and cured it for home use. This was done by first scalding and rubbing the bristles off in a vat or wooden tub after the intestines had been removed. These were kept in a bucket of lime water that was changed every day for three days and were then used for the skins of sausages or black puddings. The carcase was rubbed with sugar and saltpetre daily for several days and then hung up on a rafter near the chimney for later use.

The killing and dressing of the pig was usually done by the menfolk, but often the pioneering women became adept at even this task. When John Hay selected land in the Dumbalk Valley in 1884 after being engaged in paling splitting at Narracan for several years, his wife was of great assistance in the task of establishing a home and a farm. Mrs Hay carried meat from Trafalgar to Narracan, a distance of eleven miles on foot, while her husband continued splitting palings. She could kill and scald a pig as the occasion required. In their struggle to get established, wallabies were eaten by selectors at times, and Mrs Hay, who was a splendid shot with the gun, even shot lyre birds, obtaining ten shillings for their tails.[11] At that time, lyre birds, koalas and possums were not protected, and many settlers were glad of the money realised from the sale of koala and possum skins. Trapping and shooting soon depleted their numbers, and a proclamation was issued in December 1898 protecting the koala for the whole of the year. Prior to that date, koalas and possums had only been protected during the close season; that is, 1 November to 30 April.[12] At Leongatha *The Great Southern Star* of the 1890s regularly carried advertisements by the fur trade listing prices being paid for skins; for example, 'wallaby, large, 1s to 1s 1d per lb., bear skins 3s to 5s. per dozen, possum skins inferior 1s to 1s 9d per dozen'.[13]

Household furniture varied with the degree of affluence of the settler. Much of it was of necessity crude and simple. Mrs Lily Spencer, daughter of J. Blackmore who carried the mail from Mirboo North to the Koorooman Post Office at Horn's, recalled that their first bedding was of chaff bags stuffed with dry ferns.[14] In wintertime, if blankets were scarce, men would use a 'wagga'; that is, a rug made from bags stitched together to keep out the cold. Rugs were also made from possum and fox skins and proved a valuable adjunct in South Gippsland winters. As time passed, more furniture was acquired that not only had a monetary value, but also an intrinsic personal attachment. During the summer months when bush fires threatened their homes, the settlers removed the furniture from the house, stacked it in the centre of a patch of potatoes or maize grown nearby, and covered it with bags to prevent it burning. Mrs Josephine Roughead, daughter of John O'Reilly who settled on the Wilkur Creek in 1883, recalled:

> My mother often said that she would much prefer to lose her house than her furniture — after all they could always build another house but she could not replace her furniture.[15]

Unfortunately, many housewives lost both their house and furniture during the fires that swept through the area. In 1895, Maud Lyall, daughter of William Lyall of Harewood, Western Port, married Ernest Ricardo and came to live on portion of the Mt. Vernon Estate originally selected by William McPherson.

Ricardo built a new home for his bride and set to work improving his property, but he and his wife were forced to flee, abandoning everything in the face of the great fire of 1898. Taking their infant child in their arms, they took shelter in the home of their neighbour, Mr Robert Smith, where several other settlers had gathered. The worst of the fire had passed, when towards evening, a spark ignited the ceiling of this house and the inmates were forced to leave and watch it too reduced to ashes. Smith, Ricardo and their families then spent the night sheltering behind a horse-drawn wagon on a cultivated paddock nearby.[16]

Ricardo's neighbours, the Aberdeen family, early selectors in the area, had constructed a small tunnel into the hillside to store the cream during the heat of the summer. During the fires, Mrs Aberdeen, her mother and children took refuge in this half cellar until the danger had passed.[17] Another constant worry to the woman of the house during the summer months, apart from the intermittent danger of bush fires, was the very real threat of snakebite. If this happened and the doctor could be reached in time, the patient usually recovered. In 1896 a case of snakebite was reported in the Leongatha township.

> On Wed. last a girl of 8 years, daughter of Mrs. Frankland was bitten behind the knee by a reptile which first attacked two dogs. Mrs. Frankland hearing her child's screams rushed to her assistance and succeeded in killing the snake. Half an hour later the two dogs were dead. In the meantime all haste was displayed in taking the girl to Dr. Davies who injected chloride of lime, the puncture being clearly visible. During the night the child was very ill but yesterday morning the symptoms had disappeared and the patient returned home.[18]

Less fortunate was another case of snakebite reported from Strzelecki a fortnight later, also involving a young girl.

> The 8-year-old daughter of Mrs. Kelly of Strzelecki, sharing a bed with two other children awakened her mother with screaming. On going to her assistance, the girl complained that her finger was sore. On examination two punctures were found, snakebite was suspected, the room searched but no reptile found. Ligatures were applied and the affected part scarified and sucked. Another bite was found on the elbow — the child was taken from the bed but was unable to stand. She was taken immediately to Korumburra to receive medical attention but died on the way. After death another bite was found on her neck.[19]

It was subsequently reported that Mr Kelly and his son had killed upwards of 150 snakes on their property for the summer. So prevalent were the reptiles that the local branch of the ANA arranged for Dr Davies to give a special address at their lodge meeting the following month on 'Treatment of Snakebite' which proved 'interesting and informative'.[20] Some people spread newspapers on the floor of the bedrooms so that they could hear the snakes crawling around at night. Nevertheless, it must have been an unnerving experience for many. Mr Gordon Watson of Mardan, member of one of the pioneering families of that district, had vivid recollections of his childhood.

> My mother was a tailoress who had no experience of farm life before marriage. My earliest recollections are of stories told by my parents on completing the building of their first home. The noise from nailing the shingles on to the roof brought a great number of snakes from around the house. My father put a special man on a stump

outside the house who shot 35 snakes in two hours that had come out on account of the hammering. I was the youngest of ten children. There were no schools so my father employed a governess to educate the family. A special room was built for this purpose, one of the neighbours also sent two of his children. When the Koorooman East school was built three and a half miles away we children would walk both ways to school, at least half of a mile along fallen logs.[21]

Ill-health, sickness and injuries caused many anxious moments amongst pioneering women. Prior to the opening of the railway in 1891, the nearest doctors were stationed at Drouin, Morwell and Foster — in winter a twelve hour ride on horseback over muddy tracks. Babies were usually born at home attended by midwives with quite satisfactory results. *The Great Southern Star* normally carried an advertisement on the availability of midwives.

> Midwifery . . . Mrs. Neilsen of Inverloch is open for engagement in midwifery cases and general nursing in any part of the district. Mrs. Neilsen is a thoroughly experienced nurse having attended midwifery and other cases for the past 20 years. Favourable references supplied.
> Address . . . Mrs. Neilsen. Anderson's Inlet. P.O.[22]

The difficulty of obtaining medical attention, however, coupled with harsh living conditions, often resulted in death. Funerals were conducted with the simplicity befitting the pioneering period. The remains were usually carried from the homestead to the graveside where a service would be read. Frank Dodd of Dumbalk buried his wife and two of his children over a period of years in a plot on his farm on the Tarwin River. Hearses were only an urban luxury for the well-to-do. The daughter of a pioneer related her experiences while attending school at the home of Mr John Jeffrey at Leongatha in 1890.

> A sad occasion was once when four of us girls were called on to carry a small blue coffin with a baby on two towels — two girls holding each side down to the cemetery along a muddy wagon track — the other scholars following behind.[23]

In 1896 a man died at Mount Eccles and his friend brought the body, encased in a roughly made coffin lashed to a pack horse, for burial in the Leongatha

Anglican Church flower service, Koonwarra Hall, c. 1905 (from D. Bacon).

Cemetery. On arrival at the township, he was followed by mourners 'knee-deep in mud' down McCartin Street to the cemetery on Inlet Road.[24] To avoid the muddy tracks the coffin was sometimes carried for several miles across paddocks direct from the house to the cemetery. Following a death at the home of Mr P. Bellingham, who had selected on the Ruby Road, the remains were carried direct to the cemetery across the neighbouring selections of John Eccles and Peter Shingler.[25] In 1898 a young lad, Thomas McKean, of Mount Eccles tripped and fell at Adams's Falls, a near perpendicular drop of eighty foot on the West Tarwin Road. His companion went for help, but Thomas never regained consciousness. After a short service at the house by Mr G.M. Clark of the Wesleyan denomination, the remains were taken by his family and buried in the small cemetery on the Hallston-Mirboo North road (Allotment 82B).[26]

The first resident doctor in the Leongatha area was Dr Michael Carr who arrived on contractor O'Keefe's engine and began practice at McCartin's Hotel before the line was officially opened. Formerly resident surgeon at Sale Hospital, Dr Carr and his wife stayed at the Shingler homestead, The Grange, until a house was built for them adjacent to the Leongatha Railway Station. Appointed health officer by the Woorayl Shire Council soon after his arrival, Dr Carr spent considerable time on horseback travelling to patients scattered throughout the area from Waratah Bay and Inverloch to the Mount Eccles and Mardan districts. In addition to his duties as doctor, he was often called upon to act as chemist and veterinarian — a task that he was quite adept at as he was a keen farmer, despite the limited time he could spare from his medical duties.

The lack of a hospital in the district was a worry to Dr Carr, as well as to the general public, particularly in the event of an outbreak of an infectious disease. In the early 1900s diphtheria occurred in the Meeniyan-Stony Creek district. By that time there was another doctor, Dr C. H. Molloy, practising in the area. Having purchased a farm at Tarwin with a view to retirement, he was persuaded to resume practice and, in doing so, rendered valuable service in the southern section of the Shire. In order to isolate the diphtheria, Dr Molloy, with the assistance of Mr and Mrs Joe Tobin, proprietors of the Stony Creek Coffee Palace and Wine Saloon, immediately improvised a temporary tent hospital.

Nurse Dawson, a qualified nurse from Melbourne, was engaged to attend the patients but found on her arrival that one of her patients was almost on the point of death, and her nursing skills, in that particular case, proved fruitless. The work of Dr Molloy and Nurse Dawson in the tent hospital, however, confined the outbreak much to everyone's relief. Unfortunately, Nurse Dawson had difficulty in collecting her fees and had to sue the parents of one of her patients for payment with the case being heard at the Court of Petty Sessions at Leongatha. The Police Magistrate, in making his decision in favour of Dawson, stated that patients should be only too glad to pay the fees charged to nurse diphtheria cases. The nurse had come from Melbourne and should be paid her full fees. An order was made for £3 18s 9d together with £3 7s 3d paid into court and £3 3s 0d costs.[27]

8. TOWNSHIPS

The opening of the Great Southern Railway signalled the beginning of a series of townships spread out at roughly five mile intervals along the route. Between Korumburra and Stony Creek, six railway stations were surveyed and named: Kardella, Ruby, Leongatha, Koonwarra, Bongurra (Tarwin) and Meeniyan in a distance of less than twenty-five miles. At the completion of the survey, there was little difference between these township reserves — they were merely muddy clearings in the forest. Korumburra soon sprang into dominance through the discovery of black coal and the resultant influx of miners and associated workers.

Of the other six townships, Leongatha soon outgrew its neighbours. This was due to three factors. Firstly, the inherent fertility of a belt of red basalt soil surrounding it which settlers quickly recognised for its quality. Secondly, being at the junction of the railway and the connecting track between Mirboo North and Anderson's Inlet gave it a superior geographical location. The third factor was the establishment of the Labour Colony set up on the outskirts of the town in 1893 to alleviate the plight of the unemployed caused by the depression of that time. This immediately brought two to three hundred people to the town and district. Admittedly their spending power was very limited, but, nevertheless, the colonists provided manpower readily available to nearby farmers to assist them in bringing farms into production.

Few districts establish their identity without the aid of a local newspaper. Its very beginning reflects the faith and optimism of the proprietor and his financial sponsors. Often, the proprietor of a small country newspaper was a combination of printer, journalist, businessman and general live-wire in the community.

The Great Southern Star first commenced publication on 13 August 1890 under the auspices of William McPherson and Co. Little is known of McPherson, but it appears that he was financed by a well-educated local builder, Charles Chaplin, and hotel proprietor, Hugh McCartin. Thomas Musgrave stated that Chaplin

> canvassed the district for subscribers, and camped at our humble 12 × 12 ft paling hut, and my brother John introduced him to our neighbours, including Tarwin Lower and Inverloch. Chaplin afterwards built or supervised the building of the

Commercial Hotel for McCartin. He was a good tradesman, well educated, and could put his hand to anything, and no job too big for him.[1]

McPherson and Chaplin were not the only ones to realise the possibilities of a local newspaper. The newly-formed Woorayl Shire Council held its monthly meetings at Mirboo North, and its activities were reported in *The Mirboo Herald* by its new owner, William Wilson Young. Young had arrived in Victoria at the age of five years from a fishing village near Aberdeen, Scotland. After being educated at Heathcote, he was apprenticed to the printing trade, upon completion of which he operated a paper at Eaglehawk for a time. He then managed *The Rushworth Chronicle* for several years before coming to Mirboo North in 1889. In the course of reporting the district's activities, Mr Young visited Leongatha and was favourably impressed with its potential. Without loss of time, he secured premises in the township, sold *The Mirboo Herald*, and with the backing of a Mr Ingram took over *The Great Southern Star* in October 1890. The transfer of his printing plant from Mirboo North to Leongatha was not an easy task for Mr Young. On arrival at the Tarwin, it was found to be in flood with the water up to the handrail of the bridge. Young recalled,

> I hesitated about venturing to cross, but I saw a man on the other side, on rising ground and this seemed to encourage me and I decided to try my luck. My horse took to the water bravely, and we were soon safely across. But no sooner had I crossed than the whole structure of the bridge collapsed and floated down the stream. It was a difficult job getting the plant transported to Leongatha, but a Mr. Wm. Drummond, with his team of bullocks, succeeded in the undertaking, taking about three days to do it.[2]

The Great Southern Star thrived under the managership of William Young, and within a few years he was able to buy out his partner, Ingram, and become sole proprietor. This occurred in April 1894, at the same time that Mirboo Shire was severed from Woorayl Shire. Woorayl's area by that time had been more than doubled with the addition of the South Riding extending from Inverloch to Waratah Bay. *The Great Southern Star* regularly featured news stories from these coastal townships in an attempt to increase circulation.

Sales of newspapers were one thing, but collection of accounts was another. William Young inserted a rather apt poem in his paper in an attempt to overcome the problem of slow-paying subscribers.

> Lives of great men all remind us,
> Honest men don't stand a chance,
> The more we work there grows behind us,
> Bigger patches on our pants.
>
> On our pants, once new and glossy,
> Now are stripes of different hue,
> And because subscribers linger,
> And won't pay us what is due.
>
> Then let us now be up and doing,
> Send your mite however small,
> For when the frost of winter strikes us,
> We shall have no pants at all.[3]

William Young lived in a farm house a mile and a half from the town and walked to and from his office daily. This gave him the time to compose his editorial comments on the wants and needs of the new community, of which *The Great Southern Star* was the mouthpiece. The all-pervading necessity for a road network was constantly voiced in the paper. Woorayl Shire Council was doing its best with the limited amount of funds and equipment available; that is, corduroy was used extensively before metalling could be carried out. On 8 October 1889 tenders were called for the 'clearing and grubbing of roads about Koorooman, also supply 2500 pieces of corduroy at Koorooman'. At the same meeting, Councillors Smith and Allison moved 'that the Road Overseer be instructed to purchase one tip dray and three wheel barrows — suitable for Shire work'.

The formation of Woorayl Shire Council did not take place at a very opportune time from a financial point of view. Cr Robert Smith, in presenting his annual report on 3 December 1889, pointed out that

as the Shire of Woorayl had not been included in the scheme drawn up for the appropriation of the Municipal Vote, it could not participate on the highest scale viz., £3 to £1, but would be paid on the lowest scale viz., 17s 6d to the £1. This announcement came like a thunder clap upon the council — necessitating an entire revision of the scheme of expenditure.[4]

Apart from the provision of roads, the two main topics of interest featured in *The Great Southern Star* by Young were the necessity for an adequate water supply and the drainage of the township. Although Leongatha is blessed with a reliable average annual rainfall of thirty-seven inches, the provision of water was an urgent and constant problem. Cartage by rail was a common practice in other parts of the State, and in the late summer months, Leongatha was no exception. At the Woorayl Shire Council meeting of 12 April 1892, Crs McCartin and Ritchie moved 'that the offer of the Railway Department to supply Leongatha with 30,000 gallons of water per day, and sixpence per 100 gallons on any additional quantity be accepted'.[5]

Storekeeper T.S. Ridgway, in a letter to Council, pointed out the detrimental effects of the lack of a water supply in the township, as visitors were unable to water their horses and cattle during the summer months. He suggested that Council affix a pump on the spring known as 'O'Keefe's Well' on the road below the railway station. This well had been sunk by contractor O'Keefe in 1889 for the provision of water for the men and horses working along the line.

Council Engineer Griffin, after inspection, reported that 'he had found it full to within ten feet of the top of the shaft with fresh water which I believe would satisfy the wants and requirements of stock'. Following this report, Crs McCartin and Allan instructed the Shire Secretary to apply to the Lands Department for reservation of parts of Allotments 5 and 6, Section 20, township of Leongatha, for water supply purposes.[6] With the arrival of the heat of summer, horses and stock could not wait for the official consent of the Lands Department for the erection of permanent facilities, so the Engineer recommended 'that in the meantime it would be advisable to re-erect the old windlass and stand to provide for present requirements'.[7]

Although satisfied with the quality and quantity of water in O'Keefe's well, Griffin was not impressed with its accessibility for cartage purposes.

> Since the date of my last report attention has been drawn to the spring on the Ruby road about 40 chains from township of Leongatha which I consider to be a more advantageous site for the erection of a pump and watering place. Although not so near the centre of the township the water is much closer to the surface and would be available with less labour than at O'Keefe's well besides being more convenient to the traffic and to water carts being on the road. I have therefore given instructions for the sinking and timbering of a shallow shaft and will with your approval make arrangements for the erection of a pump, drinking trough, and stand pipe at that locality.[8]

Householders relied on tank water during the winter months, with access to wells as circumstances permitted. Hotels, coffee palaces and boarding houses all had underground wells in their back yards to catch the surplus winter rains. Drainage from Bair's and McCartin's hotels, together with that from the butcher's shop and coffee palace south of McCartin's, flowed out on the street. During the summer months the smell from the drains was a constant source of comment in *The Great Southern Star*. On 1 October 1897 the Engineer called the attention of Council 'to the necessity of procuring a quantity of disinfectant for the drains and gullies of the township before the summer'. 'Timotheus' in *The Great Southern Star* was more eloquent.

> Cleanse those drainings straight away,
> Odious both by night and day,
> Odious to the nose and eye,
> Of the luckless passer by.
> Dark and thick by broad daylight,
> Stirred about at birth of night
> By the frogs, whose thousand throats
> Make earth hideous with their notes.
>
> Treat the frog and treat the drain,
> Just as Abel was by Cain —
> Slaughter them! — and use quicklime;
> None will deem the act a crime;
> Let upon their graves be seen
> Tussocks of the grassiest green.
> Then upon the sacred mound
> Plant the eucalyptus round —
> Ash and wattle, elm and pine —
> Beautify this new design.
>
> Fitting start of Shire of Woo(!)
> For the Bair Street avenue;
> I could wish that street to be —
> Promenade of love and me —
>
> Sweet as the breath of dawn
> Lovely as a garden lawn!
> Fancy glen in forest glade
> Leongatha should be made.[9]

The Commercial Hotel, Leongatha, c. 1907. J.P. Rowan, Licensee (from Woorayl Shire Historical Society).

Nevertheless, without town water or adequate drainage, Leongatha township grew steadily. Within ten years of the opening of the railway, the four major religious denominations had erected churches to serve their respective communities. The Church of England and Methodist Churches had purchased blocks of land on opposite sides of Church Street at the junction of Bruce Street. The Methodists were the first to arrange for the erection of their church. Minutes of their quarterly meeting held 1 April 1891 record that 'Mr. A.W. Jones' tender for £21 10s for erection of Church (labour only) be accepted'. On 25 August it was resolved that an organ be purchased, 'the price not to exceed £25'.[10]

The builder, Mr A.W. Jones, also gained the contract to build the Church of England parsonage in Peart Street in the same year for the sum of £147 10s 0d. Arrangements were made to hold Church of England services in the Methodist Church rent-free, but a charge of £1 per quarter was made towards the cost of lighting and cleaning. Within a few months, the first St Peter's on the lower side of Church Street had been completed by Jones and Co. at a cost of

£159 10s 0d, plus £10 for extras.[11] Seating was not adequate for the opening ceremony, conducted by Archdeacon Langley on 7 January 1894, as Methodist minutes reveal that they would 'forgo night service on 7 Jan. and lend seats and organ if necessary to Church of England'.[12]

Preaching was not only done in the churches. Services were held in private homes throughout the district and at the Labour Colony. In the summer months Reverend North of the Church of England regularly preached at Leongatha on a Sunday at 11 a.m., at McKeown's Corner, Leongatha South, in the open air at 3 p.m., and then at Inverloch at 7 p.m. Reverend North was instrumental in starting a Young Men's Guild at St Peter's, at which a Bible Class was conducted at the regular monthly meetings. Debates were held and on 22 September 1895 the subject for discussion was listed as 'Should Young Men Be Footballers'. It was to be conducted by the Minister at 4 p.m. sharp.[13]

Prior to the erection of the Catholic Church in Ogilvy Street in 1895, Mass had been celebrated on a regular basis at the Mechanics' Hall by a visiting priest from Morwell. As a result of a series of fund-raising activities that included concerts and balls, building commenced early in 1895 under the supervision of Mr A. Gardiner. At the official blessing and opening of the building on 30 June 1895, it was dedicated to St Laurence O'Toole by Right Reverend Dr Corbett, Bishop of Sale. A choir was brought especially from Korumburra for the opening ceremonies, and under the conductorship of Madame Simonson,

Methodist Church, Lyre Bird Mound, reopened at Koonwarra, 1903 (from D. Bacon).

rendered 'Mass in B Flat' by Farmer.[14] Leongatha was attached to the Morwell Parish until 1901, when the Reverend Father P.J. Coyne was appointed its first resident pastor.

A large percentage of settlers in the Koorooman-Mardan districts were of Scottish extraction, and it was in this area that the first services of the Presbyterian denomination were held. The homes of Mr Robert Smith of Mardan West and of Mr Matthew Allison, adjacent to the surveyed site of Koorooman township, were used for this purpose during the 1880s. With the erection of the Koorooman Hall on Crighton's Hill in 1888, services were held there for some time under the charge of a Mr Duncan and several devoted laymen. By 1900 Mr James Forbes was appointed missionary in charge of the Leongatha territory, with Berry's Creek and Mount Eccles as outstations. The following year, 1901, the first St Andrew's Church in Peart Street, Leongatha, was built by Mr Neil Faulkiner and dedicated for public worship on 28 April 1901. The special opening service was conducted by the Reverend Professor Murdoch Macdonald, D D, of Ormond College, Melbourne, when the church was made a full charge by the Presbytery of Melbourne South. A call was extended and accepted by the Reverend H.C. Matthew who became the first resident minister.[15]

The 1890s saw the business sector of the town established to serve the surrounding farming community. In an age when the horse reigned supreme as the source of transport and motive power, it was inevitable that the industries associated with this field should gain dominance. A full hotel licence was not granted unless the proprietor made provision for the accommodation of six horses. Livery and bait stables were quickly established to cater for the growing number of horses in and around the district. 'Livery' entailed the care and attention of a horse; that is, harnessing, unharnessing and placing in stalls, while 'bait' was the provision of feed. Twelve months after the opening of the railway, there were two saddle and harness-makers operating at Leongatha. W.J. Leask commenced business in new premises next to the National Bank 'with a large assortment of saddlery etc. of the best description', while R. Bruce, saddler, of the Inlet Road, announced that he had opened for business.[16] The associated activities of blacksmithing and coach-building, although usually carried out on the same premises, were two distinct trades. The shoeing of horses was performed by a farrier who would mould and shape the shoes to fit the horse's hooves. Special types of shoes were made as the occasion demanded. Some were made with a bar across the rear, others would be weighted to one side to prevent knocking if a horse had a special gait. The blacksmith was a skilled artisan who could mould the heated metal into any desired shape or form. Ploughs could be made to suit the peculiar type of soil common to the district. In South Gippsland sledges fitted with iron runners were the blacksmith's stock in trade and met with a ready sale. For most of the year they were the only reliable means of transport available to many settlers and were a universal piece of farm equipment.

With the construction of metal roads, the skills of a wheelwright were called for in the making of iron-rimmed wheels for gigs, buggies, carts, wagons etc. The wooden section of the wheel was assembled by the coach-builder from fellies and spokes, a heated iron tyre made to fit the exact circumference was tapped over it quickly, and the wheel plunged into a circular trough of cold water. The rapid cooling shrank the iron rim and it fitted tightly and snugly onto the wooden wheel. This tyre lasted a considerable time depending on use, road surface and weather, until it worked loose and had to be returned to the wheelwright and the process repeated.

The blacksmith's tools of trade were an anvil and several sets of tongs which he usually made himself. A forge with a hot coke fire blown by hand bellows enabled him to hammer and mould the iron as required. The striker was often a strong young man, who worked with a selection of sledge hammers varying up to 14 lbs weight which stood handy to the anvil. A clever blacksmith could work alone with a short-handled striking hammer in his right hand and the tongs holding the hot iron in his left. For big jobs a striker with a 14 lb hammer was needed to alternate with the blacksmith's directional taps on the wheel rim or hot iron bar where needed. Verdi's 'Anvil Chorus' is a stunningly accurate portrayal of the blacksmith at work as well as being delightful listening.

The floor of the blacksmith's shop was invariably of dirt to save accidents. Hot metal could be dropped on the floor and sparks from the anvil soon died in the dirt. After years of usage, the floor of the blacksmith's shop was an iron grey silt that clung to the work clothes and was ingrained in the pores of the blacksmith's arms, neck and face. The blacksmith always wore a flannel, grey moleskin trousers, leather boots and a leather apron which was a flitch of pliable leather tied round the waist with a leather thong. At the turn of the century the blacksmith's shop in country towns was as much the centre of the town's activities as the motor garage was fifty years later.

Leongatha's blacksmith, E.T. 'Ted' Munro, had taken over the business of T.H. Brown in 1895 in McCartin Street on Allotment 13, and by 1897 he was employing six men. The old cordial factory was being utilised as a carriage factory in which buggies and gigs of high standard were being manufactured. Ted Munro was at the peak of physical condition at that time and responded to the challenge of fellow blacksmiths around Australia by attempting to create a record number of horseshoes in one hour. The previous record was held by a Mr John Kirk of Camperdown, Victoria, who, with one assistant, put up thirty-six shoes in an hour, which did not include one badly made. Mr Munro's attempt on the record, which created quite a deal of interest, was described by *The Great Southern Star*.

> The shoes made last Tuesday were the same size as those made by Mr. Kirk, and were fellowed, stamped and punched. The trial was carried out on systematic lines, and in the presence of several reputable townsmen, Mr. J.P. Rowan officiating as time keeper. The bars of iron were cut and stacked on the forge and precisely at 2.30 p.m. Mr. Munro started making shoes with Mr. W. Leahy attending to the fire and striking. The latter had a very trying ordeal, for although he worked splendidly he was handicapped by the bad quality of the coal. Mr. Munro got going in splendid style giving a fine exhibition of skill and endurance, and was going stronger than ever in the last quarter of the hour. Mr. Leahy also stuck bravely to his work, with the gratifying result that his master was enabled to turn out the record number of thirtysix in 7.40 minutes under the hour. The work was well done, and the shoes turned out just as if they were thrown off the anvil in the ordinary way of working.[17]

Munro's business continued to expand, and he was forced by pressure of space

McCartin Street, Leongatha, c. 1900 (from I. Bruce).

Ted Munro's premises in Anderson Street, Leongatha, c. 1910. Site occupied by McNiven's in 1987 (from Woorayl Shire Historical Society).

to move to new premises on Allotment 4, Anderson Street, fronting the railway trucking yards. This street was named after Robert Anderson who had erected the first store in the township on the Ruby Road adjacent to the railway tracks. After lying vacant for a short time, Munro's former premises in McCartin Street were taken over by a different type of artisan whose mechanical knowledge exceeded his literary skills. The notice on the door of the old blacksmith's shop read 'BYSICKLES REPARED'.[18]

Two other Scottish tradesmen soon set up in opposition to Ted Munro. J.H. 'Jock' Campbell arrived in Leongatha in 1897 and set up business in Roughead Street. Born at Renfrew on the Clyde, Scotland, he commenced work at ten years of age as a rivet boy at the shipbuilding yards of Elders during the American Civil War. It entailed a walk of three miles each way daily, but Campbell continued with this job until migrating to Australia at the age of seventeen. After gaining experience at several blacksmithing businesses around the State, he set up his own business in a split paling structure set amongst heavy scrub and undergrowth in Roughead Street. Like Munro, his business expanded with the district and the demand for the building of wagons, buggies and jinkers in addition to all general classes of work associated with his calling. Up to twelve men were employed at his carriage factory when in full production.

With Munro's smithy convenient for people on the western side of Leongatha and Campbell's the north, those from the southern side were well served by J. McFarlane, another Scotsman whose premises were next to that of *The Great Southern Star* in McCartin Street. Although his business was not quite as large as those of Munro and Campbell, his work was comparable. He believed in the power of advertising and often inserted a verse or two in conjunction with his weekly notice in *The Great Southern Star*.

The presence of such a large number of horses in and around the town caused other problems. One lady voiced her need in a letter to *The Great Southern Star*.

> Why does not the Council or some prominent citizen not place a block in front of the Leongatha P.O. from which ladies might mount their horses. At present ladies who are unattended have to lead their horses for some distance to a friendly spot before they can get into the saddle. We hope the Council will adopt this sensible suggestion as the cost would be trifling.[19]

Woorayl Shire Council had a similar request at their September meeting of 1906 from N.B. Fraser, newly-appointed Manager of the Bank of Victoria. He asked for permission to erect two tethering posts in the street in front of the new premises in McCartin Street then being built. This was immediately granted, but there is no record of whether the ladies got their mounting block in front of the post office. When the new post office was officially opened in February 1907, Council erected a hitching rail directly in front of it that did service for many decades. The new building, which was staffed by permanent PMG employees under the charge of Mr Brash, replaced a contract office that had been carried on in premises further up McCartin Street under the charge of Miss Gregory and staff.

Food trades have always been a major source of employment in every township. With the commencement of the railway, Phillip Bellingham opened his first butcher's shop on the Ruby Road near Anderson's store but soon shifted to more central premises in McCartin Street. A small cordial factory operated for a short period next to the bakery started by R.A. Bazley on Allotment 14, while another butchery was established on Allotment 17 by Ted Higgs. No refrigeration was available at that time, with the result that a large percentage of the meat was pickled in brine and then boiled by the purchaser.

The major trading banks were quick to realise the potential of the Leongatha district and soon commenced operations. Their establishment benefited the district in two ways. It facilitated the financial transactions necessary for the carrying on of business and also contributed to the growth of the community, by bringing in men of a different type who filled a very real need in the district. The role played by bankers and school teachers in the formation of new communities is often unrecognised and unnoticed. Although the primary producers and the service trades associated with them provided the basic strength and wealth of a district, it was often the bankers and school teachers who facilitated and organised the running of the newly-formed social and sporting organisations that quickly emerged.

The first bank to begin operations at Leongatha, the Bank of Australasia, opened an agency from Mirboo North under the charge of Mr C.E. McCay in 1890.[20] Their premises were in a wooden building owned by Hugh McCartin in Bair Street. Mr C.E. McCay was appointed Treasurer of the newly-formed Mechanics' Institute Committee but resigned on leaving the district in July 1890.[21] His position was taken by Mr G. Greig, who played an active role in the building and subsequent opening of the Institute on 4 March 1891. The secretarial work of the Mechanics' Institute was ably carried out by John Jeffrey, headmaster of the local school. Shortly after the opening of the Australasia agency in 1890, the National Bank opened for business in adjoining premises under the managership of Mr G.E. Peart. Peart was also active on the committee of the Mechanics' Institute in the initial years of its formation, serving first as Auditor and then as Treasurer until his transfer in June 1893.[22] Bankers often played a leading role in the formation of the different Churches, giving valuable advice to Church committees on financial matters. Mr Peart was active on the committee that arranged for the building of the Methodist Church in Leongatha in 1891, while another banker, Mr R. de C. Shaw, appointed Manager of the Bank of Australasia in 1894, was a strong supporter and active worker for the Church of England.

By reason of their talents, bankers were often appointed to fill the position of treasurer of any sporting bodies they joined, and Mr R. Shaw was quickly appointed Treasurer to the Leongatha Rifle Club, a post which he held for many years. A keen tennis player, Shaw joined the newly-formed Leongatha Tennis Club that played on the first courts situated in the goods yard of the railway station. As a result of concerted efforts by members of the club, of which he was president, new asphalt courts were constructed on the eastern side of the line and opened in August 1900. At the official opening Mr Shaw said,

it was a red letter day for Leongatha tennis players. The courts would not only prove a source of pleasure to lovers of the game but would be an ornament to the township — serving to assist in rubbing out that countrified appearance so perceptible to the railway traveller.[23]

There was one serious drawback to the site of the new courts. They were built adjacent to the main drain from Bair Street that flowed under the railway and out on to the railway reserve above Long Street. In the summertime the stench from these drains became rather overpowering. *The Great Southern Star* constantly admonished the Council on the situation, pointing out the danger to the health of the community. Engineer Callaway recommended that Council provide a deodorising fluid to be sent down the main drain across the railway, which hopefully would minimise the smell. He also recommended that the wooden drains along Bair Street be replaced by stone, brick or concrete. The main drain could then be taken across the railway and down onto a Council reserve of five acres that could be converted into a sewerage farm.[24]

Woorayl Shire councillors had plenty of worries with a growing township. There was no town water supply to flush out the drains or quell the outbreak of a fire, and the poor state of the drains led to periodic outbreaks of typhoid amongst the inhabitants. Under the *Health Act*, Councils were directly and financially liable for the cost of treating any outbreak of infectious diseases which occurred within their boundaries. Half of the expenditure incurred by Councils for hospital accommodation was refunded by the Government, and if the Councils failed to make provision for these cases, the Government could provide accommodation and sue for the recovery of the Council's quota.[25]

In the absence of a public hospital, any cases of infectious diseases had to be sent to Melbourne for treatment. This led to comment in the report of the Medical Superintendent of the Melbourne Hospital 'that a very considerable portion of bad cases came from the neighbourhood of South Gippsland'.[26] Periodic outbreaks of typhoid occurred at Leongatha — some fatal. In August 1903 local dairyman, M. Frazer, lost his eldest son Reginald, aged fourteen, after a short illness. He had been working on a farm near the town before being taken ill. This was the second death in the family from typhoid in six months.[27] Health Officer Dr Carr, in his reports to Council, was constantly pointing out the necessity for a proper drainage network of brick, concrete or bluestone pitchers. Another cause of typhoid, according to Dr Carr, was the prevalence of a large number of cattle sale yards in the township. In summertime the soil in these yards pulverised into dust and blew onto the roofs of the adjoining houses, thus contaminating the drinking water. This factor, combined with flies from the numerous pan closets, made such outbreaks inevitable.

The worst year for Leongatha was in 1903 when eighty-four cases were reported. Dr Carr believed this was partly brought about by the presence of a large number of 'starvers' in and around the township. These were very poor cattle brought into the district by stock agents from drought-stricken areas in the north of the State. Many were turned loose and died on the roads, and it may have been days or weeks before the carcases could be burnt. From an analysis of dates of outbreaks of the disease, Dr Carr was still adamant that drains were the main cause of the outbreaks. March was the worst month of the year, and it was in this month that Council employees cleaned out the town drains. This theory of Dr Carr was subsequently borne out in March 1909 when Shire Engineer, A.E. Callaway, was stricken with typhoid and had to be moved to St Vincent's Hospital, Melbourne. Callaway had been inspecting the recently opened drain in Bair Street, preparatory to it being relaid with bluestone pitchers.[28]

The initial moves to obtain a town water supply started at a public meeting convened by Shire President H. McCartin in the last week of February 1901. Various schemes were suggested, the most popular being that of obtaining it from Korumburra as that town was five hundred foot higher than Leongatha. The cost of this scheme was estimated at £6,000. A second scheme for the building of a reservoir on the Ruby Creek at Hamann's was estimated to cost £4,800 for the pipes alone. A sub-committee under Engineer Callaway was instructed to investigate the various proposals and report back to a further meeting. This was held almost twelve months later when the Korumburra scheme was dismissed as being too expensive. Callaway favoured the Ruby Creek scheme, as the quality and supply of the water was excellent with the creek running at the rate of 90,000 gallons per day even in the driest summer months. The site of the weir was very suitable with an excellent foundation of hard grey sandstone. Total cost was estimated at £6,490 which was made up of[29]

Pipe track,	£5,100
Head Weir	£ 200
Reticulation	£ 600
Contingencies	£ 590

On 9 April 1902 an application by councillors of the West Riding to the Governor-in-Council for the grant of a loan of £6,000 was made on their behalf by G.F. Michael, Shire Secretary, to carry out the proposed water supply scheme. Another eighteen months elapsed before tenders could be called for supply of pipes and earthworks. By this time total cost had risen to £7,600 with an estimated life of the pipes being thirty-three years. At the first meeting of the Leongatha Waterworks Trust held on 21 March 1905, Mr G.F. Michael was appointed Secretary at £35 for the first year. Trust members comprised Messrs Smith, McCartin, Livingston, Carbarns and Johnson. The offer of Mr Beard for the required land at £25 per acre was accepted and tenders were called for

(1) Clearing of three acres on site of head works.
(2) Carting of 300 yards of spawls and sand to weir site on Ruby creek.
(3) Supply of cast and wrought iron 6in. pipes.[30]

By June the Trust had accepted the tender of R. Linton of Melbourne of £1,984 4s 0d for the supply of wrought iron pipes. This tender was not approved by the Department of Water Supply because wrought iron pipes, although cheaper, had only half the life of cast iron pipes which were estimated at sixty years life expectancy. The Trust was then forced to accept the tender of Austral Otis for 360 tons of cast iron pipes at £7 10s 0d per ton. By September 1906 the laying of the mains was almost completed, and house connections were being installed in several of the main streets. The following notice was then served on owners by Trust Chairman H. McCartin:

Owners of tenements in the following streets, Roughead, McCartin, Anderson, Brown, Watt, Gray, Quarry, Church, Bair, Koonwarra Road, Ogilvy and Jeffrey are

J. Hill's bullock team ploughing for water main , Leongatha, 1906 (from D. Bacon).

H. Dannock's first shop, Roughead Street, Leongatha, 1903 (from Woorayl Shire Historical Society).

required by law before 1 October to cause a proper pipe and stop cocks to be laid so as to supply water within such tenements from the main pipe.[31]

House connections were done by local plumbers, the best known of whom was Harry Dannock at that time. Dannock arrived in Leongatha in 1899 and had built a small plumber's shop next to his house in Roughead Street on Allotment 3 Section 19. His daughter Vera recalled

> There was thick bush on both sides of this block, only about four houses at that time. My father walked many miles out to farmers, through the bush to work. Many times he had to stay the night as he could not finish the work in one day. He often came home with a side of lamb or such to pay for what he had done. No one had much money in those days and no such thing as a 40 hour week. There was a beautiful spring about where the McIndoe Park board now is. I remember Dad bringing water up from there before we had pipe water. Also my mother did her washing there a few times when the house tank was low in the summertime. Dad being the only plumber at the time he was made the turncock which meant he had to look after the pipe track into the town from Fairbank, in case of leaks. He walked that track once a week. Many times we, (my two young sisters and self) went with him to Fairbank in the jinker and horse then Dad would start to walk the track while we drove home. I remember we had one tap in the house but the water wasn't so good, and we had a filter put on. Everyone had house tanks for drinking water. Many times eels got into the pipe and blocked the flow.[32]

There were numerous complaints regarding the quality of the water, and no doubt they were justified. In the absence of a settling pond or filter basin it was inevitable that at times pollution with vegetable matter occurred, particularly during periods of heavy rainfall. Many householders like Dannock simply installed filters. The Railways Department asked whether the Trust could supply 1,000,000 gallons for local use and at what price. Commissioners Johnson and Harden moved that the price be 9d per 1,000 gallons for the first million gallons then 6d for additional 1,000s, with the contract being let for five years.[33] By October the Railways Department had replied that the water supplied by the Trust was of rather a hard nature and not adapted for locomotive purposes.[34]

If the Railways Department was not appreciative of the Leongatha water, the local fire brigade certainly was. The first movement for the formation of a fire brigade had been made at a public meeting held in February 1902 but did not meet with any success. With the arrival of town water in 1906, a brigade was formed at an enthusiastic meeting held in January 1907, at which Inspector Marshall from the Fire Brigade Board outlined the duties and responsibilities of volunteer firemen. The Board agreed to supply uniforms consisting of coat, cap, belt and spanner but no trousers! Local dentist E.S. Callanan was elected Captain, with R. Jones, Lieutenant, and W. Carmody, Secretary.[35]

The brigade had their first taste of action in December 1907, when the home of local solicitor J.W. Sutherland on Inlet Road caught fire. Through prompt action of nearby residents, including two members of the brigade, the fire was brought under control without serious damage to the house. Other members of the brigade could not be contacted owing to lack of a bell. A house to house collection was then undertaken to finance purchase of this necessity. It met with

Laying footpaths in Leongatha, c. 1900 (from Woorayl Shire Historical Society).

McCartin Street, Leongatha, 1911 (from Woorayl Shire Historical Society).

a ready response, and the bell was quickly purchased and installed. A more severe test of the prowess of the brigade occurred at 4.15 a.m. on a Saturday morning in April 1908 when four shops on the lower side of Bair Street were destroyed. When the brigade was called, they had great difficulty in locating the fire plugs to attach their hoses as there were no indicators. When eventually found and hoses connected, the pressure was not satisfactory until fireman Nicholls turned off the water to McCartin Street thus giving better pressure to Bair Street. If nothing else it illustrated the wisdom and necessity of having a well-equipped brigade in a town with practically all wooden buildings. Although the loss was considerable, it would have been much worse had it occurred before the formation of the brigade.

In March 1909 Cr P. Johnson officiated at the opening of the new fire station in Anderson Street in the presence of a large gathering. Costing £140, the fifty foot by twenty foot building was lined and varnished, fitted with lockers and lit with electricity. After the band had played several numbers, Captain Callanan lined up the brigade and marched them into the building and then asked Cr Johnson to officially open it. Cr Johnson said that the Fire Brigade Board had contributed £50, but the balance had to be raised locally, and Captain Callanan stated that property owners had already benefited by the existence of the brigade through having their insurance premiums reduced by fifteen percent. The Water Trust took credit for the reduction, but it was not made until after the brigade was formed. Progressive euchre was then played for some time, and then all adjourned to the Mechanics' Hall for a ball to celebrate the occasion.[36]

A fortnight later the brigade was called on to quell a serious fire in McCartin Street. First noticed at 3.30 a.m. in the premises of *The Great Southern Star*, the brigade was hampered by the usual custom of turning off water mains at night. It was some time before sufficient pressure could be obtained, but gradually the fire was brought under control. All early editions of the paper were destroyed, together with all the plant. Fortunately, the contents were insured and the brigade was instrumental in saving the coach-building premises next door occupied by J. McFarlane.[37]

Next to the provision of a water supply for a township, the most desired amenity is lighting. In February 1902 the Leongatha Progress Association approached Council requesting provision of street lighting. It was stated that if over twenty lamps were installed, acetylene lights would be cheaper and better, but under twenty, kerosene lamps would be cheaper but with inferior light. Cr McCartin said that 'the main streets were undoubtedly in a most unsatisfactory state but he thought lamps would assist townspeople to tolerate them'. Cr Kindellan considered 'the townspeople should strive to give outsiders means of getting to the town first'.[38] Engineer Callaway reported back to a meeting later in April that the price of red gum posts fitted with cast iron chains and lamps was £2 17s 6d, cast iron posts fitted with lamps, complete as supplied by City Council, was £3 and the cost of rail freight and fitting was £1.

No decision was made on the question until the July meeting, when Cr McCartin moved 'that the Engineer be empowered to have an incandescent kerosene lamp erected as a trial at Leongatha'. This was done at the corner of McCartin and Bair Streets later in the month, while an arc lamp was suspended at the corner of McCartin and Peart Streets for a comparison. At the November meeting the Engineer reported that 'the arc lamp gave a better reflection, and although installation costs averaged £5, the annual running costs were the same'. Council decided to retain the arc lamp which used a special type of oil known as 'Optimol', and this remained the sole lighting in the township until August 1904. Jarratt Brothers, who conducted a butchery adjacent to the Commercial Hotel on the southern side, then installed a twenty horsepower Simplex engine to run their refrigeration plant. An offer was made to Council to light the town with electricity from this plant. After inspection by Engineer Callaway, agreement was reached with Jarratt Brothers to supply lighting for a period of three years at £6 10s 0d per annum.[39] Poles and wiring were erected, and six Lilliput arc lamps of 160 candle power were placed in suitable positions along the main streets. A large gathering attended Jarratt's Butcher shop for the initial switching-on ceremony which was done by Miss McCartin, daughter of Cr Hugh McCartin who was Shire President at the time. Cr McCartin said that, fifteen years previous, Leongatha was 'a howling wilderness and yet now had the benefits of all mod-cons'. Fellow hotelier Robert Bair had shown his confidence in the new scheme by having the Otago Hotel wired, and both hotels were a blaze of light for the first time.

Six lights were hardly sufficient for the growing township, and in the following month of September 1904, a petition signed by fifty residents was presented to Council asking for an additional light near the Methodist and Church of England Churches. The initial success of Jarratt's scheme led to more town houses having lights installed. Although the overall scheme was soundly based, the plant was under-powered, under-serviced and suffered from constant breakdowns. As the end of the three year contract approached, requests were made by Council to directors of the Leongatha Butter Factory to consider supplying power and lighting on a more permanent basis.

Factory Manager Stewart Curtis Wilson investigated the proposal and put forward a detailed scheme, outlining the benefits to be derived by the company in embarking on the project. At an extraordinary meeting of shareholders at Leongatha on 1 September 1907, Chairman Peter Johnson explained the scheme and urged shareholders to alter the Articles of Association of the company to include

> . . . the business of an electric light Company in all its branches, in particular to construct, lay down, establish, fix, and carry out all necessary cables, wires, lines, accumulators, lamps and works, and to generate, accumulate, distribute electricity, for the purpose of light, heat, motive power or otherwise, to light towns, streets, buildings of places, both public and private.[40]

Johnson explained to shareholders that, using Wilson's estimates, the company, for an outlay of £1,000 would generate a net profit of £83 10s 0d annually, excluding the benefits accruing from its use in their own factory. The motion to change the Articles of Association was carried with only four dissenting. By February 1908 William Watson, Secretary, was calling tenders for the supply of forty-five poles of 'sound messmate, 28 feet long and not less than 7 ins at the small end'. When Jarratt's contract expired in August, the Leongatha Butter Factory had their plant and lines installed to continue the power supply. They wisely did not overload their generating plant as Vera Dannock recalled. 'We

Neil's Hotel, Sandymount Avenue, Inverloch, c. 1910 (from D. Bacon).

were allowed to have only one light burning at a time and the street lighting was very few and far between. But it was just wonderful to press a little button and have light'.[41]

With the opening of the new Leongatha Post Office in 1906, trunk line .telephonic communication was available to the community. Originally connected only to the post office, the service was nevertheless greatly appreciated by townsfolk and business people. The network included Korumburra, Outtrim and Inverloch, and by September 1908 Postmaster Brash was able to state that 'word has been received that towns on the eastern side of Leongatha will be connected in the next few days'.[42]

Inverloch and Meeniyan townships had not experienced the same rapid growth as Leongatha. The main complaint of Inverloch residents was that of total neglect by Council, while 'a lavish expenditure continues on the Tarwin Road and township near which two councillors reside'.[43] As a result of this neglect, a petition was circulated calling for a severance from Woorayl Shire and junction with Poowong and Jeetho Shire, but nothing further was heard of this action.

A regular shipping service to the Inlet was conducted on a monthly basis from Melbourne by the small ketch *Ripple*. This was a shallow draft vessel, fifty foot long, capable of loading up to thirty tons but which drew only four foot of water when fully laden. This enabled it to negotiate the shallow bar at the entrance of the Inlet and deposit goods at the small wharves of Inverloch, Maher's Landing and Tarwin Lower. Later a regular service was run by steamships S.S. *Despatch*, S.S. *Wyrallah*, S.S. *Moonah*, S.S. *Ellen* and the S.S. *Manawatu*. The latter three ran aground on the bar at different times without suffering serious damage. The S.S. *Manawatu* was stuck on the bar for several weeks before being winched free.

A Rocket Brigade was formed for use in shipping emergencies with members practising regularly on a weekly basis. A shed was built adjacent to the track from the hotel to the jetty to house the necessary equipment. The only time the brigade was called on in an emergency, one of the crew members became entangled in the rocket rope and was swept overboard. Fellow members went to his assistance, and all were rescued by the crew of the vessel that was supposed to be in distress.[44]

The Inverloch jetty was difficult to reach for wheeled traffic and Engineer Callaway recommended Council purchase Allotments 55 and 56. This would give the Council and public a right of way along a private street called Hopetoun Street. Callaway said that

> if this were done it would be far superior to any road which could be made over the heavy sand and which would always be liable to drift should a fire destroy the natural herbage which retains it in place.[45]

Callaway's action in this matter was thoroughly vindicated several years later when Inverloch sprang into prominence with the development of the Wonthaggi coalfield in 1909. Such was the shortage of black coal in Victoria at the time that coal was hauled by bullock wagon and steam traction engine from the

Loading Wonthaggi coal at Inverloch jetty 1910 (from Wonthaggi Historical Society).

coalfield to Inverloch. Steamers made regular weekly visits to take the coal to Melbourne for use in power stations and railway engines, until such time as the connecting rail link between Wonthaggi and Nyora was completed. The first load of coal from the newly-opened field reached Inverloch by bullock wagon on 29 November 1909. Woorayl Council President Peter Johnson claimed the honour of driving the team through the town to the jetty. On passing Neil's Hotel in Sandymount Avenue, a stop was made and the drivers were treated by the host and hostess. School turned out and photographs were taken before proceeding down a'Beckett Street where another stop was made at Lohr's Hotel. Here the drivers were invited in to toast the occasion with champagne before proceeding on their way to the jetty.[46] Six weeks later the bullock teams were joined by a steam traction engine, and four hundred tons of coal was being shipped from Inverloch weekly. Six steamers and two sailing vessels were reported in the Inlet the week before shipping ceased as a result of the completion of the railway from Nyora to Wonthaggi in February 1910.

In its infancy the two hotels were the largest buildings in Inverloch, as had been the first two hotels in Leongatha. The Inverloch Hotel in Sandymount Avenue and the Esplanade at the lower end of a'Beckett Street were both licensed in 1896. The first church in the seaside township was the Catholic Church in Scarborough Street. This was blessed and dedicated to Our Lady Star of the Sea by Bishop Corbett on 11 February 1906.[47]

Other denominations held services at the Inverloch Hall at infrequent intervals, while on Christmas Day 1910, an open-air service was held at the jetty. Following the distribution of handbills in the area during preceding weeks by members of the Salvation Army, a large gathering assembled on the wharf. The familiar melodies of Sankey's and Moody's hymns, played by a brass band from the nearby coal-mining township of Outtrim, filled the air while the audience listened with attention to the words of the preacher. It was a scene reminiscent of biblical days, and no doubt, many present drew a comparison with Christ's journeying among the fishermen of Galilee. The service was disrupted by the untimely arrival of a fishing party at the wharf with a fine haul of perch. This, unfortunately, diverted the attention of those present from the spiritual to the material needs of the hour. The brass band from Outtrim played on, but the congregation dispersed to inspect the perch recently caught in the Inlet.[48]

The growth of the Meeniyan township followed a similar pattern to that of Inverloch. Hector Campbell obtained a full licence for the Meeniyan Hotel in 1896 while the first church, St. Kevin's Catholic Church, was blessed and dedicated by Bishop Corbett on 14 December 1902.[49] The Methodists followed the next year with the opening of their church in October 1903.[50] The Church of England opened their parsonage in 1905 but continued to hold services in the Mechanics' Institute or the Methodist Church. This practice was also followed by the Presbyterians for many years until the erection of their own respective churches.

Meeniyan township never received the stimulus of a butter factory as did neighbouring towns. It did, however, develop into a good stock selling centre by reasons of its geographical location relative to the Dumbalk Valley, Stony Creek and Nerrena hinterland. As a result of the failure of the first selling firm

Meeniyan, 1905 (from Woorayl Shire Historical Society).

in the township, a Progress Association was formed by Messrs Norris, Dike, George and Patrick Griffin. These gentlemen leased the sale yards to Messrs Grieve, Hamilton and Co. who began sales on 30 August 1904.[51]

A small bacon curing factory was established in Meeniyan in 1904 with Mr T.A. Perkins, the proprietor, advertising that he was 'now prepared to supply purchasers at reasonable prices Prime Sides of Bacon, Ham, Middles, Shoulders, Pigs Cheeks, Pigs Feet, Pork German, Lard etc'.[52] Trading banks established agencies at Meeniyan at the turn of the century, but it was not until 1910 that permanent branches were established by the Colonial Bank and the Commercial Banking Company of Sydney. The Bank of Australasia decided to bypass Meeniyan in favour of Stony Creek, where it erected an imposing branch office in 1910 after carrying on an agency for several years. Stony Creek had been fortunate in having a butter factory established to serve the surrounding district since 1896, and no doubt this influenced the Bank of Australasia in establishing a permanent branch in the town.

The other townships in the Woorayl Shire, Ruby, Dumbalk, Tarwin Lower and Walkerville, all made limited progress after their formation. At the turn of the century, Ruby boasted a butter factory, wine shop, general store, blacksmith's, butcher's and baker's shop. Dumbalk boasted a butter factory, blacksmith's shop and general store, while a similar situation prevailed at Tarwin Lower with the addition of a hotel.

The early start that Leongatha had gained over these other townships in the first decade of its existence was never really challenged. The geographical and economic advantages enjoyed by it were only magnified in later decades. Subsequent development vindicated the decision made by Woorayl Shire councillors soon after its formation, that the administrative centre should be located in Leongatha.

Although Inverloch residents might have complained about 'the lavish

Bridge over Little Tarwin at the rear of the Dollar Post Office, 1910 (from F. Mackie).

expenditure on the Tarwin Road and township near which two councillors reside', no ratepayer could complain about such lavish expenditure on Council buildings at Leongatha. The yard in front of the Shire offices was cluttered with drainage pipes and other items of equipment necessary for road maintenance, and the section nearest the Mechanics' Institute had been occupied for many years by the clothes lines of the Commercial Hotel opposite, of which Mr P.J. Rowan was the licensee from 1901 to 1909. The damp clothes were carried across McCartin Street in cane baskets by local washerwomen and returned when dry. On 8 July 1904 minutes of the Institute reveal

> that notice be given to Mr. Rowan that owing to the damage done to the breaking of gates by the constant traffic through the vacant land adjoining the Institute he desist in using the yard for drying clothes. One Month's notice to be given.[53]

Fortunately, a sense of civic pride was emerging that found expression in verse published through the medium of *The Great Southern Star*.

The Old Shire Hall.

Oh we point with pride to our tree girt roads,
To the strangers in our town,
And we boast of our electric lights,
When rivals run us down.
We skite about our tip top land
And our 'yards' where salesmen bawl
But we cannot brag about the looks
Of our old Shire Hall.

Our 'factory' is run on model lines
Our 'links' are up to date;
Our Show Ground soon will beat them all
We never forget to state.

Our school is run on model lines,
Though 'tis a trifle small
But we cannot boast of modern paint
On the old Shire Hall.

Oh our 'progress board' is up to snuff
Naught's beyond its reach;
We're going to run a park and a lake
P'raps a tram to Inverloch beach.
We run a 'toney' bowling green
"Where soft the footsteps fall",
But we cannot run to a pot of paint
On the old Shire Hall.

Oh a peacock's pride is naught to ours,
When we show our Savings bank,
And the trim little home of the Fire Brigade,
Where all looks spick and spank.
But the town firebell on its lofty perch,
Ready to clang its call,
Looks down with scorn on the unwashed face,
Of the old Shire Hall.[54]   (Bluey)

(N.B. 'Bluey' was the pen-name of Mr H. Trotman, a well-known builder in the Leongatha district who contributed several poems to *The Great Southern Star* and also had items published in the Sydney *Bulletin*.)

Councillors must have been thinking along similar lines to Bluey, as the first tender dealt with at their November 1909 meeting was for renovations to the Shire offices. For many years they had sacrificed the external appearance of the Shire offices so that funds could be conserved for road construction in outlying areas.[55]

9. RECREATION

In township reserves there is always a certain area set aside for the recreation of the community. At Leongatha, Surveyor Lardner reserved two areas, one of thirty-two acres for a park and recreation reserve and another of fifteen acres for showgrounds. At a public meeting held on 24 June 1892 dissatisfaction was expressed about the suitability of these areas, and it was decided to ask the Lands Department to reserve an area on the north boundary of the town in exchange for them. This the Lands Department agreed to do, and an area of 107 acres was set aside for public recreation and show yards. On 11 March 1893 this site was placed under the control of Thomas Ridgway, George Roughead, Robert Bair, Hugh McCartin and Michael Carr.[1] In order to establish a race track on the land, the trustees again applied for a variation of the allotted area by agreeing to forego land on the northern side of the reserve in exchange for a similar area on the southern side nearer the centre of the township. This variation was agreed to by the Lands Department, but in the exchange the total area was reduced from 107 acres to 81 acres made up of 57 acres for public recreation and 24 acres for show yards reserve.

Although reserved for public use, the public first had to clear it of its natural bush. On 4 December 1896 tenders were called by William Young on behalf of the committee 'for cutting all scrub and timber up to 2ft on 25 acres more or less on Leongatha Recreation Reserve'.[2] This was done over the summer months, and by March 1897 William Young was again calling for 'Tenders for Ploughing, Forming and Draining the course on the above Reserve'.[3]

This tender was only for 'the course', an area of three to four acres of the most level land adjacent to Roughead Street. Vera Dannock recalled that 'There was only a small oval cleared where the first Shows were held. All the rest of the "Rec." as it was known was all bush'.[4] This small oval did enable cricket and football matches to be played by local teams. Other than rifle shooting, cricket appears to be the first sport played on a team basis in the Shire. The presence of a large number of men at the newly-formed Labour Colony led to a challenge match with the locals.

> The local club again tried conclusion with the Labour Colony on Saturday last, the game resulting in a win for the Colony by three wickets.

The opening of the Leongatha tennis courts on Railway Reserve, 1900. The Otago Hotel is in the background (from Woorayl Shire Historical Society).

Leongatha football team, c. 1900 (from M. Kindellan).

Leongatha Town 1st Innings . . . 33 runs, 2nd 67.
Labour Colony 1st Innings . . . 49 runs, 2nd 52, 3 to go.
The winning run being scored at 6.30 p.m. at which time it was decided to draw
stumps. At the conclusion of the match hearty cheers were given for each other and
the captains.[5]

The clearing and sowing down of the oval led to the Leongatha Cricket Club
gradually gaining strength and joining a competition that comprised Korumburra, Jumbunna and Outtrim teams. The parochial rivalry latent in small
country communities often overflowed on to the sporting arena, judging by the
report of a match between Leongatha and Jumbunna.

The match between Leongatha and Jumbunna was played last Saturday under the
liberal patronage of 40-50 representatives from the coal mines — leather lunged
larrikins who created a din that would do credit to bedlam. Most of them have a
supreme contempt for what they term 'teat jerkers'. When one of our stoutish players
chased a ball for 50 yards it was 'poddy, step it out or the Jersey bull will biff you'! It
was a sore disappointment to the barrackers when our boys made such a good stand
at the wickets and when the bowlers could not dispose of Chalmers the advice was
freely given to 'hit him on the milking side' and 'place him on the sore teat'. When
Chalmers was finally bowled at 31 the storm of keen sarcasm, innuendo and coarse
jokes developed into a hurricane. Cheers and groans rent the air from all quarters
and echoed and re-echoed in the hills. Altogether an amusing and unique
experience.[6]

Parochial rivalry was also manifest in the report of the Stony Creek correspondent of *The Great Southern Star* of 22 May 1896, advising the Leongatha
football players 'that should they ever have to play Fish Creek on their own
ground to take plenty of splints, coffins and crutches!'. Travel to outlying
districts had its hazards even in the summer months. On one occasion, Leongatha Cricket Club members were journeying to Fairbank for a friendly match
with T. Gibson driving a double-seated buggy containing seven of the players.
Going down Beisterfeldt's Hill to the Ruby Creek, his brakes failed to hold, and
the horses bolted. Rounding a bend, the buggy capsized and the team were
thrown out. The four in the front seat, Messrs Cooper, Ellis, Molloy and
Gibson, suffered painful injuries to the face and concussion, while the others
suffered severe bruising. Messrs Hicks and Molloy were rendered unconscious
and the buggy ended up in the creek utterly wrecked. The horses escaped with
cut fetlocks while the cricket team, with the assistance of neighbours, managed
to return to Leongatha where they were treated by Dr Carr.[7]

Wintertime, with its short days and muddy roads, made travelling for football
teams even more onerous. In June 1902 the Leongatha Football Team journeyed
to Mirboo North in a horse-drawn drag for a Sunday match. On their return
journey they encountered trouble.

While yet several miles from their destination, the vehicle in which they were
travelling lost the off hind wheel. The men undaunted, improvised a skid from a
sapling, and with the back portion of the drag once more raised to the horizontal the
useless wheel was taken on board and the journey thus completed. Needless to say
that on arrival in the township the scene caused a good deal of amusement.[8]

First recorded evidence of formation of Leongatha Football Club is of a notice of a public meeting to be held at McCartin's Hotel on 20 April 1894 at which Mr T. Ridgway was elected President. By 1896 Leongatha had entered into the Great Southern Football Association, comprising the Black Diamonds (Korumburra), Strzelecki, Jumbunna and Outtrim.[9] A similar association was formed to cater for teams along the coastal area, and *The Great Southern Star* carried a rather unusual report of the first match of the season at Inverloch played between Wonthaggi and Pound Creek. 'It was well contested by both sides and ended in a draw in favour of Pound Creek'.[10]

After a few years, Leongatha withdrew from the Korumburra-Outtrim League and formed another which included Mount Eccles, Meeniyan and Tarwin Lower. When Leongatha played Mount Eccles in 1902, the terrain took its toll on the players.

> The team started out before noon and after ten miles found it unable to proceed further as the road was impassable for vehicles. Shank's pony was used for the last mile on a mountainous track which was only a pipe opener. On reaching the ground the Mount Eccles players, suitably mustered were indulging in vigorous practice — their only opportunity in that hilly locality. After a very even game the results were . . .
>
> Mt Eccles   3 goals 7 behinds . . . 25 pts.
> Leongatha   2   ,,   3   ,,   . . . 15 ,,
>
> Before leaving the ground, tea scones and sandwiches were thoughtfully provided and thus fortified the Leongatha team made their way homeward reaching the township at 8.15 p.m.[11]

One of the leading Leongatha players at the time, and a man who subsequently played a leading role in sporting and community life in the district, was the late James Howard who provided this memory of football before the days of motor cars:

> I played one game with the 2nds against Jumbunna, later on getting selection with the 1sts. There was no real association until 1905 when Tarwin Lower, Meeniyan, Mount Eccles and Leongatha formed a league. My word Mount Eccles had a good team. Playing for Tarwin Lower were the Black Bros — Archie and Murray and Jack Bond. These three had come from college and were pretty good. Matches were played in front of where the (Leongatha) butter factory now is — known as 'Aberdeens'. The team travelled by butter factory wagon to Tarwin Lower where we played near the old bridge at 'Manuka' — one end of the oval was under water. Flynn, our forward, took his boots off and played without them — kicking quite a few goals. After dinner at the Tarwin 'pub' horses were harnessed up and the 'Gatha team, tired but still chirpy arrived home about midnight.[12]

Before Meeniyan joined this league in 1905, sporadic games had been played with Dumbalk and Stony Creek. Matches were played on land opposite the Meeniyan Hotel, while at Dumbalk they were played on a private property opposite the old Nerrena East school site. In order to strengthen the Meeniyan side, many of the Stony Creek footballers played with that team for several years until Stony Creek was able to field a team of their own.

Not everyone followed football or cricket. During the summer months Cole's

A scratch football team, Woorayl Shire, c. 1900 (from Woorayl Shire Historical Society).

Livery Stables at Leongatha ran a four-horse drag every Sunday morning to Inverloch beach, 'fare 4s — with fishing and picnic parties arranged for any day'.[13] Woorayl Shire Council had numerous requests for permission to erect private bathing boxes along the beach reserve. Engineer Callaway, after inspection, noted

> that the locality appears to be well adapted for the purpose, but in order to secure to bathers proper privacy it will be necessary to have a section of the beach set apart for the purpose, notices erected fixing convenient hours and a by law passed providing for the enforcement of same.[14]

Council gave permission for the erection of bathing boxes, and these were a prominent feature along the beach for many years. The only attempt made to reserve any special section of beach for bathers was the provision of a shark proof enclosure made from wooden pickets to ward off attack from the occasional marauder. Tidal action resulted in this enclosure gradually silting up, by which time the danger from sharks had greatly diminished.

Fishing and sailing on the Inlet was always a popular pastime. Peter Shingler from The Grange at Leongatha owned another property, Floraston, overlooking the Inlet, where he kept an ocean-going yacht. On one occasion he took a party of friends out of the Inlet but was unable to return through bad weather. He continued southwards and anchored at the Waratah Bay lime kilns. His

Lady riders ready for judging on Leongatha Show Day, 1905. Mary Heintz is on the right (from Mrs Anderson).

Dumbalk North Rifle Club, 1902 (from D. Dodd).

passengers, anxious to return homewards, walked back to Tarwin Lower and hired horses for the remainder of the journey.[15]

Rifle shooting was always a very popular sport in Woorayl Shire. At Leongatha the first meeting called to form a club was held at Bair's Otago Hotel on 29 July 1892, when local headmaster John Jeffrey stated that permission had been granted for formation of a club. A minimum of twenty members was necessary aged between eighteen and thirty-five years.[16] A small band of enthusiasts worked steadily towards formation of a club, but it was not until 23 September 1898 that the club was officially begun. Original members were G.E. Matthewman, E. and J. Munro, R. de C. Shaw, W. Allison, G.W. Williams, J. Hassett, E.W., C.F. and P. Johnson, J. Jeffrey, G.F. Roughead and W. Watson.[17] A small strip of land on the northern edge of the Labour Colony was obtained for use as a range, and tenders were called for the erection of mounds and the felling of trees. As an enticement for young men to join the club, Secretary E.T. Munro advised that

> for an annual subscription of one pound members get 100 rounds of ammunition a year free. If he chooses to go into camp for four days he gets another 100. Cartridges are 5s per 100 and will shortly be 2s 6d. Martini rifles are issued at 11s 6d apiece.[18]

With the Government granting full subsidies, *The Great Southern Star* stated 'there is now no excuse for young men who should be spending their spare time more profitably than watching cricket and football matches by improving their shooting skills'.[19]

At the third annual meeting held on 6 July 1900, club President Mr R. de C. Shaw said 'the club held the range only on sufferance from the Labour Colony but he hoped that the Government would allow them to remain in possession'. Through the Government actively encouraging the formation of rifle clubs by subsidising the cost of the ammunition, some clubs were becoming semi-military by holding regular drills, parades etc.

In 1898 rifle clubs were formed at Inverloch and at Meeniyan, while at Stony Creek a detachment of the famous Victorian Mounted Rifles had been formed earlier in 1896. This unit was attached to the Mirboo North detachment formed in 1887 under commanding officer C.S. Ogilvy, later Secretary of Woorayl Shire. When the Boer War broke out in 1899, two members of this detachment, Private Lindsay M. Inglis of Lyre Bird Mound, Koonwarra, and Private Victor H. Payne of Stony Creek, volunteered and took part in this campaign. Inglis was wounded at Randsberg, South Africa, and returned to a hero's welcome at Leongatha at the end of May 1900. The Leongatha Brass Band met him at the station and provided an escort to the Otago where 'suitable toasts were drunk with uproarious enthusiasm'.[20] Dumbalk Rifle Club was first formed on 27 April 1900 when Mr W. Hughes, Senior, was elected President and Mr E.J. Newton Secretary. W.B. Benn was appointed Captain for the first shoot which took place on Goldsmith's farm; the shooters firing across the river into Goad's paddock.[21]

At Mardan rifle shooting began in earnest on 14 July 1900. Despite inclement weather over sixty residents assembled for the opening on the property of Mr R. McIndoe. After being welcomed by Captain Wilson Coulter, a procession was formed, and to the strains of the bagpipes, the crowd marched to the site of the range led by members of the club. It had been arranged for Mr John Smith, Senior, to fire the first shot, but in his absence, the honour was given to Mrs R.E. McIndoe. That lady 'gallantly shouldered the rifle, "as to the manner born", and as the report of the first shot echoed and re-echoed from the surrounding hills, the company gave vent to their feelings in enthusiastic cheers'.[22]

In an era when horse transport was the norm, it was inevitable that the sport of kings should be followed on suitable occasions. Thomas Lees, an early settler in the Tarwin Lower district, who owned the Evergreen Estate, was a keen horse breeder who supplied horses for the Indian market. By 1896 hundreds of well-bred horses were being run on this property, and it naturally followed that race meetings should be organised for the district. By the time of the second meeting held in early February 1900, 'a saddling paddock had been made and the fences fronting the straight had pickets put on them'. A certain amount of publicity must have been given because the meeting was enlivened by the presence of a circus whose members 'gave exhibitions of their skill in tight rope walking, trapeze and sleight of hand work during intervals of the races'. Bookmakers were in attendance, as were spinning jennies and promoters of sweeps, 'all trying to get the better of a too confiding public'.[23]

A fortnight after the meeting at Tarwin Lower, the Inverloch Turf Club held a successful meeting on 21 February 1900. An estimated four to five hundred people attended, many of them holiday-makers camping around the Inlet. The race meeting was followed by a Grand Ball at night at the Esplanade Hotel.[24] At Stony Creek the inaugural meeting of the Great Southern Jockey Club was held in December 1895 and attracted a crowd of over 750 people with special trains being run from Port Albert and Korumburra.[25] As a result of this meeting, Secretary Barry Boys made application to the Lands Department to reserve an area for a racecourse. However, it was not until 1910 when E.W. Murphy was Secretary of the club that this area was reserved for racing.[26] At Meeniyan in March 1899 a race meeting was held on a course adjoining the railway station under an energetic committee headed by L.P. Tuomey, President, with W.B. Hughes and E. Coates Vice-presidents.[27]

At Leongatha an initial move to form a race club was held on 21 October 1898, when a committee of three was appointed to interview the trustees of the Recreation Reserve to make arrangements for facilities at the course. Negotiations dragged on for several months, but the Leongatha Turf Club was soon formed, and it arranged for a race meeting to be held at Bair's paddock on the Nerrena Road (Allotment 12). This was held on the last week of March 1899, and it was not until the following autumn that the first race meeting was held on the Leongatha Recreation Reserve on St Patrick's Day, 17 March 1900, when a crowd of over 600 people attended.[28]

There is an old axiom that it is easier to start an organisation than it is to maintain it, and this is particularly true of the race clubs that were formed about the turn of the century in the Woorayl Shire. The initial meetings were often successful, but gradually attendances fell, enthusiasm waned and most of these newly-formed clubs lapsed for several years and then reformed. Many of the younger generation, who fancied themselves as riders, did not wait until they were near a racecourse to try out their flighty steeds. Constable Gorman of Leongatha had to issue a stern warning against these 'young gentlemen who are so fond of trying the speed of their horses in the main street'.[29]

On a wet day in March 1900 a large number of these young gentlemen stood outside the Leongatha Shire Hall in pouring rain. They were waiting to be interviewed by a selection committee for inclusion in the Imperial Australian Contingent that was being raised for despatch to South Africa. Out of 200 applications, 125 presented themselves and 55 were accepted. The successful applicants were given free passes to Headquarters at Melbourne and were expected to report immediately.[30]

For those keen shooters who were not interested in embarking for South Africa, the rifle and gun clubs were a good substitute. The Leongatha Gun Club commenced in a small way in 1894, but by November 1896 it had a strong rival in the Inverloch Gun Club. This club held a handicap sweepstake for the Hayes Trophy at the club grounds at Inverloch on 9 November 1896. Melbourne Gun Club rules were followed; that is, 'Sparrows — ten birds, handicap distances 18-28 yards'.[31] Either there were more sparrows at Inverloch than at Leongatha or they were becoming scarcer in general, because Leongatha Gun Club held their shoot on the Recreation Reserve on 18 November 1899 using glass balls for targets.[32]

The Leongatha Town Band, 1908 (from R.D. Watson).

The rifle club made its presence felt in Leongatha streets at the lifting of the siege of Mafeking in May 1900. The relief of Colonel Baden-Powell and his men was the occasion of great rejoicing in the township. The Leongatha Band turned out and played martial and patriotic music up and down the main streets. Church bells were rung and 'the Rifle Club kept up a continuous roll of musketry. Torchlights were improvised and those who had no ammunition to expend joined in singing patriotic songs and cheering lustily'.[33]

Like the race clubs, the Leongatha Brass Band had a rather erratic existence in its early years. It was first formed as a result of a public meeting in February 1892, at which Mr J.W. Simmons was elected President and Mr Roberts appointed Secretary. The committee comprised Messrs King, Bryce and Crook with Mr King appointed Bandmaster.[34] It struggled bravely through its first decade of existence until it was reformed at another public meeting held in the middle of June 1902. Mr E. Johnson said 'the old band had eight instruments which could be used by new members'. Membership was fixed at five shillings, and it was stated that twenty players were available.[35] By the end of the year the band was in good form playing the old year out and the new year in on New Year's eve. By October 1905 another public meeting had to be called for it to be reformed under the charge of Mr William Allison. A concert in aid of band funds was held the following May, 1906, at which Alex Gunn and his Royal Bioscope presented 'Orchestral Selections and Illustrated Songs. Celebrated New Living Picture — the first time here'.

The opening of the tennis courts in the goods yard of the Leongatha Railway Station in 1892 provided the first opportunity for women to partake in outdoor sport other than riding, fishing and shooting. Tennis quickly became a popular sport, and courts were established at private homes in the country when financial circumstances permitted. Amy Griffin in her diary notes that Shinglers at

Visitors off to the train at Dumbalk North, c. 1910 (from D. Dodd).

The Grange possessed 'a smooth lawn tennis court and a most delightful garden rich in bloom'. This was in 1895 when many settlers had not progressed much further than two rooms and a skillion for their homestead. Picnics in the summer months, church meetings, concerts, sewing meetings and visiting comprised the main form of relaxation and social intercourse for women.

Concerts were a favourite form of entertainment, and the presence of over two hundred men at the Leongatha Labour Colony inevitably produced a reservoir of talent. This was made good use of in the production of concerts that were appreciated by the townsfolk.

> The moon did not rise until late so we took a lantern to keep clear of crab holes on our way to one of the Labour Colony concerts — destination Music Hall on foot — ladies following in darkness. Our guide got lost and fell into the claypits, we negotiated drains, logs and fences etc. — eventually arrived at Music Hall for an enjoyable evening.[36]

Encouraged by the success of this concert, the colonists again entertained a large number of the local citizens at their Music Hall the following month. William Young from *The Great Southern Star* was evidently given a seat in the front row.

> Stage manager Jack Crofts had his company well drilled. The corners were occupied by Messrs Crofts (bones) and Corrigan (banjo) whose antics were side splitting in their ludicrousness. The drollness of 'Jack' was hard to surpass and as the negro minstrel he would be hard to beat. The dining hall was packed with an appreciative audience comprising visitors from town and country including Colonel Goldstein, superintendent, who came in for his share of criticism. Owing to length of programme it was a late hour before conclusion and it is to be hoped an earlier start will be made at subsequent concerts.[37]

As in every age, music and dancing proved extremely popular. If a ball, concert or dance was organised at any of the outlying halls which served these communities, bad weather or muddy roads would not keep the locals from attending. In the Dollar-Milford area, when roads were practically impassable, Mrs York would regularly travel to the dances at the local hall on a horse-drawn sledge seated in a cane chair specially roped on for the occasion.[38]

When people went out for an evening's entertainment, the evening often was prolonged into an all-night session. In May 1896 the ladies of Tarwin Lower gave a concert and social in the Mechanics' Hall, where their 'songs and recitations were much appreciated. Dancing was entered into with great spirit and kept going till daylight'.[39]

Dance music was usually provided by piano, violin and drums. The violin retained its popularity for many decades, because it could be carried in a sugar bag on horseback across paddocks or along muddy tracks for the evening's entertainment.

The love of music is invariably passed on from parents to children. The original settlers themselves were soon searching for teachers who could impart their knowledge to the new generation springing up in the homesteads carved from the forest. Many of the first settlers in the Koorooman-Mardan area were of Scottish extraction. The skirl of the bagpipes echoed through the hills whenever a descendant of the clans, proficient in this ancient art, found time off from the ever-pressing needs of daily life. In the early 1900s Hugh Fraser, a master of the pipes, travelled around the homes of the Scottish settlers giving instruction. When sufficient pupils were interested, he located his class in the Rechabite Hall at Leongatha.

Mr E. Eggington, a music teacher from Murrumbeena, began his weekly train journeys to the Woorayl Shire in 1905. Leaving the train at Ruby, he walked to Fairbank where junior members of the McLennan, Calder, Black and Beard families awaited his weekly visit. Their parents eventually provided Mr Eggington with a pony for the long and uphill climb to Fairbank — a mode of conveyance strange to the city born musician but one which he mastered, although only after several mishaps.

The following day Mr Eggington taught morning, afternoon and evening in a small room attached to the Mechanic's Hall at Leongatha. As word of his teaching spread about the district, he added a third day to his weekly visit to South Gippsland by travelling on to Meeniyan where he taught pupils in the Dumbalk-Stony Creek districts. Former pupil Arthur Ashenden of Dumbalk recalled 'Mr Eggington always wore a red flannel — he claimed it kept arthritis at bay and he always liked to keep his hands and fingers supple for use on instruments'.[40] There were also other music teachers catering for the latent talent of the district's youth. Advertisements in *The Great Southern Star* reveal that Miss A.W. Nicholls, LRAM, Teacher of Singing, 'Will visit Leongatha once a week. Terms on Application. Opening lesson on 8 March at Hull's Coffee Palace between 11 a.m. and 4 p.m.', while Miss J.S. Laing of Ritchie Street, 'Teacher of Piano and Singing. Prepares pupils for all examinations'.[41]

Evidence of the love of music by the inhabitants of Leongatha and district was provided by the visit of world famous singer Ada Crossley to Leongatha in October 1908. News of the impending visit galvanised the community into action. A special committee was formed to organise the program. The Leongatha Butter Factory, which was in the process of wiring the township in readiness for the supply of electric current, was asked to expedite the work in order to have the Mechanics' Hall lit with electricity for the occasion. A capacity audience was guaranteed, because all available tickets were sold within one week of printing to subscribers along the South Gippsland line. A special train was ordered to be run from Korumburra, but numbers had to be limited owing to the capacity of the Mechanics' Hall.

On arrival at the Leongatha Station on the morning of Friday 23 October, Miss Crossley was presented with an address of welcome by Shire President, Cr John Wills, on behalf of district residents. The headmaster of the State school, Mr Cowling, welcomed her to the town on behalf of the ANA. A decorated drag preceded by the Leongatha Town Band took her and the accompanying artists to McCartin's hotel for lunch, after which a tour of the district was taken in buggies. The newly-built butter factory on Yarragon Road was inspected, and then the party continued on past the Labour Colony towards the Koorooman-Mardan area. On her return to the township, a stop was made at Veronica, the home of Mr John Lardner in Ogilvy Street, where over 100 ladies of the district were gathered in the garden to welcome the famous singer. Miss Crossley, dressed 'in an emperor frock of heliotrope silk, with a vest of blue chiffon with

Leongatha Bowling Green, c. 1910. President John Lardner, centre (from Woorayl Shire Historical Society).

Mr E. Eggington, itinerant music teacher, Woorayl Shire 1905-45 (from Woorayl Shire Historical Society).

ostrich feather boa and hat to match', was presented with a bouquet of flowers by Mrs H.J. Rossiter, wife of the proprietor of *The Great Southern Star*.[42]

The evening concert in the Mechanics' Hall was performed to a capacity crowd and was a memorable event for Leongatha. It was fitting that a world class artist should be the first to enjoy the benefit of the electric lighting in the hall, which replaced the kerosene and acetylene lamps used since 1891. Miss Crossley's program included Handel's famous 'Largo' and Lewis Carey's 'Nearer My God to Thee'. Tenor John Harrison, sang 'Bonnie Mary of Argyle', much to the pleasure of those of Scottish descent, while Baritone Hamilton Earle sang 'Pagliacci'. Violinist Leon Samentini enthralled all present, while Miss Crossley's accompanist on the piano, young Percy Grainger, entertained with solos 'Polonaise' from Chopin and 'Hungarian Rhapsody' from Liszt. Percy Grainger, who was later to attain fame as a composer, recorded his impressions of his short visit to Leongatha in a letter to his mother that afternoon.

> Commercial Hotel,
> Leongatha. Gippsland.
> (16 miles from Coast)

(To Rose Grainger)
23.10.08. Friday.
      My Loved one,
I am quite happy in such a place as this. Glorious district, and really admirable Australian types riding about freely and carelessly on the same dear easy going horses. Everyone kindly and careful, no flippancy. Grand meals, melting chicken and maddeningly good rhubarb pie with floods of local cream, and flirtless unconversational women waitresses. You and I could spend such a fine holiday here, living at this very Hotel and taking drives, and maybe even rides. There is also a tennis court, (asphalt) where I'm going to play a game this afternoon with 3 locals. There's a nice old Irishman from County Connaught, who can speak Irish. He has told me the sound of some Gaelic words I wanted to know.[43]

Grainger was fortunate that he arrived soon after Leongatha had gained two of the basic amenities that were taken for granted by metropolitan visitors: town water and electricity. The provision of town water, some two years previously, even though murky at times, immediately led to the establishment of another sporting amenity greatly appreciated by the senior citizens of the community. The 'nice old Irishman' whom Grainger spoke to during his short visit was in all probability retired government surveyor John Lardner. Before retiring to Leongatha, Lardner had spent several years at Bairnsdale where he had taken up bowling, and he was very keen to see the sport established at Leongatha. With the arrival of town water in 1906, the building of a bowling green in the township became possible. The first public meeting called to form a bowling club was held on 22 June 1906, at which John Lardner produced figures estimating the cost of the proposed rinks. He also read a letter from his friend at Bairnsdale, Reverend F. Milne, who averred 'that the game added ten years to a man's life'.[44] At this first meeting in June there were three clergymen present: Reverend A.E. Young, Reverend W.S. Whiteside and Father P.J. Coyne. Of the other eleven gentlemen present, the majority were drawn from the business and professional class of Leongatha. Messrs T. Gibson, J. Baker and H. Caffin were storekeepers, E.S. Callanan was the local dentist, J.P. Rowan the publican, while the Secretary, *pro tem*, was R.J. Kewish. Mr Kewish had arrived in Leongatha in August 1902, when he purchased the newly-founded *Leongatha Sun* that had commenced operations the year before under a Mr E.J. Green. Kewish played an active role in the business and social life of Leongatha becoming Secretary of the rifle club, the newly-formed Leongatha Bowling Club and was one of the local justices of the peace.

Kewish contacted the Railways Department seeking to lease a small area adjacent to the Leongatha Tennis Club courts on the Railway Reserve as a site for rinks. The Railways Department agreed to the suggestion on the condition that a rent of £10 a year was paid. After further negotiations the lease was finally granted at the rate of £4 per annum paid half yearly. By July Kewish reported promises of forty-three members and thirty-nine debenture holders guaranteeing £84 towards the cost of the new rinks.[45] A considerable amount of filling was necessary to build up the sloping site, and tenders were called for the 'cartage of 100 yards of filling from near Butter Factory to the Bowling green and spreading as directed'.[46] This was done under the watchful eye of John Lardner who took the necessary levels and laid out the new rinks. After sowing to grass, the rinks were sufficiently stable by January 1907 for the first match which was played between the smoking and non-smoking members of the club, with victory going to the non-smokers.

At the first annual meeting of the club, opinion was equally divided about the choice of the club colours, and it was left to the casting vote of President Lardner to decide between blue and white or green and gold. After choosing the latter, arrangements were made for the official opening of the new club which was fixed for 7 November 1907. Father P.J. Coyne lent a marquee, and a flag-pole was erected on which was hung the Australian flag, while the Union Jack and the Irish flag were displayed in prominent positions. The Hon. J.E. Mackey, MLA, Minister for Lands, left an important Cabinet meeting to be present at the opening at which there were over 200 present. The Leongatha Bowling Club was the first to be established on the South Gippsland line; the only others in Gippsland at that time being at Warragul and Bairnsdale. Mrs Mackey was invited to put down the first jack, and John Lardner bowled the first bowl. Mr Mackey congratulated the club 'in providing such a wonderful amenity in such an attractive spot'.[47] The Leongatha Brass Band added variety to the proceedings with several items, and photographs were taken to record the occasion. A concert was held in the Mechanics' Hall in the evening, where visitors and locals were entertained by 'Chester Bros, conjurers and mind readers, Scottish dancers, and solo items by local artists'.[48]

The year 1909 saw the beginnings of the Leongatha Golf Club when a meeting was convened for that purpose by Horace J. Rossiter, proprietor of *The Great Southern Star*. In May 1906 William Young had sold his paper to Rossiter Brothers of Yarram, who also owned *The Foster Mirror* at that time. Horace Rossiter managed *The Great Southern Star* and like the proprietor of *The Leongatha Sun*, R.J. Kewish, played an important role in the town's affairs. It was Rossiter, through his membership of the Mechanics' Institute committee, who was instrumental in arranging for the visit of Ada Crossley which proved such an outstanding success. Rossiter gathered together a small band of keen golf

Supplement to "Great Southern Star."   "NOTHING IS IMPOSSIBLE WITH INDUSTRY."

SECOND
SHOW OF THE MEENIYAN AGRICULTURAL SOCIETY
FRIDAY, DECEMBER 3, 1897.

Patrons: F. C. Mason, Esq., M.L.A., G. J. Turner, Esq., M.L.A.   President: G. Griffin, Esq.   Vice-Presidents: Cr Tack, Mr W. Geale. Committee: Messrs Alf. Butterworth, Alex. McDonald, Wilden, P. Griffin, C. Holder, Dodd, B. McKittrick, W. Little, W Cashin, Owers, G. Henderson. Young, E. Hughes.

PRIZE LIST.

Class A—Dairy Produce,
ETC.

Entrance, 1s.

Sec 1—Best 5lbs Fresh Butter First prize, 5s; second, certificate

Sec 2—Best 5lbs Salt Butter First prize, 5s; second, certificate (To be left at Mr A. McDonald's store, Meeniyan, not later than 11th November)

Sec 3—Best 10lbs Cheese First prize, 5s; second, certificate

Sec 4—Best Dozen Hen Eggs First prize, 2s 6d; second, 1s

Sec 5—Best Dozen Duck Eggs First prize, 2s 6d; second, 1s

Sec 6—Best Flitch of Bacon First prize, 5s; second, certificate

Sec 7—Best Ham First prize, 5s; second, certificate

Sec 8—Best 4lbs or over Home-made Bread, in not more than two loaves First prize, 5s; second, certificate

Sec 9—Best 4lbs Currant Loaf First prize, 5s; second, certificate

Sec 10—Best Plate Scones First prize, 2s 6d; second, 1s

Sec 11—Best Collection Home-made Preserves First prize, 5s; second, 1s

Sec 12—Best Home-made Pastry. First prize, 2s 6d; second, 1s

Sec 13—Best Collection Pickles. First prize, 5s; second, 1s

Class B.—Kitchen Garden.
Entrance, 1s.

Sec 1—Best Collection Vegetables First prize, 5s; second, 2s 6d

Sec 2—Best Six Bunches Turnips

Sec 3—Best Six Bunches Carrots

Sec 4—Best Six Bunches Parsnips

Sec 5—Best Six Bunches Swedes

Sec 6—Best Three Cabbages

Sec 7—Best 5lbs Green Peas

Sec 8—Best 5lbs French Beans

Sec 9—B st 3 Bundles Rhubarb

First prize, 2s 6d; second, 1s

Sec 10—Best Quarter Cwt Potatoes First prize, 5s; second, 2s 6d

Sec 11—Best Strawberries and Fruits in season First prize, 2s 6d; second, 1s

Sec 12—Any other variety of Vegetables First prize, 2s 6d; second, 1s

Class C.—Flower Garden.
Entrance, 1s.

Sec 1—Best Bouquet Garden Flowers First prize, 5s; second, certificate

Sec 2—Best Six Button Holes First prize, 2s 6d; second, 1s

Sec 3—Best Collection Cut Flowers - First prize, 2s 6d; second, 1s

Sec 4—Best Collection Pot Plants First prize, 5s; second, 2s 6d

Class D.
Entrance Free

Sec 1—Best kept Exercise Book by child under 13 years First prize, 2s; second, 1s

Sec 2—Best kept Exercise Book by child under 10 years First prize, 2s; second, 1s

Sec 3—Best Map of Victoria First prize, 2s; second, 1s

Sec 4—Best piece Plain Sewing by child under 13 years First prize, 3s; second, 1s q

Sec 5—Best Plain Sewing by child under 10 years First prize, 2s; second, 1s

Sec 6—Best piece of Darning by child under 13 years First prize, 2s; second, 1s

Sec 7—Best piece of Darning by child under 11 years First prize, 2s; second, 1s

Sec 8—Best piece of Knitting by child under 14 years First prize, 2s; second, 1s

Sec 9—Best Collection Cotton Fancy Work by child under 14 years First prize, 2s; second, 1s

Sec 10—Best Collection Wool Work by child under 14 years First prize, 2s; second, 1s

Class E.—Ladies' Plain & Fancy Work.
Entrance, 1s.

Sec 1—Best Collection Plain Needle and Machine Work First prize, 4s; second, 2s

Sec 2—Best Collection Fancy Work First prize, 4s; second, 2s

Sec 3—Best Collection Knitting First prize, 2s 6d; second, 1s

Sec 4—Best Collection Wool Crotchet. First prize, 2s 6d; second, 1s

Class F.—Poultry.
Entrance, 1s.

Sec 1—Best Cochin China Cock and Hen

Sec 2—Brahma Cock and Hen

Sec 3—Plymouth Rock Cock and Hen

Sec 4—Spanish Cock and Hen

Sec 5—Leghorn Cock and Hen

Sec 6—Game Cock and Hen

Sec 7—Wyandots Cock and Hen

Sec 8—Andalusian Cock and Hen

Sec 9—Hamburg Cock and Hen

Sec 10—Minorca Cock and Hen

Sec 11—Goose and Gander

Sec 12—Duck and Drake

Sec 13—Turkey Cock and Hen

Sec 14—Other Varieties, not enumerated

Prizes in this Class: First prize, 5s; second, certificate. Exhibitors to find their own coops.

Class G.—Dairy Stock.

Entrance, 5s; Members, 2s 6d.

Sec 1—Best Dairy Cow, to give the best Butter Results between the hours of 8.30 a.m. and 4 p.m. First prize, silver medal, the gift of His Excellency, Lord Brassey; second prize, 15s; third, certificate. Cows to be in the bails and milked dry at 8.30 a.m. and again at 4 p.m. For testing the Babcock test will be used.

Sec 2—Best Ayrshire Bull, any age First prize, silver medal, the gift of the president, G. Griffin, Esq; second, certificate

Sec 3—Best Shorthorn Bull, any age. First prize, £1 1s, the gift of Cr Hughes; second, certificate

Class H.—Swine.
Entrance, 2s 6d.

Sec 1—Best Large Berkshire Boar First prize, Society's silver medal; second, 5s

Sec 2—Best Large Berkshire Sow First prize, Society's silver medal; second, 5s

Sec 3—Best Improved Berkshire Boar First prize, silver medal, the gift of the Proprietor of the GREAT SOUTHERN STAR; second, 5s

Sec 4—Best Improved Berkshire Sow First prize, silver medal, the gift of the Vice-President (Mr W. Geale); second, 5s

Class I.—Horses.
Entrance, 2s 6d.

Sec 1—Best Pony under 13 hands First prize, the Society's silver medal; second, 5s; third, certificate

Sec 2—Best Lady's Hack First prize, Society's silver medal; second, 5s; third, certificate

Sec 3—Best Hunter, to carry 11st First prize, Society's silver medal; second, 5s; third, certificate

Sec 4—Best Draught Stallion First prize, Society's silver medal; second, 5s; third, certificate

Class J.—Miscellaneous.

Rules and Regulations.

Entries close for Classes G, H, and I on November 26th. Late entries received until 30th November at 50 per cent. above scheduled rates. There are no entry forms—just send along name and address, together with entrance fees, class, and section for registration.

Member's Tickets, 2s 6d, may be obtained from any of the Committee, or from Mr W. Wilson Young, STAR Office, Leongatha.

Exhibits of every description will be received for show purposes subject to the approval of the Committee.

All exhibits must have been grown, manufactured, or been the property of the exhibitor for at least one month prior to the date of Show.

There must be three entries in each section, or no prize will be given.

Bouquets, cut flowers, etc., under section C, to be in the hands of the Committee before 10 a.m. All other exhibits will be received on 1st and 2nd December, and to 8 a.m. on 3rd Dec.

Exhibits sent from a distance by train or otherwise, care of the secretary, will be well looked after, but it must be distinctly understood that no responsibility will be incurred through loss, damage in transit, etc.

Prizes will be sent out after 14 days from date of Show, unless a protest in writing, together with a deposit of 10s, has been lodged with the secretary before 4 p.m. on date of show, in which case they shall be held subject to the decision of the Committee. If the protest be deemed frivolous, the deposit to be absolutely forfeited.

The judges' decision shall be final. They shall have power to supplement prizes where they think advisable. They shall have power to withhold any prize from any article not deemed worthy, and may award the Society's certificate to any exhibit which they may consider deserving.

The Committee may substitute goods to the value of prize money.

Address all Communications to "Secretary, Agricultural Society, Meeniyan."

Concert and Ball in the Evening in aid of the funds of the Society.

A. McDONALD, Hon. Treasurer.   N. R. DIKE. Hon. Sec.

enthusiasts and attempts were made to construct a course on portion of the Recreation Reserve. Mr J.N. Baker, who conducted a general store on the lower corner of Roughead and Long Streets, was elected first President with Mr Norman Fraser as Secretary.[49]

A great deal of voluntary labour was necessary for the establishment of the first course, but it slowly took shape. Instruction was given by a professional from Melbourne, Rowley Banks, to new players at three shillings per hour. The official opening of the new course took place on 18 May 1910, when the four-somes handicap over eleven holes was won by Mr W.P. Lardner and Miss E. McPherson.[50] Membership steadily increased, and by means of working-bees held over a period of years, the club gradually converted an area of scrub and bush into a first-class golf course.

Portion of the land being converted for use as a golf course was controlled by trustees of the Recreation Reserve and portion by the Agricultural and Pastoral Society. This divided control of the Reserve led to a degree of dissatisfaction in subsequent years. For many years the grounds were divided by a nine strand wire fence, but eventually commonsense prevailed and a Joint Committee of Management was established and the fence removed.

The first Show that was held by the Leongatha Agricultural and Pastoral Society, on Wednesday 18 February 1903, at which there were over 2,500 present, was not the first held in the Woorayl Shire. Both Meeniyan and Stony Creek had held Shows several years earlier. The initial meeting to consider the holding of a Show at Meeniyan took place on 23 May 1896, when Mr Baldwin was elected President with Cr Cashin of Tarwin Lower and Mr Jones of Buffalo Creek Vice-presidents. It was decided to name the newly-formed organisation the Meeniyan Horticultural and Agricultural Products Society, and the Secretary, N.R. Dike, was instructed to obtain rules from other societies for future guidance.[51] Their first Show, held at Meeniyan on 9 December 1896, was a great success. There were separate classes for dairy stock, horses, swine and poultry, while other sections catered for home produce, ladies' plain and fancy work, kitchen and flower garden exhibits.

At Stony Creek a Show was held under the auspices of the Horticultural Society in the Stony Creek Hall on 11 and 12 March 1897. It did not include any entries in the livestock section but concentrated on horticultural and home exhibits. One notable section was devoted to exhibits executed by bachelors. In this section the prize for a home-made loaf of bread attracted four entries, with first prize being awarded to R. Campbell and second prize to F. Michael. Other entries in this section were for the best darned sock and best patched garment. Both of these divisions were won by J. Leishman.[52]

The first provisional meeting to consider the formation of an Agricultural and Pastoral Society at Leongatha was held in the Mechanics' Institute Hall on 18 June 1894. It was convened by Mr D. Spencer of Inlet Road, a leading farmer of the district, but insufficient interest was expressed to warrant formation. It was not until eight years later that another meeting was held on 9 July 1902, when those present decided to canvass for members. The result of the canvass revealed that 170 had already promised membership. It was decided that a committee of fifty be formed and that election of office bearers take place at the August meeting. The result of the poll saw Cr R. Smith, JP, elected President, H.

McCartin, J. Martin, Vice-presidents, T.M. Gibson, Secretary, R. de C. Shaw, Treasurer, and Messrs J. Henderson, R. Lester, T. Carbarns, W. Tack, W. Irwin and W. Livingston elected as officials.[53]

On 17 September tenders were called for construction of 50 cattle and horse pens, 150 sheep hurdles and the clearing of five chains of track on the Showground. It soon became evident that the preparations could not be completed in time for the planned opening Show in December 1902 with the result that it was postponed until 18 February 1903. The Secretary reported that the publican's booth had been submitted for auction, but no bids were made. The committee then sold the right privately to Mr Prior for £35. Thomas Lees of Tarwin suggested that auctioneers should be asked to conduct sales of stock at the Show and give the society a commission — sales to commence at 4 p.m. The Concert Committee reported that the Edisonia Company had been engaged for Show night to provide entertainment for Show patrons at the Leongatha Mechanics' Hall.[54]

This first Show attracted over 900 entries, 100 of which were from the Leongatha Labour Colony. Some criticism was expressed at a subsequent committee meeting that these entries were under the name of Colonel Goldstein, and as such he was personally entitled to the prize money therefrom.[55] The following year, 1904, entries increased from 900 to over 1,300, notwithstanding the fact that the Labour Colony did not submit any. The outstanding success of the Leongatha Show led to the early demise of the Meeniyan and Stony Creek Shows. In July 1904 the Leongatha A and P Society made formal application to the Minister for Lands to have the northern part of the Reserve excised and vested in separate trustees for Show purposes. This was agreed to by the Minister, and on 13 October 1905 a separate Committee of Management for the Show Yards Reserve was appointed, consisting of Messrs Robert Smith, Matthew Allison, William H. Livingston, Peter Johnson and Arthur Simmons. For the Recreation Reserve, Messrs Arthur Simmons, Hugh McCartin, Robert Bair, John P. Rowan and William W. Young were appointed as trustees.[56]

As a result of an enthusiastic and energetic committee, the Leongatha Show became the event of the year. In 1905, on a very hot day, over 3,500 people attended the Show. The committee had arranged for the cartage of 3,000 gallons of water to the ground, plus copious supplies of ale and soft drink. By mid-afternoon there was nothing but hot whisky and green ginger available, with the result that 'there were more "red letters" floating on the atmosphere than would fill a moderately sized Webster's'.[57] A special train from Alberton brought over 300 visitors and another from Lang Lang brought a further 180 to swell the crowd. The three blacksmiths from Leongatha, Messrs Munro, McFarlane and Campbell, all displayed their craftsmanship in the exhibition of double buggies, spring carts and jinkers. A competition was held for guessing the weight of a bullock, and when the ballot box was opened, it was found that two entrants, Messrs E. Begg and C.M. Watt, had each guessed to within half a pound of the correct weight, 1,015 lbs. As the prize for this competition was a sewing machine, these two gentlemen had to divide it as best they could.[58]

A concert was regularly held in the Mechanics' Hall on Show night to cater for the large number of visitors to the town and always attracted a good crowd. Leongatha was a popular venue for visiting artists, and the Mechanics' Hall was

The Leongatha Show, lower oval, c. 1910 (from L. Johnson).

filled to capacity when well-known singers and musicians staged a concert. When singer Amy Castles, accompanied by baritone Peter Dawson, visited the town on 5 November 1909, arrangements similar to the visit of Ada Crossley were put into operation. Dr Howden read the address of welcome at the gaily decorated railway station, while the children from the State school serenaded Miss Castles with 'Bright are the Glories'. The concert in the evening attracted a capacity crowd, and the numbers presented by the five artists in the party proved very popular. Tosti's 'Goodbye' and Gounod's 'Serenade', in which Miss Castles was accompanied by Master Amadio on the flute and Victor Busst on the piano, called for double encores. Unfortunately, a 'local yokel', not sufficiently appreciative of good music and alive to the fact that it was Guy Fawkes night, lit a double-bunger cracker in the middle of one of the items.[59]

The Mechanics' Institute was always the centre of the town and district's cultural and recreational activities. Poetry reading and recitation was quite a popular form of entertainment. The Leongatha branch of the Australian Natives' Association issued an invitation to all ladies and gentlemen to come along to the reading room of the Mechanics' Institute to 'sing, read, recite, tell a story or pay 3d.'. Dr Davies rendered a solo, Mr G.M. Nelson gave a discourse on philosophy, while a visitor, Mr Johnson, had the audience in convulsions with his descriptions of a fight between John L. Sullivan and Signor Sylvestor.[60]

With the passage of time and the growth of the town and district, it was found necessary to make additions to the original building. The main hall erected in 1891 measured ninety-five foot by thirty-five foot with stage and dressing rooms attached, and had a mean height of twenty-two foot. The second portion immediately in front comprised a two-storey building, forty-five foot by twenty foot with a mean height from floor level of twenty-eight foot. This was erected in 1901 by local builder E.P. Harden and comprised a large central passage with offices on the ground floor, while the upper floor was used by the various lodges for meetings. These additions were greatly appreciated by lodge members judging by a letter from the MUIOOF Lodge to the President and committee of the Mechanics' Institute inviting them 'to share a friendly glass of wine to celebrate the opening of the new lodge room'.[61]

The Institute was used by a variety of clubs for recreational purposes. In 1904 the Secretary was instructed to write to the ANA, the MUIOOF and the Irish National Foresters Lodges asking them to 'use their influence whereby the noise created by playing quoits be minimised'.[62] As a result of continued use by the community, a new floor in the original hall of four inches by one and one eighth inches Kauri was installed in 1908. This proved extremely popular for roller skating, although there was a division of opinion amongst committee members as to whether it should be allowed. The offer of £1 per week rent by E.A. Cole for use of the hall for skating purposes persuaded the committee to allow its use for this form of indoor sport. Letters were soon received from the Secretary of the Lodges complaining of the noise made by skating, and the Secretary was instructed to ensure that the hall not be let for skating purposes on Lodge meeting nights.

Draughts were a popular form of indoor entertainment at the Mechanics' Institute. In 1899 the Woorayl Draughts Club had forty paid-up members and had acquired eighteen new boards. Tournaments were held during the winter months, and matches were arranged with neighbouring clubs. In January 1899 world champion draughts player Mr A. Jordan visited the town, and secretary R.A. Bazley had a busy time during the day and evening arranging the contests. At one stage the champion had twenty games in progress against local contenders. Over seventy games were played of which Jordan won sixty-four with drawn matches being played by O'Bryan (2), Hulls (1), Smith (2), Harrison (1) and Devling (1).[63] The contest created great interest amongst the public, and after play the gentlemen adjourned to Rowan's Hotel where the President, Mr Devling, proposed the toast to the champion. Mr Jordan in reply said that it was a creditable performance by country players, and the standard was well up to that of other clubs he had played.

The perfection of the motion film industry took place over a period of several decades. At the turn of the century, pictures could be illustrated on a wall or screen by the use of a 'magic lantern'. This was merely a kerosene lantern with a series of large wicks set in parallel to provide a bright light behind the camera negative. In September 1900 the Picturama Company made their first appearance at the Leongatha Mechanics' Hall with pictures of the Transvaal war. The program included views of 'Lord Roberts arrival at Cape Town, Lancers crossing Modder River, Armoured Train captured by Boers, Battle of Glencoe and many others. Battle scenes described by Chas. Richardson, late 1st Battn. 44th Essex Regt'.[64]

In April 1903 the Institute received a request from the British Biograph Co. for permission to show 'Living pictures same as Real Life. Coronation Films, Cricket Match (England v. Aust.), War pictures, Paris Exhibitions and Fire Scenes in America'.[65] The installation of electricity in the hall in 1908 resulted in more frequent use by biograph companies. In February 1912 the American Speaking Picture Co. hired the hall to introduce South Gippslanders to the wonders of the new medium.

McCartin Street, Leongatha, 1914 (from Woorayl Shire Historical Society).

Marvellous Bio Megaphone Pictures that live, breathe and speak. Come, see and hear the most famous artists in their greatest successes. Everything done by electricity. Also will be displayed over 8,000 ft of latest animated pictures. Meet Sydney Henry, Eminent English Elocutionist who will deliver descriptive lecture on notable pictures. Our own electric light. No Flicker. Watch for searchlight thrown from Hall next Friday. Popular Prices 2s and 1s. Children half price. Syd Henry, Manager. A.H. Tasman, Touring manager.[66]

The continued and frequent use of the hall facilities enabled the committee of the Institute to launch out and erect an ornate cement brick building adjoining their wooden structure. Five members of the committee gave their names to the bank as guarantors for the overdraft necessary to complete the project, which was recognised as an ornament to the town. It comprised a library and reading room fronting on to McCartin Street, a committee room and a well appointed billiard room. This building, which was erected by Messrs Loring and Spiers at a cost of £1,186, was officially opened by the Hon. J.E. Mackey, MLA, on 26 March 1912.[67] Mr Mackey paid tribute to the citizens of the district in erecting such a fine building and hoped they would purchase many good books of the best class available. After formally opening the building, he called on the wife of the President (Mrs H.J. Rossiter) to open the tables by delivering the first stroke with the cue.[68] The internal walls of the new Institute were made of plaster of paris reinforced with river reeds gathered from nearby swamps. This rather unusual mode of wall construction proved to be quite satisfactory, although it was not adopted elsewhere in the Shire. The new building proved extremely popular and was used by all sections of the community. The billiard tables were constantly in use, and the committee carried a motion moved by William

Russell and seconded by E. Begg that 'the billiard tables be reserved for use of ladies on Friday afternoons for one month'.[69]

Residents of the Stony Creek area were also keen on billiards and purchased tables for installation at their Farmer's Club formed in 1911. Application by the club committee for a liquor licence in 1912 met with determined opposition from the Independent Order of Rechabites, but the application was successful and the club soon became a virile social centre for the district.

Not all men and women were keen on club activities such as billiards, cards and draughts. Many found relaxation and recreation in Church choirs that met regularly. On Good Friday night, 1912, the Mechanics' Hall was crowded with an appreciative audience to hear the combined Church choirs render Stainer's 'Crucifixion' under the baton of Dr Howden. Dr Howden had come to Leongatha as a young man in 1905 and quickly established a practice through his conscientious work in the community. Tenor, Mr Prout, Manager of the orchard at the Labour Colony and Bass, Mr Marshall, were the leading solo singers while Soprano, Mrs Rossiter, and Alto, Miss Prideaux, performed creditably.[70] Mr Arthur Mesley, newly-appointed headmaster of Leongatha High School, read the connecting scriptural readings. At the conclusion of the cantata, a collection was taken up and the proceeds forwarded to the Children's Hospital, Melbourne. Dr Howden stated that he hoped the members of the choirs would seriously consider the matter of creating a philharmonic society which would be open to all singers. This expressed hope of Dr Howden was not fulfilled, but nevertheless, Church music and choirs continued to flourish in the township.

10. SETTLING IN

At the beginning of the twentieth century, government-sponsored welfare was minimal. The Leongatha Labour Colony provided a temporary respite for able-bodied men who later moved around the country searching for work. Many of these men would erect a tent or primitive hut and eke out a living trapping or performing odd jobs whenever available. It was a harsh life with little return as illustrated in a letter to *The Great Southern Star*.

> About three months ago I got sacked from the Labour Colony since when I have been trying to make a living close to Leongatha as a wallaby trapper and possum catcher. But some person besides coming into my hut and stealing skins, keeps on robbing my traps. Perhaps the publication of this or a word from your pen would cause them to be ashamed of making a living by thieving from an exiled Labour Colonist. Yours etc . . .
>
> Robert Searle. Leongatha 20.7.95.[1]

Other men who had acquired a little capital purchased a small area of bush land and endeavoured to become self-supporting. At a sale of Leongatha township blocks in Melbourne in 1894, a small area of three acres on the southern edge of the town just below the railway land (Allotments 4 and 5, Section 6) was purchased by W. Feighrey. At that time it was in its virgin state, covered with a heavy growth of timber, hazel scrub and ferns. Feighrey slept under a log on a bed of ferns and hazel branches for the first year or two until he managed to erect a small hut with timber cut from his block. It had no chimney, the smoke finding its way through cracks in the roof. The furniture was comparable in its simplicity — the bed made of blackwood slabs, boarded up like a cot while old tins were used for cooking purposes.

Feighrey kept to himself, asking favours of no one. Gradually, he cleared his small allotment with the use of only an axe, spade and crowbar. As his land was cleared, he dug it over with a spade and sowed oats, potatoes and peas which were all harvested by hand. The oats and peas were threshed and sold about the township. Every year the land would be again dug and rolled with a small roller made from a log cut on the property and drawn by himself. Feighrey paid cash for what little purchases he made in the township and gradually acquired a considerable number of sovereigns which he kept on his body at all times. Periodically, he would walk eight miles to Korumburra and carry back goods, if they could be purchased cheaper there. He made no friends in the eighteen years of his residence on his block, becoming known in the township as 'The Hermit'. Water rarely touched his body, and his clothes consisted of rags and other people's cast-offs. With advancing years, he disposed of his block of land to neighbour Mr R. Bair but insisted that he be paid in gold. Unable to sign his name, his mark had to be witnessed by a local justice of the peace. By some means or another, he made his way to Sunshine, where he collapsed on the road and was taken by ambulance to the Melbourne Hospital. Upon being washed, 118 gold sovereigns were found wrapped in rotten strips of rags wound around his body. They were stuck together in lots of ten with an accumulation of years of dirt, filth and cobbler's wax. Receipts from the sale of his land led to his identification as W. Feighrey of Leongatha.[2]

There were many similar cases such as Feighrey of men living alone in small slab huts or tents that were often built on unused roads. Eight miles north-east of Leongatha, one man had a small partly-cleared block on which he ran a few sheep and a horse. A small waterhole on the property provided his only water supply, and one hot summer his old horse became stuck in it and drowned. Not wishing to worry his neighbours for assistance, he set to work with an axe and crosscut saw, cut the horse into pieces and pulled the remains out with a wire-strainer.[3]

The Great Southern Star regularly carried death notices of men who were found dead from causes unknown:

> A man was found dead in McCartin's sale yards rotunda yesterday morning. He evidently passed away in his sleep for when found he was lying on his back with one arm across his chest, and a bag drawn over the lower portion of his body.[4]

Undoubtedly, many deaths were the result of alcohol, some of malnutrition, while a frequent cause was that of burning. If medical treatment were available, the patient stood a good chance of recovering.

> A man named Cornelius Gallagher working at the gravel pits near Foster was found on Monday morning about 2 a.m. enveloped in flames. It appears he returned to bed leaving a fire in the fireplace and by some unexplained reason the tent caught fire and he was severely burned. He was attended by Dr Hayden of Foster and Dr Carr of Leongatha. The man improved wonderfully on his way to Melbourne although one of his ears was nearly burnt off, his knees and hands also being burnt. He was admitted to Melbourne Hospital where he now lies.[5]

The first private hospital to be opened in Leongatha was in Peart Street in 1903 by a Miss Caparm-Jones, Certificated Midwife, who announced that she 'is now prepared to accommodate ladies at her newly-erected private hospital. Terms on application'.[6] Accident and general illness cases were still sent off to Melbourne hospitals, and the community met in February 1905 to decide what form of activity should be held to assist these hospitals with financial support. A division of opinion existed as to the most suitable function and as to how the proceeds should be divided. Mr R. Bair, Senior, considered that race meetings

Above: F. Fredericksen's bush camp, Tarwin Lower, 1925 (from Woorayl Shire Historical Society).

Right: Second Annual Sports Programme, Leongatha, 1904.

brought in six times as much as athletic meetings. The money at the athletic sports went to 'a lot of spielers who left five minutes after their race', said Mr Bair. He believed that the proceeds should be devoted towards improvements of the ground and not to the hospitals. It was finally decided to hold a race meeting with fifty percent of proceeds going towards the Melbourne Hospital and twenty-five percent each towards the Alfred and the Children's Hospital.[7]

A further step in the provision of health care was made in February 1907 when the Leongatha Progress Association elected a sub-committee to report on ways and means of establishing a cottage hospital in the town. Storekeeper J. Baker, President of the Association, had obtained figures from the Castlemaine Hospital which showed that it could be run at a cost per patient of £64 per annum.[8] Mr McCartin said he felt they had been overtaxing the Melbourne institutions by sending down too many patients. As a life governor of the Melbourne Hospital, he personally had sent down many patients, as there was no other alternative. In March McCartin offered to donate £200 plus an acre of land towards the proposed cottage hospital or £300 without the land. This offer was conditional on the community collecting £2,000 prior to 1 July. On being questioned by Mr Daniel Spencer as to whether he would give his donation if only £1,200 were raised, Mr McCartin said 'No!'.

A committee was formed locally to investigate the proposal and report back to a further meeting. Collectors were appointed to canvass the town and Shire for donations towards the project. This committee reported that

> it was compelled by severe logic to write "impracticable" against the project. There was insufficient support in the district due to the close proximity to Melbourne and

Leading Leongatha onion grower Daniel Spencer with his wife Lily Spencer (nee Blackmore) and son Dan, junior, 1908 (from Woorayl Shire Historical Society).

the fact there were hospital movements at Korumburra and Yarram. The cost of maintenance was another point put forward by those interviewed.[9]

Miss Caparm-Jones's hospital in Peart Street was taken over by Miss Oldham in March 1907, while Nurse Florence Good, member of the Royal Victorian Trained Nurses' Association and formerly of the Alfred and Women's Hospital, opened a private hospital in Church Street adjacent to the Methodist Church. Nurse Good had 'excellent testimonials from leading Melbourne Physicians and Surgeons after eight years of private nursing'.[10] Both of these hospitals catered for medical and surgical cases as well as midwifery. Another private hospital in Roughead Street, Tara, was opened in June 1907 by Miss Picket for ladies only.[11]

The decision to remain at home or send a patient to hospital must often have been extremely difficult. When Mrs H. Dannock was taken ill at her home in Roughead Street, Dr Carr was immediately called and diagnosed a case of acute laryngitis. This was followed by pleurisy, and yet after three days of careful watching with a private nurse in attendance, she passed away leaving a family of six children, the youngest being ten months old.[12]

Although the bulk of the populace was reasonably catered for with hospital facilities, there were still indigent cases whose means of access to hospital treatment was through the public system. This led to a movement in Leongatha to set up a fund to endow a bed in one of the Melbourne public hospitals or in one of the local private hospitals. Added impetus to this movement was given by a letter read by Dr Carr at a public meeting in the Mechanics' Institute from the Board of Health in October 1911 complaining 'of the number of infectious cases sent from the district, and that steps should be taken to have them treated locally'. Bank Manager Mr R. de C. Shaw doubted whether the district would support a hospital, 'for when a patient were once put on a train, it would be considered just as well to send the patient to Melbourne, in lieu of getting out at Leongatha'.[13]

At a further meeting of twenty-three residents at Leongatha in February 1912 under the chairmanship of Reverend Jackson, it was formally resolved to establish a fund known as the 'Leongatha Hospital Charity Fund' to be raised by hospital collections in the churches, concerts etc. to relieve cases of distress in the district. Mr J.M. Molloy, Chemist, (brother of Dr C.H. Molloy) said he was opposed to the establishment of a hospital for many years to come. He considered it would be far better to sink parochial differences and support one at Korumburra. The most economical method was to subsidise a bed in one of the local private hospitals and to continue with the practice of sending infectious cases elsewhere. On the motion of Messrs Begg and O'Toole, it was decided 'that half of the amount collected on Hospital Sunday be sent to Melbourne institutions and half retained for the fund to be created'.[14]

At Meeniyan a small private hospital to cater for midwifery cases was opened by Mrs Clemann, wife of one of the village settlers on the outskirts of the town. Village settlements were another attempt by the Victorian Government to alleviate the effects of the widespread unemployment prevalent in the 1890s. Set up under the same Act of 1893 that legally constituted labour colonies, they catered for people of a slightly different category. Areas of Crown land were sub-divided into allotments of up to twenty acres on which settlers were obliged to live for at least eight months of the year, using it for 'agriculture, gardening, grazing, dairying, farming or other like purposes'.[15]

Tools supplied by the Government comprised a plough, harrows, spades, pickaxes, forks, rakes, scythes, hoes, axes plus two incubators. Seven of these settlements were established in South Gippsland during the 1890s at Darlimurla, Koornork (Hoddle Range), Kardella, Mardan, Tarwin, Strzelecki and at Meeniyan. Many of the settlers were tradesmen forced out of work by the depression. They quickly established themselves on their small, twenty-acre blocks and contributed in no small measure to the development of their respective communities. At Meeniyan Mrs Clemann's maternity home on the Village Settlement was followed by the opening of a private hospital in 1910 by Nurse Britten. She was soon given great assistance in community health care by the arrival of Nurse Quatreman in March 1912 who acted as Bush Nurse.

The Bush Nursing Association was established only twelve months previously to cater for families of settlers who were striving to create homes and farms in remote districts without access to medical facilities. The first to be established was at Beech Forest in 1911, and within twelve months four more were set up, with Meeniyan being the fifth. On 8 March 1912 a special train carrying Lady Denman and the Vice-Regal party including Mrs Murray (wife of the Premier), the Hon. J. Mackey and Mrs Mackey, Dr Barrett, Mesdames Burston and Saddler, Miss Michaelis and Dr Janet Greig arrived at Meeniyan to mark the inauguration of the scheme.

After an official welcome at the station by the Shire President, Cr Mummery, the party moved across to the newly-finished Mechanics' Hall which was suitably decorated for the occasion and where a banquet was prepared. Mr P. Griffin, one of the village settlers, in an address of welcome, outlined the difficulties that confronted the original settlers and how appreciative they were of the new service being provided. Dr Barrett, Secretary of the scheme, said that it was a co-operative movement that enabled members, through making a small payment regularly, to partake of medical benefits. Dr Nicholls said he had attended in order to express his appreciation of the work done by the newly-formed Bush Nursing Association. He said the medical profession had one aim which although 'some people thought that was to make money their primary aim was to fight the three D's, Dirt, Disease and Death'.[16]

First Secretary of the Meeniyan scheme was Mr H. Bennett, headteacher at the State school. He arranged for transport of the district nurse, first on horse-back and later through the purchase of a horse and gig. Nurse Quatreman was followed by Sisters Hurnall, Boniface, Carson and Buckley. So successful was the Meeniyan scheme that residents of the Pound Creek, Tarwin Lower and Waratah districts soon joined together and asked for a nurse to be sent there under a similar arrangement. A meeting to arrange for the introduction of the scheme was held at Tarwin Lower on 18 April 1913 and another at Waratah the following day. At these meetings Sister Hurnall outlined the benefits which accrued to the area through having a nurse stationed there. Waratah residents agreed to combine with Tarwin Lower and Pound Creek in the scheme and elected Mrs Kelly and Mr A. Dewar to represent them on the committee.[17] By July Nurse Sprott arrived at Tarwin Lower to launch the scheme in that area,

Meeniyan State School and Catholic Church, 1905 (from Woorayl Shire Historical Society).

Scrub cutting on Tarwin River flats, c. 1910 (from D. Dodd).

and she was welcomed by Mr A.M. Black of Tarwin Meadows at an 'at home' given on her behalf by the eighty residents present. As a result of a visit by Nurse Sprott to the Tarwin Lower school, a wagon load of children arrived at Leongatha shortly afterwards for dental treatment.[18]

In 1913 Bush Nursing Centres were also established at Dumbalk, Dumbalk North and Buffalo. At a special meeting of subscribers held at Meeniyan in January 1914, it was decided that the incoming nurse should reside at Dumbalk for the ensuing year as an offer had been made of a suitable residence close to the Dumbalk butter factory. The scale of charges to subscribers was fixed at £2 per annum, which gave a fifty percent reduction in nursing fees; at £1 per annum a forty percent reduction; at 10s per annum a twenty percent reduction. Non-subscribers were charged the scale of fees as set by the Victorian Trained Nurses' Association.[19]

While doctors and nurses could attend to the physical ailments of children, teachers were necessary to supply their educational needs. Once primary schooling had been established throughout the Shire, a movement soon emerged for some form of secondary education. As early as 1905 suggestions had been made for an Agricultural High School to be established on portion of the Labour Colony. With upwards of 200 men as a labour force in the Colony, in the space of a decade the 820 acres had been transformed from an area of virgin

Lodge's Bridge, East Tarwin, c. 1910 (from D. Dodd).

bush into a clean, well-managed farm. The absence of any more timbered areas led to problems in keeping the men gainfully employed. Criticism was expressed publicly about the running of the Colony, and a Parliamentary Committee of Inquiry was set up to investigate the complaints. During the course of this Inquiry, Superintendent Goldstein stated that the Colony should be closed and moved onto another site where the men could be more gainfully employed in bringing virgin land into production.[20]

Perhaps the chief reason why this obvious course was not taken was that it was uneconomic. After seven years of existence, the Colony was becoming self-supporting and less of a drain on the Government's finances. The report of the Select Committee of Inquiry was criticial that 'no systematic method was followed in providing work for the men'. Yet it was satisfied that Colonel Goldstein had 'shown energy and enthusiasm throughout his association with the Colony'. It recommended that experimental cropping be discontinued and that dairying, pig raising and food growing for the colonists be the main activity.[21]

In 1904 portions of the Colony on the north side of the Yarragon Road were sold, with twenty acres known as the 'Scent Farm' being purchased by the Leongatha Butter Factory. This was an area that had been set aside specifically for the growing of flowers to be converted into perfume. Sponsored by the Department of Agriculture, it was an attempt to introduce another primary industry into Gippsland in the hope of increasing returns to settlers. Plots were set out with artemisia, aniseed, geranium, cassia, lavender, pennyroyal, rose, sage, pansy, tuberose, thyme and verbena. Lavender met with a ready market for use as a deodorant in hospitals, and returns of the Colony for 1912 show that 32,600 cuttings of this plant were sold for that year.[22]

After repeated representations from Woorayl Shire Council for the establishment of an Agricultural High School on the remainder of the Colony, the Government agreed on the condition that half of the cost of the school building was provided locally. Woorayl Shire Council decided at a special meeting in September 1907 to raise the rate to 1s 9d to allow for the accumulation of £750 for this purpose over a period of three years. No action was forthcoming by the Government until further representations were made through local Member, the Hon. J.E. Mackey, MLA. This resulted in the Government agreeing to the establishment of the new school, provided there was a minimum attendance of fifty pupils.

Tenders were called for new buildings, and the Leongatha Agricultural High School formally began on 6 February 1912 in one of the rooms made available by the headmaster of the State School, Mr M. Clanchy. Principal of the new school was Arthur Mesley, TTC, Dip.Agr.Sc., a young man who was to play an important role in the life of the district in subsequent years. During 1912 the new school buildings were erected at the corner of Horn Street and Nerrena Road on forty acres of land excised from the Labour Colony. Attendance had increased from the original fifty-five pupils to sixty-seven, necessitating some classes being held in the Rechabite Hall in Roughead Street during 1912. The new school buildings were officially opened the following year on 7 March 1913 by the Minister of Education, Mr F. Tate, before a crowd of 600 people. A special train from Foster was run to mark the occasion, and forty primary schools within the district displayed samples of school work done by pupils. Mr Tate said

> It required more than an elementary education to equip a child for this 20th century battle of life . . . It was hoped that an Agricultural High School would do something to turn the thoughts of boys and girls towards the big primary industries upon which the future of this province depends.[23]

In addition to the influence he exercised on students at the school, Mesley played an active role in fostering adult education. In conjunction with the Department of Agriculture, he arranged for a series of classes to be held at the High School on Thursday afternoons for the instruction of farmers on up-to-date methods of formation and manuring of pastures. He was instrumental in the formation of the Jersey Breeders' Association of which he was Secretary.[24] On Mesley's suggestion the Leongatha Mechanics' Institute arranged for a series of University Extension Lectures to be held on a regular basis during 1913-14. The first of these was held on 9 July 1913, the lecturer being Dean Stephen, MA, on the subject of 'A Fair Day's Wage for a Fair Day's Work'.[25] At the September lecture the Mechanics' Institute was fortunate to obtain the services of Professor W. Baldwin Spencer, with bioscope and phonograph. Professor Spencer's lecture on 'The Northern Territory and Its Aborigines' had drawn crowded houses in Melbourne and proved equally popular at Leongatha.

This series of lectures in 1913 proved so popular with Leongatha residents that Mesley set about repeating the program for 1914. By June of that year he had arranged four more interesting and varied lectures. Invitations were sent to Professor Tucker to deliver two lectures, 'A Walk Through Imperial Rome' and 'A Walk Through Ancient Athens'. Professor Berry was invited to lecture on 'Red, Yellow and White Races', while Mr J. McRae was asked to speak on 'The Poetry of Burns'.[26] It can be seen from the choice of subjects that Mesley saw his position as Principal of the Agricultural High School as only part of his role in educational matters. His energy and enthusiasm for adult education were of great benefit to the community generally.

Prior to the opening of the Agricultural High School in 1912, there were small private schools operating in Leongatha for a time. In April 1903 Miss Shields opened a private school close to the Presbyterian Church in Peart Street for primary children. She was associated with Miss Townsend who conducted classes for music, singing and painting on the same premises. In May 1905 Miss Tabor opened a private school in a forty foot by twenty foot building below the Masonic Hall in Bruce Street which she named 'Woorayl College'.[27] This school developed into a day and boarding school with Miss Sherwin as Principal. The curriculum was all embracing.

> Woorayl College . . . Pupils prepared for all examinations — scholastic and musical. Dressmaking and Millinery. Classes 10s 6d. Night School Tues. and Fridays. Drawing and Painting on Sat. Morning. Kindergarten class being formed for children under 7. Full day £1 1s. Prospectus on application. New term begins 25 January 1910.[28]

Until the high school attained its full quota of teachers and classes, the only

Dumbalk Hall, c. 1913 (from D. Bacon).

means of preparation for university was through private schools such as the Iona Private School conducted by Miss M. Chapman at Leongatha in 1912. Miss Chapman's advertisement in *The Great Southern Star* states she was a 'Registered Teacher, First Class honors, Melbourne University' and that 'Pupils will be prepared for University and other examinations'.[29]

Classes for shorthand were held from time to time at the Mechanics' Institute by visiting teachers, but with the growth of the high school, these small private schools quickly declined. The major exception to this trend was the convent school opened by the Sisters of St Joseph in Ogilvy Street in February 1914. To make way for the erection of their new brick church, the Catholic community had shifted their original wooden building by bullock wagon to a site on the eastern side of the presbytery. This was converted into a school which commenced with an enrolment of 42 pupils in 1914 but quickly increased to 104 in 1915.[30] In *The Great Southern Star* of 27 January 1914, the Sisters announced that 'Tuition in Music, Singing, Painting, Stencilling and Pen Painting, Fancy Work will be given; also Type writing, Shorthand and Bookkeeping will be given at reasonable terms'.[31]

These private schools were financed through direct charges on students. At the new Agricultural High School no fees were charged for pupils under the age of fourteen years. For those over fourteen, there was a provision made for those whose parents' income fell below a certain level, in which case the fees could be waived. In 1913 fees at the high school were as follows: £6 per annum for each of three terms with £2 per term to be paid in advance.[32]

The problems confronting pupils from the outlying areas of the Shire in making use of these educational facilities were formidable. Those adjacent to the railway line made use of the goods train that left Korumburra daily at 6.40 a.m. to get to school, returning on the passenger train that left at 4 p.m. in the evening. Others rode on horseback anything up to ten miles to and from school daily. Many boarded from Monday to Friday at private homes in Leongatha, with the result that the School Council pressed the Education Department for the provision of hostels in the town. Owing to lack of funds, plans for a new building were abandoned, and an old weatherboard structure from Wonthaggi was resited on the corner of Horn and Ogilvy Streets and remodelled for use as a girls' hostel. This was opened in 1917, but it was several years later before a boys' hostel was completed and opened further up Ogilvy Street.

When John Jeffrey retired in May 1905 as Principal of the Leongatha State School, he was succeeded by Mr J.E. Cowling who quickly assumed many of Jeffrey's positions in various community organisations. A keen rifle shot, Cowling joined the Leongatha Rifle Club and inevitably passed on some of his enthusiasm for this sport to his pupils. A Cadet Corps was formed at the Leongatha State School, and on 5 May 1908 Cowling embarked a detachment of cadets from his school for Dandenong, where they spent four days in military training.[33] Having formed a Cadet Corps, Cowling found it necessary to purchase a drum to improve their marching abilities. An appeal was made through the columns of *The Great Southern Star* for donations towards the cost of the drum. Donations could be left at the post office where Postmaster Mr Brash 'will be glad to receive the cash'.[34]

Cadets were subject to strict military discipline and could be charged for non-attendance at drills. At Korumburra in November 1912, Captain Olden of the Defence Department proceeded against sixteen boys at the Court of Petty Sessions for failing to attend compulsory drills. Captain Olden said that most of the lads on being interviewed had promised to make up the deficiencies, which varied from twelve to fifty-five hours. The Police Magistrate, Mr Cohen, granted an adjournment of three months but pointed out to the lads that they would be liable to heavy penalties if they did not live up to their promises.[35]

At this time the Lands Department had been prosecuting landowners for non-clearance of ragwort, a noxious weed that thrives exceptionally well in South Gippsland. The Police Magistrate for the area, Mr Read Murphy, evidently perturbed at the number of cases of prosecution regularly coming before the Bench, contacted Cowling and asked him to encourage his pupils to eradicate this weed. Mr Murphy offered a prize to the pupils of the Leongatha State School who could gather up and bring to the school the greatest number of ragwort plants. Mr Cowling agreed to keep a tally of the numbers brought and encouraged the students in their task.

At the end of August 1908, Mr Murphy visited the State School and expressed his appreciation of the good work done by the students in this praise-worthy task. Their work was of benefit to the district and 'they were increasing their habits of industry and observation in themselves', said Mr Murphy. Prize winners in the competition were Willie O'Donnell and Leo Canty who gathered over 11,000 plants each.[36] The following year Headmaster Cowling declined to take part in a similar competition, and the ragwort continued to flourish on

Fairbank, S.S. 3171, 1907 (from W. Calder).

Mount Eccles-Leongatha Road, c. 1910 (from Woorayl Shire Historical Society).

district farms. As Police Magistrate, Mr Murphy did his best to interpret the law as it related to the elimination of noxious weeds, and *The Great Southern Star* contains numerous references to fines imposed on landowners for failure to eradicate ragwort. Solicitor Richard Little of Leongatha challenged the Police Magistrate on a technical point of law, with the result that Mr Murphy was stood down from the Bench for several weeks while subject to a departmental inquiry. After hearing evidence from all parties concerned, the technicality was dismissed and Mr Murphy re-instated to the Bench.

Upon his return on 17 November 1908, Cr Wills, Shire President, and Mr Johnson, JP, congratulated him on the way he had come out of the inquiry. Mr McColl, on behalf of thirty-six residents of the Mardan district, read a joint letter expressing sympathy for Mr Murphy. They were glad to see him back again and were satisfied justice would be impartially administered. In reply Mr Murphy thanked the speakers for their sentiments and stated that he would value the letter presented by Mr McColl higher than gold and diamonds. In a rather oblique pun on Mr Little who brought the accusations against him, Mr Murphy referred to 'the littleness of the charges' which led to the inquiry.[37]

Mr Richard Little had a keen mind when it came to points of law. In 1904, before Mr Read Murphy was Police Magistrate, Little had been proceeded against under the *Truancy Act* for failing to send his children to school. Little

Koonwarra State School, c. 1912 (from L. Johnson).

advised the Inspector that he was instructing his children at home and was quite capable of doing so. He could not be fined for neglecting to send his children to school, as they were receiving instruction which he contended was far superior to that received at the State school. The Bench, after examining the Act on the subject, stated that the defendant, although technically correct, would still have to see his children obtained the State school percentage.[38]

The highlight of the school year at the Leongatha State School was the annual picnic. Picnics at that time were a major social event. Church picnics, Lodge picnics, school picnics all helped to create a social cohesion as well as providing an opportunity for renewal of friendship, family ties etc. Beginning in 1909 under an energetic committee headed by G.F. Michael, Shire Secretary, the Leongatha State School picnic was held at St Kilda beach. A special train was hired for the occasion, and the pupils were accompanied by a team of bowlers who played a friendly game at the St Kilda Bowling Club. As a result of this excursion to St Kilda, a return visit from that city was arranged. In March 1910, 600 children from the fourth, fifth and sixth grades of the St Kilda State School, together with a number of civic officials, teachers and parents, arrived by special train to spend a day at Leongatha. The Commercial Hotel prepared over 100 meals for the visitors, while the children were marched to the Recreation Reserve where they were entertained with various sports and games. Twenty gallons of milk were ordered from the Labour Colony, as well as other large quantities of liquid refreshments. A team of bowlers played a match against the local team, while another party was taken for a buggy trip around the district.[39]

The following year pupils from other district schools joined in the train trip to St Kilda beach, with over 600 adults and children from stations between Ruby and Stony Creek taking part. On embarking for the return trip to Leongatha, one child, the son of Mr and Mrs C. Simon, was missing — he was last seen wandering off in the shallow water towards Albert Park but could not be found when the main party left. Fortunately, he was located by the police and returned to Leongatha the following day. Possibly as a result of this mishap, later picnics were held at Mordialloc, Kilcunda and Waratah Bay, all of which proved equally popular with children and parents alike.

For farm children, the attraction of the annual picnic was rivalled only by that of the annual Show. Thirteen-year-old Alex le Maitre recorded his impressions of that event in his composition book in 1908.

12.2.08.

I went to the Korumburra Show on Wednesday, it was a very smoky day as there were several bush-fires around. I got to the showground about one o'clock. I had a look at the separators, and engines and ploughs first. Then we went to the sheep and cows and had a look at them. Soon the horses and buggies came out in the ring and were parading about till the trotting and high jumping commenced. There were a lot of circuses and booths on the ground.[40]

Horses and buggies were soon to be rivalled as the universal means of transport. In December 1910 former President of Woorayl Shire, Cr W.H. Livingston of Willinvale property, Ruby, purchased a motor vehicle to assist him in his journeys to another property at Ultima. During his term as Shire

President, Livingston had become embroiled in a court action for slander against fellow councillor Hugh McCartin. Differences of opinion arose during one Council meeting when Cr McCartin had stated that 'birds of a feather stick together'. On being asked by Livingston to whom he referred, McCartin said 'if the cap fits, wear it'. McCartin further stated 'that he thanked God that he had no convict blood running in his veins'. President Livingston replied 'if only on account of your age I would hit hard'. The result of this rather stormy meeting of Woorayl Shire Council was a slander action against McCartin by Livingston which was heard in the Supreme Court.[41] The verdict was given in favour of Livingston for £5, with costs on a special scale fixed by the contending parties. Hugh McCartin thereupon submitted his resignation from Woorayl Shire Council after sixteen years of notable service.

As one swallow does not make a summer, so one motor car in the district did not affect the mode of travel of the vast majority. Horse transport, plus railway travel when necessary, was standard practice. When the Leongatha Co-operative Society commenced business in 1911, in the store formerly operated by Baker Bros. at the corner of Long and Roughead Streets, one of their first activities was to build extensive stabling for their customers at the rear of the building. At the first half yearly report of the activities at their new Co-operative store, Chairman W. Coulter said

> For the convenience of country customers a large stable for their horses has been erected with 32 stalls, with feed boxes in each. These will be in use every Thursday which is the principal business day in the town. The yard which has often been a mud hole in winter, has been gravelled and is now well set so that water now flows over it like a brick foundation. Some 60 loads of gravel from Mrs Bond's quarry were carted for the purpose.[42]

The Co-op store, as it soon became known, was started from funds subscribed by farmers and others who were dissatisfied with the service provided by the existing storekeepers. After canvassing the district for the sale of shares in the project, the directors found that it would be more practical to purchase an existing business than start one of their own as originally intended. The land and buildings occupied by Baker Bros. store were purchased for £1,675, together with the stock valued at £3,500. Alterations were made to the main building, Chairman Coulter stating that 'the drapery dept. has been enlarged a further 27 ft, and is now a commodious room 60 ft by 33 ft. Cash wire carriers have been installed, and a cash desk has been placed in the centre of the floor'.[43]

The provision of stabling for such a large number of horse-drawn vehicles, together with other facilities provided by the Co-op, quickly led to it becoming an important business in the township and a major employer of labour. Dressmaking and millinery were added to the store's activities, and permission was sought from the Shire Council to install a 1½ horsepower electric motor and to have the premises approved for use as a factory or workroom.[44]

The electricity supply from the Leongatha Butter Factory to the township had proved very reliable and satisfactory, although there were minor breakdowns. When local carrier T. Collis was driving a lorry past the Leongatha Post Office in August 1912, his horse stood on a live electricity wire that had fallen loose. The horse leapt into the air and then fell prostrate on the roadway. *The Great*

Leongatha Bowling Club, c. 1910 (from Woorayl Shire Historical Society).

Southern Star noted that 'Pegasus was then taken to his stable, not being fit for further work after such a shock'.[45] Senior Constable Evans was called for and stood guard until the electrician from the butter factory arrived to replace the fallen wire.

Although telephonic communication with Melbourne had been possible since 1906, private telephone calls could only be made from the post office to Melbourne and other exchanges as there was no subscriber network in the area. In 1910 the Leongatha Traders' Association persuaded an officer from the Postal Department to visit the town with a view to arranging for the installation of a telephone exchange. Secretary, J.T. Lardner, introduced the officer to business people in the town, and promises of connection were made by over thirty people. Cost to the subscribers was to be £4 per annum with a free service between numbers on the exchange in the town.[46]

Another two years elapsed before any concrete action was taken for installation of the exchange and house connections. Numbers were then issued to those who had paid their subscription, and their names were listed in the *Victorian Telephone Guide* of 1913. Unfortunately, the Guide was issued and in circulation before the necessary exchange was installed at Leongatha. All during 1913 when a Leongatha number was called, a messenger had to be sent from the post office requesting the desired person to come to the office as soon as possible. Naturally, this situation caused considerable resentment from those who had paid their money in anticipation of being connected to an exchange. By October 1913 the necessary telephone poles and equipment had arrived at the Leongatha Railway Station, and residents were noticeably elated when the exchange was installed at the end of that year. *The Great Southern Star* of 24

December 1913 published a list of subscribers to the newly-installed exchange, which gave a comprehensive picture of the activities carried on in the township at that time.

The Great Southern Star 24 December 1913.
Subscribers to Leongatha Telephone Exchange.
1. Shire of Woorayl.
2. Butter Factory and manager's residence.
3. Co-operative Society's Store.
4. W.G. Walker, storekeeper.
5. J.M. Peck and Sons, auctioneers.
6. J.M. Molloy, chemist.
7. P. Johnson, butcher.
8. Dr Howden, physician.
9. Nurse Morris, private hospital.
10. Lardner and Co., ironmongers.
11. Colvin and Co., drapers.
12. A.E. Edney, storekeeper.
13. Rossiter and Co. 'Star' Office.
14. Pearce and Jarratt, butchers.
15. S. Maddern, Commercial Hotel.
16. Neal Bros., storekeepers.
17. R. Bair, Otago Hotel.
18. E. Manders, agent.
19. Nurse Good, Private Hospital.
20. Rev. P.J. Coyne, Presbytery.
21. J.W. Rumpf, quarry.

Bair Street, Leongatha, 1910 (from Woorayl Shire Historical Society).

22. J. McFarlane, coachbuilder.
23. E.F. McNamara, baker.
24. H. Kelly, undertaker.
25. Jno. Lardner, private residence.
26. Dr Pern, physician.
27. E.A. Cole, auction mart.
28. McCartin and Co., auctioneers.
29. R.J. Kewish, 'Sun' Office.
30. P. Johnson's slaughter yards.
31. McGowan and Due, dentists.
32. J. Conway, carrier.
33. G.E. Matthewman, tailor.
34. R. Little, solicitor.
35. Government Labour Colony.
36. W. Watson, private residence.

The full benefits to subscribers could not be realised until the outlying areas were connected to the Leongatha exchange, and for that purpose telephone leagues were established to hasten the installation of this service. Under these schemes, the league purchased the necessary wire, insulators and poles for connection to the different farms. The lines were erected and maintained by voluntary labour, with usually two to three farms being on the one line — the so called 'party line.' Different call signals were used by the exchange operator; that is, either two long or two short rings or a combination of both if there were more than two subscribers on the one line. The temptation to listen in to the conversation of neighbours sometimes proved too great and often led to a rift in friendships. Nevertheless, party lines did provide an improvement in communication services throughout the district until a comprehensive network of individual lines could be installed.

A financial guarantee had to be entered into between these Leagues and the Postal Department to ensure sufficient revenue for the first five years after installation. If the revenue from the service failed to meet the guarantee, then hours of service would be reduced. When the line to Mirboo North through Mardan was completed in 1914, a League was formed in that district that led to the installation of a telephone exchange at the home of James McKinnon and family, pioneer settlers of that district. First subscribers to the McKinnons' exchange were 1) W. Coulter, J.H. McColl, W.J. Coulter, T.W. Coulter; 2) P.J. O'Malley; 3) J.H. Potter, P. Miller; 4) D.S. Campbell, W.C. Couper, J.J. Blundell; 5) Mrs Ramsay, Steele Bros., W.E. Steele; 6) John McKinnon; 7) Campbell Bros.[47]

Even before the installation of the new telephone exchange, the advantages of trunk line communication were demonstrated in cases of emergency. Such an emergency occurred in the Leongatha township on New Year's Day 1913. At 8.15 p.m. fire broke out in the upper storey of the wooden coffee palace owned by Mr Harrison in the centre of McCartin Street. Surrounded by other wooden buildings, it appeared that the whole street of shops and dwellings would be wiped out. To make matters worse, a fire brigade competition had been held at Korumburra that day, and the major portion of the Leongatha Fire Brigade was in that town with some of the equipment. Korumburra was hastily contacted,

McCartin Street, Leongatha, 1913, after the fire (from Woorayl Shire Historical Society).

and the announcement that Leongatha was burning was made just after the beginning of the night's entertainment. The Leongatha brigade, together with representatives of the Korumburra and Wonthaggi brigades, were rushed to Leongatha by special train in the record time of twelve minutes.[48]

Within half an hour of the ringing of the firebell, the two-storey coffee palace was a heap of ruins, with only chimneys still standing. The greatest danger was that the fire would spread across the right-of-way on to Jarratt's butchery and so engulf all the wooden shops that extended down Bair Street. Had there been a wind this would certainly have occurred, as sparks ignited the Bank of Victoria and O'Toole's store on the opposite side of McCartin Street several times. The newly-built brick buildings of the Colonial Bank and Mr W. Field's saddlery prevented the fire from spreading up McCartin Street, but the three wooden shops of Mrs Tomlin and Messrs Hehir and Molloy were destroyed. It was only by the heroic efforts of the Leongatha, Korumburra and Wonthaggi Fire Brigade members that the fire was finally brought under control by 11 p.m.

At the time of this fire, ninety percent of the buildings in Leongatha were of wooden construction. Brickworks had been commenced by G. Mewburn in 1890 in Hughes Street (Allotment 19, Section 18), but most of his output was used for chimneys, floors, drains, cellars etc. Hayes's store, only three hundred yards from the kiln in Roughead Street, was the first building erected with Mewburn's bricks and contained a large cellar underneath for storage of food-stuffs. A small brickworks operated at the Labour Colony below the Scent Farm for a time, but these bricks were only used on the Colony. Another brickworks was started by E. Trigg of Jeffrey Street in 1909 who stated that he had 10,000 bricks ready for a trial. The price of these bricks was quoted at £2 5s 0d per thousand as against the price of Melbourne bricks at £3 15s 0d.[49]

Wood was used in the kilns to fire these bricks, but evidently the finished product was not up to standard and neither enterprise continued. The new Presbytery in Ogilvy Street built in 1904, and the new butter factory in Yarragon Road built in 1905, were both made of Melbourne bricks. The first public building to be built of brick was the new railway station in 1910, followed by the Court House in 1912. St Peter's Parish Hall in Church Street, opened in March of that year, was of wooden construction costing £500, but it fulfilled a long felt need by the congregation and was to serve its original purpose for many decades. Dr Pain, Bishop of the Diocese, was welcomed at the opening by the resident minister Reverend A. Gamble in the presence of a large congregation. Dr Pain said the hall and the Sunday school that would be held in it were an integral part of parish life and that Leongatha parishioners were 'loyal, zealous and enterprising'.[50]

The Catholic community, under the leadership of Father P.J. Coyne, their first resident parish priest, decided to erect a substantial brick church in place of the original wooden one built in 1895. Plans for the new church were of a romanesque structure with a belfry to cost almost £7,000. The foundation stone was laid by Bishop Phelan on 26 April 1913, but it was decided to proceed with only part of the original plan, omitting the belfry, sanctuary and part of the nave. The modified building was constructed by Messrs F. and E. Deague of Fitzroy for the sum of £3,200, under plans prepared by Architect Charles I. Rice of Melbourne.

A special train was run from Fish Creek for the opening ceremonies on 16

The opening of St Laurence O'Toole's Catholic Church, Leongatha, 16 November 1913. The bell and stand were erected in 1909 having been donated by Mrs Jeremiah Hanley (from Woorayl Shire Historical Society).

November 1913, and seating accommodation in the church was taxed to the utmost. Dr Mannix, Coadjutor Archbishop of Melbourne, preached the occasional sermon at the Pontifical High Mass which was celebrated by Bishop Phelan of the Sale Diocese. A special choir was brought from the city for the occasion, and the church was dedicated by Bishop Phelan to St Laurence O'Toole the Irish Saint.[51] Church functions at this time provided suitable news material for country newspaper proprietors to fill their columns. Sermons of visiting bishops were reported verbatim while the minutiae of a local wedding was enjoyed by residents who were not able to attend in person.

In 1910 a wedding in the original wooden Catholic Church in Ogilvy Street was reported by R.J. Kewish, proprietor of *The Leongatha Sun*. It is reprinted here in its entirety because not only does it provide all possible details relative to the occasion, but it illustrates the extent to which Kewish and his rival, Horace Rossiter of *The Great Southern Star*, went to fill their weekly columns. In the absence of techniques for reproducing photographs for their readers, these newspaper men provided word pictures of current events.

The Leongatha Sun, Feby. 17, 1910.

WEDDING
COLLIER-CARTY

A pretty wedding in which much much local interest was taken was celebrated at the Catholic Church, Leongatha, on Wednesday, 2nd inst., when Miss Maud Elizabeth Carty, third daughter of Mr and Mrs J. Carty, of Hallston, and Mr William Ernest Collier, younger son of the late Mr J.W. Collier and Mrs R. Richardson, of Allambee East, were united in the bonds of holy matrimony, the Rev. Father Coyne officiating. The bride entered the church on her father's arm, wearing a most becoming semi-Empire bridal gown of creme silk, which fell in soft, graceful folds, and was trimmed with beautiful silk lace and silk applique, and embroidered with true lovers' knots. The full court train was handsomely embroidered with true lovers' knots, and fastened with clusters of orange blossoms. The long tulle veil was softly draped over a coronet of orange blossoms. She carried a shower bouquet of white carnations and lillies of the valley and asparagus fern, and white satin streamers. The bridesmaids were the Misses Winnie and Cecily Carty (sisters of the bride). They looked charming in Empire gowns of soft creme silk prettily trimmed with silk insertion and soft creme ribbon, and wore creme tulle hats trimmed with soft satin ribbon, and clusters of pale blue wisteria. They carried shower bouquets of La France roses, and asparagus softened with tulle, and finished with pale blue satin streamers, and wore gold brooches, the gift of the bridegroom. Mr M. O'Bryan was best man, and Mr Will Gilbert (Melbourne) groomsman. The bride's mother wore a handsome dress of rich black silk, and hat with ruched tulle with osprey mount. After the ceremony a reception and wedding tea was held in the lodge-room of the Mechanics' hall, at which a number of intimate friends and relatives partook of the good things provided. The usual toasts were proposed and honored. The happy couple left by the afternoon train for Melbourne, where the honeymoon is being spent, amidst showers of confetti and good wishes from their numerous friends. The bride's travelling dress was a smart coat and skirt of creme serge, and hat of creme satin straw, trimmed with satin ribbon and white flowers. Some costly and handsome presents were received, chief amongst which were:—

Bride to Bridegroom, gold sleeve links
Bridegroom to Bride, silver mounted brushes and comb
Father of Bride, cheque
Mother of Bride, household linen and cutlery
Mr and Mrs O'Mara, cheque

,, ,, T.W. Clarke, silver biscuit barrel and butter dish
,, ,, B. Mitchell, silver and cut glass pickle jar
,, ,, H. Charlton, cheque
,, ,, A.J. Hall, cutlery
,, ,, J. Harrison, silver and cut glass salt cellars
,, ,, R. McKay, silver jardiners
,, ,, J. Davis, cheque
,, ,, B. Fowles, silver and cut glass toilet jars
,, ,, J. Loughrey, silver and cut glass salt cellars
,, ,, T. Moroney, afternoon tea set
,, ,, H. Williams, silver and cut glass honey jar
,, ,, J. Griggs, silver jam dish
,, ,, J. O'Bryan, silver and cut glass fruit dish
,, ,, J. O'Neill, case of carvers
,, ,, Tourrier, silver fruit stand
Mr W. and Miss O'Neill, silver and cut glass biscuit barrel
Mrs and Miss Walford, silver bread knife and fork
Mrs J. Griggs, silver tray
Miss Harold, silver bread fork
,, Frances Carty, cheque
,, Connie Carty, pair pillow shams
,, Amy Harrison, silver hand mirror
,, J. Hall, silver and hand-painted biscuit barrel
,, Cecily Carty, glassware
,, Winnie Carty, silver and ruby epergne
,, Dorothy Carty, silver jewel case
Misses Alice and Ada Griggs, silver and cut glass toilet jars
Misses Creta and Mamie McGrath, handsome silver and cut glass combination flower and fruit stand
Mr McKinnon, cheque
,, R. Forrest, silver and hand painted biscuit barrel
,, T.A. Hall, cheque
,, J.N. Baker, silver and cut glass salad bowl
,, D. McDonald, pair silver butter dishes
,, Edgar Marks, silver and cameo biscuit barrel
,, Will Gilbert, silver teapot
,, Harrie Tanner, pair pictures
,, F. Knaws, silverware
,, L. Dietrich, dessert knives
,, J. O'Neill, silver dinner cruet
,, J. Hill, silver and cut glass stand

Walkerville from the end of the jetty, c. 1920 (from Woorayl Shire).

Blackbutt stump at Hamann's property, Fairbank, c. 1910 (from D. Bacon).

11. THE 1914-18 WAR

The year 1914 commenced with south-eastern Australia in the grip of one of its periodic droughts. Although Woorayl Shire is in one of the most favoured parts of the Australian continent as far as the reliability of rainfall is concerned, it too felt the effects of the dry season. From an average of thirty-seven inches annually, Leongatha's rainfall for that year dropped to an all time low of twenty-five inches. Many cattle and sheep from the northern parts of the State were sent to Woorayl Shire on agistment while others wandered the roads in search of feed and water. Fortunately, Engineer Callaway had regularly travelled around the Shire and kept in mind available water reserves. In his report on their importance to Council for travelling stock he stated:

> On the way (to Waratah) I noticed that the public watering places are enclosed with post and wire fences, both at Brandy Swamp and Five Tree Hammock. The first is not of much importance as it is dry in summer, but the latter is permanent water, at which there is a reserve of 10 acres with a one chain road on the west side of Cashin's fence. I think this reserve should be left open as water for travelling stock is scarce in dry seasons.[1]

At the December 1913 meeting of Woorayl Council, the Engineer was instructed 'to inspect the council water hole at Inverloch and endeavour to have it working for the summer'. The presence of feed and water on 'the long paddock' was a sore temptation to stockowners to let their stock wander, much to the annoyance of others. Following complaints from farmers in the Mount Eccles area, Shire Ranger, Mr Bishop, went out and impounded sixteen horses including one entire. He then reported that 'if there were any more complaints he would prosecute the owners'. Council was constantly bombarded with letters and deputations for stricter enforcement of by-laws regarding wandering stock.

The situation was particularly bad around Inverloch where it was not uncommon to see mobs of fifty to sixty head of cattle wandering in the area. Mr Bishop was stationed at Leongatha and it meant an early morning ride of sixteen miles to Inverloch to catch the offending cattle. As in all country towns, there was a 'bush telegraph' in existence, because Mr Bishop complained that 'he had visited Inverloch several times with the object of impounding the stock;

but word had been sent that he was coming and a notice posted up warning owners'.[2] One summer morning he left Leongatha before daylight and collected twenty-seven cattle at Inverloch township before the owners had any idea he was in the vicinity. The difficulty caused by the absence of a pound at Inverloch was realised by councillors, but its establishment at that seaside resort was well down on their list of priorities.

Shire Engineer Callaway resigned from Woorayl Shire Council in July 1913 after fifteen years of service to take up a position with the newly-formed Country Roads Board. He was replaced in August by Mr D. Gray, one of whose first tasks was to try and enforce the *Width of Tires Act*.

The Chairman of the Country Roads Board, Mr Calder, was adamant that great damage was being done to roads through non-enforcement of this Act and called on Councils to enforce it. Under the Act there was a strict limit on the load of vehicles depending on the width of their tyres. Engineer Gray reported to the February 1914 meeting of Woorayl Shire Council that 'I strongly recommend the enforcement of *Width of Tires Act* at once. I have put off one of Rumpf's wagons carrying five tons on 2¼ inch tyres. Already some of the metal roads have been greatly damaged'.[3]

The maintenance of roads was all important for the cartage of cream to butter factories. At Leongatha South there was a particularly bad stretch of road, and Mr S.J. Williams recalled

> Private contractors were employed by the L.B.F. to collect the cream before the company ran their own waggons. In the Leongatha South area Mr H. Cleman used three ponies in a light waggon with two inch tyres to get through the mud in the winter time. He found that the mud did not cling to the wheels so much and the light ponies were able to flounder through it much better than the heavier horses. He would leave his home on the Inlet Road and collect cream from the farms past the Leongatha South school and would always arrive at the Norton homestead in time for morning tea. By lunch time he would be back to his own place where his wife would have three more ponies ready and harnessed for the final pull into Leongatha.[4]

The 1914 drought encouraged the proliferation of rabbits in the Woorayl Shire. They were first introduced into the area by Mr George Black of Tarwin Meadows before the turn of the century for sporting purposes. When they became a problem there after several years, Mr Black used a cheap and novel method of eradication. He persuaded the master of the small schooner that plied between the Inlet and Melbourne to bring back as many cats as possible from the metropolitan area in the hold of the vessel. On arrival the half starved, half mad creatures were released on the Meadows, and within a few years, had eliminated the rabbits completely. The second invasion of rabbits commenced in 1907, when they were noticed on Mr Carl Hamann's property at Fairbank, and within seven years, they had reached plague proportions. Few realised the massive expenditure in time, labour and money that would be necessary to control them or the damage that would be done to pastures through their presence.

On their first appearance in the Leongatha area, they were merely regarded as good shooting targets. Members of the Leongatha Gun Club had no difficulty in obtaining 'bags' of fifty for a day's shooting. Others could not see the point in using cartridges when dogs could do the same job more cheaply. At a meeting held at the Commercial Hotel in October 1914, it was decided to form a Fox Terrier Club at Leongatha. Mr W. Lindner's tender to wire net the Recreation Reserve oval at 2s 9d per chain was accepted, and two hundred copies of rule books for the club were procured.[5] Tenders were called for the supply of sixty pair of rabbits to be delivered in crates to the Secretary, George Hewett, on 27 October. The meeting was held on the Recreation Reserve on 28 October — admission for gents was 1s and ladies 6d. A publican's booth was arranged for the occasion, and an enjoyable time was had by all, except the rabbits.

> The coursing was on the whole, exceptionally good, some fairly long courses being run. One feature of the afternoon was the strength of the rabbits, which, contrary to the general opinion ran well; and it is safe to say that had the enclosure not been wire-netted the terriers would have been outclassed. There is no doubt that the committee made a mistake in deciding that the judge's decision should be given on points, for it would have been far more satisfactory had the judge's verdict been given on the kill and there is no doubt that those connected with the club will benefit by the experience of the first meeting and that they will decide all contests in the future on the kill.[6]

Unfortunately, such diversions as coursing were overshadowed by bigger clouds on the horizon before 1914 came to a close. In July of that year the Immigration and Labour Bureau of 555 Flinders Street, Melbourne, was advertising in *The Great Southern Star* that there were 380 British lads arriving on the S.S. *Hawke's Bay* and the S.S. *Berrima* who were seeking employment in Victoria. Their ages ranged from sixteen to twenty years, and although the majority were without rural experience, 'they readily adapt themselves to country work and rapidly become good helpers, having come out specially to be employed in country districts'.[7] Wages asked for these migrants were ten shillings per week and keep, and the Bureau was anxious 'that those employers who wish to take advantage of their services should apply without delay'.

Within nine months the tide of young men leaving Europe to seek employment in the country districts of Victoria had been reversed, and thousands of Victorians were leaving the State in response to a call from the motherland.

> Take up the white man's burden,
> Have done with childish days;
> The lightly proffered laurel,
> The easy ungrudged praise,
> Comes now to search your manhood
> Through all the thankless years,
> Cold, edged with dear-bought wisdom,
> The judgement of your peers.
>
> Your country calls!
> Will you respond?[8]

Many young men responded immediately to the call to arms thinking, perhaps, that this war would be similar in its duration to that of the Boer War. There was no real personal hatred or animosity to Germany or Germans at the beginning of the war. Fourteen years earlier, when the German barque *Magnat* of 1,120 tons under the command of Captain Ostermann ran ashore on Venus Bay at midnight on 9 March 1900, its crew of sixteen young German sailors was given every assistance by local inhabitants and the authorities. Attempts were made to tow the ship clear, but unfortunately, the lines from the tug snapped and the *Magnat* beached again permanently. Provisions for the ship's crew were supplied by the Tarwin Lower hotelkeeper, Mr Munro, and a dance was held on board one evening to relieve the crew's monotony.

Ostermann, worried by the loss of his ship, became ill and died on 20 August 1900. As there was no doctor in attendance to issue a death certificate, a magisterial inquiry was held by J.H. Inglis, JP, of Lyre Bird Mound, Koonwarra, and a verdict of death from natural causes was given. Ostermann was buried in the Tarwin Lower Cemetery at which it was stated that 'there was a large attendance and many beautiful wreaths covered the coffin when laid to rest'.[9]

In 1913 the committee of the Leongatha Mechanics' Institute was in a quandary as to the best piano to purchase for the hall. Eventually, it was decided that a preferential vote be taken on the issue with several British pianos being included on the ballot paper. The final result was in favour of the German Lipp upright grand piano which had been used for the recent Caledonian concert. Voting was nine in favour of the Lipp and seven for its nearest rival the Wertheim. *The Great Southern Star* commended the decision.

> The committee are to be congratulated upon the selection of such a well known and popular piano. Inquiries proved that Lipp pianos by reason of the refinement of their tone, their perfect mechanism, superior workmanship, and strength of construction are regarded as the most popular pianos known.[10]

On an individual level, human nature usually triumphs over man-made political divisions. At Inverloch on 14 November 1914, a young girl got into difficulties whilst bathing too near the channel. Two Sisters of St Joseph went to her assistance but were unable to prevent her being carried out by the swift current. Fortunately, a young German who was on the beach at the time rushed into the water, taking off only his coat, and managed to bring her back safely to land. On being thanked for his heroic action, he could only reply in broken English 'It was nothing'.[11]

Until the casualty lists started to appear after the landing at Gallipoli in April 1915, the terrible reality of war did not really strike home. Efforts were made to assist the Belgian Relief Fund by means of patriotic concerts, and the Leongatha Gun Club organised a rabbit shoot at which 340 rabbits were bagged. These were placed temporarily in the freezing chamber at the Leongatha Butter Factory, through the courtesy of Board member Peter Johnson, and subsequently, forwarded to Melbourne for the benefit of the Relief Fund.[12]

At Stony Creek a picnic race meeting was held early in March 1915 in aid of this Fund. A carnival atmosphere pervaded throughout the day with auction sales of stock and produce taking place between races, with the proceeds going to the Relief Fund. Articles of fancy work were disposed of by raffles, and guessing the weight of a sheep brought in several pounds with the result that the overall benefit to the fund was in excess of £100.[13]

Horse racing had experienced a resurgence of interest within the Shire during

Dempsey's homestead, Stony Creek, c. 1914 (from M. McGlead).

German barque Magnat *beached at Tarwin beach, 1900 (from F. Mackie).*

the preceding few years. At Leongatha the Recreation Reserve was the venue for meetings of the reformed Leongatha Racing Club. After a lapse of a decade or more, the club reformed in 1912 and held three successful meetings on the Reserve. Members and participants were not satisfied with the small oval for horse racing and decided to purchase a 110 acre property on Brown's Road, two miles to the south of the town. Debentures were issued to finance the purchase, and a great deal of work was done by voluntary workers under the direction of Mr A. Simmons. By November 1914 the committee had cleared the track, installed necessary drainage and laid out a course that was four chains over the mile.

The first meeting was held on the new course on a Friday in early February 1915, but considerable difficulty was experienced in getting the people actually on to the racecourse. Brown's Road had not been formed, but that did not deter the committee from going ahead with the meeting. Special trains were run from Melbourne and Foster, and both were crowded upon reaching Leongatha. Double-seated buggies, drags and motor cars ran from the station to the course on the big day, covering the passengers with dust. Such minor details did not mar the success of the meeting or dampen the enthusiasm of the crowd. The three trustees of the club, Messrs John Smith, Arthur Simmons and Thomas Riggall, were well pleased with the first meeting on the new course, and further improvements were planned to cater for future meetings.[14]

Black's dairies, Tarwin Lower, c. 1914 (from M. Armstrong).

Twelve months after the declaration of war, letters were received from some of the Wooarayl Shire soldiers who had been through the holocaust of Gallipoli. Corporal Eddie Keane described his experiences as follows:

The night we landed we had to charge up hills like Chalmers's hill at the old 'Gatha. I carried a machine gun on my back, 20 lbs of cartridges, and my full pack of 115 lbs altogether, and the terrible strain has told on me now. I was in charge of a machine gun section, and I am No. 1 gunner in the trenches where I was. I have had five different machine guns to fire out of, and I have stood with my hands on my gun for 75 hours at a time. Just imagine standing for days on dead bodies and blood in the trenches. Phew, the smell is horrible, especially the Turks. They are big men, and good fighters. Our losses are bad, but we will hold our own against the best the world can produce. Like Johnnie Walker, "still going Strong."[15]

Another soldier from Leongatha South, Private W.H. Williams, wrote to his parents while recuperating at Luna Park Hospital, Heliopolis, after being wounded at Gallipoli.

I am off back for another smack now. I suppose the Turks will stop me altogether this trip. I got a bullet through my cap, two shrapnel bullets in my rifle, one in my 48 hours iron rations on my back and the case of the shell nearly knocked my leg off below the knee. I used 200 rounds of ammunition before I was counted out; but I am prepared to have another fly at them. I came to push the bayonet and fight for my country and I am going to do it and chance getting knocked over. A man has only to die once. Tell Mr McFarlane to keep a few clay pigeons for me — that is if I have a chance to come back. If I can shoot Turks I think I can manage to shoot the clay pigeons. Remember me to all my friends in Leongatha and Leongatha South.[16]

The heavy toll of casualties encountered in the Gallipoli campaign called for a step-up in recruiting activities. Special meetings were called by Shire President Cr McDonald in 1915 to form committees to assist the Government in its recruiting drive. At Leongatha in July the Mechanics' Hall, suitably decorated with the Union Jack, the Australian flag and those of the allied nations, was filled with a capacity crowd of men and women. Patriotic numbers were played by an orchestra before the commencement of proceedings. Local member, the Hon. J.E. Mackey, MLA, spoke of the Government's task in ensuring a continuous supply of reinforcements and urged each municipality to contribute its share.

Mr E.L. Warriner, headmaster of the Leongatha State School, announced that all teachers were giving a percentage of their salaries to the patriotic fund, while Messrs Cole and Begg offered the use of their cars for patriotic work. Cr G.M. Black of Tarwin Meadows offered timber for the making of splints, crutches etc. for wounded soldiers. At the Leongatha Labour Colony five men had enlisted within a fortnight, making a total of nineteen from the Colony, and there were now only old men and 'physical rejects' left. Manager Mr Willoughby said that one man was rejected on account of two toes being defective, but after having these removed, he again presented himself and was accepted.[17]

At the end of August 1915 residents of Tarwin Lower were thrown into a state of confusion by the announcement that Cr G.M. Black had enlisted, together with ten of his staff from the dairy farming complex at the Meadows. After the death of Mr George Black, Senior, in 1902, his sons, Murray and Archibald, converted this rich property of some 2,000 acres from a beef producing enterprise into a series of eight share dairy farms. Homes were built for the share farmers, while milking sheds and piggeries were established on the sandy rises overlooking the extensive flats. Three miles of horse-drawn tramways were laid down so that milk could be hauled to a centrally situated cheese factory. Some was separated on the farms, and the skim milk was used in piggeries that were also served by the tramway. The cream was first sent to the nearby butter factory at Tarwin Lower, but later a full wagon load of cream was taken to the Tarwin Railway Station for despatch to the Leongatha Butter Factory. The dairy farms averaged 200 acres in size with herds of 120 cows that were hand milked by the share farmers and members of their families. Share farmers received eight shillings in the pound of butterfat proceeds together with a share of the returns from the pigs. Additional homes were built at the The Meadows for the manager, stockmen, blacksmith, butcher and general farm hands. A school and store with a post office agency were opened in 1913 to cater for the needs of the people engaged in this intensive farming operation.[18]

The news that Mr Black had enlisted and proposed to sell off his extensive dairy and pig herds caused dismay to many in the district. J.M. Peck and Sons who were handling the sale described it as 'Probably the most extensive sale of dairy stock ever held in Australia on one property'.[19] A public meeting was called by Cr Alex McDonald at the Meeniyan Mechanics' Institute, at which concern was expressed at the damage that would be done to the district by the closure of the enterprise. Cr McDonald said he believed that 1,000 of the cows to be sold would go to the Western District, and this would mean a big financial loss to the Leongatha Butter Factory.[20]

Butter factory managers estimated at the time that it took eighteen to twenty cows to ensure the production of one ton of butter annually. This figure varied with type and breed of cow, seasonal fluctuations etc., but the loss of 1,000 cows from a factory's intake would be reflected in a decline of at least fifty tons of butter annually. Up to 700 bacon pigs each year were also produced at The Meadows, and their loss would be detrimental to the operations of the Dandenong Bacon Factory. As a result of this meeting at Meeniyan, a deputation was appointed to wait on Mr Black and ask him to reconsider his decision in the light of the economic loss to the district, as well as the loss of eight or nine families from the area.

On Friday 17 September 1915, Mr G.M. Black accompanied by his Manager, Mr Hay McDowell, met the deputation at the Shire Hall at a meeting convened by Shire President Peter Johnson. Other members of the deputation were Crs Donald, McDonald and Henderson together with Messrs J.E. Lees, E.A. Cole and C. Moore representing district residents. Mr Black said he realised that, if he reverted to grazing, the property could be worked with two to three men compared with up to 100 on share dairies. For this reason and the economic loss to the district, he agreed to defer enlistment and continue with the dairying operation for at least another season. Mr Lees stated that as a representative of the Tarwin Lower residents, the War Fund and recruiting would be helped more by Mr Black remaining than by enlisting. Subscribers to patriotic funds

1. ATTACHING A WIRE ROPE TO PULL DOWN A TREE WITH BULLOCK TEAM.   2. A TREE PULLED DOWN.
MACHINE.   4. MACHINE FORMING UP THE ROAD.   ?. PORTION OF CLEARED ROAD READY FOR ROAD
ROAD-MAKING IN SOUTH GIPPSLAND   (Photographs by R. Evans).

Road-making in South Gippsland, Weekly Times, *17 November 1917.*

had immediately dropped their subscriptions when they heard the news that the share dairies were to be closed. Cr McDonald congratulated Mr Black on his decision which would be of great benefit to the district. 'His loyalty had been proved, and if the time did come that Mr Black's services were required he would not be found wanting'.[21]

Woorayl Shire councillors had other problems to contend with in the Tarwin Lower area even though it was one of the most fertile parts of the Shire. To enable construction of all-weather roads, large quantities of bluestone had to be hauled from Cuttriss's quarry further up the Inlet near Screw Creek. In 1910, at the instigation of Engineer Callaway, Council purchased the barge *Lizzie* from San Remo for the sum of £106, this amount being debited to the South Riding.[22] *Lizzie* did good service for several years, hauling the bluestone spalls from Cuttriss's quarry to the jetty at Tarwin Lower where they could be crushed for use on roadworks.

In September 1915, while anchored off Screw Creek, *Lizzie* was wrecked by an explosion which destroyed the stern portion. Constable Hehir from Inverloch called in detectives from Melbourne to investigate the matter. Black trackers were sent to the scene in an endeavour to find the culprits, but no clues were left. Newly-appointed Engineer Clifford Bate inspected *Lizzie* and 'found the stern badly damaged, most of the planks being forced completely away from the stern post. Extensive repairs are required to make her seaworthy. The damage appeared to be the result of an explosion'.[23] Bate was instructed to secure the services of a marine expert with a view to preparing an estimate of the cost of raising and repairing *Lizzie*. The demands being made on such personnel due to the war effort precluded any attention being given to *Lizzie*, and she slowly settled into the mud at Screw Creek.

Explosives, commonly used by farmers and road contractors to remove tree stumps, were readily available to all and freely advertised; for example:

> 'Rackarock' . . . Federal Brand . . . Clear your land with 'Rackarock.' The cheapest and Most Effective explosive for this purpose. Absolutely safe and non-explosive until mixed. Can be fired either by time fuse or electrically. 'Federal' Rackarock, Gelignite and other requisites for clearing timber, sub-soiling etc. as well as leaflets and full information can be obtained from The Leongatha and District Co-operative Society Ltd. Local agents.[24]

In all probability the destruction of *Lizzie* was caused by Rackarock purchased at the Co-op store and used by some misguided individual either as a lark or with malicious intent. Woorayl Shire Council was deprived of the use of its barge as a cheap means of transporting road-making material along the Inlet and was forced to use more expensive road transport. No attempts were made to refloat *Lizzie*, and at the June 1918 Council meeting Crs Henderson and Donald moved 'that the Engineer be instructed to collect at Pound Creek Jetty all material connected with the barge Lizzie with the object of having same disposed of by sale'.[25]

Rifle shooting maintained its popularity as a sport both indoors and outdoors. In the event of a bazaar or similar function, a rifle shoot was often included in the program of events. At Stony Creek a 'Gorgeous Japanese Fair' was held in July 1913 to raise funds for the hall committee. The Leongatha Brass Band was engaged for the opening night and Mr Eggington's String Band for other nights together with a variety of entertainments. Not everyone approved of such frivolities. Reverend Seamer of the Leongatha Branch of Social Reform Bureau chided the hall committee on their fund raising methods.

> It is said that a shooting gallery or some such device or game of skill or chance was used at the recent Japanese fair for the purpose of disposing of certain articles. So hurtful to the community is this method of disposing of goods that public opinion reflected by the law decrees that a first offence deserves a fine 'not exceeding two hundred pounds'. The penalty is only mentioned to prove how serious a moral wrong it is known to be by those who think.[26]

The Stony Creek Hall Committee was not too perturbed by having their wayward habits brought to the notice of the district at large by Reverend Seamer. A rather lengthy letter in reply appeared in *The Great Southern Star* a few weeks later pointing out that

> there are greater evils than the harmless church lottery calling for the daily attention of the clergy amongst the members and 'heathens' of our own community. If such attention were given to those evils there would be no time for newspaper controversy, and the clergy of every denomination would be kept busy casting out the beams, so as to clearly see the motes elsewhere. Yours etc . . . Another Jolly.[27]

The Leongatha Mechanics' Institute had constant requests for use of the Lodge room for indoor shooting activities but were refused permission by the Public Health Department for such use. In 1915 the application by the Woorayl War Fund for permission to erect a miniature rifle range in the grounds adjoining the Institute was immediately granted by the committee.[28] This miniature range proved immediately popular for young and old, being opened on Friday and Saturday evenings while a ladies' shoot was organised for Thursday evenings. In its first six weeks of operation over £4 was raised for the Woorayl War Fund after payment of initial expenses. Realising that the range could not continue indefinitely in such a prominent site in the township, application was made to the railway authorities for excision of a small strip of land granted to the bowling club on the Long Street boundary.[29] The bowling club made no objection to the excision, but the range continued in operation on the Mechanics' Institute site for some considerable time and did not utilise the ground made available on Long Street.

A special committee sponsored by the Woorayl War Fund arranged for wool, flannel and calico to be distributed from shops to all who were prepared to work. Cut out garments were distributed every Thursday from the Mechanics' hall. By December 1915 J.M. Molloy reported on the work done by the women of the Woorayl Shire in connection with the fund.

> 1596 pairs of sox, 288 scarves, 440 flannel shirts, 246 handkerchiefs, 23 cardigans, 100 underpants, 301 washers, 7 belts, 462 sheets, 1490 pillow slips, 14 pyjamas, 1157 bandages, 196 kit bags, 221 Hospital bags, 79 helmets, 121 cushions, cuffs, mittens etc. Total 6736.

A report sent in by Mr Sagar of the high school lists the work done by the

Stony Creek, Main Street, c. 1917 (from D. Helms).

Men's Red Cross club: 200 walking sticks, 50 deck chairs, 57 trays, 65 pairs of crutches, 50 bandage winders, 12 splints, 50 bed rests, 560 bed foot rests, 50 leg rests, 50 four fold bed screens and 100 bed cradles.

Meanwhile, the basic industry of farming in the Shire continued in different forms, one of which was apiculture. The Leongatha Apiary was established by Mr A. Salmon on a small area of vacant land at the entrance to the goods yard of the railway station in 1913. So successful was this apiary that Mr Salmon called a public meeting to form a large scale apiary to exploit 'the thousands of acres of nectar bearing pastures surrounding the little town of Leongatha'.[30] Although considerable interest was shown in the project, nothing eventuated, although bee-keeping continued to be conducted on a small scale within the Shire. One enthusiastic bee-keeper, Tarlton Rayment, was employed as a painter and signwriter with Mr McFarlane's blacksmith and coach-building business at Leongatha for several years. Rayment used his extensive knowledge of bees and their habits in the publication of various articles on the subject. During his stay in Leongatha, he married Clarice Begg, daughter of James Begg, one of the pioneers of the district. Rayment later achieved distinction as author of *The Valley of the Sky*, a novel based on the life of Angus McMillan, the Gippsland explorer.[31]

The creation of light horse regiments within the Australian Imperial Forces led to a strong demand for horses throughout the country. Periodically, buyers acting on behalf of the Government would visit Leongatha and Meeniyan in search of these animals. Advertisements such as appeared in *The Great Southern Star* of 4 February 1916 were common.

Joseph Clarke and Co. will have a Government buyer at Leongatha on the above date for Military Horses of the following descriptions —

Bee-keeper Tarlton Rayment making frames (from Woorayl Shire Historical Society).

Strong CAVALRY Horses
Gunners and Artillery Horses (Ages 5 to 12 years).
Persons having any of these classes of horses will have good offers made for suitable animals, as the Government are in need of them.
E.A. Cole, Local Rep.

The proliferation of rabbits from 1914 onwards led to the inauguration of another industry in the harvesting and processing of them. In February 1916 a freezing works was established at the Leongatha Butter Factory, where rabbits were purchased and stored before being railed to Melbourne for export to Europe. The numbers handled by this works were phenomenal when it is considered that these were only the rabbits that were trapped or ferreted. Within a month of opening, 2,000 rabbits a day were being handled, representing a cash return to trappers of £450 per week. In the first fifteen weeks of operation, the Leongatha freezing works handled 360,000 rabbits for export.[32] By July the total was estimated at half a million.

As a means of eradication, trapping was ineffective. When catches declined, the trappers moved further afield, leaving sufficient in the trapped area to regenerate within a year or two. Wire netting of boundary fences and then poisoning within was the only really satisfactory method of clearing farms of the pest. Demonstrations of poisoning by means of apples and strychnine were organised by government inspectors for the benefit of farmers. A plough furrow was made through the infected area, untreated baits were laid for two nights, and then on the third night, strychnine was added to the apples or carrots and used as bait. At Stony Creek Inspector A. Brown organised a trial demonstration on Mr C. Charlton's property in August 1916. On a paddock of fifty-seven acres upwards of 300 rabbits were poisoned even after the paddock had been trapped and shot over. Although some controversy arose over the question of birds being killed from the taking of baits, not one dead bird was found after this trial.[33]

Even though some financial return was obtained through the sale of rabbits and their skins, this was more than offset by the damage done to the major grazing industries. At the Leongatha Butter Factory output dropped from a total of 592 tons of butter in 1910-11 to 380 tons for the year 1914-15.[34] Although this decline was accentuated by the poor season of 1914-15, a major factor was the depredations of rabbits on pastures. Eight rabbits eat as much as one sheep, and if half a million rabbits were handled through the freezing works at Leongatha in the first six months of operation, the rabbit population of Woorayl Shire in 1915-1916 must have been counted in millions.

The effect of the war in Europe was becoming more and more evident in the daily life of the people at home. As the recruiting campaign was stepped up, passions were aroused that led to recriminations amongst former friends. In December 1915 a Military Court of Inquiry was conducted at the Leongatha Court House by Major T.P. McInerney concerning disloyal utterances by a local resident, A.A. Hitchiner. E.W. Johnson of Koonwarra alleged that Hitchiner, in the course of conversation during a card evening at Mr Prosser's house, said that 'the Germans were no worse than the others in warfare'. Upon hearing that Hitchiner intended to enlist, Johnson had contacted the military authorities thinking that Hitchiner would be a traitor if accepted by the Armed Forces. In evidence given before the Court, Hitchiner stated that both his parents were born in England and there was no German blood in him. He could not imagine why he was rejected and could not see that it was anything else than what was said at Prosser's. Solicitor Richard Little of Leongatha called witnesses on behalf of Hitchiner who had been a member of the Patriotic Committee at Koonwarra. After an adjournment of two weeks to study the evidence, Major McInerney stated that the Military Department would now place no obstacle in the way of Mr Hitchiner enlisting.

> Hitchiner impressed me as being a truthful man. E.W. Johnson and A.A. Hitchiner are of opposite parties in politics, and both Johnson and Hitchiner appear to have followers, and in a way they are rivals for leadership in little local movements. On the evidence I find that Alfred Hitchiner is neither disaffected nor disloyal.[35]

The establishment of a recruiting office at Leongatha at the end of 1915 resulted in a steady flow of men into the Armed Forces. A horse and vehicle were provided for the recruiting Sergeant in charge to travel around the district. Quotas were fixed by the Government with Woorayl Shire's being thirteen per month. Enlistments were published in the weekly issue of *The Great Southern Star*, and by the end of March 1916, 330 men had enlisted from Woorayl Shire.[36] The great majority were from farming backgrounds, educated at small one-teacher schools until the age of fourteen when they left to work on their parents' farms.

Several young men met their deaths before participating in the war. In June 1915 a young man named James Lamb of Hallston was carting his last load of rabbits to Leongatha to forward to Melbourne before enlisting. On passing a tree near the quarry on the property of Mr Alf Griggs, a limb fell across the dray, striking Lamb who was walking alongside on the head, killing him instantly. The body was taken to a nearby residence where an inquiry was conducted by Mr J. O'Bryan, JP, who recorded a verdict of accidental death.

Two enlisted men home on final leave, William Geddes and William McKay, were crossing Anderson's Inlet to Point Smythe with their uncle in a twenty foot boat with a load of timber when it overturned. All three were drowned and the bodies never recovered.[37]

At Tarwin Lower in November 1915 the three Emmerson brothers of Meeniyan set out in a boat for a day's fishing on the Inlet. A strong wind sprang up overturning the boat and throwing the boys into deep water. Two of the brothers, Arthur and Frank, were drowned, but after clinging to the boat for several hours, Ernest Emmerson managed to swim ashore near The Bluff. He arrived in an exhausted condition at Mr Black's property, Halewood, at 5.30 p.m. in the afternoon — ten hours after the fatality had occurred.[38]

As the reservoir of able-bodied men willing to enlist became depleted, renewed agitation took place for the introduction of conscription. The Federal Government arranged for a referendum to be taken on the issue in October 1916. The Leongatha Mechanics' Institute benefited to a minor degree from the campaign in that several meetings were held by proponents of both sides. The first in favour of conscription was held on 7 October 1916 at which a crowded

Leongatha Scouts with Reverend P.W. Robinson and Reverend H.J. Harvey, c. 1917.

gathering gave enthusiastic support to the speakers in favour of it. A week later the Hall was again crowded by supporters of both sides to hear the anti-conscriptionists state their case.

Senator Anstey was listed to address the meeting but was replaced at the last moment by Senator Blakey. It was 9.30 p.m. before the meeting got under way, with Senator Blakey receiving the full force of a cabbage on his head before completing his address. Many interruptions and interjections took place during the evening before the meeting eventually broke up in disorder — the conscriptionist element preventing the anti-conscriptionists from presenting their case publicly.[39] Further meetings were held throughout the Shire by the Conscription Committee, including an open-air one at the cross-roads at Allambee. The anti-conscriptionists booked the Mechanics' Hall at Leongatha for 26 October for another meeting and managed to present their side of the argument without any major disruptions. Whether by accident or design, the electric light failed during the meeting plunging the hall into darkness. Fortunately, someone produced candles and lamps that enabled the meeting to continue.

So confident was the Government that the referendum would be carried that a proclamation was issued calling on all young men between the ages of twenty-one and thirty-five years to present themselves for medical examination. On 10 October 1916 there were 208 men in attendance at the Leongatha Hall where they were examined by Drs Wood, Molloy and Green. Of the total number, only a third, 72, were passed as fit, 56 were doubtful and 80 unfit.[40] Over 100 applications were made for exemption, and these were heard before the Police Magistrate, Mr Cohen, on 25 and 26 October. All men passed as fit were asked why they did not enlist, although exemptions were automatically granted to married men and unmarried only sons. Many claimed exemption due to the heavy farm work being too much for their parents. The military officer in attendance stated that 'eighty percent of exemptions applied for in Gippsland the reason is given that the father is a cripple'.[41]

Mr Cohen was very strict and only granted exemptions in exceptional circumstances, such as J.A. O'Loughlin who had two brothers at the front and to A.L. Sherry, a grader and tester at the local butter factory. Manager S.C. Wilson appeared on behalf of Sherry and stated that he had tried unsuccessfully to get a man to take his place, and even then it would take six months to train a substitute.

As a result of the defeat of the conscription referendum at the end of October, the Government was forced to release those men who had been drafted into the Armed Forces against their wishes. Although the overall result of the referendum ended in a victory for the anti-conscriptionists, the figures for the Leongatha sub-division showed a two to one majority in favour of conscription.[42]

Electors enrolled			Yes	No	Informal	Total
Male	Female	Total				
1253	993	2,246	1,058	489	24	1,571

While men were still being despatched overseas as reinforcements, others were arriving back from the war wounded or sick. By 1916 the question of preference

Stone crusher, Simon's Lane, Leongatha, c. 1920 (from D. Bacon).

to returned men had arisen in different spheres. When the committee of the Mechanics' Institute advertised for a billiard marker for their room in 1916 on a salary of 45s a week, there were thirty applicants for the position which was advertised in the Melbourne daily papers. One applicant claimed to have lost £2,000 in a bank and had been privileged with 'a coledge scooling'. The committee decided to give preference to returned soldiers and appointed Mr T. Rayne to the position.[43]

Even with the absence of so many young men from the district, no difficulty was experienced in gathering a crowd of spectators for an exhibition of billiards staged in August of that year. Clark McConachy, New Zealand champion, demonstrated his prowess against two of the local champions, Hugh McLennan of Fairbank and W. Stanton of Mirboo. After giving McLennan 450 start, McConachy scored 750 to McLennan's 604 even though McLennan played in his usual fine style. Stanton played a good game but could not match the champion who made 200 off the red in 13 minutes. McConachy's command over the balls was 'an eye-opener to the majority of onlookers who followed every movement of the champion with great interest'.[44]

The Mechanics' Institute Committee had a difficult decision to make regarding preference to returned men when it came to a lease of the hall for picture purposes. The hall had been let on a weekly basis to Mr Hayes, proprietor of Lux Picture Co., who was over the military age himself and had one son at the front. In 1916 the Institute received an application from Messrs Makeham and Witton of Korumburra, both returned men, for permission to use the hall for the showing of pictures. Although the committee knew the Lux Co. was running at a loss through depleted audiences, they were forced to lease the hall to Makeham and Witton on a similar basis. Leongatha residents then had two picture shows weekly for a period of twelve months, until Messrs Makeham and Witton decided to withdraw from the district.[45]

Woorayl Shire Council, fortunately, did not encounter any problems with preferential employment when they advertised the position of lamplighter at Inverloch. Three acetylene street lamps had been erected for the benefit of residents following requests from the progress association. G.F. Michael, Shire Secretary, called tenders for lighting of these three lights on a monthly basis in August 1916.[46] George Michael had virtually run the Shire offices single-handed since his appointment in October 1900. As no typewriter was owned by Council, Michael dealt with all correspondence using pen and ink in a very fluent and readable longhand. Until 1913 no telephone was connected to the Shire offices, and it was not until 1918 that Council decided to connect this amenity to the homes of the Shire Secretary and Engineer.[47]

During 1916 a Queen Carnival was held at Leongatha to raise funds for patriotic purposes. Committees associated with each Queen worked hard in the running of concerts, entertainments, sale of goods etc. on behalf of their candidate. The grand finale took place at the Recreation Reserve on 27 October, at which a large crowd rivalling that of the annual Show was present. The Victorian Police Band was in attendance, a boxing tournament was conducted while a buckjumping contest was held on the arena after the finish of the high school sports. Numerous stalls sold everything from dairy produce,

The Herbert and McDonald families of Meeniyan travelling to East Gippsland on holidays in 1917 (from F. Mackie).

Riverview Hotel, Tarwin Lower, c. 1914 (from D. Bacon).

dressed lamb, poultry to home cooked cakes, wearing apparel and ornaments. In the evening a concert was held in the Mechanics' Hall at which the crowning of the winning Queen took place. Final results were

Scotland (Miss McIndoe)	96,144 votes	400 pounds 12s	
England (Mrs Gwyther)	72,804 ,,	303 ,,	7s 2d
Australia (Miss Griffiths)	59,606 ,,	248 ,,	7s
Ireland (Miss N. Hogan)	33,588 ,,	139 ,,	19s 4d

Secretary of the Scots Queen was Mr J.C. Campbell; the English, Miss Ethel Prideaux; the Australian, Mrs Mesley and Mr W.R. Moyle, and the Irish, Mr J.P. O'Toole.[48]

The Scottish influence on the district was particularly strong during the period up to and including the 1914-18 War. The Caledonian Society held their annual 'Hielan Gatherin' at the Recreation Reserve at which the skirl of bagpipes brought back memories of their homeland and the heather. Old friendships were renewed often with the aid of a little spirits. Chief of the society for several years during the war was blacksmith Jock Campbell who would forget his business rivalry with fellow Scotsmen, Ted Munro and James McFarlane, in the enjoyment of the music and the traditional Scottish dancing and games. At the 1917 meeting of the society held for the benefit of War Relief Funds, pipe bands from South and Port Melbourne took part at the daytime activities, and a grand Scottish concert was held in the Mechanics' Hall in the evening.

Functions were held in other parts of the Shire for the benefit of the War Relief Fund. At Tarwin Lower a garden fete and jumble fair was held at the home of Mr Murray Black on The Meadows in December 1916 and opened by local member Hon. J.E. Mackey, MLA. The Wonthaggi State Coal Mine Band was procured for the occasion, and a concert party from Leongatha added variety to the program. Tarwin Lower residents needed a fete and concert party to revive their spirits after the destruction of the Riverview Hotel by fire five weeks earlier on 9 November. One of Black's employees, Alfred Miles, had been charged with having 'wilfully and maliciously set fire to the Riverview Hotel, the property of Michael Healy on 9 November'.[49] After trial at the Supreme Court, Melbourne, in December before a jury, Miles was acquitted of the charge. Healy lost no time in recommencing business at Riverview. He arranged for a thirteen-roomed building from Bright in north-eastern Victoria to be dismantled and railed to the Tarwin Railway Station. It was then hauled to Tarwin Lower by bullock wagon and re-erected on the site of the former premises.[50]

Recruiting continued throughout 1917, but as numbers were declining, the Federal Government decided to proceed with another referendum to introduce conscription. No effort was spared to ensure a 'Yes' vote, and a similar pattern of meetings for and against the proposal took place throughout the country. When the vote was taken on 20 December 1917, the 'No' vote again recorded a majority with figures for the Leongatha sub-division being practically identical to that of 1916 with 987 in favour and 489 against.[51]

With the periodic return of injured and sick soldiers from the war, the question of a war memorial to the members of the Armed Forces was soon under discussion. Several schemes were suggested, but the one finally adopted was that put forward by Mr W. Watson of planting an avenue of trees along Roughead Street and then between the butter factory and the Labour Colony. When a working-bee was arranged for 22 June 1918, over 200 people attended with spades, shovels, hammers etc. to plant trees and erect guards.[52] All callings were represented, with farmers, contractors, business and professional men participating. The Hon. J.E. Mackey, MLA, was present and displayed a keen interest in the proceedings. The ladies of the town and district arranged refreshments under the verandah of the butter factory, and at a blast of the factory whistle, all adjourned to this area. Mr R. de C. Shaw, Chairman of the Tree Planting Committee, welcomed Mr Mackey who gave a stirring address, paying tribute to the soldiers who had gone abroad to fight for the British Empire. Mr Mackey was then asked to plant the first of the 170 trees that had been obtained from Moss Vale nursery. Mr Mackey said he hoped that within a year they would be able to meet and celebrate peace, and that each soldier would be able to return and say this is 'My' tree. Similar tree plantings in honour of enlisted soldiers were undertaken at Wooreen and at Meeniyan in August.[53]

During October 1918 an armoured tank was brought to the district by goods train and paraded through the streets of Leongatha, much to the delight of the school children who romped all over it. Cr Alex McDonald welcomed the War Loan representatives who accompanied the tank on its journey throughout the State. Lieutenant Pickett, who was in charge of the tank, congratulated Cr McDonald on the £1,200 raised at Meeniyan which he said was an excellent result for 'a one horse town', especially as the people had only one hour's notice of their arrival.[54] Lieutenant Pickett hoped that the full quota of £31,000 would be raised in Leongatha before the tank left so that an honour flag could be raised. The following day the tank was taken to the high school in the morning and then to the sale yards in the afternoon, where a direct appeal for subscriptions to the War Loan was made to farmers. Another appeal was made in the streets in the afternoon resulting in the sum of £26,790 being raised, a record amount for the trip.[55]

A little over a month later, the same streets of Leongatha were thronged with crowds celebrating the end of hostilities on 11 November 1918. On Friday 15 November the streets were decorated with flags and bunting from every vantage point. All business houses closed for the day so that staff could take part in the festivities. A procession started from Ogilvy Street at the Catholic Church corner where scholars from the State, convent and high schools assembled. Sergeant Wells, 'on a sprightly steed', led the procession which comprised returned soldiers, the town band, members of the fire brigade and the general public. At the town hall the Shire President, Cr A.J. Hall, addressed the gathering and expressed the hope that all would soon be able to welcome back 'those who had left their native land and covered themselves with glory'. He also made special reference to the work done by the womenfolk of the Shire in connection with the war effort. In the evening a special thanksgiving service was held in the Mechanics' Hall where Archdeacon Harvey presided, and appropriate hymns were sung by the combined church choirs.[56]

At Meeniyan a public holiday was celebrated with business closing for the day

Armoured tank, Whitelaw Street, Meeniyan, during War Loan Appeal, October 1918 (from F. Mackie).

Anzac Day, Leongatha, 1919 (from D. Bacon).

and the children being granted a holiday. Headteacher Mr Doubleday marched his pupils down to the station where the National Anthem was sung as the morning train from Melbourne came in, and this was repeated on the arrival of the afternoon train. The populace assembled at the Mechanics' Hall with Cr L. Donald, JP, in the Chair. Addresses were given by Messrs T.A. Welsford, W. Freeman, W.J. Farrell, William Doubleday and Reverend Sortell with refreshments being distributed to the children.[57]

Extracts taken from the composition book of Alex Le Maitre, born 1895, signaller in the 22nd Battalion. Served at Gallipoli and was killed in action 4 August 1916 Pozieres, France.

In November 1916 Alex Le Maitre's parents, Mr and Mrs P. Le Maitre, received the following letter from their son's unit signed by Lt L. McCartin, Sergt S.W. Wicks and fourteen privates.

As comrades and brother signallers of your son Alex, we have to tender you and family our sincerest condolences in your bereavement. It was in the recent severe fighting at Pozieres that Alex was struck by a piece of shell and killed instantly. He was in charge at the time, on 4 August. We who are left feel his loss very much, especially as he had only recently got his first step in promotion.[58]

12. RECOVERY

One of the organisations least affected by the 1914-18 War was the Leongatha Agricultural and Pastoral Society. The annual Show in February continued to be a major event in the township drawing the greatest crowds for any one day. A difference of opinion arose amongst committee members in 1918 about whether the next Show should be 'dry' or 'wet'. At the September meeting of the society, E. Begg moved 'that Leongatha should follow the example of the Royal Show and ban intoxicating liquor'. He was prepared to donate a guinea if no publican's booth were allowed. William Russell supported the motion saying that they 'wanted a class of men to breed a physically sound generation for the next war'.[1] A. Mesley said that drinking to excess was a decided evil. On some afternoons a dozen or so men could be seen in Leongatha streets affected by drink. G.H. Brown opposed the motion and instanced the local Caledonian Society which had decided to have a 'dry' sports, and someone had brought along a thirty-six gallon barrel in a buggy. John Eccles said if they stopped a man from taking a glass of ale, they should stop others from having a cup of tea, which was worse than a glass of ale for a man. Voting on the motion was sixteen to seven in favour of a 'dry' Show for February 1919.

Tickets were sold over the summer months in anticipation of a 'dry' Show, and after the cessation of hostilities in November 1918, committee members worked with a will to make the peace-time Show of 1919 a huge success. But the tide of events swept over the Agricultural and Pastoral Society along with the rest of the community, and all the plans for the first peace-time Show came to naught. The arrival of transports from the war theatre of Europe with discharged soldiers brought about an outbreak of pneumonic influenza in Victoria, resulting in 600 cases being reported with 30 deaths occurring by the end of January 1919.[2]

The Government of the day closed all military camps and introduced other measures to combat the flu and minimise its impact on the populace. General vaccination was introduced together with strict isolation of infected patients. Many sporting events were abandoned and places of amusement closed. At Leongatha the Show, the race meeting, the Presbyterian sale of gifts and weekly

Fairbank, S.S. 3171, 1919 (from W. Ryan).

Meeniyan State School, 1920. French Consul presenting a flag to head girl Mary Neish in appreciation of aid given by Meeniyan residents during the war (from F. Mackie).

Lux pictures were cancelled. Special regulations applied to Church services, and the community was advised to avoid crowds if possible. The billiard room at the Mechanics' Institute was closed for a time, but after representations were made to Health Officer, Dr Wood, it was re-opened on condition that all windows were left open and attendance limited to twelve. Strict quarantine provisions were introduced, and all cases had to be reported to the Shire Secretary. A committee under Dr Wood arranged for each section of the town to be patrolled to ensure those provisions were carried out. The re-opening of the schools was delayed, and the Leongatha High School was converted into a ten-bed, temporary hospital. The telephone was immediately connected to the school, and two nurses arrived to deal with any outbreak. Fortunately, these precautions together with an extensive program of vaccination prevented a general outbreak in Woorayl Shire.

Other areas were not so fortunate. At Wonthaggi in the first week of March 1919, there were nineteen patients in the temporary hospital set up in the Town Hall; twenty-one in isolation tents and at least thirty patients who should have been in hospital but were unable to be admitted.[3] When schools were re-opened on 10 March, the worst of the outbreak had passed, although isolated cases continued to occur in the district, sometimes resulting in death. A young returned soldier, Douglas Curnick, after spending four years overseas with the AIF, died as a result of pneumonic flu. Nursed privately at the home of Frank Lester of Koorooman, he received every attention from Dr Horace Pern who made fifteen visits to his bedside during the course of his short illness.[4] Dr Pern stated that had a hospital been set up in the town, he would have sent Curnick there. Health Officer Dr Wood considered it was better to nurse patients in their own homes and approved of payment to Voluntary Aid Detachment helpers to assist in this work. By July Dr Wood reported that there had been seventy cases of influenza in the Shire with only two deaths.

During the flu epidemic 'Welcome Home' concerts and celebrations for the returned men were suspended, but on the first Sunday in July, a large crowd attended a thanksgiving service in the Mechanics' Hall. Shire President, Cr Hall, Archdeacon Harvey, Reverend P.C. Lusted and Reverend R. Whitford were in attendance when the Peace Proclamation was read at 3.30 p.m. On Saturday 19 July a procession, led by Major Pern as Marshall, which included the town band, cadets, returned soldiers and school children, passed along Ogilvy and Bair Streets and assembled in front of the Mechanics' Hall for Peace Day celebrations. Road contractor McGuinness had stationed a pile driving derrick outside the hall which was suitably decorated with flags, bunting and gum leaves. Arthur Mesley read a special oration written by official war historian, C.E.W. Bean, while a distribution of medals and sweets was made to the children. A Grand Peace Night Concert was held in the evening at which the combined Church choirs and orchestra rendered 'Hallelujah Chorus' and 'The Heavens are Telling' interspersed with patriotic songs by leading amateurs.[5]

The Government of the day introduced a scheme of land settlement to provide employment for returned soldiers and make better use of large estates that were not being worked to maximum efficiency. The Leongatha Labour Colony was closed in 1919 after twenty-five years of operation and sub-divided into four dairy farms of up to 100 acres each and one orchard block fronting the

Coalition Creek of 25 acres. At a two day clearing sale held on the Colony on 29 and 30 April, all the buildings with the exception of the Manager's residence and dairyman's cottage were sold for removal. Over 2,000 people attended the clearing sale which was the largest from the point of view of numbers attending ever held in the district. The Manager of the Colony for the past decade, J.M. Willoughby, had built up the Colony's reputation by reason of good farming practices, and the stock and plant sold exceptionally well.

One of the first properties to be purchased for group settlement by soldiers was the Mt Vernon Estate fronting Berry's Creek, originally selected by William McPherson. The sub-division into suitable blocks was contingent on the provision of access roads. The Soldier Settlement Commission wanted the Country Roads Board to provide these roads, while the CRB passed the responsibility on to local Councils. In the meantime, considerable hardship was caused to the returned men by their inability to gain access to their blocks. At Mt Vernon the absence of sub-divisional roads meant that some soldiers had to camp in tents and sledge the building materials for their homes to the required site before building could commence.

When this estate was sub-divided into twelve blocks, the local repatriation committee did not receive a plan of sub-division until after the blocks had been allocated. This caused a certain amount of dissatisfaction, particularly as only three of the twelve men were from the Woorayl Shire. When Gunnersen's Hollyside Estate on the Wilkur Creek was sub-divided by the Commission in November 1920 into five blocks, applications were received from ex-soldiers from all over Victoria. This time none of these blocks went to local applicants. At a meeting convened by Shire President, Cr A. McDonald, in December 1920, it was pointed out that there were farmers' sons in the city anxious to obtain land in the district in which they had been born and reared. It was claimed that insufficient land was being purchased to cater for the large number of ex-soldiers desirous of going on the land. A deputation was arranged to wait on the Minister and explain the situation regarding the treatment of local applicants in the allocation of blocks. Other large properties were purchased around the Leongatha district by the Soldier Settlement Commission during the next few years. At Leongatha South, Martin's Springdale Estate, originally taken up by James Nation, was acquired in 1921 and sub-divided into eight blocks. A local repatriation committee assisted in the allocation which resulted in two of the eight blocks going to local ex-soldiers, Messrs L.T. Gwyther and R.T. Maddern. The Boorool Estate at Mardan of 2,221 acres, originally selected by Robert Smith in 1878, was purchased in 1924 and sub-divided into 22 soldier settlement blocks. The following year Floraston of 841 acres, which overlooked Anderson's Inlet and was formerly the property of Peter Shingler, was acquired and sub-divided into five blocks.[6]

Within a few years many of these settlers were in dire financial straits. The collapse of the London butter market in 1921 led to a substantial drop in returns to dairy farmers in 1922. Chairman of Directors of the Leongatha factory, Robert Watson, at the annual meeting of shareholders in September 1922, reported a record production of 583 tons for the year ending June 1921, an increase on the previous year of 156 tons.[7] Mr Watson said that usually two-thirds of the total production was consumed in Australia, but as a result of

Picnic at Koonwarra, c. 1920 (from L. Johnson).

increased production, this proportion had fallen to half. The depressed export market resulted in returns to farmers of one shilling per pound, less than half that obtained the previous season.

Many soldier settlers who had purchased stock at high prices in expectation of good returns had great difficulty in meeting repayments. As a result of pressure from returned soldier associations, a Royal Commission was established by the Government in 1925 to investigate the complaints of the soldier settlers. Evidence was presented to a sitting of the Royal Commission in the Victory Hall, Leongatha, on 23 April 1925 by soldier settlers outlining their difficulties. Edward Roy Harding, a soldier settler on the Labour Colony, said that the average income from dairying for the last two years was £8 for each head of cattle. Arrears of fifteen settlers totalled £4,785, and nine had no personal capital to begin with and were in serious financial difficulties. A large percentage of the cows purchased by the settlers were other farmers' culls bought at high prices. Harding, speaking on behalf of the local association, called for a complete abolition of interest repayments and a general relaxation of terms. Following the report of this Commission, the Government revalued the blocks to allow for a decrease in land values and liberalised the terms of repayment for others. The re-classification came too late for many, as figures presented by the Returned Soldiers' League in 1927 showed that of the 11,991 returned soldiers who took up land under *The Australian Soldiers' Repatriation Acts* of 1920, 1921 and 1922, no less than 2,885 had abandoned or transferred their blocks.[8]

Many of the abandoned blocks were re-allotted to neighbouring settlers or to British migrants with a small amount of capital. Some of these were soon in financial trouble, and another Royal Commission was set up in 1931 to investigate their complaints. Two men who had taken up blocks on the Boorool Estate in 1925 gave evidence to the Commission of their experiences. Harold Thompson stated that

> He and a man who had taken an adjoining block had to sleep under sheets of galvanised iron while their wives slept in the only completed room of the house. The creek which had been represented to him as a permanent watercourse, dried up after the winter, and he had to cart water three miles. The grass also dried up and disappeared and as he could not provide feed for his stock he had to give up the block after eleven months. Nineteen cows, for which he had been charged £143, were then valued at £57 by the inspector who had bought them for him.[9]

A similar story was told by William McCarthy who took up another block on Boorool at the same time and eventually abandoned it as hopeless. He had 'not neglected his block and cows, and had not drunk to excess'. The Commission sat for four days at Leongatha in May 1931 and heard evidence from settlers from Koo-Wee-Rup, Poowong and Fish Creek, in addition to that presented from the Leongatha area. Mr J.A. McDonald, sworn valuer of Meeniyan, stated that 'some of the land at Boorool was worth £40 per acre and some not worth six. Only five men of the original 18 settlers were now on the estate and were only making a bare living'.[10] The financial straits experienced by many of the settlers on the Boorool Estate did not prevent them from running a ball in their new hall which had been shifted from Koorooman in 1930.

C. Hoult carting onions, Wooreen Road, c. 1924 (from D. Bacon).

Plain and Fancy Dress Ball . . . Prize for Best Lubra and Partner. Best Sustained
Character. Best Dressed Couple. Best Exhibition and Fancy Dancing. Belle of Ball
and Novelty Dances. Good Music, Splendid Supper. Gents 3s. Ladies 1s . . . A.W.
Palmer. Hon. Sec.[11]

In the 1920s very few farm families possessed motor vehicles. As trips to townships for shopping purposes were not frequent, the regular visits of a travelling
salesman were looked forward to by adults and children alike. Some specialised
in the one product. The Griffiths Tea salesman was a regular visitor in a horse-
drawn gig with the brand name painted in large letters across the back of the gig
seat. The Rawleighs man specialised in household and stock medicines. Professional piano tuners made regular calls on families that were known, or judged
to be, owners of pianos. Indian hawkers travelled in covered-in horse-drawn
vans fitted out as a drapery shop in which they slept at night. Overalls, trousers,
flannels, shirts, suits, razors and strops were standard stock for men and Indian
cotton, soaps, towels, sheets and blankets, together with frocks, skirts, blouses
and underwear for ladies. A special drawer containing ribbons, laces, perfume,
jewellery, hair clasps, combs etc. was brought in to the farm kitchen and
displayed before the admiring and inquisitive eyes of farm children.

Some hawkers carried a few fowls in a small cage slung under the axles of the
van. The birds were released for a run of an evening. At intervals one was
traded in part payment for a prime rooster that would be killed and eaten
according to ritual methods of food preparation. Johnny cakes were other
traditional hawker fare and a treat for children. Indian hawkers were renowned
as good judges of horseflesh and took a pride in their animals. They often led a
spare horse with them which was sold at a profit in the course of their travels.
Goolam Ali Khan, better known as 'Chunda', was a regular trader to homesteads in the Nerrena-Meeniyan district in the 1920s and the 1930s. Many are
the stories told of this much loved and respected caller and his useful and
interesting wares. Together with the swaggie and seasonal worker, these
salesmen brought colour and interest to lives that were often harsh and
monotonous in their daily routines.

While the Indian hawker broke the solitude of isolated farm families in the
early 1920s, a placename of the North American Indians was a common subject
of conversation in the Leongatha township at that time. In the United States
there is a lake called 'Chatauqua' by the American Indians. On the shores of
this lake a musical festival was held regularly that gradually developed in a
similar way to the Welsh Eisteddfod. Leading lecturers, orators and musical
artists took part in this annual event, and its influence gradually extended to
England, New Zealand and Australia. The Chatauqua program was basically
non-sectarian and non-partisan from a political viewpoint and aimed to promote the civic, educational and social advancement of the community. First
held in Australia in 1918, a series of four Chatauqua lectures arranged at the
Leongatha Mechanics' Hall in November 1921 attracted large audiences.
Leading musical artists were matched by gifted speakers on matters of topical
interest. Subjects included 'The Bolshevik Bubble', 'Corner Stones of
Character', 'Reconstruction through Anglo-Saxon Eyes — Different Problems
around the Colonies'. In 1923 a further series of Chatauqua lectures was held at

the Mechanics' Hall with such diverse subjects as 'The Oriental Pageant' by Julius Caesar Mayphee and 'The World and Ourselves' by Dr Frank Bohn being well received by the local populace.[12]

The return of the soldiers from overseas led to increased demands for building materials of all kinds throughout the State. Although timber was in plentiful supply, demand for bricks increased greatly in the period immediately after the war. The presence of good brick-making clay at Koonwarra had been known for many years, where Mr Thomas Buckingham had commenced operations with a small kiln. In 1921 the Leongatha Brick Co. was formed to develop the clay deposits on a commercial basis. Directors of the company were Messrs E.W. Johnson, F. Morris, E. Begg, R.J. Shaw and Tom Buckingham with J.W. Sutherland as Secretary. Seven acres of land were purchased from John Holt, an up-to-date brick-making plant installed and the company officially opened by retired government surveyor, John Lardner, on 14 January 1922.[13] Capacity of the plant was 50,000 bricks per week with the plant running eight hours a day for five days. Wood and coal were used to fire the bricks, and the average percentage of 'firsts'; that is, those suitable for external walls, was seventy-five percent. These bricks, although made at Koonwarra, had the imprint 'Leongatha' on them, and many were used in the construction of buildings in and around the district. Others were railed to stations up and down the Great Southern Railway line as far as Dandenong.

The first public building to be built of Leongatha bricks was the grandstand at the Leongatha Recreation Reserve which was erected in 1921. Money for this long-awaited amenity at the Reserve was raised by means of a King Carnival held during that year. Committees were appointed to support Kings of Commerce, Sport, Agriculture, Pastoral and Dairying. These committees ran a variety of functions during 1921 for raising funds; for example, at the Leongatha Show of 1921, the King of Commerce ran a baby creche.

> WANTED . . . 250 BABIES . . . to take care of on Show Day. Age no object. Those not claimed by 6 p.m. will be sold to defray expenses. Apply Baby Creche — in charge of Ladies of King of Commerce.[14]

The King of Sports Committee arranged for leading Victorian professional tennis players, G. Patterson, P. O'Hara Wood, I.D. McInnes and R.V. Thomas (SA) to visit Leongatha on 19 March 1921. Wood and Thomas were partners when they won the world championship at Wimbledon, and their presence attracted a large crowd of tennis enthusiasts from surrounding districts. Seating capacity of 400 was provided, and the prowess of the champions created a favourable impression on all present. Shire President, Cr A. McDonald, entertained the players in the evening at the Otago Hotel, while the committee arranging the function benefited by a profit of over £50. Raffles of a jinker, bullock, sewing machine and two ponies proved very popular and realised considerable sums. Gymkhanas, concerts, pony races and trotting events were conducted by the various committees, with the result that over £2,000 was raised during 1921 towards the cost of the proposed grandstand.

At the close of the Carnival on 18 May, the amounts raised by the different committees were:

Right: Goolam Ali Khan, hawker, 1930s (from Mrs Anderson).

Below: Boiler installation, Koonwarra Brickworks, 1921 (from L. Johnson).

King of Commerce (Mr E.F. McNamara)	738 pounds 7s 2d
King of Sport (Mr A. Simmons)	528 „ 8s 3d
King of Agriculture (Mr D. Spencer)	366 „ 8s 3d
King of Pastoral and Dairying (Mr K. Macdonald)	311 „ 18s [15]

By the end of the year, building of the grandstand had commenced. Bricks from the newly-opened Koonwarra brickworks were subject to a stringent government test before being used. Under this test bricks should absorb not more than 16 ozs of water when submerged for twenty-four hours. The Leongatha bricks when subjected to this test absorbed only 8½ ozs and were therefore used with confidence. The official opening of the stand took place at a gala sports meeting on 7 March 1922 and was performed by the Hon. J.E. Mackey, MLA. Mr T.E. Molloy, Architect, presented a gold brooch in the form of a trowel bordered with Australian pearls to Mrs E.F. McNamara, wife of the winning King, for her efforts during the Carnival period.

The brickworks at Koonwarra operated satisfactorily for a time but soon ran into financial difficulties. One of the directors, Mr Thomas Buckingham, left the company and commenced operations on his own behalf closer to Leongatha. His enterprise was short-lived, but the original company carried on until 1926. Director E.W. Johnson then announced that, although the quality of the bricks being produced was excellent, insufficient orders were being received to operate efficiently. Over £120 a week was being paid in wages when in full production, so the directors had decided to close down the works and sell the plant.[16]

The erection of such a fine grandstand enabled Leongatha to stage sporting fixtures in a manner that otherwise would not have been possible. The grandstand was filled to capacity on Saturday, 11 October 1924 when a football match was played between the local team and Association Premiers of that year, Footscray. The Association team and thirty-five supporters, including the Mayor of Footscray, Cr T.B. Drew, arrived by train on the Saturday morning and were given a civic welcome by Woorayl Shire Council at Sheehan's Commercial Hotel. Cr Drew thanked the Council for the welcome extended and said he was proud of the team, 'for they were gentlemen both on and off the field'. The match was played in the afternoon under rather adverse weather conditions. During the first half of the match, the visitors were slightly ahead of the locals, with the score at half-time being Footscray 4 goals 5 behinds to 3 goals 3 behinds. In the third quarter Leongatha played splendidly, with the scores at three-quarter time being Leongatha 5 goals 6 behinds to Footscray 4 goals 6 behinds. Drizzling rain made the ball very slippery, and the Footscray Captain, Con McCarthy, was heard to say to Alex Eason the rover, 'By God, Alex, we had better get a move on, these fellows are better footballers than we thought they were'.[17] The final quarter provided one of the most exciting finishes witnessed by district residents. Footscray extended themselves to the limit in an effort to reduce the lead gained by Leongatha but could only score behinds, and when the bell rang, the scores were Leongatha 6 goals 7 behinds (43 points) to Footscray 4 goals 14 behinds (38 points). Best players for Leongatha were Alex Crombie, the Larkin brothers, Cotter, Kerr, Parnell, Alp, Barnes, Hodgkiss, Brumley, Little and Hayes.[18]

During the 1920s three organisations represented the returned soldiers'

Leongatha golfers, c. 1928 (from Woorayl Shire Historical Society).

interests in the Woorayl Shire. These were the Returned Sailors', Soldiers', & Airmen's League of Australia, The Soldiers', Sailors' and Fathers' Association and the Repatriation Committee. All had the interests of the returned men at heart, but each had different priorities. Many suggestions as to an appropriate war memorial were canvassed, with the first tangible result being a planned memorial obelisk for the main street of Meeniyan. A special committee representing the Meeniyan-Stony Creek returned soldiers accepted a tender for construction of this monument in August 1922 at a sum of £360. The official unveiling took place on 1 May 1923 when guests included Sir John Mackey, MLA, Mr T. Patterson, Dr Pern of the Leongatha RSL, J.M. Molloy, Secretary of the local branch of the Soldier Settlement Board, and Cr John Eccles.

The Leongatha branch of the RSL was undecided as to what form their memorial should take. Initially, it was proposed to make additions and alterations to their clubrooms in Bair Street, but after calling tenders for these works in October 1920, this project was abandoned. At this time the committee of the Leongatha Mechanics' Institute broached plans for the erection of a new hall to replace the original one built in 1891. The Institute Committee envisaged selling the site of the existing hall and building a new one on the vacant corner of McCartin and Bruce Streets. Before the original site could be sold, a freehold title had to be obtained by the trustees from the Lands Department. When news of this proposal circulated through the town and district, there immediately developed a movement to oppose the change.

The Leongatha branch of the RSL dropped plans for the additions to their premises in Bair Street and offered to contribute £1,000 towards the erection of a new hall and offices, provided they could have permanent use of one section. In October 1923 Woorayl Shire Council, after long consideration, agreed to 'build a memorial hall and council chambers provided the public provide one third of the capital required and that the cost of the building be approved by this council'. Two months later in December, a circular was distributed throughout the Shire appealing for funds to build a new hall on the corner of McCartin and Bruce Streets. On Tuesday, 19 February 1924 at 1.40 a.m. fire broke out in one of the ante rooms of the Mechanics' Institute and quickly spread to the main hall and Shire offices. Fortunately, there was time to rescue all the Shire's books and documents, and a large iron safe was removed by chopping a hole in the wooden wall with axes.

The cement brick building adjoining was saved, although the wooden skylight caught fire repeatedly, and damage was done to the billiard tables by water. The Institute Committee immediately altered their plans to build a new hall on the McCartin-Bruce Streets corner, and at their March meeting a resolution was carried

> That the Mechanics' committee is prepared to hand over to the Woorayl Shire Council for the purpose of a memorial hall its contract for the purchase of land at the corner of Bruce and McCartin Streets, together with £300 in cash, and the allotments of land on which the old hall was built.[19]

Council business was being conducted in temporary offices in Bair Street by Secretary George Michael and his new assistant Annie Johnson, who had been appointed by Council in February 1921 to help with the secretarial work at a

Bringing in the sheaves, Koonwarra, 1919 (from D. Bacon).

salary of £109 4s 0d per annum.[20] Community functions such as concerts, dances, pictures etc. were held in the Victory Hall, a large wooden building in Bair Street opposite the Otago Hotel. This simple weatherboard structure was built by James Palmer in 1921 and used as a skating rink and for other recreational purposes but was totally inadequate for the needs of the growing district.

The urgent and immediate need for a new hall and Shire offices helped resolve the differences of opinion amongst the community. A competition for design of the new complex was initiated, the winning entry being from local architect, T.E. Molloy. Following the transfer of title from the Mechanics' Institute trustees, tenders were called for erection of the new hall and Council offices. In April 1925 the tender of R.V. Ritchie for the sum of £14,000 was accepted by Council for the project. Council instructed Secretary Michael to visit Melbourne with a view to obtaining a loan for this amount by the issue of debentures to be charged upon the security of the Municipal Fund.[21]

Good progress was made during 1925 with the construction of the buildings. A Carnival Committee was formed to raise money to augment the loan, and a public subscription list was opened that added £1,500 to the total. The official opening on 24 May 1926 was a gala day for the Shire. Cr D. Gibson, Shire President, said that

> It is a memorial that will be evidence to the sight and senses of future generations that their forerunners had gratitude in their hearts and recognised the courage of their men and the great sacrifices made for liberty and freedom during the years 1914-1918.[22]

The Great Southern Star brought out a special issue to mark the occasion on the following day. High quality paper was used to improve the standard of the photographs and to allow it to be kept as a memento of the opening of the Shire's most significant building. To celebrate the opening of the hall, a special ball was held. Present was Mrs Ilma Burchell, who still has vivid memories of the night.

> I was living at Mirboo North at the time. My husband Archie left early as he was playing in the band that provided the music for the opening night. The Tarwin river was across the road at Wightman's that evening but eventually we got through safely in the hire car that was bringing the rest of the party. It was a wonderful night and we returned to Mirboo North just at daylight.[23]

Woorayl Shire Council had the same problem choosing a suitable piano as did the Mechanics' Institute Committee of 1913 when it purchased the German Lipp. A sub-committee was formed and advice sought from music teacher Mr E. Eggington. After investigation, Eggington reported that he favoured the purchase of a German-made piano at £165 compared to an English one at £350. Councillors were in a quandary as they did not wish to offend the returned soldiers over the matter, and yet they wanted the best value for their money. Cr Hyland summed up the situation by saying that 'although the Germans were dogs, their pianos were the best'.[24] In the end the ties of blood and patriotism proved stronger than economic and musical considerations, and a British piano was purchased.

Six months after the opening of the Memorial Hall, residents of Leongatha South had the pleasure of attending a concert and dance to mark the opening of their new hall. The fifty foot by twenty-five foot wooden building right on the edge of the main Leongatha-Inverloch Road replaced an earlier hall destroyed by fire the previous summer. Cr K. Macdonald carried out the opening ceremony, while the music was supplied by Messrs Eggington, Hefford, D. Norton and Miss Eva Watson.

A third hall in the district was in the course of construction during 1926. Architect T.E. Molloy had been commissioned by Dean P.J. Coyne to build a large hall adjacent to St Laurence O'Toole's Church in Ogilvy Street. Opened in May 1927 by the newly-elected member for the district, Mr W.G. McKenzie, MLA, it marked the completion of a building program initiated by Dean Coyne when first appointed pastor in 1901. In that time he was instrumental in arranging for the erection of the presbytery in 1904, the new brick church in 1913, the renovation and opening of the school in 1914 and the opening of the convent in 1915.

New churches at Inverloch, Meeniyan and Fish Creek had all been built during his stay at Leongatha as parish priest. Popular amongst the parishioners and townspeople alike, Dean Coyne adhered to the sentiments expressed in the words of Father O'Flynn's song 'Why should the gaiety be left to the laity?'. He sometimes opened the annual Catholic ball by having a dance with one of the leading ladies of the parish. Regarded as the patriarch of the district, no one took exception to this minor transgression of canon law. 'The Dean', as he was widely known, was on very friendly terms with Health Officer Dr Francis Aldersley Wood. Each year at Christmas, these elderly gentlemen took it in turns to have dinner together so that their housekeepers could at least have every second Christmas day off. Publican Arthur Bair regularly sent around a bottle of top-shelf whisky with best wishes from The Otago to 'the two most eligible bachelors in Leongatha'.[25]

The resurgence of building activities after the 1914-18 War led to the experimentation in the use of new materials. The gradual introduction of reinforced concrete for use in major buildings such as bridges led to increased demand for blue metal, sand and cement. The quarry on Simon's Lane adjacent to the railway line, that had been operated by Rumpf since opening in the 1890s, was purchased in 1916 by Civil Engineer J.T. Knox. Knox greatly increased the output of crushed rock from this quarry which was used extensively by Woorayl and neighbouring Shire Councils for roadworks. After a trip to America in 1922, Knox sought to develop the use of concrete blocks for building purposes and thereby increase the demand for the bluestone aggregate produced at the quarry. Due to increased problems with water seepage at the Simon's Lane quarry, Knox purchased the massive bluestone outcrop at Nerrena known as 'Chalmers's Hill', so named after its original selector, David Chalmers from Ballarat.

Top left: Rear view of presbytery, Ogilvy Street, c. 1929 (from Woorayl Shire Historical Society). Centre left: IOR picnic, Inverloch, c. 1922 (from Woorayl Shire Historical Society). Bottom left: Knox's Rockhill Farm, 1977 (from Woorayl Shire Historical Society).

An adjoining property, Rockhill Farm, was also purchased from Mr M. Holloway, and here Mr Knox built an extensive dairying complex modelled on those which he had seen operating in America. Made from the cement blocks that Knox wished to popularise, it comprised two enclosed double-sided sheds parallel to each other capable of each holding 100 cows. Two large silos, seventy foot high and sixteen foot in diameter, for storage of ensilage together with an up-to-date milk processing plant were installed. Completed in 1926 at an overall cost of £16,000, the complex operated for over a decade, but the basic design was not suitable for Australian conditions at the time. Farms which employed labour found it increasingly difficult to operate profitably, and the majority of dairy farms that survived those rigorous years did so mainly by the use of unpaid family labour. The general consensus of opinion amongst farmers and officers of the Department of Agriculture favoured grassland farming with a minimum of bail feeding.

Nevertheless, the secondary aim of J.T. Knox of increasing the use of concrete block construction was slowly being achieved. In 1925 work was begun on a band rotunda at Leongatha on the railway reserve opposite the Court House. Designed by architect T.E. Molloy, concrete blocks made at Knox's works were used in the construction of this fine circular bandstand. Accommodation was provided for thirty bandsmen with a concert stage suitable for a choir of thirty. This addition to the town's civic amenities was officially opened in November 1926 by Cr H.J. Hyland, in the absence of the President Cr H. York, before a large gathering. In addition to the bandstand, Knox was also responsible for the construction of the cairn adjacent to the railway station. This was erected in 1927 by the Victorian Government as one of a series to commemorate Count Strzelecki's epic journey through the South and West Gippsland forest in 1840.

The year 1927 saw the end of the Leongatha and District Co-operative Society that had been started with such high hopes in 1911. The Co-op store was a prominent feature of the business scene at Leongatha until 2 April 1925 when the major portion of the premises at the corner of Roughead and Long Streets was destroyed by fire. The books of the society were salvaged from the fire which broke out at 8.05 on a Thursday morning. Suspicion fell on the Accountant, Charles Haigmair, as the safe was found open and the money missing. At the Leongatha Court on 30 July, G.A. Perry, Manager of the store, stated that Haigmair had charge of all books and monies belonging to the firm. He was to have left the firm on the day the fire occurred. Haigmair was charged with theft and committed for trial at the Supreme Court on 27 August, where he was sentenced to eighteen months jail. Judge Cussen said Haigmair seemed to be a man of exceptional ability, and he was unable to understand why he had committed the offences.[26] The society lost heavily through the fire and the defalcations of Haigmair. Although the store re-opened for a short time in rented premises in McCartin Street, it never recovered from the major financial setback of 1925. In November 1927 the society was wound up and the assets liquidated.

The Co-operative Society was not the only organisation to have its assets liquidated. The Leongatha Race Club, after several successful meetings on their new course on Brown's Road during the 1914-18 War, entered into a slow decline. The 1925 and 1926 annual meetings of the club were held at the

Leongatha High School students at Knox's Quarry, Simon's Lane, 1927 (from Woorayl Shire Historical Society).

Pakenham Racecourse of Bourke brothers, as it was found that there was little financial profit being made from meetings on the Leongatha course. At meetings of debenture holders in 1928 and 1929, it was finally decided to sell off the land on Brown's Road that had been used as a racecourse since 1915 and use the proceeds to indemnify the debenture holders.[27]

Amid the fluctuations experienced by business and sporting organisations, the steady growth and stability of the Leongatha Butter Factory proved a bastion to the district's economy. Under capable management, the service it provided in changing the farmer's raw material into a finished, saleable product with a cash return was often overlooked. The fortnightly cheques posted to the farmers by the butter factories operating within the Shire were the very life blood of the small service industries and shopkeepers in the towns. Since 1908 the Leongatha Butter Factory had supplied the town with electricity on a reliable and economic basis. With the inauguration of the Yallourn scheme in 1923, directors realised that this sideline to the company's activities was nearing its end. On being approached by the SEC, Woorayl Shire Council tentatively agreed to terminate its agreement with the butter factory and connect with the SEC grid.

There was some argument over the price at which the power would be supplied from the new scheme. A deputation consisting of councillors representing the Woorayl, Korumburra and Mirboo Shires was reported to have advised the Commission

> that unless the S.E.C. definitely state that the price for electricity will not be more than 10d for light, and 4d for power, they would stay as they were and have electricity supplied to them by the local butter factories.[28]

Councillors were not pleased when the SEC decided to locate the sub-station for the town on a corner of the Recreation Reserve. Minutes of the meeting of 17 March 1924 Council meeting record that

> Council strongly objects to the alienation of an area of the Leongatha Recreation Reserve by the Electricity Commission for purposes of erecting a sub station, as this area is urgently required for recreation purposes. Council offers no objection to an area being used further westerly.

The following month an engineer from the Electricity Commission visited the area, where he conferred with councillors and representatives of sporting groups in the township. The engineer was taken further along the reserve to a site eight chains from the Roughead Street corner, in the scrub portion of the Reserve, which he agreed to accept. Fortunately for the future residents of the township, this alienation of public land did not take place, as the Commission purchased another site at the junction of Horn and Turner Streets for its sub-station. During 1924 gangs of men erected new power lines in the township in readiness for Yallourn power, which formally replaced that of the Leongatha Butter Factory on 15 February 1925.[29]

The site originally chosen by the Electricity Commission on the Reserve at the corner of Roughead and Turner Streets was granted by the trustees to the Leongatha Tennis Club, which laid out new courts during 1928-29 to replace those adjacent to the railway station that had been in use since 1900. At the same time as these new tennis courts were being built, a croquet club was formed with Mrs A. Mesley as President and arranged for levelling and sowing down of a suitable lawn next to the tennis courts. Much of the preparatory work was done by road contractor James McGuiness at minimal cost, and lawns were

SEC pole lifting gang, Leongatha, 1924 (from P. Alford).

officially opened in December 1930 by Cr D.D. Gibson.[30] The club house, erected in conjunction with the golf club, was used for the first time, and the croquet club soon became a favoured spot for the ladies of the district.

The trustees of the Recreation Reserve were finding it impossible to finance improvements to the ground or make any impression on the outstanding debt caused by the erection of the brick grandstand. Accordingly, an approach was made to the trustees of the Show Yards Reserve requesting them to assume control of the whole ground and thereby accept responsibility for the outstanding debt. This action was endorsed at a public meeting called by the Shire President on 22 October 1931. The Minister for Lands initially refused the request, as the proposal would have given the Agricultural and Pastoral Society, through their trustees, sole control over both reserves to the exclusion of the general public.

Following an inquiry conducted by the Local Land Board at Leongatha on 23 August 1932, it was finally agreed by all representatives of sporting bodies and the Agricultural and Pastoral Society that the two reserves be amalgamated and controlled by a committee comprising:

Shire of Woorayl	1 member (to be Chairman)
Agricultural and Pastoral Society	3 ,,
Golf club	1 ,,
Tennis and croquet clubs	1 ,,
Cricket and football clubs	1 ,,

Regulations to give effect to the amalgamation were drawn up and published in the Government *Gazette* of 26 October 1932, while regulations as to its use were drawn up and published in the *Gazette* of 17 May 1933.[31]

Stony Creek Butter Factory, c. 1927 (from W. Helms).

Tarwin Lower football team, 1928 (from F. Mackie).

The steady growth of Leongatha during the 1920s brought about demand for other services besides sporting facilities. Health Officer Dr Wood was constantly reminding Council of the necessity for improved drainage, not only at Leongatha but also at Meeniyan and Inverloch. An outbreak of typhoid at Meeniyan in March 1920, when five cases had to be sent off to Melbourne hospitals, led to Dr Wood closing a large boarding house in that town. A pall of gloom was cast over Meeniyan a fortnight later when it was learnt that Mr H.D. Mackay, the popular manager of the National Bank and one of the five cases sent to Melbourne, had died as a result of typhoid. Mackay had been Secretary of the Bush Nursing Association and a prominent member of the Presbyterian Church. His death emphasised the warnings that were repeatedly being given by the Health Officer. Despite these occasional outbreaks of infectious diseases, the health of Woorayl Shire residents was remarkably good. Dr Wood read with pleasure a report that appeared in the Melbourne *Herald* of March 1924 concerning the health of police recruits from country districts.

> Gippsland raises the best type of policeman from a physical standpoint. That is the opinion of the doctor who is travelling throughout the state examining recruits for the force. He says the climate is the main factor in Gippsland's record. At Echuca the first 13 were rejected whereas at Leongatha (Sth Gipps.) the first 20 were selected.[32]

Another aspect that was constantly being urged on Council by Dr Wood was the provision of a morgue in the township. As Health Officer he had to issue death certificates and sometimes undertake post mortems in whatever premises were available. This usually took place in a back room of the Otago Hotel at Leongatha. At Meeniyan, as a result of a car accident in 1926, the body of a sixteen-year-old boy from a well-known family was held in the local police cells until an inquest could be held.[33] Council eventually obtained permission from the Crown Lands Department in September 1926 to erect a small building at the rear of the Court House that could be used as a morgue and ambulance station on payment of a rental of £1 per annum.

Dr Wood's tenth annual report to Council in February 1929 gave him a sense of satisfaction. The list of infectious diseases was remarkably low with diphtheria and scarlet fever being almost absent; for example, scarlet fever 2 cases, no deaths; tuberculosis 1 case, 1 death; diphtheria, 1 case, no deaths, acute poliomyelitis 2 cases, no deaths. Births totalled 99, with 54 males and 45 females. Fifteen males died and 10 females. Approximate population of the Shire was 6,300; the birth rate was 15.7814 per thousand; the death rate 3.968 per thousand; the infant mortality rate 0.47 per thousand.[34]

Nevertheless, there were some who were not satisfied even with these exemplary figures. Six months after their publication, a meeting was called in Leongatha to discuss the formation of a baby health centre. Dr Wood and his fellow medical officer, Dr Horace Pern, were not impressed with the necessity of such new-fangled schemes encroaching on their domain. They immediately used their literary skills to ensure that the proposed baby health centre be strangled at birth.

> We wish to point out that in this district we have the fittest and most beautiful babies in the world; that they are wonderfully free from infantile troubles. The infantile mortality rate during the last four years has been less than 1 per 1,000 of population. We both treat our maternity cases during their ante natal period free of charge. We watch them, and if need be, treat them. We do our midwifery in private hospitals, under ideal conditions. The mothers and babies are well looked after; the mothers are taught how to bring up their babies and how to feed them. Most of the babies, we are glad to say, are brought up on the food the Almighty ordained that they should have. If the babies are not thriving they are brought either to the sisters at the hospitals or to us.
>
> The whole state of affairs is highly satisfactory. We point out that we have given our whole lives to our work, and we are more competent to meet the requirements of both mother and baby than a nurse. Baby Health Centres are undoubtedly of value in large centres where mothers cannot get the same care, and do not understand the value of the different foods, and are unable, in a good many cases, to obtain these in sufficient amounts. In this district where food of all sorts is abundant, we state definitely, in our judgment the formation of a Baby Health Centre is quite unnecessary. We are absolutely adverse to it, and do not intend to give it any support. Yours etc.,
>
> F. Aldersley Wood,
> Horace Pern.   9 Sept 1929.[35]

In a small town like Leongatha, such a blast coming from the two local and highly esteemed doctors was more than enough to quench the ardour of any zealots for some considerable time. It was not until the passage of time had brought new conditions and a new doctor to the town that a baby health centre could be formed.

Dr F.A. Wood was born in Cawthorn, Yorkshire, England, but went to Leipzig, Germany, at eleven years of age to study music. In 1889 he emigrated to Victoria with his sister, Edith, and brother, Ernest Wood, who was brought to

Melbourne from Lincoln Cathedral to occupy the position of organist and organiser of the choral work of St Paul's Cathedral, Melbourne. After graduating with honors at Melbourne University, Dr Wood was appointed resident doctor at the Royal Melbourne Hospital and then practised at Cressy before coming to Leongatha in 1916. Having been reared in the atmosphere of the Church, he expressed to a marked degree the characteristics of a Christian gentleman. The author can recall words spoken to his mother by Dr Wood in his distinct Yorkshire accent: 'Mrs Murphy, if I were paid for half of my work I would be a wealthy man'. He was not a wealthy man but gave generously to a variety of causes, living in a simple weatherboard house in Long Street near the railway station. Unmarried, he kept a housekeeper, and not being able to master the intricacies of motor vehicles, he employed a chauffeur to drive him about the district when visiting patients. After minor operations, such as the removal of tonsils, it was the task of the chauffeur to return patients to their respective homes with no charge being made for this service.

Dr Horace Pern was also born in England, coming to Australia in 1902. His father, Dr Alfred Pern, of Botley, near Southampton, married twice, and each of his wives had seven children. The first seven sons all became doctors, and after spending some time in South Africa, Dr Horace Pern came to Australia where he practised at Smythesdale. He was the first man to purchase a motor vehicle in that township before the 1914-18 War. One day the local parson was walking past the stationary car and saw a pair of legs protruding from underneath it. On hearing a string of blasphemous oaths, the parson said, 'I am sorry to hear you swearing like that'. Pern said, 'Buy a bloody car and you will become a willing learner!'.[36]

After serving with the AIF at Gallipoli and other theatres of war, Horce Pern commenced practice at Leongatha in 1918 where he played a leading role in the RSL. Having witnessed the trauma of the battlefield, he was most considerate in the treatment of these returned men and always stressed that allowances should be made for them as a result of their war experiences. During his stay at Leongatha, Dr Pern made a careful study of arthritis, the results of which he published regularly in the Medical Journal of Australia. His 1933 article was selected by the Medical Annual of Britain (1934, p.414) from 500 articles submitted as the best in the world. He made no allowances for himself in the course of his treatment of patients in the Leongatha district, and on his death in 1936, the citizens of the district subscribed to a fund which was used for the purchase of a large clock that was dedicated to his memory and mounted on the facade above the entrance to Memorial Hall. A former patient penned a fitting tribute entitled 'The Beloved Physician', the last verse of which epitomises the feeling of the district residents on his death.

> And we who loved you, love you still. With tears
> And laughter mingling, we'll tell again
> The jokes and stories that you told us.
> Your humour, kindly, quick; your piquant speech;
> Your anger hot, or coldly withering;
> Your scorn of those who failed to play the game,
> Your patience, and your tenderness to those
> On whom the shadow of the Cross had fall'n;

*Above: Leongatha Post Office corner, 1926
(from Woorayl Shire Historical Society).*

*Right: Dr H. Pern, Leongatha, 1918-36
(from Woorayl Shire Historical Society).*

Of this we'll tell physician-soldier-friend,
When we together meet and talk of you;
And if our heart-ache finds relief in tears
You'll know we do not mourn, we're glad for you.[37]

The growth of townships mirrors the development and wealth of the district surrounding them. The Woorayl Shire is primarily a farming district, and although sporadic attempts were made at mining, little success was achieved. Scarlett's coal seam at Berry's Creek discovered in 1882 did not prove commercially viable, although a company was formed to develop it and a shaft sunk to a depth of ninety foot. During the 1920s extensive drilling was done to the south of Leongatha in search of oil, but again nothing of consequence was discovered. The real wealth of the district lay in its topsoil and its suitability for farming purposes. While dairying and stock raising have always been the main farming enterprises, several other crops have been grown successfully.

Onion and potato growing quickly became established as an integral part of district farming. Onion growing was usually conducted on a share basis on the red soils around Leongatha, Mardan, Koonwarra and Dumbalk districts. Although some land was leased on a fixed annual rent, the usual practice was

Harvest Sunday, Meeniyan Methodist Church, 1920 (from F. Mackie).

for it to be let on a one in six basis. Under this arrangement every sixth bag of the harvested crop was left in the paddock for the owner of the land. This system worked quite satisfactorily, because in the event of a slump in prices, both owner and tenant bore the brunt, while conversely, in a good year both reaped the benefit. Many wage earners used this method of share cropping in an attempt to become independent farmers with varying degrees of success. One man who tried onion growing around Leongatha was John Neilson, father of the poet John Shaw Neilson. After the death of his first wife, John Neilson married Elizabeth McFarlane from Leongatha in 1912. He lived in the district for several years assisting his brother-in-law, Willie McFarlane, at onion growing. Two daughters were born of this second marriage at Leongatha, and during these years he was occasionally visited by his grown-up son John Shaw Neilson. The Yallourn Power Station was in the course of construction in the early 1920s, and John Shaw Neilson spent some time there engaged in labouring work. Both father and son had published poetry by this time, although neither had many years of schooling. After several years of general farm work in the Leongatha district, John Neilson, Senior, died after a short illness in 1922 and was buried in the Leongatha Cemetery.[38]

Other crops besides onions and potatoes have been grown successfully within the Shire at different times. Wheat, oats, barley, flax, maize and peas have all been grown on a limited scale. During the 1920s a determined effort was made to establish a sugar beet industry in the Leongatha district. The first trial plot was grown on the Rubybank property formerly owned by the Begg family in 1921. The roots were of good shape, and when sent to the beet factory at Maffra, showed a purity of 87 percent and a sugar content of 7.2 percent.[39] After visits by officers of the Department of Agriculture and the Manager of the Maffra factory, it was agreed to establish several trial plots of five acres each so that the suitability of the district could be ascertained before a factory was built. First crops were harvested from these areas in May 1926 and forwarded by rail to the Maffra factory. Average yield ranged up to ten tons per acre while one acre on the flat adjoining the Coalition Creek, yielded twenty tons per acre. The sugar content was quite satisfactory, and the trials were continued for another two years. The 1928 crop was adversely affected by cutworm, with the result that the beets were very forky and fibrous. Through a political decision made at the Federal level, sugar production from cane in Queensland and northern NSW was encouraged to the detriment of beet growing in Gippsland. The trials at Leongatha were discontinued, although the Maffra factory continued to handle produce from that area until 1945.[40]

While the bulk of the cropping was done on the red soils of the Shire, the lighter soils of Nerrena and the South Riding were slowly being brought into production. When bullocks and horses had to be used for land clearing purposes, the area cleared annually was relatively small, yet nevertheless, some progress was achieved. Bullock teams were used regularly up until the 1930s on this coastal country. When the yacht Four Winds of twenty-six tons was wrecked at Venus Bay on 1 July 1923, the salvage operations were performed by bullock teams. With twenty-eight bullocks in the lead and sometimes ten or fourteen on the back axle to prevent the boat slipping, the Four Winds was hauled along the beach to Point Smythe where it was refloated and taken to the wharf at Tarwin

Lower.[41] The gradual introduction of traction engines for land clearing in the 1930s soon led to the disappearance of the bullock teams that had served the first generation of settlers for so long.

Two other factors helped in bringing the Nerrena and South Riding areas into production. One was the realisation that with adequate use of artificial fertilisers applied on a scientific basis, quite good pastures could be grown on land that had been considered relatively worthless. Officers of the Department of Agriculture, through field trials designed to test the responses of various types and mixtures of fertilisers, developed techniques that were to transform the lighter soils of the Woorayl Shire. Large areas of second-class land were covered with messmate and peppermint gum which could be cut and sold for mine props to the Wonthaggi State Coal Mine. The money obtained from this timber enabled many farmers to increase the use of their fertiliser and establish first-class pastures on what was once thought to be second-class land.

This slow but steady improvement in the carrying capacity of all sections of the Woorayl Shire led to the establishment of the Gippsland and Northern Co-operative Co. in the district. Originally formed in 1905 to market dairy produce from co-operative butter factories, it gradually enlarged its scope of activities to include the sale of livestock, real estate and insurance. Its directors were men of vision and enterprise who foresaw the emergence of Woorayl Shire as one of the prime cattle breeding and fattening areas of Victoria. In September 1928 the 'G and N', as the Co-op was commonly known, applied to Woorayl Shire Council for permission to erect sale yards at Leongatha. The site chosen immediately aroused the ire of Health Officer Dr Wood.

> The site, as well as others in the heart of the town, is not suitable, if only for sanitary reasons, but when, as in this case they abut on the back premises of a bakery, two cafes, and a butcher's shop, I cannot enter too strong a protest against this being allowed. I expect the council to wholeheartedly support me in refusing this application.[42]

The Council was in a dilemma. The president, Cr H. Hyland, said that Council desired that the G and N erect yards at Leongatha, and would grant the application, but must abide by the decision of their Health Officer. A further application by the G and N in January 1929 for permission to erect sale yards on Allotments 4 and 5, Section 13, on the Melbourne road was agreed to by Dr Wood, provided that a pitched drain was installed to carry the effluent away. Subsequent extension of the commercial shopping area and the necessity for provision of car-parking space have validated Dr Wood's refusal to sanction the erection of sale yards on such a central site.

Events have also proved the wisdom of the G and N establishing a branch office at Leongatha. Since its inception the Co-operative has played a major role in the livestock industry in the area. By bringing together buyer and seller on a regular basis and by providing facilities and finance to complete the transaction, it has played almost as important a role in the livestock industry as the Leongatha Butter Factory has done in the processing of milk and cream. Other stock selling firms have operated at Leongatha and Meeniyan with a reasonable degree of success from time to time, but none has surpassed the G and N in its record of providing service to livestock producers within the Woorayl Shire.

Harvest time, Koonwarra, c. 1920 (from L. Johnson).

Cream collection, Stony Creek, c. 1927 (from W. Helms).

The 1920s saw the beginning of mechanisation by Woorayl Shire Council. At the July 1926 meeting Crs Gibson and Henderson successfully moved that

> Council purchase two Baby Winner road graders with 5ft blades for two horses, one Leyland 50 cwt motor truck, one Dennis 30 cwt motor truck and one 10/12 motor of a type to be decided upon. The necessary housing accommodation be provided and that Council borrow the sum of 3,500 pounds to finance the above contract and works.[43]

Both trucks gave reliable service, but Council decided in 1930 to replace the Dennis with

> One Albion 30-cwt truck, steel hand operated end tipping body, complete with driver's cab, windscreen, storm curtains and with mechanically operated tyre pump fitted to gear box, paraffin side lamps and tail lamp, with bulb horn.[44]

Whether through economic pressures or the novelty and prestige associated with driving the new vehicle, Council received 189 applications for the position of truck driver when it advertised in April 1930.[45]

Bair Street, Leongatha, c. 1930 (from D. Bacon).

13. THE 1930s

Although the 1930s was a period of financial stringency for farmers and associated trades, there were other sectors less affected. Many service industries experienced relatively stable and prosperous growth. At Inverloch in 1930 Cal Wyeth embarked on an ambitious project of building Pine Lodge, a high class restaurant and guest house that catered for visitors from all over the Commonwealth. In an ideal location overlooking the Inlet, Pine Lodge with its tiled swimming pool and quality bands for evening entertainment attracted a large number of young people, particularly during the holiday season. The increasing use of motor vehicles made it a popular week-end resort for metropolitan visitors.

Even though many people were subject to the trauma of unemployment during this decade, a few small industries such as ladies millinery were not adversely affected. At Leongatha during this decade McCartin Street boasted a ladies millinery establishment employing two women permanently.

Men's hairdressing was a very active trade during the 1930s with many young men visiting the barber at least once a fortnight — short back and sides were all the vogue, and for special occasions it was common practice to be shaved at the barber's with a 'cut-throat' razor. In Bair Street Mr J.F. 'Frank' Goldsworthy's hairdressing salon was a favoured meeting place for locals where town gossip would be exchanged. Football matches were replayed with the advantage of hindsight, while other sporting activities were thoroughly analysed. As a result of a spirited discussion on physical prowess, forty-nine-year-old Frank Goldsworthy wagered he could hop around the Leongatha Recreation Reserve without putting more than one foot to the ground. The attempt was made during half time at the football match Yallourn versus Leongatha in May 1936. He was allowed to stop for a breather but was not to touch the railing. Over 900 people cheered him as he hopped his way around the ground accomplishing the course of a third of a mile in eight and a half minutes.[1]

Wages were low, and those young men who had jobs could get good value for what little money they received. For the sum of 1s 6d in the 1930s, one of three things could be obtained: a haircut, a pound of butter or a gallon of petrol. The Leongatha Caledonian Society fixed admission prices for their annual ball to be

held in the Catholic Hall on Easter Monday 1933 at 3s for gents and 1s 6d for
ladies. This was a reduction on the 1929 price when the charge was 5s for gents
and 2s 5½d for ladies.[2]

Few young men possessed motor cars, and many had difficulty in buying
enough petrol for their motor bikes. Enoch (Eenie) Hodgkiss, popular footballer
and Captain of the Leongatha Fire Brigade, worked at Edney's garage in Bair
Street. When asked by one of his teammates to supply one shilling's worth of
petrol for a motor bike, Eenie replied jokingly, 'What are you trying to do —
wean it?'.[3]

Although some young men might have been able to afford a motor bike, their
younger brothers and sisters still rode to school on horseback — the care and
attention of horses being part and parcel of their lives. On 3 February 1932
nine-year-old Lennie Gwyther, son of Captain and Mrs Leo Tennyson Gwyther
and grandson of pioneer James Gwyther of Koonwarra, set off on his pony,
Ginger Meggs, to ride to Sydney. Taking only a saddle bag and an oilskin coat,
he accomplished the 600 mile journey in time to witness the opening of the
famed Sydney Harbour Bridge at Easter. His father arranged overnight stops for
Lennie as far as Bombala, where he and a neighbour travelling in an A-Model
Ford caught up with him. As word of his travels became public, people kindly
offered him accommodation. On his arrival back at Leongatha on 10 June after
his 1,400 mile journey, he was met a mile outside the town by three of the oldest
residents of the district, Messrs J.J. O'Reilly, C.B. Hamann and Charles Simon,
mounted on their respective steeds. Escorted to the Memorial Hall by these
three pioneers, Lennie was given a civic welcome by the Shire President, Cr R.E.
McIndoe, Junior, in the presence of a large crowd.[4]

Not all school children were as fortunate or as capable as Lennie Gwyther in
being able to ride to Sydney and view the opening of the harbour bridge. Their
teachers, nevertheless, devised appropriate means of interesting their pupils in
local events. A yearly exercise on the part of pupils of the Leongatha State
School was the census of koalas within the township boundary. The 1931
census revealed a total of seventeen koalas, but after two counts in 1932, it was
found that only five koalas were still to be found within the same area.[5] The
town was divided into sections and systematically explored by selected groups of
pupils with the two counts being taken a fortnight apart. The reason for the
decline in numbers was probably due to a combination of causes such as disease,
migration or illicit destruction. Five years earlier in 1927, at their annual picnic
at Waratah Bay, Leongatha State School pupils were fortunate in capturing a
white native koala. This albino variety of the common koala is very rare and
was forwarded to the Melbourne Zoo, where it aroused considerable interest
and comment from the general public.[6]

A troop of boy scouts was formed at Leongatha as early as 1917 by the
Reverend H.J. Harvey, and flourished under his care and direction for several
years, but then lapsed through lack of leaders. Re-formed in 1927, the same
pattern of events occurred, and the troop had to be re-formed again in 1936
under the guidance of local dentist, Mr R.N. Peverill. Mr Peverill persuaded Mr
Gordon Simons, with the assistance of four or five of the original scouts as
instructors, to become Patrol Leaders and use some of the equipment from the
old troop to begin training.[7]

Shire President, Cr R.E. McIndoe, Junior, welcoming Lennie Gwyther on his return from Sydney, June 1932 (from D. Bacon).

The Girl Guide movement was initiated in Leongatha through the efforts and enthusiasm of Miss Daisy McKinnon, grand-daughter of Mardan pioneer Mr Alexander McKinnon. After completing her secondary education at Leongatha High School, followed by three years at Teacher's College, Daisy McKinnon taught at several metropolitan high schools. In 1932 she arranged for parties of Guides from metropolitan branches to visit Leongatha where they enjoyed the new experience of travelling on one of South Gippsland's earliest forms of transport — the horse-drawn sledge. As a means of raising funds for the Guide movement and of occupying the girls' spare time, Miss McKinnon encouraged the girls to collect dead snakes. These were boiled in kerosene tins until all the flesh parted from the vertebrae. With the addition of coloured beads, these vertebrae were then made into necklaces which were sold in Melbourne.[8] As a result of these visits by metropolitan Guides and the encouragement of Miss McKinnon, Leongatha's first Guide company was formed in 1932 with Miss Alice Watson as Captain and Mrs Aberdeen the District Commissioner. Members of this first company included Marion and Dorothy Steele, Phyllis Morris, Ivy Brown, Mary and Ellen Markley, Annie Wilson, Gladys Marshall, Bernie and Rita Warfe, Bonnie Goldsworthy, Phyllis Groube and Thelma Sangster.[9]

While the Scout and Guide movements catered mainly for boys and girls resident in the townships, those living on farms were well occupied during non-school hours. When not assisting their parents in the multitude of tasks common to farming in South Gippsland, most boys engaged in rabbiting as a relaxing and money-making activity. Trapping, ferreting and shooting were standard methods employed with farmers' sons usually having access to .22 calibre rifles at fourteen years of age. Through a combination of these methods, together with netting of boundaries, digging out or fumigating of warrens, poisoning with apples and strychnine, rabbit numbers were being slowly reduced.

The era of horse transport was gradually drawing to a close. Blacksmiths' shops were being converted into garages, while oil and petrol depots were replacing the livery and bait stables. Technology was introducing new industries into townships to supplant the old. The film industry was gaining in momentum with major improvements being made in film-making and projection. At the Memorial Hall the silent movie with the musical accompaniment being provided by either one of three local pianists, Mrs L. Clarke, Mrs C. Edney or Miss F. McCully, was being supplanted by new techniques. Proprietor Terry Ahern, not satisfied with obsolete methods, installed a modern Movietone Plant in 1932 which ironed out a lot of the imperfections of the earlier 'talkies'. Wireless was becoming increasingly popular, particularly during Test cricket matches and overseas air races.

Aeroplanes were gradually making their appearance in the district. The first recorded visit of an aeroplane to Leongatha was at the Caledonian Sports Carnival in 1920. It landed on the outskirts of the town in Sol Maddern's paddock on Koonwarra Road with the intention of taking passengers for joyrides, but the weather proved too boisterous. The aviators, nevertheless, made a good harvest by charging 1s 6d just to view the new machine. Other planes visited the town at different intervals, and Mr Maddern renamed his property Aeroview. On Sunday 30 October 1932 Sir Charles Kingsford-Smith in the famed *Southern Cross* landed on Sullivan's paddock nearby in the presence of over 1,000 people. A brisk business was done with joyrides at ten shillings per head, but again the wind intervened and flying had to be discontinued for two hours during the afternoon.

House removing, Dumbalk, 1930 (from D. Dodd).

Reverend C. Harland, speaking at the Presbyterian Church on the same morning, made a strong protest against the practice of airmen coming to the town to run business trips on a Sunday. Parliament rightly forced places of business to close on a Sunday and yet allowed others 'to desecrate the day as they liked'.[10] Harland appreciated the fact that, while the Church services were in progress, the airmen courteously kept their machines away from the vicinity. Kingsford-Smith left Leongatha in the *Southern Cross* the following day with a group of Leongatha residents to view the Melbourne Cup at Flemington on the Tuesday. Owing to a heavy head wind, the flight to Melbourne took almost two hours, but fortunately, the return trip on the Wednesday took less than one hour. There is an element of irony in the fact that the first commercial flight from Leongatha took place in order that residents might view the Melbourne Cup. Forty-one years earlier in 1891, contractor A. O'Keefe ran the first commercial passenger train on the South Gippsland line for the very same reason.[11]

Another service industry that flourished during the 1930s was the supply and fitting of milking machines on dairy farms. Since their first introduction in the early 1900s, milking machines had improved in efficiency and were slowly replacing the famous, or infamous, MDK method (Mum, Dad and Kids) so prevalent on dairy farms for many years. Due to the downturn in the price of beef and lamb, many grazing properties were forced by economic pressure into dairying. Although the returns were meagre, it did at least ensure a constant cash flow and also provided employment for growing families. Increased cow numbers inevitably led to a greater number of pigs being kept on farms to utilise the skim milk available. Pigs were a reasonably satisfactory sideline for dairy farmers and contributed in no small measure to the profitability of business enterprises in Leongatha and Meeniyan. They were brought to the sale yards in drays, carts, wagons, four-wheeled buggies and trucks, or if in close proximity to the town, they would be walked. In the 1930s it was a common sight to see a herd of pigs being driven up Roughead Street by Mr H. Rolfe from his farm on the old Labour Colony.

Cattle were driven to sale yards at Leongatha and Meeniyan by professional drovers with good dogs. Large mobs of cattle were brought to Leongatha for the special store sales held in spring and autumn and some of the droving feats were quite remarkable. Vic Land who operated as a professional drover and stock agent at Leongatha for many years recalled.

> I would leave Leongatha on horseback between 2 and 3 a.m. with my three dogs and be at Marrabel's paddock near Warragul at daylight. There would be upwards of 300 store bullocks there for me to bring to Leongatha. With the help of my dogs I would have that mob penned in the G. and N.'s yards at Leongatha by 5 p.m. in readiness for the sale the next day. I had two 'soft' dogs trained for sheep, and a 'hard' dog for nipping the heels of the cattle and hurrying them along. I came down Ross's hill and along the Wild Dog Valley road. At cross roads I would send a 'soft' dog to block each side road while I followed on behind with the 'hard' dog. If I met another mob one drover would ride to the head of his mob and turn them into a side lane or hold them steady while the others passed.[12]

Droving required skill and patience. Whilst taking a mob of heifers to Mirboo

Cropping at Mardan, 1935 (from W. Coulter).

North, Vic Land found that floods had washed all the decking from the Berry's Creek bridge with the exception of four planks. With the benefit of age, experience and patience, Vic held his mob bunched at the bridge for an hour and a half until one heifer eventually plucked up courage and walked nervously across the planks to be soon followed by the rest of the mob. Vic Land's skill with horses and cattle was utilised for many years at the rodeos which were later held at the Leongatha Recreation Reserve where he filled the role of 'pick-up man' with distinction.

Many cattle were brought to the Woorayl Shire from the East Gippsland districts, and these also would be driven in mobs of several hundred before livestock transport was introduced. The lack of metalled tracks from roads to farm buildings mitigated against motor transport of all kinds, including stock. Mr D.W. 'Jock' Findlay remembers loading his first truck of pigs at Mr W.M. Gunn's property Wilkur, Leongatha North, in the 1930s.

> Billy Gunn met me at the road with three horses and waders on as the mud was over his gum boots. He hooked the team to the truck and we ploughed through the mud to the pig sty and loaded up. I never thought we would make it back to the road but Billy stood those horses up and we got back on the metal with the mud sometimes up to the tray of the truck.[13]

The Government implemented various road-making schemes to provide work for the unemployed during this decade. In 1931 a gang of sixty men was housed in tents for several months at Ashdale, the property of the Ashenden family at Dumbalk North. They were engaged in widening the road to the Dollar Post Office. Little machinery was used in this task other than horse-drawn scoops. The sandstone was loosened with picks or explosives, and much of this material

1934 floods, Koonwarra viaduct (from M. Wightman).

was shifted with wheelbarrows. Woorayl Shire Council had regular gangs of unemployed men engaged on road-making and bridge building schemes during these years.

The record flood of December 1934 caused severe damage to the road network of Woorayl Shire. Shire Engineer C. Bate reported that as a result of ten inches of rain in the first week of December, eighteen bridges and culverts had been washed away. The estimated cost of repairs for these together with damage caused by landslips, scours and washaways was £9,650.[14] The torrential rain caused a large petrol tank at the Vacuum Oil Co. depot in Bair Street Leongatha to be forced from its bed by seepage. The tank measuring eighteen foot long by ten foot, with a capacity of 6,500 gallons, was buried four foot in the ground. It rose to ground level where it floated on the water in the pit from which it had risen, breaking the connecting pipes. The company then requested the permission of Woorayl Shire Council to place all tanks above ground level on concrete stands.[15]

The railway bridge at Koonwarra was partly washed away in the flood, and the repairs to this and other bridges and roads within the Shire resulted in increased employment for some considerable time. Several young men in the area obtained their first regular employment on the Shire Council in this repair work during 1935. Men camped on the job site and returned to their homes at weekends thus obviating loss of time in travelling. One camp site of Woorayl Shire workmen at Dumbalk was visited by policemen and detectives in December 1935. They were investigating the brutal murder of a six-year-old girl at Leongatha the week before. Harry Money of Roughead Street, Leongatha, had passed information to the police that he had seen fellow Council workman and tent-mate Arnold Karl Sodeman in the vicinity of the crime in the evening

Bill and Leo Hogan during 1934 floods with snakes killed on high ground, Koonwarra (from J. Hogan).

1934 floods, Meeniyan (from M. Wightman).

of 1 December. Sodeman, who lived in a weatherboard house in Bair Street, Leongatha, was arrested, and after questioning, confessed to the murder of June Rushmer at Leongatha, Ethel Belshaw at Inverloch on 1 January 1935, Mena Griffiths at Ormond on 9 November 1930 and Hazel Wilson at Ormond on 9 January 1931. After trial in the Criminal Court in Melbourne in February 1936, Sodeman was sentenced to death and hanged in June 1936.[16]

The 1934 flood led to increased pressure from landholders along the Tarwin for snagging of the river to minimise the damage done by floodwaters. In the lower reaches of the Tarwin, this work had been commenced forty-five years earlier in 1889. Undertaken by the Water Supply Department, a tract of thirty miles of the river was snagged in the five year period 1889-1894. Starting at Stewart's at Tarwin Lower and continuing to within one mile from Meeniyan, the banks were cleared on each side for a distance of 1½ chains, and all trees likely to fall into the river were removed. A punt on which an eight horsepower engine with winch was installed was used for the purpose, with the logs from the stream being left on the banks to be burnt by landowners when dry.[17] As a result of the devastation caused by the December flood of 1934, a public meeting was held at the Middle Tarwin Hall on 8 May 1935. A large gathering of farmers requested from the Minister for Water Supply, Mr Old, government assistance in the snagging of the Tarwin from the junction of the East and West branches with cuts through the bends where necessary.[18]

There was a difference of opinion as to the wisdom of cutting bends in the river. It speeded up the flow of water but resulted in increased erosion. At Dunlop's cut the water was running at fifteen miles per hour but was sluggish further downstream. Mr Wyeth of Inverloch stated that there was four to five foot more water coming down the river than twenty-five years ago, and the Inlet was becoming silted up with mud. A small government grant enabled snagging to be commenced in 1935, but the following year landowners again approached Woorayl Shire Council urging it to make further application for grants so that the work could be continued. Council succeeded in their application as a further £300 was made available by the Government for this work 'on condition that Council co-operate by undertaking supervision and payment of men'.[19] The heavy winter rainfall of South Gippsland rendered many Woorayl Shire roads impassable. Council was constantly refusing requests by carriers and farmers along certain roads for the carriage of firewood and mine props. Minutes of the Council meeting of 12 June 1936 recorded the following requests.

1 . . . From A.J. Butcher, Nerrena, asking permission to cart limited loads. He had bought a truck and would be unemployed if he could not supply the Leongatha Butter Factory from Mackieson's or from his own property; the truck only weighed 25 cwt. — Refused.
2 . . . From G.B. Croatto, asking to be allowed to cart firewood on Cummins' road, using a four wheeled horse drawn vehicle. — Refused.
3 . . . From Norman E. Smith, Inverloch, asking for permit to cart firewood on portion of Leongatha road in small ½-ton truck, from McKeown's paddock. — Refused.
4 . . . From J. McLeish, general manager Vic. State Coal Mine, Wonthaggi, re J.A. Russell's application to cart 120 props, 8ft long by 12in diameter. He could deliver in ten days, and asked that restrictions be suspended for that period. — Refused.

The financial pressure on many families during this decade was acute. Some families paid their debts in goods in lieu of cash. Laurie Trotman who drove the mail car on the Hallston route during these years recalled that every Thursday there would be a dressed chicken on the gatepost of an isolated farmhouse with instructions that it be delivered to the residence of Dr Wood.[20] Reduced incomes of families resulted in a decline in attendance at the Leongatha High School. As an economy measure the Government closed the farm enterprise in 1930, and the word 'Agricultural' was dropped from the official title. In 1932, when attendance dropped below 100, School Council took steps to inaugurate a bus service from Kongwak through Korumburra. This catered for students above year ten as Korumburra had only a Higher Elementary School that ceased at that level. The bus service, which was operated by Leongatha garage proprietor Mr Charles Edney, was instrumental in immediately bringing attendance back over the 100 mark.

After the disastrous fire of 16 September 1933, when all Leongatha High School buildings except the sloyd room were destroyed, a concerted attempt was made by Korumburra residents to have their school made into a high school. This would dispense with the necessity of bussing their senior students to Leongatha. Korumburra had a strong claim, as the population of their Shire of 8,060 exceeded that of Woorayl which totalled 6,300. An active committee was formed at Leongatha comprising representatives of all organisations in an attempt to prevent loss of the school from the district. Donations were made to the fund from the Caledonian Society, the ANA Lodge, Country Women's Association and many private donors. Circulars were printed outlining the potential loss to Leongatha, and canvassing by committee members took place within the district. Woorayl Shire Council contributed £30 and the Electricity Commission agreed to install electric stoves in the domestic arts section of the new school free.

Fortunately for Leongatha, regulations specified that funds from the Government Buildings' Fire Insurance Fund could only be used to replace buildings on the original site. Tenders were then let for the erection of new buildings that were completed during 1934 and officially opened on 4 February 1935. To assist with the beautification of the school grounds, Leongatha Country Women's Association donated sixty trees for planting adjacent to the new buildings. The first of these was planted on 2 August 1935 by Mrs H.J. Rossiter, Branch President, with further plantings in 1936.

The Leongatha branch of the Country Women's Association was formed at Leongatha on 10 February 1931 when Group President of South Gippsland, Mrs Murray Black of Tarwin Lower, addressed the meeting. The basic objective of the CWA members was to make the country a better and more enjoyable place in which to live. Demonstrations and competitions in domestic arts were held regularly, while branch funds were used for the relief of distressed cases that occurred within the community. Quite apart from these practical aspects of the CWA's activities, it also played a valuable role in the development of social contacts among members from different walks of life.

For the young men and women of the Shire, the highlight of the social calendar was the Bachelor's Ball. In 1933 over 400 people from all parts of the Shire and neighbouring townships thronged the gaily decorated Memorial Hall

Sunday afternoon at Dempsey's woodheap, Stony Creek, c. 1930. Champion axeman Frank Dempsey is on the extreme right (from M. McGlead).

at Leongatha for this auspicious occasion. Fern fronds were used to sub-divide the hall, stage and foyer which 'was a veritable fairy dell'. President George Beilby received the guests who were presented with a souvenir card to commemorate the occasion. George Beilby was ably assisted by a committee comprising Messrs Eric Little (Secretary), Lance Mason, Jack Lester, Frank Moore, Pat Bollard, Tony Cavagna, Fred Harley, Tasman O'Brien, Jack Rochford and George Warfe. 'The Gloomchasers' orchestra from Yallourn supplied the music and were still going strong when daylight brought festivities to an end.[21]

The Bachelor Girls Committee returned the compliment by staging their annual ball in the same style and received the same patronage. In 1936, under the Presidency of Miss Ena Maddern with Miss Phyllis Rossiter as Secretary, the Bachelor Girls' Ball held at the Memorial Hall attracted 450 dancers from all parts of Gippsland and even from Melbourne. Miss Maddern, wearing 'a smartly cut frock of prairie leaf green blistered matalasse, with a frilled cape to match', received the guests and was ably assisted by Miss Rossiter who wore 'a floral sand crepe frock with a tight-fitting bodice and frilled skirt'.[22] There were five 'sittings' of supper, with an unlimited supply of sandwiches, cakes, fruit salad, trifle and other good things on the menu supplied by the bachelor girls. To recapture the spirit of the occasion, an enterprising photographer took flashlight photographs during the evening, prints of which were available before the guests returned home. The Bachelor Girls Committee assisting Miss Maddern and Miss Rossiter were Misses Alma Morris (Vice-president) Alice Watson, Kathleen Moloney, Betty Mitchell, Jean Knox, Audrey Hagan and Madge Mitchell.[23]

Residents of the Shire were receiving good dividends through the use of the Memorial Hall, even though it was not a paying proposition to Woorayl Shire Council. Following the loss of the Victory Hall in Bair Street by fire in June 1934, the Memorial Hall was the only suitable venue for major social events. Although it was let on a five year basis to picture show proprietors, the rent from the hall did not recompense Council for the funds outlayed and the necessary maintenance. Accordingly, in 1933 Council leased the two front rooms adjoining the main entrance to local dentist Norman Poulton as a means of increasing revenue. Poulton had a neat method of disposing of the teeth which he extracted. He simply bored a hole in the floor of his work room and dropped them down the hole. Twenty-five years later local plumber Vic Hemming, doing repair work underneath the hall, found a large pile of human teeth — the result of over a decade of extractions.

At the front of the Shire offices in McCartin Street, wooden seats had been placed for the benefit of passers-by. These seats were directly beneath the window where Miss Annie Johnson, Assistant Shire Secretary for many years, performed her duties. The prevalence in the township of many itinerants who occasionally overindulged in liquor at the Commercial and Otago Hotels made these seats a favoured resting place for inebriates. The resultant bad language drifting through Miss Johnson's window led to her requesting Council to remove these wooden benches as the comments interfered with her work. Council, realising the valued work which Miss Johnson was doing on their behalf, readily acceded to her request.[24]

Itinerant workmen were a notable feature of Leongatha during the summer months when they were in good demand for potato digging and onion bagging.

Leongatha Cycle Club, Inverloch Road Race, 1939 (from L. Ralph).

Many camped at the Recreation Reserve or in tents on unused roads while awaiting employment. Woorayl Shire councillors were sympathetic to these men and even considered erecting an iron building in the vicinity of the Council sheep-dip on the northern extremity of the Recreation Reserve for their benefit. The majority of councillors, however, felt that this would aggravate the problem by increasing the number around the township, so no action was taken on the matter.[25] The local police constables did their best to ensure that these itinerants did not cause any trouble to the resident community. As a general rule, these men were honest and trustworthy and did more harm to themselves than anyone else. Rather than charge them through the Courts under the *Vagrancy Act* or for being 'Under the Influence', Senior Constable McMillan would put them on manual work at the police station cutting wood or attending to the garden.

One frequent offender was Clarence Skidmore, and after one such session in the Senior Constable's vegetable garden, 'Skiddy', as he was known around Leongatha, boasted to his fellow inebriates at the Otago, 'I fixed that bloody McMillan this time. He had me on planting out his cabbages. But when he wasn't looking I bit the roots off them before putting them in the ground'.[26] No doubt Senior Constable McMillan had his revenge on 'Skiddy' when the cabbages failed to thrive. After several years of service at Leongatha, Senior Constable McMillan was honoured with a farewell dinner given by Leongatha residents. Appreciation was expressed by speakers of the Boy's Cycle Club and the Caledonian Society, in both of which McMillan had taken an active interest. Senior Constable Campbell of Foster said he had applied for the position at Leongatha but being Scottish it was decided to send a 'Pat'.[27]

Although the English, Scots and Irish were well represented in the police force, there were many members of other nationalities represented in Woorayl Shire. August Bruno, a Swedish migrant who had been domiciled in the Shire since 1899, had worked at a variety of jobs during his lifetime. For many years he was curator of the billiard room at the Leongatha Mechanics' Institute but left to start his own billiard saloon in the Victory Hall in Bair Street. After this hall was destroyed by fire in 1934, Bruno did casual work until he obtained the lease of the brick building at the corner of Roughead and Hughes Streets, originally known as 'Hayes's store'. A large brick cellar of 365 square feet underneath this building was used by Bruno for the growing of mushrooms during 1937. Stable manure that had been exposed to the open air for some time was placed in trays on which the spawn was sown at six weekly intervals. Average yield of two to three pounds per square foot of bed area was obtained in the course of three to five months of continuous cropping.[28] Although moderately successful from a financial viewpoint, Bruno did not continue with the venture for any length of time.

On the opposite side of Roughead Street, the small brick structure adjacent to the Rechabite Hall was used for a variety of business enterprises during the 1930s. First built by the Leongatha and District Co-operative Society Ltd in the 1920s to house its dress-making and tailoring department, it survived the disastrous fire of 1925 that practically destroyed the viability of this co-operative movement. After the liquidation of the Society, it was leased for a time by a Mr Dobell from Korumburra who had recently commenced the production of the

Lyre Bird brand cordial and soft drinks. In July 1934 it was again leased by Mr G.F. Hopkins who, with the assistance of his son Keith, began production of the weekly newspaper *The Leongatha Echo*. The Hopkins family quickly established their paper as 'The Voice of Public Opinion' in the district in opposition to *The Great Southern Star*. But they soon found that their location in Roughead Street was too distant from the town's business area, and after a short time moved to premises in McCartin Street opposite *The Great Southern Star*.

In the 1930s, due to the succession of good onion crops with resultant low prices to producers, attempts were made to lift growers' returns by the establishment of a 'pool'. Under this scheme onions from each onion-growing district in Victoria were stored in a central location, and regular amounts released monthly on to the market, thereby eliminating gluts. Initial moves for the formation of the pool came from growers in the Colac and Warrnambool districts, and delegates from these areas visited Leongatha on several occasions to convince fellow growers of the advantages of the proposed scheme. W. Kiely summed up the plight of the onion-grower in verse.

> Under the spreading bankruptcy,
> The farmer's homestead stands;
> Its lord a mournful man is he,
> As he ploughs his mortgaged lands.
> For laws that cramp his industry
> Are as strong as iron bands.
>
> Week in week out, in ragged pants,
> He toils, his shirt to keep;
> He ploughs, he harrows, and he plants,
> For thieves and sharks to reap;
> And the only time he fails the ants,
> Is when he is asleep.
>
> Toiling, a sight for others' mirth,
> A slave through life he goes,
> Content to work for all he's worth
> Till his creditors foreclose;
> And in six feet by two of earth,
> He earns a long repose.[29]

A voluntary onion pool was brought into operation in 1934 and immediately had the effect of raising the return to growers to £6 per ton, considerably in excess of that obtained in previous years. At Leongatha the pool onions were stacked on an area of land fronting Horn Street, an area now occupied by Leongatha State School. The bulk of the onions were of the Brown Spanish variety, and after bagging were stacked on wooden decking consisting of poles from four to six inches in diameter. The bags, known as onion 'gunnies', which when filled averaged fourteen to the ton, were stacked in tiers six high with a ridge in the centre and protected from the weather by wooden shutters made from palings. Before delivery to the railway station, they were regraded over a slatted table — this work being known as 'picking-over'. In April 1936 Mr James Howard, Manager of the local pool, presented a statement of onions on hand

Brown Spanish onions, Boorool, c. 1930 (from I. Burchell).

that gives a clear indication of the extent of onion growing in Woorayl Shire at that time.

	Marketable Onions	Picklers
Leongatha	21,120 bags	868
Gwyther's Siding	864 ,,	49
Meeniyan	1,605 ,,	100
	23,589 ,,	1,017

Globe onions picked over, 540 bags; trucked, 498 bags.
Lease of land for depot, 4½ acres, £20.
Sawn timber for making storage shed. 3,000 ft at 19s — £28 10s.
Palings, 10,110 at 24s per 100, £121 6s., total £169 16s.[30]

After operating for two years under a voluntary scheme, the pool was replaced by the formation of the Victorian Onion Marketing Board in 1936. At the first election of grower representatives to the Board, Cr R.E. McIndoe, Junior, of Leongatha was elected to represent growers of Gippsland and the metropolitan area, a position he held for over twenty years. The variation in tonnage of the onion crop from year to year caused severe problems to the newly-formed Onion Board. The 1937 crop exceeded estimates, and the Board was left with over 10,000 bags of unsaleable onions at the end of the selling season in October of that year. Money advanced to growers on this crop exceeded the Board's returns from sales, and the Board had great difficulty in recovering this money from growers in subsequent years. Nevertheless, the Board did bring a measure of stability into the onion growing industry in the 1930s with considerable benefit to growers.

While most agricultural products were in over-supply during the 1930s, the demand for flax remained strong. The flax mill at Drouin regularly sponsored advertisements in *The Great Southern Star*: 'Flax Wanted . . . 250 acres. £4 per ton cash being paid for standard flax at Drouin Mill. Clean seed supplied. Farmers! Inquire Now!'[31] The very fact that it was necessary to advertise for flax growers during the depression years proved that there were difficulties associated with the growing of the crop. Flax did not normally fit into Woorayl Shire farming operations, which were predominantly grassland based. Yield per acre was much lighter than onions and potatoes, and it was harder to harvest than oats. For these reasons flax growing made slow progress in the Leongatha district during the 1930s. At Koonwarra Mr R. Stockdale grew flax consistently during these years and encouraged others to do likewise. On the fertile red soil of Mardan, Messrs Robert and Frank Lester harvested forty-eight and fifty acres of flax respectively in 1937. The Drouin factory to which the flax was sent by railway truck had been purchased by Messrs Millar and Kinnear. This firm was keen to introduce a finer twine than had been customary up to that time. By cutting crops slightly before maturity, a percentage of oil is retained in the fibre, tending to make it soft like silk.

Flax was previously imported into Australia, mainly from Belgium and Russia, but Messrs Millar and Kinnear made available finest Egyptian seed to farmers for planting at reduced prices. Due to this incentive, the production of flax in the district for 1937 resulted in the despatch of twenty-five railway trucks (twenty-five tons) to Drouin from Gwyther's Siding and seventeen trucks (fifty-

Leongatha Athletic Club, 1930s (from R. Horne).

nine tons) from the Leongatha station.[32] The expertise gained by farmers in the growing of this crop proved advantageous when the outbreak of hostilities in 1939 caused an unprecedented demand for flax to be used for military purposes.

The 1930s saw the gradual extension of electricity to outlying districts of Woorayl Shire. In 1936 a branch line from Mirboo North connected the Dumbalk, Meeniyan and Stony Creek townships together with many farms along the route. On 6 August Yallourn power was used for the first time at the Dumbalk Butter Factory, replacing the suction gas engine that had been in constant use for the past twenty-eight years. Housewives along the route were delighted with the new-found convenience of electric jugs, irons, lights etc. that had been the privilege of urban dwellers for many decades. Battery wireless sets were quickly replaced by electric sets, and the dairy farmers appreciated the convenience of reliable power and lighting for milking purposes. Temperamental engines and hurricane lamps were quickly replaced by electric motors and incandescent lights. Woorayl Shire Council acceded to the request of the Electricity Commission and agreed to provide twelve streetlights each at Meeniyan, Dumbalk and Stony Creek, the cost of the latter to be shared by South Gippsland Shire as half of the town was in their territory.[33]

The gradual improvement in main roads brought about by increased government expenditure during the 1930s led to the provision of 'service car' facilities on the South Gippsland route. In June 1933 Messrs Steinfort and Ragg began a regular service car run from Leongatha through Korumburra and Poowong to Melbourne. Other service cars operated on the Melbourne route, and competition was keen. Passengers were called for and delivered free of charge within one mile of the booking office.[34]

Although the number of motor cars using the roads was relatively small, there were other driving hazards. When the Yarram service car was proceeding down Beilby's hill near Gwyther's swamp on the Koonwarra Road in June 1936, it encountered a mob of seventy cattle being driven from Meeniyan to Leongatha. The seven passengers, all school teachers from the Yarram district, were returning to school after the winter holidays. The car crashed into the mob of cattle, skidded along the side of the bank throwing the three female passengers in the 'dickie' seat to the roadway and breaking every window in the car. Fortunately, only one teacher, Miss Hearne, had to be treated at St Mary's Private Hospital, Leongatha, by Dr Donoghue, where it was found necessary to insert thirty-two stitches in a head wound. The other teachers proceeded to their respective schools the following morning by train after spending the night at the Otago Hotel.[35]

The leisure activities of older boys and young men of the district were catered for by the formation of a unit of the militia at Leongatha in August 1936. At the initial meeting over fifty young men from Leongatha, Dumbalk and Meeniyan signified their willingness to undergo training. Colonel C. Carre-Riddell of the 29/22nd Battalion attended and stated that, with sufficient support, a machine gun and trench mortar company would be formed. There would be eight Vickers machine guns and twice as many Lewis guns to each company, as well as trench mortars. Training began in earnest in November at the Leongatha Recreation Reserve under Captain W.B. Cook, Sergeant Major Dyke and Lieutenant Haysom when rifles and other equipment were issued.

Three months later the Leongatha unit was joined by 200 members of 29/22nd Battalion from Fitzroy who arrived by transport for a weekend bivouac at the Recreation Reserve. During their stay 600 blankets were issued to the men as no tents are taken on bivouac, and the men sleep on their groundsheets. Field manoeuvres including practice with machine guns, trench mortars and rifle drill were watched by local residents. On Sunday morning a Church parade was held with the battalion band leading the parade along Roughead, Bair and Long Streets before returning to the Reserve. The military authorities approached the Agricultural and Pastoral Society for the lease of the society's pavilion on the Reserve in May 1937 for training purposes on condition that 'six lights be placed in the building, one outside the secretary's office and two large lights on the ground'. This was agreed to by the society, and the following month the Leongatha unit of the 29/22nd Battalion, now over 100 strong, formally moved into the pavilion. Warrant Officer Fletcher, AIC, the 'permanent soldier' instructor with the unit, said he was very relieved to see the men under shelter at last as 'they had trained in pitch darkness on the oval, often in the rain'.[36]

The militia unit became a very pronounced feature of life in the district from then on with training bivouacs taking place at Inverloch and an annual camp at Mornington. Examination for promotion took place regularly, and one of the first men to gain his 'pips' was Lieutenant Bill Owen, teller at the State Savings Bank, who later led the battalion in the defence of Rabaul. Another member of the Leongatha militia unit at that time was local carpenter George Warfe who rapidly gained promotion. Both men displayed leadership qualities that in a few short years saw them promoted to the rank of Colonel.

With the death of Dr Horace Pern in 1936, his practice was purchased by Dr F.P. Donoghue, a younger man with a farming background from the Sale-Nambrok area. When another move was made to form an infant welfare centre at Leongatha in 1937, Dr Donoghue supported the idea and Dr Wood remained non-committal. Shire Council was divided on the issue principally on economic grounds. Local chemist M.E. McGillivray added his weight to the campaign by a letter to the press in which he stated that 'old people think it all so much new-fangled nonsense'.[37]

The task of councillors in apportioning Shire revenue was a difficult, and often thankless, one. While one section of ratepayers was pressing for improved health services, Council was closing roads for goods traffic in the wintertime through lack of funds for maintenance. After prolonged deliberation, Woorayl Shire Council finally carried a motion at their January meeting of 1938 'to establish an Infant Welfare Centre jointly with the Shire of Mirboo, the cost to this shire not to exceed £120 (excluding travelling allowance)'.

Six applications were received for the position of Sister in Charge with Sister K. Lewis being the successful applicant. A committee to assist in the running of the centre was formed as a result of an enthusiastic meeting in July 1938 with Mrs F. Moore as President, Mrs J. Gray Vice-president, Mrs F. Donoghue

Top right: Leongatha blacksmith 'Jock' Campbell, 1933 (from Woorayl Shire Historical Society). Bottom right: Militia in Michael Place, Leongatha, 1938 (from M. Wightman).

Secretary, Mrs F. Williams Treasurer and Mrs T. Ahern Assistant Secretary. At the official opening of the centre on 7 September 1938, the Director of Infant Welfare, Dr Scantlebury, said that there were now 175 centres established in the State which showed how the movement was flourishing.[38]

Health Officer Dr Wood had other problems to worry about during 1938. An epidemic of infantile paralysis in Victoria resulted in the first case being reported in Woorayl Shire in February of that year. As Fairfield Infectious Diseases Hospital was already full to capacity, Dr Wood immediately issued instructions that no children under sixteen years of age be permitted to attend the cinema or swimming pools.[39] He also ordered the onion depot in Horn Street to be moved to a site outside the township boundary. The Agricultural and Pastoral Society, at a hastily convened meeting, agreed to cancel their annual Show, as did the committee arranging the Tarwin Lower aquatic sports for 19 February. Fortunately, these precautions proved effective as Woorayl Shire escaped the epidemic with a relatively minor number of cases.

In his annual reports to Council, Dr Wood frequently alluded to the unsatisfactory system of pan disposal practised at Leongatha and stressed the importance of Council obtaining a sanitary site further removed from the township. Nothing had been done to remedy the situation, and the Health Officer viewed with delight the move to form a sewerage trust at Leongatha. Through the vigilance of local Member Herbert Hyland, MLA, a government scheme to assist municipalities in the installation of sewerage schemes was brought to the notice of councillors and the public generally. Under this scheme, the Government grant increased in inverse ratio to the population, with the greatest subsidy of forty percent going to towns of under 2,000 population. Leongatha's population of 1,700 in 1938 was under this number and so qualified for the maximum subsidy.[40]

Engineer C. Bate presented a comprehensive report on the scheme that entailed driving a tunnel under the railway line from the Strzelecki monument to Young Street, with an outfall to treatment works past the cemetery. Bate estimated that the quantity of extra water required should not exceed six gallons of water per person per day. On an estimated capital cost of £34,600, the grant would amount to £13,840, and the balance could be obtained through loans at four and a half percent. As a result of a further public meeting held in December 1938, a poll of ratepayers on the adoption of the scheme was held. The issue was keenly fought, and although it resulted in a victory for those in favour of the scheme, the margin was small — 380 for 'Yes' and 347 for 'No', a majority of 33 votes.[41]

As a result of the poll, a sewerage authority was formed on 29 March 1939 with authority to borrow up to £50,000 on loan. The commissioners of the Waterworks Trust automatically became commissioners of the new Authority. Engineer C. Bate reported that Messrs Scott and Furphy, Engineers of Melbourne, had suggested that all houses in Leongatha should be numbered to facilitate their work when sewerage was being carried out. Mr Bate said that the estimated cost of numbering all the residences in the township, approximately 500, would be £100 or about four shillings each. Mr Bate said it was really the responsibility of the Council, and allowance would have to be made for future buildings on vacant blocks. At the May meeting of the Authority, the offer of a

Rabbit buyer at Mount Eccles, 1933 (from F. Helliwell).

vacant house in Bair Street for use as offices was accepted at a rental of twenty-one shillings per week. The tender of local cabinet-maker, H.J. Marriner, for the supply of a plan press at £14 13s 0d, drafting table at £17 17s 0d and three stools at £4 10s 0d was also accepted.[42]

Although endowed with a reliable annual rainfall, water shortages occur occasionally in Woorayl Shire. The rainfall during 1938 was well below average, and water boring plants were busy towards the end of that year. In March 1939 the Leongatha Butter Factory, in an endeavour to augment its supply, sank a bore adjacent to its butter room which yielded in excess of 1,000 gallons per hour at a depth of 150 foot. Meeniyan township was suffering from an acute water shortage, and Cr H.P. Williams convinced his fellow councillors that an experimental shaft should be sunk in the main street. Old residents knew of the existence of a well in the railway yards, and after obtaining the services of a water diviner, a shaft was sunk in the main street in the vicinity of Cr Williams's store. Water was struck at a depth of thirty foot and entered the shaft with such force that workmen were forced to temporarily abandon the job.[43] It quickly rose to within eight foot of the surface and provided Meeniyan township with ample supply for the cleaning of the sale yards, for street plantations and in the event of outbreak of fire.

Meeniyan residents were particularly fire conscious after seeing their Mechanics' Hall destroyed on Sunday morning, 21 August 1938. A bucket brigade managed to prevent the fire from spreading along Whitelaw Street, and although the Leongatha Fire Brigade made a quick dash to the scene, nothing could be done to save the hall in the absence of an adequate supply of water. Two months later, the same situation prevailed at Koonwarra. On 26 October 1938 the Koonwarra Hall, built in 1892, was consumed by fire, blame for which was laid on a passing swagman. The loss of the hall was a big blow to Koonwarra citizens. Although insured for £350 and the piano and furniture for £80, it was three years before residents were able to attend the opening of the new building that replaced it. Meeniyan residents were able to finance the rebuilding of their hall in a much shorter time. This was opened at a gala ball on 18 July 1939 when Mr W.G. McKenzie, MLA, performed the opening ceremony, and the whole proceedings were broadcast over 3UL Warragul radio station.[44]

The devastating bushfires of January 1939 that followed the 1938 drought fortunately missed the Woorayl Shire. Minor outbreaks at Koonwarra and Buffalo caused severe local damage to farms but only a small number of stock perished. The severe drought had led to an increased numbers of stock grazing 'the long paddock'. Cal Wyeth, proprietor of Pine Lodge, was particularly upset about the situation at Inverloch and led a deputation to Council complaining of the depredations of wandering cattle. He had spent a lot of money improving the grounds and gardens at Pine Lodge, but hungry cattle had ruined them. Mr Wyeth said it cost him ten shillings per week to buy cut flowers for the tables at Pine Lodge and urged Council to establish a pound at Inverloch to eliminate the herds of wandering cattle. Cows got stuck in his cattle pit and calves managed to get through it. Mr Wyeth said that 'cows with bells on their necks were nice in a way, but when this method of locating them extended to about fifty, it meant sleepless nights for visitors and residents'.[45] Council did not accede to his request for the establishment of a pound but instructed the ranger to be more vigilant in this area and also agreed to bitumen the road to the gate of Pine Lodge.

The minor drawback of wandering stock did not detract from the attraction of Inverloch as a holiday and fishing resort during the 1930s. Each summer the foreshore was crowded with the tents of holiday-makers occupying every available cleared area. Periodically, the Inlet claimed victims through drowning accidents, the worst chapter being the summer of 1939-40 when eight lives were lost. The former owner of the Esplanade Hotel, Mr A.J. Frongered, his wife Christine and two sons, Kurt twelve and Oleman ten, were drowned in a boating accident while attempting to cross the bar after travelling in his yacht from San Remo. After operating an ironmongery business at Wonthaggi for many years, Frongered had re-built the Esplanade Hotel with Wonthaggi redstone bricks after its destruction by fire in 1934. He had also built a unique home at Inverloch of pulverised stone that resembled a ship. After the accident the body of Mrs Frongered was washed up on the beach at Eagle's Nest three miles from Inverloch, while those of her husband and son Oleman were later found at Pound Creek and Maher's Landing respectively.[46]

14. THE 1940s

The ominous war clouds gathering over Europe during 1939 were beginning to affect the lives of Woorayl Shire residents. The Minister for Defence, Mr Street, announced in July that three new militia battalions were to be established in country districts, one in Victoria and two in NSW. The Victorian unit was to be the 22nd Battalion drawn from the South Gippsland area with headquarters at Leongatha.[1] With the outbreak of hostilities in September 1939, recruits were soon accepted by the three branches of the Armed Forces for service overseas. In February 1940 membership of the militia was made compulsory for the twenty to twenty-one age group who were liable for service within Australia and the New Guinea area.

During the last week of February 1940, Leongatha residents were more preoccupied with their long planned 'Back-to' celebrations than the war effort. These were held from 24 February to 2 March. A warm welcome was accorded to visitors who arrived by special train from Melbourne at a fare of 11s 8d on the Saturday afternoon. Church services, band recitals at the Recreation Reserve, Flower and Baby Shows at the Memorial Hall, Costume Cavalcade, School Sports, an Athletic Carnival and a Centenary Ball all helped to awaken memories of past years and renew friendships severed by time. The gathering struggle between nations that was to cost the lives of so many of the young men of the Shire was forgotten during this week of celebrations.

Within a month of the ending of the 'Back-to-Leongatha' festivities, the first thirteen men from the Shire were given a send-off at a social arranged by the Welfare Committee. The war quickly altered other district activities. It brought about an immediate and urgent need for flax fibre. Increased production was vital to fulfil the needs for canvas, aeroplane fabric, twine, parachute harness, gaiters, binding, fire hoses etc. At a public meeting called by Woorayl Shire President, Cr H.P. Williams of Meeniyan in June 1940, Mr R.B. Hogg of the Department of Supply and Development stated that, whereas 70,000 tons had been grown annually in Australia, it was now necessary to grow 300,000 tons of fibre for war purposes. Gippsland had been allocated an area of 2,000 acres with the Leongatha district 550 acres. Promises of 1,400 acres to be grown for the coming season were made by district farmers at this meeting.[2] In 1941 the

MEENIYAN WARTIME

MERRYMAKERS

PRESENT

Sparklets
Revue

MEENIYAN   **THURSDAY, Aug. 8**
HALL   **1940**

Meeniyan   Merrymakers
Programme, 1940 (from
Woorayl Shire Historical
Society).

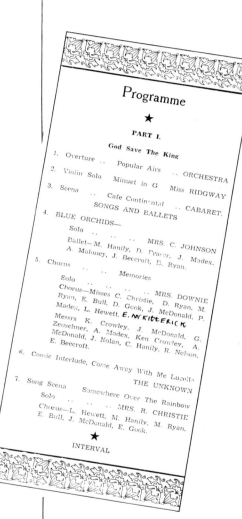

Programme

★

PART I.

God Save The King

1. Overture .. Popular Airs .. ORCHESTRA
2. Violin Solo   Minuet in G   Miss RIDGWAY
3. Scena .. Cafe Continental .. CABARET.
   SONGS AND BALLETS
4. BLUE ORCHIDS—
   Solo .. .. .. MRS. C. JOHNSON
   Ballet— M. Hanily, D. Fraser, J. Madex,
   A. Maloney, J. Beecroft, D. Ryan.
5. Chorus .. .. Memories
   Solo .. .. .. MRS. DOWNIE
   Chorus—Misses C. Christie, D. Ryan, M.
   Ryan, E. Bull, D. Gook, J. McDonald, P.
   Madex, L. Hewett. E. McKitterick
   Messrs K. Crowley, J. McDonald, G.
   Zeuschner, A. Madex, Ken Crowley, A.
   McDonald, J. Nolan, C. Hanily, R. Nelson,
   E. Beecroft.
6. Comic Interlude, Come Away With Me Lucelle
   THE UNKNOWN
7. Song Scena   Somewhere Over The Rainbow
   Solo .. .. MRS. R. CHRISTIE
   Chorus—L. Hewett, M. Hanily, M. Ryan,
   E. Bull, J. McDonald, E. Gook.

★

INTERVAL

nearest flax mill to Woorayl Shire was at Koo-Wee-Rup which necessitated double handling of the sheaves from the paddock to the railway station and then to the mill. By February 1941 the Koo-Wee-Rup mill was employing ninety people working two shifts, and it was reported that the best samples were coming from the Meeniyan, Dumbalk and Berwick districts, with yields of seed being 5½ bushells to the ton.³ Average crop yield in the Leongatha district was 1½ tons per acre for which the Government paid £5 per ton. The cost of freight to Koo-Wee-Rup led to Leongatha growers urging the Government to establish a de-seeding mill in the district. Following increased plantings in 1941, tenders were called by the Government for erection of a mill for de-seeding purposes at the corner of Yarragon Road and Horn Street, Leongatha, in December 1941.⁴

Meanwhile, wartime demands were changing other aspects of life in the township. The militia battalion centred at Leongatha continued with exercises and training on the Recreation Reserve during 1940, but in April 1941 the Reserve was taken over by the 13th Light Horse Regiment. The grandstand was adapted for cooking purposes, while the exhibition pavilion was used for administration and training purposes. Over 150 tents were erected on the Reserve, and on Monday 5 May 1941, 450 horsemen who had recently completed a three month training camp at Geelong arrived in batches of 50 to take up quarters on the Reserve. In addition to the mounted men, there were 200 men on foot who received ground training before taking part in horse manoeuvres. Training took place on roads and paddocks adjacent to the township, the chief area being Rockhill Farm, the property of Mr J.T. Knox at Nerrena. A military hospital, under canvas, of twenty-five beds was set up on the Reserve to cater for accidents and illness.⁵

The Leongatha branch of the CWA, under the leadership of Mrs Gladys Rutherford, was the first to organise a social gathering for members of the Light Horse unit. This was held in St Peter's Parish Hall a week after their arrival and proved a great success — the new floor receiving a rough baptism with the tramp of military boots.⁶

The onset of winter rains soon created mud problems on the Reserve with the presence of such a large number of men and horses. Although no reasons were given by the military authorities, it was thought that this may have influenced the decision to transfer the 13th Light Horse unit to Mt Martha on 1 July 1941. The Reserve then reverted back to the militia for six months until December when the 13th Light Horse arrived back at Leongatha — without its horses.⁷

One of the many Leongatha residents who took pleasure in watching the manoeuvring of the Light Horse on the Reserve during its stay was sawmiller, Mr A.W. 'Bill' Smith. A keen lover of horses, Bill Smith had purchased the site of the old Co-operative store at the corner of Roughead and Long Streets in 1940 as a base for his sawmilling and hardware business. When he took possession of the site, Bill Smith recalled the time he stabled his horses there, twenty-four years previously. In 1916 he and his wife were living on a small property, Roseneath, just near the Allambee turnoff at Mirboo North. Mrs Smith had to be brought to Nurse Good's private hospital in Church Street, Leongatha, for confinement. With his two well-bred buggy horses in good fettle, Bill Smith made record time on the journey. Nearing Leongatha he galloped his horses at full speed along Crighton's flat and up the Labour Colony hill to the township. He arrived at Nurse Good's hospital with his horses white with foam after their thirteen mile dash. Mrs Smith went straight to the labour ward where twin sons, Roy and George, were born. Realising the value of his horses, Bill Smith walked them around the side streets of Leongatha for an hour and a half allowing them to cool down before un-harnessing them in the Co-operative store stables in Roughead Street.[8]

With two more sons, Bert and Clarrie, to assist the twins, Bill Smith commenced sawmilling in a small way at Mirboo North in 1934. They had only been in business a week when the Woorayl Shire placed an order with them for the supply of bridge timber required because of losses in the disastrous floods of December of that year. Sensing the potential for the growth of Leongatha, Bill Smith and his four sons transferred their sawmilling operations there during the summer of 1940-1. The cutting of logs, cartage to the mill and the ripping and stacking of the scantling initially provided employment for fifteen men and proved a welcome addition to Leongatha's industry. In order to provide storage space for logs, Clarrie Smith recalls that one of his first tasks was to fill in O'Keefe's well. This had been dug in 1890 during the building of the railway line by contractor Andrew O'Keefe and was the only water supply for the township for many years.[9]

A further demand for labour in Leongatha in 1941 was caused by the decision of the Leongatha Butter Factory to commence cheese-making operations. As a result of an appeal by the Government, cheese-making facilities were built at Leongatha and Dumbalk in 1941-2. Leongatha's plant was designed to treat 10,000 gallons of milk daily working one shift, while Dumbalk was designed to treat 8,000 gallons in two shifts.[10] At Leongatha an additional fifteen men were needed for this operation, and coupled with enlistments in the Armed Forces, a labour shortage quickly developed in the district. One of the first projects to feel the effects of this shortage was the Leongatha sewerage scheme.

By September 1940 the Sewerage Authority, which consisted of Commissioners C.A. Bond (Chairman), Dr F.A. Wood, E.T. Munro, C. Edney, R.J. Hagan, J. Rowden, T. Sangster, Engineer C. Bate and Secretary J.F. Odlum, had completed a series of test bores about the township. Arrangements had been made by the Secretary for the procurement of loan money to finance the scheme, and in December 1940 the tender of S.P. Stackpoole of Sunshine for the construction of sewers and manholes for the sum of £23,840 5s 3d was accepted. Some criticism was expressed by members of the community that the project should be deferred because of the war effort. Mr H. Hyland, MLA, advised the Authority that if the loan money was not taken up by Leongatha, it would be allocated to another town and not voted again. The Authority, therefore, accepted the offer of the National Bank of Australasia Ltd Provident Fund for a loan of £20,000 for twenty years at £3 15s 0d percent.[11]

The tender of Hoffman Brick and Pottery Co. of South Melbourne for the supply of pipes and fittings for the sum of £6,160 7s 7d was accepted, together with one from Gatic Engineering Co. Pty Ltd of Brunswick for the supply and delivery of manhole covers for the sum of £562 10s 0d.[12] Stackpoole began work almost immediately to take advantage of the summer weather. The driving of a tunnel underneath the railway line necessitated the sinking of two deep shafts, one near the overhead railway bridge and another adjacent to the Strzelecki monument. This latter shaft caused Stackpoole considerable difficulty. It tapped an artesian spring at a depth of sixty foot that flowed at the rate of 4,000 gallons per hour and rose to within twenty foot of the surface.[13]

Engineer Bate had samples of the water forwarded to Melbourne for analysis. This showed that the water had no injurious substances and would be fit for bathing purposes providing it was filtered and chlorinated. Commissioners Phillips and Pounder moved that the necessary steps be taken by the Engineer to conserve the flow of water. It could later be used for a swimming pool for which a suitable site was in close proximity.[14] Stackpoole continued with the tunnelling and deep trenching, but the Authority was unable to obtain a tender for the treatment works even after extensive advertising.

The deterioration of the war situation towards the end of 1941 was soon reflected in the day-to-day life of Leongatha residents. Local bakers Messrs E.F. McNamara and F.W. Tilley announced that as from 1 February 1942 they would discontinue bread deliveries as both of their drivers had been called up for war service. As compensation to the housewives for the elimination of this service, they reduced the price of a large loaf from 1s 0½d to 11d.[15] Wartime regulations restricted the use of paper for wrapping goods other than for items such as butter, cheese and bacon. Townspeople were asked to bring baskets to the store and country customers advised to bring boxes to carry articles to their vehicles.

Although newsprint was scarce, Woorayl Shire continued to be served by its two newspapers. After the closure of *The Leongatha Sun* in 1929, *The Great Southern Star* had a monopoly of news until the publication of *The Leongatha Echo* began in 1934. Although *The Star* was published bi-weekly, *The Echo* came out on a weekly basis with both papers giving a comprehensive coverage of district events. For the benefit of its Meeniyan readers, *The Star* printed *The Meeniyan Record* which was basically the same paper with its front page featuring more news from the Meeniyan-Stony Creek districts.

Stringent manpower controls were introduced throughout Australia in February 1942 to cope with wartime exigencies. At Leongatha a manpower office was set up in the Court House under Lands Department officer Mr R.J. Hagan, assisted by the military area officer, Captain Blandford. Sewerage works were classed as non-essential, and Secretary J.F. Odlum received notice in mid-March that all work was to be stopped for the duration of the war. The only work permitted was that necessary to leave the project in a safe condition. This had to be done in two weeks, and the men released had to report to manpower offices to work in areas more directly connected with the war effort. Engineer Bate reported that Stackpoole had completed seven miles of sewers out of a total length of ten and a half miles at termination of work.[16]

In January 1942 workmen were busily putting the finishing touches to the cheese factory on Yarragon Road, while a quarter of a mile further along another gang of twenty men had commenced the building of the flax mill. The management of the Leongatha Butter Factory had no difficulty in persuading farmers to forward whole milk in cans in preference to sending cream. Many farmers experiencing acute labour shortages through having sons in the Armed Forces were only too glad to dispense with the task of separating the milk and feeding pigs. A small premium for butterfat in milk as against butterfat in cream was an added inducement for dairy farmers to change over to milk supply. Smaller butter factories were facing extreme difficulties. Wartime regulations stated that all factories must include a percentage of cheese in their output. The Government helped with the financing of cheese-making extensions, but the changeover was uneconomic below a certain level of production. The Tarwin Lower factory, which had been operated by the Excelsior Butter Factory Co. since 1926, was purchased by the Leongatha Butter and Cheese Factory Co. in June 1941 and ceased operations in March 1942.[17]

The Tarwin Lower butter factory was not the first in the Woorayl Shire to succumb to forces beyond its control. Stony Creek farmers lost their factory on 17 April 1930 through a disastrous fire and were unable to arrange sufficient finance for re-building. Cream was then collected by contract carrier P. Fielder and forwarded to Leongatha factory. The Ruby factory closed in April 1935 after operating since 1897. A privately-owned factory, it had a series of owners, most successful of whom was Victor Brumley who conducted it until 1931 when he sold to Messrs Moser and Wilson. The freezing works at the factory continued to be operated by the Logan family for many more years as a storage depot for rabbits. The closure of the Ruby and Tarwin Lower factories was only the beginning of a slow rationalisation of dairy manufacturing facilities brought about by the increased use of motor transport for the cartage of cream and milk.

The completion of the flax mill on Yarragon Road in 1942 brought to light a new problem for the management. Although within the town boundary, it was outside the Water Trust area. Manager W.R. Cook stated in April there were 653 tons of flax stacked in the yard adjoining the mill, and if a fire should break out there was no means of extinguishing it without a water supply. A request by Mr Cook on behalf of the Flax Production Committee to the Water Trust for the installation of 2,740 foot of one inch water main from the existing town supply was granted at the May meeting of the Trust. The price charged was ten shillings per 1,000 gallons.[18]

The autumn of 1942 was the nadir of the 1939-45 War for Australia. Following the bombing of Darwin in February, air-raid precautions were introduced throughout Australia. Regulations were promulgated stating that all motor car headlights were to be shaded with black paint, cardboard or metal discs. Strict petrol rationing was enforced with many cars and trucks in essential services being fitted with gas producers. Woorayl Shire Council had their Ford and Chevrolet trucks fitted with gas production units. A special meeting convened by Shire President Cr R.E. McIndoe arranged for a committee to oversee the production of charcoal within the Shire. Mr A.J. McVicar said that 'there was any quantity of wood at Buffalo, sufficient for thousands of tons of charcoal, but labour was the trouble'.[19] Air-raid tests were introduced at Leongatha in March 1942, the details of which were published in *The Great Southern Star* on 20 March.

> Signals . . . Prepare for Air Raid . . . Series of short and long blasts. Raid Impending . . . Series of short blasts of five seconds on with two second intervals. All Clear . . . Continuous blast of two minutes. These will be given by the Butter Factory whistle and the bells from the Anglican and Roman Catholic Churches.
> C.A. Bond, District Warden. C.H. Lyon and F.R. Moore, Assistant Wardens.

Major W.T. Owen, 2/22nd Battalion, New Britain, 1941 (from D. Lawson).

Special meetings of school councils were called to discuss provision of slit trenches for the children. Engineer C. Bate said he favoured slit trenches of the U Shape, more zig-zag type than straight trenches. Trenches should be four foot nine inches deep, three foot wide at the top and two foot at the bottom. Three foot of trench was necessary for each person. Meeniyan State School Committee was the first to dig trenches in the Shire. On 21 March, at an enthusiastic working-bee of parents at the school, Mr W. McIlwaine with his team of horses and Tom Hamilton with plough, scooped out the top half of the trench while others followed with pick and shovel. Similar working-bees were held at the Leongatha State and High Schools, while Shire President, Cr R.E. McIndoe, called a public working-bee for the digging of trenches at the Court House site and at the rear of the Memorial Hall. These were quickly completed and were sufficient for ninety people. Heavy winter rains resulted in several inches of water lying in the bottom of the trenches, but fortunately their use was never required.

By June Major Bill Owen and the remnants of the 2/22nd Battalion were back at Leongatha recuperating after their escape from New Britain. The 2/22nd Battalion had borne the brunt of the Japanese attack on Rabaul. With other units of the AIF and members of the anti-tank corps, they were over-whelmed by an invading Japanese force. Inadequately equipped with only two anti-aircraft guns to match the formidable Japanese Zeros, the men fought bravely before yielding this important position. Many were captured, but a small party of eighteen men under their leader, Major Owen, cut their way through 300 miles of jungle southwards, living mostly on food supplied by the natives — kow kow, a kind of sweet potato, and occasionally a pig or two. Malaria took its toll, and by the time they had made contact with Allied Forces some, including Owen, had lost two stone in weight on their trek through the jungle. Private Owen Hughes from Dumbalk, Private Phil Hillis of Mount Eccles and Private Dave Lawson of Leongatha were in a similar group which made its way southwards, but other members of the 2/22nd from Leongatha were not so fortunate, and amongst those captured by the Japanese were Jack Howard, Fred Ketels and Quartermaster Thomas Sangster. Two months later the sad news was received at Leongatha that Bill Owen, newly promoted to Lieutenant-Colonel, had been mortally wounded in the fighting in Papua.[20]

A steady stream of wounded personnel was returning from the war zone necessitating increased hospital facilities. Cal Wyeth's Pine Lodge at Inverloch was taken over by the naval authorities for use as a hospital, with an immediate appeal by them to Red Cross branches at Wonthaggi, Korumburra and Leongatha for the supply of sixteen nursing aides for staffing purposes. Surgeon Captain Scott McKenzie said the boys in the hospital had been to Dakkar, Greece, Crete, the Coral Sea battle and Darwin, and any aid the Red Cross could give would be only a small measure of what these boys had done for the Australian community.[21]

Manpower shortages created by the war quickly led to the employment of women in most branches of industry and as auxiliaries to the Armed Forces. On 13 February 1942 Captain Beath of the Australian Women's Legion addressed a meeting of sixty women at the Leongatha Memorial Hall and gave an interesting and instructive address on the AWL. The main purpose of the Australian Women's Legion was to train women to be of service, whether in the auxiliaries to the fighting forces, namely the Women's Australian Auxiliary Air Force, the Australian Women's Army Service or as Air-Raid Precaution workers. Many young women of Woorayl Shire volunteered for these services, while others performed valuable war work in their home district. At Leongatha the flax mill proved a ready employer of female labour during the war years. The work appealed to women who were loath to commit themselves to service life and yet wished to contribute to the war effort. Adult women workers were paid approximately £3 per week, and many preferred this activity to that of factory work in the city. But as Ellen Lyndon described, it was back-breaking work.

> Waterproof clothes, gum boots, overalls, gardening gloves (flax is rough on the hands) were real necessities and the workers had to provide their own. The ripened flax is cut, tied in sheaves and stacked like oats. After the linseed had been threshed from the straw this was carted back again and spread out to rot on the paddocks. This process is called 'retting'. The shell of the straw rots away from the fibre that is the flax. A smart little red tractor would draw loads of sheaves into the paddocks, often getting bogged to the axles in the soft wet soil and cutting slit trenches in its efforts to free itself. The sheaves were tossed off in rows, a girl appointed band cutter, and the team spread the clean yellow straw, a thin layer of it, in even rows until the paddock was covered.

There was an art in throwing the unrolling sheaf so that it would cover the longest possible strip of ground, and we became very skilful at this in time. At first any thicknesses, and there were plenty, had to be thinned out by hand with the worker bent from the waist, and it was in this attitude that we spent most of our working hours. At first it was sheer agony to straighten up those backs and it had to be done very gradually in case they broke! For the first week, at least, we suffered excruciating backache and by knockoff time were all so stiff that we had difficulty in mounting the truck for the homeward journey. We were allowed ten minutes smoko and the same in the afternoon, with fifty minutes for lunch, knocking off for the day at 5 p.m. and wishing heartily that tomorrow was Sunday.

When the flax had weathered six to eight weeks and leached to a dirty brown it was all turned with the aid of long poles. The men did this and after them came the girls to do the 'gaiting'. In gaiting the worker picks up just the right amount of straw and flips it round her knee with the seed heads tangled together at the top. This forms a little wigwam that stands up unaided and allows the wind to dry it thoroughly. Later, it is gathered again into sheaves and tied, to be carted to the mill to be scutched — a mechanical process that divides the unwanted straw from the wanted fibre. The amount of manual handling was terrific. The finest grade flax was then worth 900 pounds per ton. It takes about 20 tons of straw to produce one ton of fibre.[22]

One hazard for the flax straw while lying out was excessive wind. Gale force winds at Leongatha in August 1942 lifted the flax from paddocks adjoining Nerrena Road where it had been spread out and deposited it along the roadside almost to the height of the electricity lines. On the north side of the Recreation Reserve, Welsford's paddock was swept bare with the flax straw piled high along the dividing fence of the Reserve. The girls had an unenviable job trying to 'gait' it back into order before it could be forwarded to the scutching mill at Koo-Wee-Rup.[23]

The Leongatha branch of the Australian Women's Legion was active during the war years. A vacant block of land lent by Mrs Fletcher was used for a herb garden, camouflage nets were made by members, first aid and home nursing courses conducted by the Red Cross Emergency Company were regularly attended. Many members of the AWL took their part in the air-watch from the observation tower erected on the vacant block of land at the corner of McCartin and Bruce Streets. This was staffed on a twenty-four hour basis by members of the Volunteer Air Observers Corps on two hour rosters. Observers were trained in aircraft identification so that any aircraft seen could be immediately reported to the authorities. On one occasion the observers had more than a silhouette to help them identify the aircraft. In August 1943 a fighter-bomber made a forced landing on the property of Mr J. Charlton one mile south-west of Leongatha. Fortunately, only minor damage was done and the crew escaped unhurt.[24]

The enlistment of many school teachers in the Armed Forces created a serious staff shortage in district schools. Many married women who had formerly taught school returned to the classrooms at this time, often under extreme difficulties. When the teacher at Mount Eccles South State School, six miles north of Leongatha, enlisted in 1941, his place was taken by Mrs Adeline Wisdom of Leongatha. Mrs Wisdom lived on a small farm in Bazley Street

Leongatha Dive Bombers Revue, 1941. Left to right: Sheila Conway, Roma Hagan, Timmy Bate, Sylvia Smith, Betty Pratt, Doris Howard and Joy Hopkins (from Woorayl Shire Historical Society).

where she and her husband, who worked on the railways, milked a dozen cows by hand to supplement their income. When she re-commenced teaching, Mrs Wisdom rose soon after 5 a.m., cut six lunches for members of her family, gave the children their breakfast and then rode a bicycle up steep hills to Mount Eccles South to have the school open at 9 a.m. The following year she taught at Mackey State School on the Nerrena-Dumbalk Road seven miles from Leongatha. Nerrena Road at that time was not sealed, and often she would ride through deep water when the river flooded. In 1944 Mrs Wisdom was transferred to Leongatha East State School. Whilst stationed there she found it much easier to walk down the railway line almost to Gwyther's siding, and then to the school rather than ride the bicycle around the road. After school she would often ride home on the railway trolley with her ganger husband.[25]

During the war, balls and dances were usually held only in conjunction with patriotic fund-raising activities. Proceeds from the various functions were amalgamated into the Woorayl War Fund that was formed in April 1940 and used for provision of amenities to armed personnel and assistance, if necessary, to their dependants. The Leongatha Dramatic Society organised several concerts in aid of this fund. Their stage show, the 'Dive Bomber's Revue', included in its cast a White Russian refugee, Mrs Olga Ray, who with her brother, N. Kamper, had settled in Leongatha during the 1930s.[26] Mrs Ray, who had previous experience with the Moscow Ballet, trained many Leongatha girls in dancing techniques with Sylvia Smith assisting her in the tap dancing numbers. A seven piece orchestra comprising Mrs K.S. Hopkins (piano), Mrs H.J. Baker, Miss K. Farmer and Mr R.E. McIndoe (violin), Mr G. Rayson (cornet), Mr G.C. Milnes (saxophone), with Mr V. Slater (drums) introduced their Third Revue on 22 October 1941 with 'Alexander's Ragtime Band' and 'Everybody's Doin' It' for the opening chorus.[27]

Radio station 3UL Warragul formed a Friendly Circle of Listeners during the war years. This group of ladies met on Thursdays at Leongatha to pool their wartime efforts in the raising of funds for patriotic and charitable purposes. Red Cross, Church and CWA work associated with the war effort occupied the activities of other women. On 29 September 1943 the Leongatha Memorial Hall was crowded with members of the CWA from South Gippsland branches when famous author Mary Grant Bruce addressed the meeting. Mrs Bruce spoke of her love for Gippsland, the need to combat soil erosion, plant more trees and better educate country children.[28]

Government rationing of petrol and superphosphate in 1942 was followed by food and clothing rationing. Ration books were issued to all adults, and shopkeepers were forced to spend endless hours in explanation, collection and counting of coupons. In Woorayl Shire food rationing had minimal impact on the everyday lives of residents. Butter and meat were readily available on farms, and most town residents had close contact with farming families. Rabbits and poultry could easily fill any shortfall in meat coupons. Tea, sugar and clothing coupons were more closely guarded, but little real hardship resulted from the scarcity of these commodities.

The shortage of manpower on farms was alleviated to a small extent in 1943 by the arrival of the first batch of Italian prisoners-of-war in September. Arrangements for their arrival had been made at a meeting held in August at which Mr Don Cameron, Deputy Director of Manpower, stated he was receiving 275 letters a day asking that men be released from war service to work on farms.[29] Depots for prisoners had been established at Colac and Hamilton and were working satisfactorily. A local committee to supervise allocation was formed to work with Manpower Officer Mr R.J. Hagan. Temporary accommodation was set up at the Recreation Reserve, and a maximum of three prisoners per farm was permitted. Prisoners were allocated as quickly as possible after arrival and were easily recognisable by their army issue uniforms that were dyed red. They soon became an accepted part of daily life, and little trouble was experienced by those farmers who engaged them.

Some criticism was expressed from time to time that they were given too much freedom, such as having wine parties, riding bicycles, 'even driving cockies' cars!'. At a meeting of Leongatha Traders and Progress Association, one member said 'Why, these fellows even wander into barbers' shops to get their hair cut!'.[30] Around Leongatha, many of the POWs tried to attend the 11 o'clock Mass at St Laurence O'Toole's Church on a Sunday where parish priest, Reverend Father P.M. O'Donnell, preached his sermon in English and then repeated it in fluent Italian for the benefit of the POWs.

Units of the Volunteer Defence Corps were formed at Leongatha, Dumbalk and Meeniyan. Manoeuvres were held on the Recreation Reserve when members were instructed in the techniques of unarmed combat, Vickers machine gun practice, mortar firing, grenade throwing etc. Bivouacs were held at Inverloch and a mock battle at Beilby's Hill took place between the units of Meeniyan, Dumbalk and Mardan against volunteers from Leongatha Inverloch, Mirboo North, Mount Eccles and Berry's Creek. Over 250 men took part in the exercise which was important enough from the military point of view to warrant the presence of Brigadier Scott from the city. One member of the VDC was armed with a walking stick instead of a rifle, while another appeared in full 'war paint' with an array of medals and uniform from past wars. Some medals were 'the wrong side up' with the result that a fellow VDC member asked him which way he was walking.[31]

The severe drought of 1944 over Victoria affected Leongatha residents more than food and clothing rationing. The two reservoirs supplying Leongatha were showing signs of depletion by the end of the year, and the Commissioners were forced to impose restrictions to conserve supply. Visitors to Leongatha complained of having to carry water upstairs at the two hotels to perform their ablutions. Engineer C. Bate produced figures at the Water Trust meeting showing that per head of population residents were using 268 gallons per day. As the people living in the high portion of the town were unable to obtain water from the mains, the amount per head per day by those who did get water was considerably more. Commissioner R.J. Hagan expressed the opinion that the ideal time to water gardens was between 2 and 3 a.m. 'There was something wrong with a man who was not prepared to do that to keep his garden in good order', said Mr Hagan.[32]

As in previous droughts in the northern part of the State, hundreds of horses were forwarded to Woorayl Shire for agistment. Some of these were used by farmers in Woorayl Shire for the cultivation of potatoes. In its efforts to ensure sufficient food for the Armed Forces, the Government instituted a contract system for the growing of potatoes. Each grower nominated the acreage to be grown and the Government paid for the produce, landed at the railhead at £12 10s 0d per ton, provided it passed inspection by an officer of the Department of Agriculture. It was a form of orderly marketing never before experienced by farmers in South Gippsland. Production of potatoes increased dramatically around Leongatha. By 1944 there were 231 contracting growers responsible for 1,850 acres, with an estimated yield of 7,000 tons. Loading figures for the Leongatha Railway Station for 1942 and 1943 were 1,600 and 3,356 tons respectively.[33]

The dairy industry did not share in any expansion during the war years. Mr H. Jones, Secretary of the Leongatha Butter Factory, stated that peak output of the company occurred in 1942 with 1,815 tons of butter. Even allowing for the diversion of milk for cheese-making, production had dropped to the equivalent of 1,680 tons of butter in 1943 with a further drop to 1,516 tons for 1944. Between 1941 and 1944 there was a decline from 684 to 618 in the number of dairy farms operating, with the number of cows being milked declining from 22,166 to 19,956.[34] There were several factors contributing towards this decline. Severe rationing of superphosphate for grassland purposes, scarcity of labour on farms and the decline of herd testing all played their part. Herd testing associations had been formed at Tarwin Lower in 1921, at Leongatha and Dumbalk in 1922, and had played an important role in increasing production within the Shire. At Dumbalk North the average butterfat yield per cow had risen from 167 lbs of fat from 800 cows in 1922-3 to 310 lbs of fat from 1,087 cows in 1940.[35] The majority of herd testing units closed down in 1941-42 because of a lack of testers. The policy of the Department of Agriculture of including women in their twice-yearly training classes enabled the Leongatha Association to re-open in 1943 with the appointment of Miss Ann Wilson of Pakenham as official tester.[36]

The summer of 1944 which brought water restrictions to Leongatha residents also brought several outbreaks of grass fires within the Shire that caused considerable damage. On 21 and 22 January outbreaks at Nerrena, Hallston and Wooreen were only quelled by the strenuous efforts of over 100 volunteers from Leongatha. First Constable Longmuir and Mounted Constable Polwarth co-operated with ex-Captain Hodgkiss and Foreman T. McGaw of the Leongatha Fire Brigade in directing operations over a forty-eight hour period. With temperatures over the century and a strong north wind blowing, the fires brought home to everyone the necessity for efficient brigades to stamp out fires quickly.

Unloading milk cans, Leongatha Butter Factory, 1948 (from Woorayl Shire Historical Society).

Three weeks later on 14 February, another outbreak occurred at Boorool in which 3,000 acres of grassland were burnt in a few hours. First noticed on the property of Mr J.A. McIndoe where a haystack ignited, it spread quickly across grassland towards Mardan where Mr D.W. Findlay suffered extensive losses of stock and fencing. Over sixty volunteers from Leongatha managed to save Mr Findlay's house after heroic efforts. His dairy herd escaped unharmed, because they fled before the flames to the safety of the cow yard. All fencing and sixty sheep were lost in a matter of minutes. The fire then raced several hundred yards to the property of Mr T.W. Coulter, and in a matter of minutes, the commodious home with all contents, together with the machinery shed and implements, were destroyed.[37] Frantic efforts by volunteers prevented further loss of the home of Mr W.J. Coulter, where the garage was destroyed. Fortunately, a car and truck had been driven into a crop of millet as a precaution, while the women and children had been removed to Dumbalk for safety. The fire swept through McColl's property and, only after strenuous efforts by volunteers, was diverted from the Presbyterian Church.

On their return to Leongatha at 10 p.m., the firefighters found the town in semi-darkness. Other fires had destroyed power lines between Yinnar and Boolarra, and it was not until 7 a.m. the following morning that Leongatha residents were re-connected to Yallourn. As a result of these fires, volunteer bush fire brigades were formed at Leongatha and Meeniyan. A small government grant enabled these brigades to purchase fire-fighting equipment, and each brigade was allocated an ex-army vehicle. Fees for members of the Leongatha brigade were fixed at five shillings for landholders and one shilling for non-landholders.[38]

The Leongatha Flaxgrowers' Association continued its attempts to have a full scutching mill established to save transport costs to Koo-Wee-Rup and provide further employment in the district. These attempts were unsuccessful, as new methods of harvesting the crop, developed as a result of wartime labour shortages, had eliminated much of the work associated with retting and gaiting of the straw. By January 1945 the flax crops were being de-seeded with a stripper while standing. The crop was then cut with a binder fitted with special rollers that crushed the straw and left it spread out evenly for paddock retting. When dried sufficiently, the straw was then gathered and carted direct to the mill for extraction of the fibre. This new harvesting technique signalled the end of the age-old practice of hand spreading and gaiting. Acreage sown to flax in Woorayl Shire fluctuated around 700 to 800 acres during the 1940s, whereas the minimum required for a scutching mill was 1,200 to 1,500 acres.[39]

A shortage of hospital facilities in Woorayl Shire became apparent during the war. St Mary's Hospital at 73 McCartin Street, that had been conducted in an exemplary manner for many years by the Dodd sisters, closed on 30 June 1942, leaving only the private hospital Stradbroke in Church Street to service the town and district. Acting Shire President, Cr Bond, called a public meeting to discuss the formation of a bush nursing hospital on 13 August at which over 100 people attended. Cr H.P. Williams of Meeniyan said that the whole Shire would be behind the scheme so there would be no doubt over finance. On the motion of Postmaster J.C. Luckie and draper Norman J. Wilson, it was resolved that steps be taken to ascertain how many people would be prepared to subscribe 30s or £2 per annum towards the cost of such a hospital.[40] A strong committee, headed by J.C. Luckie as Chairman and Bank Managers H.J. Baker and A.E. Jamieson, soon had over £600 in hand for the project from 412 contributors. The committee quickly arranged for the lease of St Mary's Hospital, the provision of staff, registration of premises and fixing of appropriate fees.

Sister Pyle was appointed first Matron, and at the official opening on 8 December 1942, the town band marched along McCartin Street to the hospital followed by members of the VDC in uniform. Shire President, Cr A.C. Ashenden, welcomed Sir James and Lady Barrett and introduced Cr H.P. Williams, President of the Hospital Committee, and Mrs H.J. Rossiter, President of the Women's Auxiliary. Sir James said that it cost between £3-4 per week to keep a patient at the hospital, and the difference between that and the fees charged had to be made up by members' subscriptions and other fund-raising activities. Bush nursing hospitals did not receive assistance from the Government, and each hospital was conducted as thought fit by the management.[41]

By January 1944 Sister Pyle reported that the average daily number of patients treated at the hospital for the month of December was 5.1, an increase of over 100 percent since opening. In November 1944, with a view to erection of new premises, the Committee arranged for the purchase of four and a half acres of land from the Curnick family in Jeffrey Street for the sum of £1,500. Several blocks were inspected, but two were outside the sewerage treatment area. The Jeffrey Street site was chosen because of its admirable position and 'the clear view of the beautiful surrounding countryside'.[42]

Postmaster J.C. Luckie held office in the Leongatha branch of the Australian Natives' Association at that time and took an active interest in movements for improvements within the community. The ANA had proved a valuable forum for debate since its inception, and many worthwhile ideas had emanated from its discussions. For many years the ANA had offered prizes in district schools for improved school gardens and essay writing. In 1935 the Leongatha branch had developed a detailed and comprehensive plan for the installation of a swimming pool in the town but was unable to obtain sufficient support for the project.[43]

In April 1945 a delegation from the Leongatha branch of the ANA, consisting of Messrs Aberdeen, Luckie and Place, waited on Woorayl Shire Council urging the acquisition by Council of the Moss Vale Park area. The delegation stressed that although the present owner, Mr J. Hayes, was amenable to the holding of sports and picnics on the area, a change of ownership could mean that this beautiful spot might be lost for use by future generations.

With the death of Francis Moss at Buninyong in 1916, the nursery that had supplied so many of the fruit and ornamental trees for district homesteads was closed, and the whole property offered for sale. It passed through several hands until purchased by Mr Les Edey in 1931. Mr Edey took an active interest in the Berry's Creek school which began holding its annual sports and picnic on the banks of the river from 1933 onwards.[44] After Les Edey sold the property to Mr J.S. Hayes in the early 1940s, approaches were made to him by Mr J. Dowling and Mr C. Aberdeen of Berry's Creek with a view to reserving the river bank area for a public park. With support from the Leongatha branch of the ANA, and subsequently from Woorayl and Mirboo Shire Councils, an area along the river bank of approximately ten acres was sold for this purpose by Mr Hayes in March 1946. At a public meeting held at Berry's Creek in April, the first Committee of Management was formed comprising five local residents, together with one representative each from Woorayl and Mirboo Councils. Initial members were Messrs C. Aberdeen Chairman, K.H. Chisholm Secretary, P. Hayes, J.R. Forrester, J.W. Dowling, G.M. Davis and J.W. Collins.[45]

The ending of hostilities on 15 August 1945 was an occasion for joy for all Woorayl Shire residents. A combined Church service of thanksgiving held at the Memorial Hall on the Wednesday afternoon preceded the official Peace Day celebrations on the following day. A special committee organised a gala procession which assembled in Ogilvy Street, then wound its leisurely way through Bair Street down Roughead Street to the Recreation Reserve. The whole community celebrated the return of peace after almost six years of hostilities. The procession included the town band, the fire brigade, members of the RSL, the VDC, horsemen in costume, swagmen and schoolchildren. There were 'nigger minstrels on a lorry' and pre-school children pushing handcarts. A crowd of between 1,500 and 2,000 had lunch on the 'Rec.' before enjoying the spectacle of a fancy dress football match and sports for the children.[46]

In attempts to keep up the supply of food for allied troops, army authorities were releasing personnel for farm work prior to the cessation of hostilities. Others returned to civilian life during the following twelve months and were accorded welcome home functions in their respective localities. Record crowds attended these events arranged at Leongatha South and Meeniyan in February 1946. At Dumbalk the welcome home took the form of a banquet which was held in the weighing room of the butter factory. As in all wars there were some men who never returned. In October 1945 a wave of sadness passed over Leongatha when three telegrams of condolence arrived for the well-known Howard, Ketels and Sangster families. They were official confirmation of the deaths of Jack Howard, Fred Ketels and Thomas Sangster who were captured at the fall of Rabaul in January 1942.[47]

At the final meeting of the Woorayl War Fund in April 1946, a Deed of Trust was adopted for the disbursement of the balance of the remaining funds. All moneys from the waste products depot that had operated so successfully during the war years in Hayes's old brick store at the corner of Roughead and Hughes Streets was transferred to the Red Cross Fund and the balance of the general fund was voted to the Soldiers' Relief Fund. A total of £26,609 was raised from the numerous wartime activities, and the trustees appointed to administer the relief fund were Messrs E.R. Harding, J.F. Couper, C.L. Brumley, V.A. Amos, J.W. Dowling, W.T. Jones and W.E. Wheeler.[48]

As in the 1914-18 War the return of the ex-servicemen led to movements within the Shire for an appropriate memorial to the fallen. Many favoured the building of a memorial hospital which would cater for all sections of the Shire. It was claimed by supporters of this scheme that a public hospital would attract greater government funding than the bush nursing hospital envisaged for the Jeffrey Street site. This claim was refuted at a public meeting in February 1946 chaired by Shire President Cr Sloan. Mr McVilly of the Hospitals and Charities Commission stated that the Government would be as generous to a bush nursing hospital as a public hospital, provided certain conditions pertaining to public patients were complied with.[49]

The outcome of this meeting, which was attended by over 100 people, was a decision to proceed with plans for the erection of a public hospital. A committee of twelve was elected of whom six were members of the proposed bush nursing hospital. At the March meeting of Woorayl Shire Council, Cr H.P. Williams of Meeniyan successfully moved a motion that Council donate £1,000 towards the future Woorayl District Memorial Hospital saying that 'no ratepayer would dare question the action of the council when the health of the community was considered'.[50]

A public appeal for funds was immediately launched, followed by a Queen Carnival that culminated in a crowning ceremony at the Leongatha Recreation Reserve on 16 November 1946. Over 3,000 people witnessed the crowning of the Queens by Hon. W. MacAulay, a member of the Hospitals and Charities Commission. Lord Chancellor P.J. O'Malley read the proclamation bringing the Queen Carnival to an end. Hospital committee President, F.R. Moore, paid tribute to the Queens whose committees raised over £10,000 towards the proposed hospital. Amounts raised by different committees were:

Queen of Transport	Elsie Knight	£2,454 12s 6d
Queen of Agriculture	Marjorie Williams	£2,352 18s 10d
Queen of Song	Norma Hancock	£2,050 3s 11d
Queen of Peace	Melvie Dunlop	£1,789 6s 2d
Queen of Sport	Anne Roughead	£1,520 8s 0d.[51]

Further fund-raising activities took place during 1947 amongst which was the raffle of a Vauxhall car donated by Melbourne philanthropist James Flood. This raffle was drawn on 18 April 1947 by Mr W.G. McKenzie, MLA, Minister for Agriculture. The winning ticket was drawn from a huge barrel made available by the Lord Mayor of Melbourne, Cr Connelly. Winner of the raffle was F.M. Glass of Carnegie, with the hospital committee profiting by over £4,000.[52]

During 1947 and 1948 a strong movement developed within the community for a change in the site of the proposed hospital from Jeffrey Street to McCartin's Hill on Koonwarra Road. The committee of the bush nursing hospital had already proceeded with the drawing of plans for the Jeffrey Street site and were loath to disrupt the program. Reasons for and against the change were advanced by different groups. The Leongatha branch of the CWA favoured the McCartin's Hill site because it would 'enable the management to keep its own cows, grow vegetables, poultry and fruit for hospital use'.[53] Many people from the Meeniyan and Dumbalk districts also favoured it because it was more visible and accessible to people entering the town.

Hospital committee Secretary E.W. Sutherland produced a letter in June 1947 from the National Trustees acting on behalf of the McCartin Estate saying that the site was 'definitely not for sale'.[54] Dr W.A. Sloss and Mr McVilly of the Hospitals and Charities Commission, after inspection of both sites, declared in favour of the Jeffrey Street site. The position altered in September when, following further representations to the Byrne family, executors of Hugh McCartin, they agreed to make available a site of four to five acres on the hill

Potato planting, Koorooman, c. 1952 (from M. Wightman).

for a hospital. When Cr H.P. Williams successfully moved a motion at the September 1948 Council meeting stating that 'in the Council's opinion the best site for a Memorial Hospital is McCartin's hill and we ask as principal subscribers to the fund that this site be adopted', the members of the Woorayl District Memorial Hospital (WDMH) Committee were in a quandary.

Many people were of the opinion that the Jeffrey Street site could be sold by the committee, but this was not so. At a crowded public meeting held at the Memorial Hall on 18 October 1948, Chairman Frank Moore revealed that under the terms of purchase the Jeffrey Street land had to be returned to the former owners if not used for a hospital. This rather rowdy meeting carried a motion by a large majority favouring the McCartin's Hill site. The situation was further complicated in February 1949 when Woorayl Shire Council received a letter from the Hospitals and Charities Commission stating that it had found 'the Jeffrey Street site to be the better and would now proceed with the development of plans and specifications for same'.[55]

At the annual meeting of the WDMH Committee in March 1949, a motion of no-confidence in the committee over the question of the site was carried, and members of the committee resigned as a body on 7 March. A new committee was elected in April composed of supporters of the McCartin's Hill site and was successful in changing the decision of the Hospitals and Charities Commission to proceed with plans for the Jeffrey Street site. The amalgamation of the Bush Nursing Hospital Committee and the WDMH Committee in May 1950 helped heal the divisions within the community caused by the dispute. Through the generosity of the Byrne family, five acres of the McCartin's Hill site was finally acquired by the WDMH Committee in 1951, and the Jeffrey Street site was returned to its former owners.[56] It was later sub-divided into building blocks serviced by a new street, Douglas Court.

The return of the ex-servicemen to civilian life led to an upsurge of farming activities within the Woorayl Shire. The expansion of acreage under potatoes during wartime led to a great increase of activity at the Leongatha Railway Station with over 5,000 tons being loaded annually in the years 1945-51.[57] Until the 1950s practically the whole crop was shifted by rail. With the termination of the contract system, a Potato Growers' Association was formed in Victoria with a strong branch at Leongatha with over 100 members. Unlike other potato growing districts, the Leongatha area is blessed with a wide variety of soils and dependable rainfall. This enabled planting and harvesting to be carried out over a very wide period of time with resultant benefits on employment within the district. When the Potato Marketing Board was formed in 1947, the South Gippsland representative was Mr L.M. Timmins who subsequently occupied the position of Board Chairman. Members of the Board worked unceasingly to bring stability to the industry with great benefit to growers and consumers alike. Unfortunately, the increased production which resulted from their efforts brought about gluts that could only be regulated by imposition of quotas on growers' deliveries.

The Board visited Leongatha in February 1949 when Chairman A.C. Boustead explained Board policy to a meeting of growers under the chairmanship of Harold Morter. Mr Boustead said forty-three percent of growers grew an average of three acres each, with twenty-seven percent growing an average of nine acres each.[58] Dissatisfaction with the imposition of quotas on delivery and the growing prevalence of motor transport enabled some growers to bypass government inspection depots at railway stations in the sale of their produce to unscrupulous merchants. This factor, coupled with Section 92 of the Commonwealth Constitution which ensured free trade between the States, ultimately led to the breakdown of the Potato Marketing Board.

Flax growing in the area reached its peak in 1945 with over 900 acres being grown. A state-wide competition sponsored by the Flax Production Committee resulted in first prize for the whole of Victoria being won by Messrs F. and A. Lester of Mardan. The prize winning crop was planted during the last week of August 1945 on second year land that had been ploughed with a mouldboard plough, well disced and consolidated by harrowing and rolling. Harvested in the third week of December, it yielded forty-six hundredweight of good quality straw per acre with only a minute percentage of weeds.[59] Flax production declined rapidly after the war, with the mill and machinery being sold by auction in May 1947.[60] The building was converted to a shearing shed complex in 1948 by its new owner, Mr J.A. McIndoe, where a four-stand plant was installed to cater for district flocks.

Onion production continued on a limited scale on the red soils around Leongatha, Mardan and Koonwarra, providing employment and reasonable returns from relatively small acreages. Onions had the advantage over potatoes in that the Brown Spanish variety could be exported. In 1947 over 1,000 tons of Leongatha onions were exported to Singapore and the Pacific islands.[61] This increased volume of outward produce from the Leongatha Railway Station in the immediate post-war years led to the purchase and installation of a new weighbridge in 1947 adjacent to the bandstand.

Although cropping played an important role in farming activities during the 1940s, the major component of Woorayl Shire's primary industries remained its dairying and stock-raising activities. It was the expansion of these that provided the stimulus to the post-war development. In August 1948 directors of the Leongatha Butter and Cheese Factory Co. Ltd laid the foundation stone for a large new butter factory to cater for the increased production of milk and cream within the district. Housing accommodation was so limited in the township at the time that workmen employed in its building were billeted in the exhibition pavilion on the nearby Recreation Reserve. Land for provision of sixteen Housing Commission homes beween Koonwarra Road and Hassett Street was purchased in 1946, and construction of the first five was completed by November 1947, with tenancy being decided by ballot.[62] Tenants moved in before street construction had been commenced following delay in negotiations between the Commission and Woorayl Shire Council. Council unanimously decided at their February 1947 meeting that the name of this first street in the post-war expansion of Leongatha should be Owen Street after the late Lieutenant-Colonel W.T. Owen, killed in the fighting in Papua in 1942.[63]

Hoeing onions, Koorooman, 1948 (from M. Wightman).

The scarcity of housing and the resultant boom in building operations caused labour shortages in other fields. Woorayl Shire Council was unable to obtain men for roadworks. In 1946 Engineer C. Bate consistently advertised for men 'at £4 19s for a 5 day week of 44 hours. 1s 8d per day camp allowance. Tents and beds provided. Meals supplied at cost'.[64] At the suggestion of the RSL, Council finally decided to nominate twelve British ex-servicemen to augment their labour force. Accommodation was provided by the purchase of the former flax mill and its conversion from a shearing shed into dormitory facilities in 1949. From the Council's point of view, the scheme was not a success. The first to arrive, an ex-paratrooper from Scotland, Robert Millar, stayed only a few days with the Council and then resigned.[65]

Council had expected the men to arrive in one batch and had engaged a cook for this purpose, but such was the scarcity of labour in Australia that the other eleven obtained jobs before reaching Leongatha. Under the post-war migration scheme only non-British migrants were bound to remain with their sponsoring employers. Council employed some of these migrants who were quartered in the converted flax mill, but with the transitory nature of workmen at that time, the scheme was not continued for long. The flax mill site was then developed as a Council machinery and storage depot.

The 1940s witnessed the beginning of a slow transition for Woorayl Shire

Soldier settler Don Lyndon moving in, 1948 (from E. Lyndon).

from being a solely agricultural and pastoral economy. Although Leongatha's annual Show which reflected the diverse nature of produce from within the area continued to draw record crowds, the composition of exhibitors, spectators and showmen was slowly changing. Whereas entries were previously drawn from within South Gippsland, motor transport enabled competitors to attend from other parts of the State. Changing farm technology was represented by vast numbers of machinery exhibits. Tractors, trucks, cars and horse transports filled the showgrounds. The boxing troupe led by Harry Johns, a showman par excellence, continued to dominate the sideshow scene. Boxing troupes added spice and variety to Show Day. To listen to Harry Johns, clad in white shirt and cream trousers, frothing at the mouth while he harangued and cajoled one of the local pugilists to step up on the board to match one of his fighters was a show on its own. Waving a £5 note as an inducement, a sum which represented a week's wages for many of his onlookers, Harry Johns always managed to entice one of the local young-bloods to 'go five rounds for the purse'. His team of fighters clad in shiny trunks and woollen dressing gowns, one ringing a bell, another banging a drum and challenging all comers, provided a sharp contrast to other sideshows such as the Fat Lady and the Snake Charmer.

But whereas outside exhibitors and showmen were interested in taking money out of the district, there were others who were prepared to put money into the town and create employment. R.V. 'Vern' Pease, draper, member of the old established firm of R.E. Pease and Co. from Wonthaggi, sensed the potential growth of Leongatha and established a branch of its drapery business in McCartin Street in October 1938. Under capable management it quickly grew to become one of the leading business establishments of the town. Mr H.S. Roberts grasped the potential advantages of a stable labour force by setting up the firm of Revelation Fashions in Elizabeth House, Bair Street, Leongatha, in May 1944.[66] The marked improvements in road transport coupled with better telephone and telegraphic services were slowly beginning to outweigh freight disadvantages for light industries. Initially employing six to eight girls in the manufacture of women's blouses and skirts, Mr Roberts hoped to double his labour force within a few years with the production of frocks and underwear. Revelation Fashions proved to be the forerunner of several more diversified industries to be established in the post-war era.

15. RESURGENCE

There were several factors favouring the development of Woorayl Shire from 1950 onwards. Some were natural while others were man-made. The natural ones included its climate, its geographical position relative to Melbourne and the Latrobe Valley, its assured rainfall and the fertility and topography of its soils. These natural assets were capitalised on by the industry of its inhabitants, the introduction of artificial fertilisers, scientific methods of farm production and the use of machinery. The successful introduction of myxomatosis in 1950 brought the depredations of the rabbit down to manageable proportions with huge benefits to farmers. During the 1950s the Federal Government's economic policies encouraged land clearing and development by means of taxation concessions. This enticed many people other than traditional farmers into embarking on the development of large areas of lighter soils in the Woorayl Shire. It entailed considerable capital expenditure in bulldozing, ploughing, fertilising, seeding and fencing that provided gainful employment for large numbers of men. The Pitman method of pasture development, whereby a fifty-fifty mixture of lime and superphosphate is drilled into virgin soils with innoculated clover seed, was widely used.

The purchase by the Government of large properties for sub-division among soldier settlers in the 1950s brought about an influx of young energetic men to the Shire who contributed greatly to community growth. On dairy farms the provision of better milking facilities enabled larger herds to be handled. The universal adoption of three-point linkage tractors on these farms was followed by new methods of fodder conservation, cultivation methods etc. As with all machinery, there was an inbuilt risk attached to their use, particularly on hilly country. Statistics showed that farming in South Gippsland was, indeed, a relatively high risk occupation. In the Leongatha-Korumburra area ten farmers were killed and several more injured in the five year period 1958-63 due to tractors capsizing.[1]

Aerial top-dressing began in the Woorayl Shire in the mid-1950s with a resultant increase in the productivity of the hill country in the north of the Shire. Techniques were soon developed for the aerial spraying of chemicals necessary for the eradication of noxious weeds and insect pests on pastures. The increase in stock carrying capacity of the Shire from these new methods benefited the dairy factories by providing increased milk and cream supply. Stock agents and carrying firms also gained from the increased stock numbers. At Leongatha two young men, Tom Richardson and Ian Leeming, built new cattle sale yards on the Melbourne road adjacent to those of the Gippsland and Northern Company. Opened by Cr C.A. Bond in June 1954, these yards were extended several years later to cope with the expansion of pig production within the district.

While milk was being separated on farms, pig raising expanded with cow numbers. A few specialist pig producers, such as Ray Cashin on the Labour Colony site, relied on purchased grain or whey from butter factories. With a turn-off of forty to fifty baconers weekly, Ray Cashin was for many years one of the largest pig producers in Gippsland. Most dairy farmers sold their pigs locally at either Meeniyan or Leongatha pig sales, which were held on the alternate week to the cattle sale. Bobby calves were also sold on this day, known throughout the Shire as 'Pig and Lady Day'. The main reason for this name was that often the proceeds from the sale of calves or pigs was given direct to the farmer's wife for shopping purposes. Even in the 1950s there were many farm women who came to the township only once a fortnight to purchase necessary supplies. Many of them had spent the intervening period in the care and treatment of young calves and were more than justified in receiving the proceeds for household and personal purchases.

Proceeds from the sale of pigs and bobby calves were greatly appreciated by shopkeepers. Even the Leongatha High School fixed the date for its annual fair in the 1930s to coincide with the first pig sale in July to take advantage of the extra money in circulation.[2] The Gippsland and Northern Company opened a new set of pig sale yards at Meeniyan in March 1948 adjacent to the railway trucking yards to cater for the district's increase in pig numbers. At Leongatha in March 1956 this firm yarded a record 1,020 pigs at their fortnightly sale.[3] Richardson and Leeming applied to Woorayl Shire Council for permission to build pig sale yards adjacent to their cattle yards in 1957. A petition to Council was immediately drawn up by 65 adjoining ratepayers objecting to their establishment, while a counter petition circulated by Richardson and Leeming was signed by 107 farmers in favour of the proposal. Permission was finally given by Council on condition that no effluent went into the town's drains. This proviso was overcome by the use of a Furphy water cart for effluent disposal, with the first sale of pigs in the new yards being conducted in September 1959.[4]

The increased income generated from the farming industries was soon reflected in the growth of townships with Leongatha deriving the greatest benefit. The extension of the school bus system to all parts of the Shire centralised the bulk of the educational facilities at Leongatha. This in turn created many more jobs for teachers and ancillary staff which further aggravated the shortage of housing.

Members of the Leongatha branch of the National Catholic Rural Movement, encouraged by Father William Caffrey, initiated plans that resulted in the formation of the first Co-operative Housing Society in Leongatha in 1953. Directors of the first society were Messrs T.P. Whelan (Chairman), R.P. O'Malley, T.W. Clark, James O'Brien and William Gleeson.[5] The money allocated to the first society was quickly taken up. Chairman Tom Whelan reported at the first annual meeting in July 1954 that the type of house on which the advances were approved was fifty percent weatherboard, thirty percent weatherboard and cement sheet, ten percent cement sheet and ten percent brick veneer.[6] Further societies were subsequently formed under the guidance of Secretary Alan Proudlock. Mr Whelan reported in 1959 that the societies had financed 111 houses in five and a half years, of which 57 had been built in Leongatha. Shire Council figures revealed that one in every three houses then being built in Leongatha was Housing Society financed.[7]

In order to cater for the demand for rental housing, thirty acres adjacent to the Woorayl District Memorial Hospital site were purchased from the Byrne family by the Housing Commission in 1956. The land acquired for the hospital by the hospital committee in 1951 was planted with potatoes to help in the raising of funds. Labour and seed were donated and the crop harvested successfully during April and May of 1952. Through the efforts of the Woorayl District Memorial Hospital Committee, Leongatha was successful in winning the Top-Town contest for 1952 with a prize of £1,000 being added to the hospital fund. When making the award, Mr J. Pacini, General Manager of the *Sun News Pictorial* which sponsored the contest, complimented all associated with the competition. Chairman of the hospital committee, Greg Welsford, said the contest had developed local talent and that residents appreciated the excellent artists that had come from the city for the various concerts. Mr Welsford also stated that the committee had £38,000 in assets and yet was unable to get permission from the Hospitals and Charities Commission to proceed with plans and specifications for a new hospital.[8]

Plans were finally approved and permission obtained for the building of a twenty-eight-bed hospital in November 1955. Construction proceeded slowly, and it was not until 24 June 1958, that the Governor, Sir Dallas Brooks, officially opened the building. Dr J. Lindell, Chairman of the Hospitals and Charities Commission, prior to handing the gold key to Sir Dallas for the opening, said that the design of hospitals could only be improved by mistakes found in others. He also said there was no such thing as free hospitals, 'You have to pay for them either by taxation or by generous giving'.[9] Mr R. Seidel, President of the Leongatha branch of the RSL, dedicated the memorial stone in the foyer of the hospital to the memory of service personnel who made the supreme sacrifice in the 1939-45 War.

The building of Housing Commission homes and the opening of the hospital on McCartin's Hill were contingent on the completion of the sewerage project begun for the town in 1939. After closing down in 1942, the Sewerage Authority was unable to recommence work on the scheme until 1956 when tenders were let for construction of treatment works in Begg Street.[10] Upon completion of these works, the Authority began house connections in April 1958, and by October 1959 it reported that 356 houses had been connected.[11]

The opening of the new Woorayl District Memorial Hospital signalled the end of the private hospitals that had served the area for the past half century. Stradbroke Private Hospital in Church Street, conducted by Sister Janet Potter for the previous thirty-six years, finally closed. A farewell party was given on 21 July 1958 in nearby St Peter's Parish Hall as a mark of appreciation of her service to the community. Sister Potter had not had a holiday for twenty-two years, and during the thirty-six years she conducted Stradbroke, over 3,000 children were born there under her care and guidance. To a crowded gathering Dr G. Bennett spoke at length of her stirling work. 'She is a nurse of the old regime who worked 24 hours of a day', said Dr Bennett.[12] It was an outstanding record that spoke volumes for her devotion to nursing and which earned Sister Potter a respected niche in the hearts and minds of Woorayl Shire residents.

The post-war growth of the Shire led to increased demands on Council. When formed originally in 1888, it comprised 240 square miles, consisting of only two ridings, East and West, with three councillors in each. Through re-alignment of boundaries by 1896, it had increased in size to 475 square miles with three ridings, West, South and Mirboo, with a predominance of farmers and graziers representing ratepayers.[13] Cr H.P. Williams, proprietor of the Red Store at Meeniyan, served on Woorayl Council for sixteen years from 1937 to 1953, with four terms as President. At the November 1950 meeting Cr Williams success-fully moved a motion to bring in compulsory voting at Council elections. In the course of a lively debate, he said 'that ratepayers show little or no interest in municipal elections. When complaints are made about something that "the silly old councillors have done" or not done, those complaints come from people who do not vote'.[14] Cr A.C. Ashenden, in supporting the motion, said

> the job is done for nothing and councillors do not ask for anything. But the least we should know is that our services are satisfactory or otherwise. When a 46 percent poll is declared the majority of the people do not give us that satisfaction.[15]

Following requests from interested ratepayers, a poll was taken in 1952 on the desirability of change from the system of improved capital value rating to the unimproved site value system. A keenly fought campaign by protagonists of both systems resulted in a resounding defeat for the proposal with 1,098 'Yes' votes and 3,119 'No' votes.[16]

The increase in the size of Leongatha township led to moves for the formation of a town or central riding. The Progress Association had officially requested Council to place the question before ratepayers at the election in August 1944, but Council replied that it 'did not consider it an opportune time for a poll to be taken'.[17] Following renewed pressure during the 1950s and the increased work load being placed on the nine councillors, it was decided to re-subdivide into four ridings in 1957 with a provision for a central riding. The first elections under the new boundaries took place in August 1958 and created great interest throughout the Shire. Seventeen candidates nominated for the twelve positions with the successful candidates being:

> Central Riding — Crs C.A. Bond, C. Hyland, J.A. McIndoe.
> North Riding — Crs R.E. McIndoe, A.C. Ashenden, W.G. Holt.
> South Riding — Crs H.G. Bird, H. Kinnish, R.A. Seidel.
> West Riding — Crs P.J. Buckley, J.A. McDonald, W.J. Hinds.[18]

Following thirty-five years of service as Shire Engineer, Mr C.E. Bate retired from that position in 1950 and was replaced by Mr F. Stansfield. As a mark of appreciation of Mr Bate's services, Council included a plaque in the new overhead railway bridge connecting Ogilvy and Bair Streets. Opened on 10 March 1955, Shire President Cr Sloan said that, when Mr Bate first came to the Shire in 1915, 'it took him two days to go Turton's Creek in a cart or buggy. Now it could be done in two hours or less'.[19]

When Fred Stansfield came to Woorayl Shire in 1950, after four years at Korumburra, his engineering responsibilities gradually increased to encompass such tasks as construction of playing areas for schools and the design of community projects. Following complaints from nearby residents regarding the disused quarry in Worthy Street, Leongatha, Council decided in 1954 to partially fill it and slope the sides for safety purposes. Engineer Stansfield reported that blasting was unsuccessful, so he had engaged road contractor Harry Anthony with bulldozer and ripper to do the job at a cost of £200.[20]

The new bridge at Tarwin Lower caused the engineering staff a great deal of worry. The lack of a suitable foundation for bridge building on the banks of the Tarwin proved a formidable problem. In March 1955 Stansfield reported that

> The weight of embankment placed at the approaches to the bridge caused a wedge of land 100 ft wide along the river bank and 60 ft back from the bank along the new road to slip towards the river and downstream. Weight of the embankment would be 5-600 tons. Deck of bridge on the southern abutment has dropped 20 ins and moved downstream 18 ins breaking the joint of R.C. piles and underside of buttresses supporting concrete crosshead. A new temporary pier to be driven and southern span lifted to remedy the situation.[21]

These temporary repairs sufficed for over thirty years until major repairs and widening of the bridge took place in 1987 at a cost of $245,777. The Tarwin Lower area was the scene of a major search by police and local residents in 1952-3 in connection with the mysterious disappearance of Margaret Clement of Tullaree in May 1952. First taken up by Francis Longmore in the 1880s, Tullaree was subsequently developed into a highly productive property by Charles Widdis, a grazier from Heyfield. Carrying out extensive drainage and land clearing works, Widdis soon transformed this low-lying area on the banks of the Tarwin. With an imposing seventeen-roomed brick homestead set on over 2,000 acres, Tullaree was purchased in 1907 by members of the Clement family, formally of Prospect Station, Seaspray. Peter Scott Clement had been a major shareholder in The Long Tunnel goldmine at Walhalla, and following his death in 1890, his family inherited considerable wealth. Jeannie and Margaret Clement purchased Tullaree from Widdis on the recommendation of their brother Peter.

Having travelled extensively overseas on the proceeds of their father's investments, the Clement sisters lived a highly gracious lifestyle at Tullaree, hosting many parties for their numerous friends and acquaintances. Peter Scott Clement, Junior, was severely wounded during the 1914-18 War, and on his return the property gradually deteriorated through bad management and insufficient attention to drainage. By the 1950s the greater portion of it had reverted to swamp land. When Jeannie Clement died in 1950, it took eight men to carry her coffin through the swamp to the nearest all-weather road. In May 1952 neighbour Stanley Livingstone found the homestead empty with no trace of Margaret Clement. Despite an extensive search by police and subsequent draining of the surrounding swamp land, her body was never recovered.[22] Her disappearance remains one of the unsolved mysteries of the district, in some respects similar to that of Martin Wiberg at Waratah Bay almost sixty years earlier.

The growth of townships within the Shire was accompanied by a diversity of interests of its residents. Service clubs attracted many and led to the initiation of projects for the betterment of towns and district. On 15 November 1952 the first meeting of the Leongatha Apex Club was held at McNamara's Cafe in McCartin Street, with local veterinarian, Goff Letts, being elected first President.[23] Imbued with a sense of service, the Apexians' first task was to clean up the area around the Strzelecki monument in Long Street. The bandstand opposite the Court House had fallen into disuse and disrepair and was used principally as a camping spot for inebriates and swagmen. Apexians cleared this area and established the Apex Park, which was formally handed over to the Shire in 1957.

For many years attempts had been made to create a caravan park in Leongatha to cater for the increasing number of tourists. In 1939 Cr Bond suggested to Council the desirability of using a park in a'Beckett Street for this purpose. Owing to objections from nearby residents, Council did not adopt this suggestion. Although several sites were considered, none could be found within the Sewerage Authority area. Apexians finally located a one and three-quarter acre block in Turner Street that had been acquired by the Army in the 1940s as a drill hall site. After a request was made by Apex to Council asking their support in the matter, the Army agreed in December 1962 to sell the land for £1,000.[24] The loan money was made available to Council by the Tourist Authority, and Apex agreed to repay the money to Council over a twenty year period. The Caravan Park was quickly developed by Apexians during 1963-4 and proved an immediate success.

After the re-alignment of the South Gippsland Highway in 1964, Council purchased a small area of land opposite the Woorayl District Memorial Hospital. Apex members established a children's playground on one half of this area, while the other half was developed as a native park by Don and Ellen Lyndon. The Lyndons came to the Leongatha district in 1951, when they took up portion of the Timmins Estate on Carmody's Road acquired by the Soldier Settlement Commission. Ellen Lyndon was a particularly keen naturalist and lover of native flora and fauna and, with her husband, took an active part in community organisations. This triangular section of land was transformed in a few years, through judicious tree planting by the Lyndons, and is fittingly known as the 'Ellen Lyndon Park'.

When Leongatha Rotary Club first received its charter in February 1954, Rotarian Bill Birch of the Korumburra Club, and the Governor's Special Representative, said 'it would be difficult to get a band of 29 men who could start off a Rotary club more efficiently than Leongatha'.[25] Within two years of its formation, Leongatha Rotary Club members embarked on a project that was to have far reaching and beneficial effects on the citizens of Woorayl Shire. When work on the new Woorayl District Memorial Hospital began in 1956, Leongatha Rotary arranged for the purchase of the Bush Nursing Hospital in

McCartin Street. Its intention was to convert it into a home for the elderly which it named 'Woorayl Lodge'. It was assisted by subsidies provided by the Government and its own fund-raising activities. When the Woorayl District Memorial Hospital opened in 1958, Rotarians worked untiringly on the renovations and alterations to Woorayl Lodge, which was officially opened on 14 December 1960 by Shire President, Cr H. Bird.[26]

Woorayl Lodge rapidly gained acceptance in the community with further accommodation being added as opportunity and finances permitted. As a mark of appreciation of the President of the first Woorayl Lodge Committee, Mr E.R. Harding, MM, JP, the service road between the flats was named Harding Place.[27] Leongatha Rotary Club members were also active in the provision of school bus shelters. Over twenty of these were placed at appropriate positions within the Shire and proved very acceptable to country students whilst waiting for buses in wintry weather.

Another community project that came to fruition during the 1950s was the Leongatha Swimming Pool. Its construction had been mooted for several decades. The ANA strove unsuccessfully for its formation in the 1930s, and another attempt was made in January 1947 when Shire President, Cr K. Macdonald, called a public meeting to discuss the project. A sub-committee was formed, but no worthwhile progress was made until 1953, when a further committee infused new life into the project. Two returned soldiers, Don Lyndon and Len Goldsworthy, succeeded in arousing sufficient enthusiasm to get the project re-started. Donations were solicited from local business groups, calf drives amongst farmers were conducted, and a crop of potatoes was grown with voluntary labour.

Further valuable assistance to the Swimming Pool Committee was provided by funds raised at the garden parties of Mr and Mrs Gordon Watson of Mardan. The first of these garden parties was held at the Watson's homestead on Nichol's Road in October 1948 to assist with the building of a Guide Hut in Leongatha. It was so successful that for thirty years, with only one exception, the Watsons opened their one and a half acre garden to the general public on the last Saturday of October each year. Funds raised from the first six parties enabled the Guide Hut in Jeffrey Street, Leongatha, to be built. Mr and Mrs Watson then devoted their efforts to assisting the Swimming Pool Committee for several years, raising over £1,750 towards the project, with Mr Gordon Watson acting as Honorary Secretary of the Committee.[28] Much of the work associated with the cementing and tiling of the pool was done by working-bees, with the pool being finally opened for use in December 1960 at a total cost of over £20,000. This amount was financed by a government grant of £6,000, a loan from Woorayl Shire Council of £6,000 that was to be paid off on an annual basis, and the balance by public funding.[29]

Residents of Mardan provided their own swimming pool in a suitable spot on Twomey's Creek on land donated by Mr Bill Campbell. First opened in 1937, the retaining wall was washed away during a flash flood in the early 1950s. In 1957, while working in the area, contractor Alan Sydenham cleaned out the silt with a trenching machine. Working-bees were held under the supervision of Engineer Stansfield that resulted in the construction of a reinforced concrete

E. Bawden paying tribute to H. Dannock, February 1955 at Recreation Reserve, Leongatha (from Woorayl Shire Historical Society).

retaining wall sixty foot by eight foot across the gully. When filled, it provided an excellent pool of 300 foot in length at a minimal cost to Mardan residents and Woorayl Shire ratepayers.[30]

The 1950s and '60s ushered in a period of church building within the Shire. The original wooden buildings erected around the turn of the century were all in need of extensive repairs or renewal. At Tarwin Lower on Sunday 22 February 1953, the Union Memorial Church was officially opened with a joint service conducted by Church of England Minister the Reverend Ackland of Won-thaggi, assisted by Reverend Evans of the Presbyterian Church Meeniyan.[31]

The following year, 1954, at Leongatha, the Methodists re-opened the former church building that originated from Lyre Bird Mound. This small wooden building had been shifted to Koonwarra in 1903, then to Wooreen in 1928 and finally to Leongatha in 1954, where it was renovated for use as a Sunday school and kindergarten. Reverend S.C. Blainey, Chairman of the District, who had ministered at Leongatha during the 1930s, conducted a short dedicatory service.[32] In April 1957 the Methodists had the pleasure of opening their new church at the corner of Church and Bruce Streets, while on 14 December 1958 members of the Church of England attended the official opening of their new St Peter's Church by the Most Reverend J.J. Booth, CMG, DDC, former Archbishop of Melbourne.[33] Built on a dominant site in the township that had been purchased twenty years previously from the Woorayl Shire, it was part of a planned new parish complex that was disrupted by the outbreak of war. The rectory was completed in 1940, and after cessation of hostilities, Reverend H.A. Cairns took up the challenge of fund-raising for the new St Peter's. The first sod for the excavations for the new church was turned on 20 January 1956 by leading parishioner Mr James Haw, while the contract was let for its erection to local builder Mr W.R. Tilson.[34] Following the successful completion of St Peter's, Mr Tilson was engaged to build the new Masonic Hall opposite the old St Peter's in Bruce Street. Completed in 1961, the new Temple of the Lord Brassey Lodge replaced the original Temple opened in 1905.[35]

In the 1960s the foundations for three more churches were laid in Leongatha. In 1964 the Presbyterians moved the original St Andrew's Church back from Peart Street and converted it for use as a hall. The foundation stone of the new St Andrew's was laid on 3 July 1965 by the Right Hon. Reverend G. Ross Williams, Moderator of Victoria, and the new church opened on 11 June 1966.[36] After meeting for several years in the old Rechabite Hall in Roughead Street and later in the Council Chambers, the Seventh Day Adventist congregation began work on their new church in a'Beckett Street in October 1965. Through voluntary working-bees, first under the charge of Pastor Parrow and later Pastor Vysma, this church was officially opened by Shire President, Cr William Tilson, in November 1969.[37] With the arrival of many Dutch migrants during the post-war period, members of the Reformed Church of South Gippsland first met at the Koonwarra Hall in November 1955 for weekly services. Following purchase of land in Peart Street, Leongatha, in 1964, plans were made for the building of a new church which was opened in August 1970.[38] These new churches were not only architecturally pleasing, but also helped provide a social infrastructure of support groups for young wives, social guilds, choirs and the charitable relief work necessary in every community.

The 1950s saw an increased demand for greater and more varied sporting facilities within the Shire. Golf proved particularly popular and new courses were formed at Leongatha South and at Meeniyan. The Leongatha Golf Club embarked on an ambitious program for the construction of a complete new eighteen hole course on a 130 acre property at Leongatha South. Although situated eleven miles from Leongatha, when the proposal for purchase in September 1955 was voted on by members, it resulted in a sixty-one to four majority.[39] Three trustees, Messrs T.A. Welsford, A.N.L. Atkinson and W.P. Shea, were appointed to complete the purchase. The new property was only semi-cleared at the time, and a great number of working-bees were necessary before the first tournament was played over the full eighteen hole course at Easter 1961. It was an outstanding success, and with the construction of its new clubhouse in 1964, Leongatha Golf Club contributed greatly to the sporting and social activities of the Shire. The original course on the Recreation Reserve was taken over by the Woorayl Golf Club, and although complaints were made to Council by players regarding odours from the town tip adjoining the course, this minor distraction did not greatly affect membership.

At Meeniyan moves for the formation of a golf course began in 1954 when interested players decided to accept the offer of Mr Jack Hughes for the use of his property on the Meeniyan-Buffalo road for a course. After purchase of the land by the newly-formed club, Mr and Mrs Jack Hughes were conferred life memberships with trustees being Messrs T. Considine, C. Carmichael and J. Luckie.[40]

Tennis and netball proved equally popular and led to the building of many courts throughout the Shire. Four new en-tout-cas tennis courts fronting Turner Street were laid adjacent to Leongatha Club's asphalt courts in 1947. Increased membership resulted in eight courts of this type being laid down with an additional three plexipave courts in subsequent years. Six new netball courts opened at Meeniyan in 1967, followed by eight at the northern end of the Leongatha Recreation Reserve in 1969, were quickly filled by competing teams at weekends. Increased membership of district bowling clubs resulted in the construction of new greens. Leongatha Bowling Club purchased one and a quarter acres of land in Hughes Street in 1946 for this purpose. Working-bees of enthusiastic members enabled the club to open on its new site in March 1948. Continued support from members resulted in the opening of substantial new club rooms in 1987.[41]

The Meeniyan Bowling Club was formed as a result of a meeting convened by Mr Fred Deering at the Mechanics' Institute Hall on 20 May 1960. Several further meetings were held before the site for the green was decided on after consultation with trustees of the Recreation Reserve. Timber from the former CBC bank was used for the building of the clubhouse, and the bowling club quickly proved a popular addition to Meeniyan's sporting facilities when opened on 18 January 1964.[42] The Inverloch bowling green was formed on a sand dune adjacent to the old jetty. Large quantities of fowl manure and topsoil were carted to the site to enable a good green to be established on the sand bank. Over a hundred players attended the opening of the new green on Saturday, 10 November 1961. Club President Mr R. Scott, in welcoming the visitors, said 'the day was a red letter one for Inverloch, as provision of bowling greens added to a town's status'.[43] Erosion of the foreshore by tidal action caused considerable anxiety to club members, particularly during a king tide on 14 May 1964. Sea water came to within fifteen yards of the new green, and members hurriedly filled 240 sandbags which they dumped in the danger spot to prevent further damage.

Horse racing was always a favourite sport in Woorayl Shire, but attempts to establish a permanent racecourse met with little success until the 1950s. The Stony Creek racecourse was used intermittently from 1894 onwards but lapsed in the 1920s. Following a meeting of racing enthusiasts in May 1947, the Stony Creek and District Racing Club was re-formed with the intention of developing the course to its full potential as the centre for racing in South Gippsland. Mr J.R. Carmichael was elected President with Messrs T. Considine and F.H. Helms Vice-presidents. Working-bees held on a weekly basis at the course over the next two years ensured the completion of a running rail, open-horse stalls and toilets, but little provision had been made for onlookers. The first meeting held on 26 April 1950 was an outstanding success, despite the absence of Melbourne caterers who had been engaged to supply the liquor booth. This deficiency was remedied in subsequent years, as further substantial buildings were erected to replace the makeshift arrangements that characterised earlier meetings. Leongatha and Foster Racing Clubs commenced using the Stony Creek course in 1951, and continued until 1964, when the three clubs were amalgamated into the South Gippsland Racing Club with Rod Carmichael as the first President.[44]

Other horse lovers less keen on racing established pony and polocrosse clubs.

Polocrosse was played regularly on the Leongatha Recreation Reserve in the early 1960s, sometimes resulting in a difference of opinion with cricket club members as to who was entitled to use of the lower oval.[45] Pony clubs at Berry's Creek under the guidance of Mrs E. Kenny and at Tarwin Lower under veterinarian Peter O'Connor drew members from all parts of the Shire. Whilst many were attracted to horse riding for leisure and recreation, others preferred riding the waves at Anderson's Inlet where the South Gippsland Yacht Club was re-formed in 1966 after a lapse of over thirty years.

South of Meeniyan an entirely different type of sport emerged. At Scadden's Run, named after a pioneering family of the 1880s, the South Gippsland Gliding Club commenced operations in March 1965. With thirty members from as far afield as Warragul, the gliding club quickly arranged for the purchase of two, two-seater gliders from Germany. These were housed in a hangar built on Scadden's Run and on suitable days were launched by means of a winch or an aeroplane pull if available. Cross-country gliding was undertaken with foundation members Lou Canobie, Tom Burchell and Arthur Nelson soaring as far afield as Yarram and Dandenong.[46]

The increased demand for sporting facilities was paralleled by a similar demand for greater educational facilities within the Shire. The Leongatha Primary School had outgrown its original site in Jeffrey Street and made a gradual transition to a new and larger area on Horn Street during the years 1957-64. The Catholic community replaced their original wooden school in

First year high school pupils at the 50th Anniversary, 1962. Includes Charles Edney, Miss A. Johnson, Don Chalmers and William Hassett (from B. Trotman).

Ogilvy Street with a fine new brick building in 1957. Not all of the pupils at these primary schools were from the township. Due to the provision of bus facilities throughout the Shire, many parents began sending their junior children to the Leongatha schools. Declining enrolments in the small one-teacher schools, coupled with staff shortages, led to the closing of many of these small schools during the post-war era. Even where there were sufficient pupils to warrant a one-teacher school, a division of opinion often arose amongst parents as to its suitability compared to a large central school.

Enrolment at Leongatha High School increased greatly during the 1950s and '60s, and in addition students tended to remain at school for a longer period. Although extra school classrooms were provided by the Education Department, an adequate assembly hall was urgently needed. Fund-raising activities, together with the formation of a Co-operative Society formed specifically for the purpose, enabled work to begin on the hall in 1964. Designed by J. Esmond Dorney, son-in-law of the first headmaster Arthur Mesley, it was built by Mr W. 'Bill' Tilson and opened by Mr Bloomfield, Minister for Education, on 2 June 1965.[47]

By reason of its size and design, Mesley Hall proved a valuable asset to the community as well as to the school. One of the first organisations to avail itself of its facilities was the Lyric Theatre group. Within six months of the opening of Mesley Hall, Lyric Theatre's production 'Why Not Sing' attracted over 1,000 people from all parts of South Gippsland during its three nights' run.[48] In succeeding years Lyric Theatre consistently staged excellent productions in Mesley Hall that contributed greatly to the enjoyment of patrons while providing a valuable outlet for local talent and enthusiasm for the stage.

Mesley Hall also provided a suitable venue for the joint Korumburra-Leongatha Eisteddfod. Revived after a lapse of twenty-five years through the efforts of Mr and Mrs Jack Hoy, this musical competition has attracted hundreds of competitors to its various sections after it became an annual event in 1972. Like Lyric Theatre, its main success is in its cultural and entertainment value, as well as providing performance experience for amateur vocalists and musicians.

Student numbers at the high school peaked at over 700 in the mid-1960s but then eased following the establishment of Leongatha Technical School in 1967 with the appointment of Mr W.H. Johnson, B.Sc., Dip.Ed., as first Principal. Siting of the new technical school was finalised in November 1968 on twenty-seven acres of land formerly used for sporting purposes by the high school. Tenders were called in October 1969 for the first stage of thirty-two classrooms covering six acres.[49] The technical school, when finished, catered for up to 800 students and became the apprenticeship centre for South Gippsland, with workshops catering for fitting and turning, panel beating, welding, farm mechanics and sheet metal work.

Leongatha High School was compensated for the loss of its playing oval by the construction of a new one facing Horn Street on what had formerly been the horse paddock. Completed in 1972, this oval, named the 'Nicholas Oval' in honour of former sportsmaster Harold Nicholas, together with the new one on the technical school site, provided a welcome addition to the sporting facilities of the town, particularly during the summer cricket season.

Although many new uses of leisure and forms of recreation developed during the post-war era, the time-honoured hobby and pastime of gardening still retained its attraction and appeal. The Leongatha Horticultural Society was formed in March 1949 with the objective of 'the promotion and encouragement of practical and experimental horticulture by exhibitions, reading, and discussion on papers of horticultural subjects'.[50] Well-known local builder and businessman, Hubert Potter, was elected first President with Miss Gwen Adams first Secretary Treasurer. The first Spring Show, the forerunner of the Daffodil Festival, was held in the old Council chambers in 1949, and the society soon demonstrated the talents of its members by its display at the annual Leongatha Show. In 1955 Miss Gladys Brumley was appointed first librarian of the society to select and loan books on gardening matters to members. The Daffodil Festival, a three day event which developed from the Spring Show, was held in the Memorial Hall for the first time in 1960 and quickly became a popular feature attracting visitors from near and far.

The Country Women's Association continued its activities during this period with emphasis on craft work by members, while a music and drama group provided an outlet for ladies interested in these activities. Fund-raising activities undertaken during the war period were continued with proceeds being used to purchase a holiday home at Inverloch in 1948. This was well used during the summer months by CWA members and their families during the '50s and '60s, but increased maintenance costs led to its subsequent disposal in 1976.

Dancing retained its attraction with the main district halls being regularly filled for hospital, Church and sporting club balls. Before the onset of electronic amplified music, The Four Aces dance band of the Kerr brothers, Doug and Johnnie, provided first-class dance music with piano, saxophone, bass and drums. With versatile Ian Richardson at the piano capable of playing ragtime, boogie-woogie or traditional waltz numbers, The Four Aces programs were normally fifty-fifty, modern and old-time.

Credit for the continuing popularity of ballroom dancing in the district was due to the training of innumerable debutante sets. For over thirty years at Leongatha, Mr Jack Roughead and his wife Shirley converted gangling, teen-age youths into well-polished partners for the annual crop of debutantes. Mr and Mrs Reg Smith of Allambee, both accomplished dancers, also trained many debutante sets and passed on their dancing skills to the next generation. At Dollar Mr and Mrs Ernie Thorson trained over 900 debutantes for presentation at annual balls.

The Saturday night dances at the Meeniyan Mechanics' Hall were the venue for young people of the Shire during the '60s and '70s. Held under the watchful eye of Meeniyan stalwart, Tom Nolan, these dances became a by-word amongst teenagers for an enjoyable night out. Mrs Madex and her band provided dance music at balls and dances in this region, and her name remained synonymous with dance music for decades. Before her marriage, Mrs Madex (nee Laura Bright) rode horseback with her sister to play at the small halls and towns of South Gippsland during the First World War. She played violin and piano without the need of sheet music — a natural musician. Describing the evolution of dance bands in the area, Mrs Madex recalled 'First it was violins, then we added a trumpet, and then a few pianos were provided around the district. The drums did not show up until the second war'.[51]

Leongatha High School Library Committee (1969) with Mrs D. Bacon (nee McKinnon). Appointed librarian in 1956, she occupied this position until retirement in 1975. As a result of her involvement in community affairs, particularly in the formation of Leongatha Guides, the Anglican Church and the Woorayl Shire Historical Society, Mrs Bacon was awarded the Order of Australia in 1986.

At the smaller halls within the Shire, many dances were still held with music provided by willing amateurs from homes nearby. At a send-off at Fairbank Mechanics' Hall in 1971 for William 'Billie' Bawden, a popular lifelong resident of the district, the grand finale was given by the guest of honour himself. Standing on the aged hall piano, a cast-off from Government House in the 1890s, Billie Bawden gave a stirring rendition of Scottish airs on his bagpipes that was greatly appreciated by the crowded gathering.[52]

Scouting and Guiding became increasingly popular in the 1950s. Neither organisation had access to large funds, but both managed to erect halls through assistance from local tradesmen and working-bees of parents. In October 1954 Leongatha Scouts commenced building their hall in Allison Street.[53] A prefabricated steel-framed building with twelve foot walls, it provided a nucleus for scouting activities that was urgently needed. A similar type of building was used for a scout hall on the Meeniyan Recreation Reserve when the first scout group under J.H. Jeffries gathered sufficient support for its commencement in 1967.[54] With financial assistance from funds raised at Mr and Mrs Gordon Watsons' annual garden parties, Leongatha Guide Hall in a'Beckett Street was completed and opened by Sir Herbert Hyland, MLA, on 13 April 1957.[55]

The Young Farmers' Movement within the Shire began in 1934 with the formation of Calf Clubs at district schools sponsored by Mr W. Yuill, Senior Dairy Supervisor of the Department of Agriculture. Although active for several years, these clubs all went into recess during the 1939-45 war years. It was not until 1949 as a result of action by leading Dollar resident, Arthur Ashenden, that the Senior Young Farmers' Movement again became established. Membership in the Tarwin Valley club, formed on March 1949, rose quickly with a varied program for meetings consisting of lectures, films and field days. Activities were divided between social, cultural and agricultural activities. Debates with other clubs improved the public speaking attributes of members and provided a springboard for later entry into other spheres of public life. Craft work, cookery, excursions and the presence of male members attracted many girls into the Young Farmers' Movement. Two other Young Farmers' clubs were formed in the Shire: Koonwarra in 1952 with the encouragement of Mr Norm Caithness and at Fairbank in 1956, where Mr Ray Sommers was elected to guide the club in its first year of operation.[56]

All of these many and varied communal activities were based on people, and Woorayl Shire was fortunate that it maintained a steady growth rate of population. While some other rural Shires experienced a decline in inhabitants as a result of farm mechanisation and amalgamation brought about by economic pressures, Woorayl Shire's population continued to increase. One major factor in this increase was the post-war influx of British and European migrants. The British 'Big Brother' movement of the 1920s and 1930s brought many valued men to the district. Family nomination by Italians and the return to Australia by some of those who had spent time on district farms as prisoners-of-war added many more.

The predominance of dairying as the major farming enterprise in the Shire led to the influx of many Dutch families during the 1950s and 1960s. Among the European migrants, the Dutch appeared to have an inbuilt liking for dairying. Many had the benefit of post-primary education at agricultural colleges and brought with them special skills in the feeding and breeding of livestock that quickly resulted in increased production on South Gippsland dairy farms. Dutch families often gained their start in farming through share-farming larger dairying properties. The relative ease of dairying in Victoria compared to Europe where stock needed to be housed for several months of the year was quickly appreciated by these migrant farmers. Coupled with the comparatively cheap price of land at that time, many soon progressed from being share farmers to landowners. There was little or no racial animosity towards migrants or problems with assimilation. Free language classes in English were conducted for a period at the Koonwarra Hall during 1957, while the first naturalisation ceremonies conducted by Woorayl Shire Council took place during the monthly Council meetings. Following suggestions by the local branch of the Australian Natives' Association, these occasions were given more prominence within the community. A special date was reserved at which members of all religious and community organisations could be present and extend a fuller and more expressive welcome to the new citizens of the Shire. On Australia Day 1961 the Council chambers were crowded as nineteen former nationals of Germany, Holland and Italy renounced their allegiance to their homelands and took the oath to become Australian citizens.[57]

At the 1963 naturalisation ceremonies held at Leongatha, veteran MLA Sir Herbert Hyland said 'He hates the word "New Australians", it should be "Naturalised Australians". We are all equal and have the same privileges, rights and responsibilities'.[58] At the 1968 ceremonies held on Australia Day, thirty-six migrants were naturalised at Leongatha. Cr W.J. Hinds, Shire President, welcomed the Hon. Peter Nixon, MHR, to the function and thanked members of the Horticultural Society, the Woorayl Municipal Band and the CWA Choir for their assistance in making the ceremony such an impressive and agreeable occasion.

Migration coupled with the natural increase was quickly reflected in the census figures for Woorayl Shire.[59]

	1954	1961
Leongatha	2,304	2,755
Rest of Shire	4,742	6,029
Totals	7,046	8,784

Although Dutch migrants tended almost exclusively towards the dairying industry, other national groupings were found throughout a variety of occupations. Sten Bergman, a Swedish migrant who came to Australia to work on the Snowy Mountains Scheme, operated a bakery in Bair Street, Leongatha, for many years. Nick Vitetta from Southern Italy, after starting business in the fruit and vegetable trade, purchased the old established drapery business of Claude Bair in Bair Street and made a success of it from the start. Peter and Amando Bolge, cabinet-makers, from Northern Italy, commenced operations as builders.

One of the best examples of the post-war assimilation of migrants was provided by the Citizen of the Year Award instituted by the Leongatha Jaycees. Inaugurated in 1969, this award was given for outstanding community service within Woorayl Shire. Selection was by an appropriate panel drawn from different groupings, and the first person to win this meritorious award was a post-war Dutch migrant, Otto Van Der Vorm. Otto and his wife Maria arrived in Australia in March 1957, and after spending six months at Williamstown, came to Leongatha where they spent four years doing farm work on the property of Mr and Mrs Alan Lester at Koorooman before coming to live in Leongatha township. Naturalised in June 1963, they were the proud parents of six young Australians. A member of the Presbyterian Church, Otto helped in the formation of youth clubs by training boys in boxing and gymnastics and was also a swimming pool instructor. During his twelve years of residence in the Shire, Otto donated twenty-two pints of blood to the Blood Bank which was formed by the Red Cross at the Woorayl District Memorial Hospital.[60]

It was appropriate that the post of Shire President at the time of this award was occupied by another post-war migrant, Cr William Tilson. After many years as a successful building contractor, during which time he carried out extensive alterations to the Memorial Hall in 1962, William Tilson was elected to Woorayl Shire Council in 1968 and filled the role of Shire President during 1969-70 with care and distinction.[61]

The role of Shire Councils changed markedly during the post-war decades. From being primarily concerned with services associated with property, such as the provision of roads and bridges, Councils became increasingly involved with services to people and provision of other amenities. Some services were relatively simple to administer and caused little trouble. For example, in 1955

Council called applications for appointment of a full-time gardener at a salary of £15 per week. Shire Secretary Clive Lyon said there was sufficient work for one man full-time in looking after parks at Meeniyan, Dumbalk and Leongatha.[62] In 1961 Council Secretary A. Beanland reported that £274 had been paid out on over 700 fox and wombat scalp bonuses for the year at 7s 6d per scalp.[63]

But councillors had bigger problems than payment of wombat bonuses or provision of a gardener. In 1959 an extensive sub-division of building blocks took place at Venus Bay by the Van Cleef Foundation, acting for Dutch-born businessman Mr Louis Roet. By 1961, 1,500 blocks were sold making some councillors wary of the scheme following problems with sub-standard housing on allotments at Inverloch. Engineer Stansfield kept a close watch on the development project and reported that all Council's requirements were being complied with regarding parks, drainage etc.[64] The Venus Bay scheme brought home to councillors the necessity for Council control over sub-division, and in June 1961 Council endorsed the interim development order on all land within the Shire giving it total and complete control over all sub-division and building.[65]

In 1960 Council agreed to commence a home help service to cater for sick mothers unable to look after their children and for those just returning home with a new baby. A housekeeper was appointed at a salary of £14 per week with Council being reimbursed by the Government for £8 and the difference being made up, if possible, by those who employed the housekeeper.[66]

Meat inspection was another area that caused problems to Council. After sharing the cost of meat inspection at local abattoirs with neighbouring

The Koonwarra tug-of-war team at the Leongatha Show, 1969. Anchorman Ian Kneebone, Knotman Ron Zaghet, Phil Shandley, Angie Sgarbossa, Ross Roycroft, Barry Shandley, Coach Allie Watt (from Woorayl Shire Historical Society).

municipalities for many years, Woorayl Shire Council decided to 'go it alone' and appoint its own inspector in 1967. Secretary Keith Brydon estimated this method would save Woorayl Council $600 per annum.[67]

A similar problem was posed by the provision of library facilities within the Shire. Since the inception of the Leongatha Mechanics' Institute in 1891, a library had always functioned there as part of the Institute with a reasonable degree of satisfaction to users. Prior to the 1960s the Institute Library operated on a small budget made up of members' fees, a government grant of £50 per annum plus a similar grant of £50 per annum from Woorayl Shire Council. After payment of wages to a librarian, there was little money left for the purchase of new books, and the standard of reading matter declined. As a means of increasing revenue, the Institute Committee leased the centre room between the library and the billiard room to hairdresser, Len Goldsworthy. Such was the shortage of business premises after the war that, when Len returned from active service, the Institute granted him occupancy on a temporary basis in 1947. Twenty years later he was still there wielding the clippers in this small room that had formerly been the members' room of the Institute. Card playing was the favourite pastime practised there by members — often for more than pennies.

Renewed interest in the library in the early 1960s, following the appointment of new members to the Committee, led to a vast improvement in the quality of books and service to members. Book depots manned by voluntary workers were established at Meeniyan and Dumbalk. Shire Council steadily increased its subsidy to the Institute Library until it reached $2,300 per annum in 1969, with the Government grant being only $438 per annum.[68] In order to obtain the maximum Government grant, it was necessary to change from subscriptions to a 'free' library scheme. Pressure was also brought on Council to join the Regional Library Scheme centred at Warragul or appoint a fully-qualified librarian to the Leongatha Library. After lengthy debate, the latter course was adopted with Council assuming full control of the Institute Library in 1973.[69]

Although Woorayl Council decided to 'go-it-alone' on meat inspection and library facilities, it did co-operate with neighbouring Korumburra Shire in the provision of an airfield. Engineer Stansfield reported in 1967 that up to five light planes daily were making use of the private airstrip adjoining the hospital. In March 1969 Council decided to raise $50,000 in loan money for the joint purchase of a 326-acre property on the boundary of the Korumburra Shire. This would allow for the construction of an all-weather airstrip suitable for two-engine aircraft.[70]

The provision of an airfield within the Shire epitomised the change that was taking place in the transport field. In the space of a little more than one generation, railways had lost their supremacy as carriers of passengers and goods. The twenty-three day railway strike of November 1950 literally forced many firms and people into the use of road transport as an alternative. The provision of better highways and arterial roads, and the increased percentage of car ownership, was soon reflected in falling tonnages of freight and number of passengers carried by rail. Large semi-trailers for stock transport, and the use of bulk tankers for farm collection, started a revolution in the dairying and livestock industries that was to have profound effects on farms, dairy factories and townships alike.

16. HARVEST

The gradual change-over by dairy farmers to the supply of whole milk rather than cream to factories, which commenced during wartime, accelerated in the 1950s and '60s. By November 1959 the Leongatha Butter Factory was receiving half its supply of butterfat in milk and half in cream. As herds became larger, the labour involved in the handling and washing of milk cans increased accordingly, and the temptation to change to bulk milk pick-up was greater amongst the largest producers. Archie's Creek was the first factory to introduce bulk pick-up in South Gippsland in 1956 followed by Mirboo North in 1957.

By October 1959 eleven Dumbalk suppliers had ordered refrigerated vats, and the company had purchased a tanker for collection.[1] Many factory directors were in a quandary whether to recommend suppliers to purchase water-cooled or refrigerated vats, as there were no firm guidelines laid down by the Department of Agriculture. At a crowded meeting of over 200 Leongatha suppliers at the Memorial Hall in April 1961, Chairman Harold Morter outlined the reasons why the Leongatha Company was marking time on the issue. Fellow director Lincoln Timmins said that the estimated cost of the changeover was £500,000 which would be borne by the company and farmers alike. Director Ed Bawden raised one of the few laughs at the meeting when he pointed out that protagonists of bulk milk pick-up claimed it saved 2½d per lb cartage when the gross cartage cost of Leongatha under existing arrangements was 2¼d per lb.[2]

Nevertheless, once started the trend to bulk pick-up continued with gathering speed. By June 1962 Dumbalk factory reported that it had achieved a 100 percent changeover to refrigerated milk, while Leongatha factory was just beginning to accept water-cooled milk. By October 1964 Leongatha had 90 suppliers on bulk pick-up as against 145 on cans, with 18,000 gallons out of the daily milk intake of 45,000 gallons being received in bulk.[3] The change to bulk pick-up had other far-reaching consequences. It enabled factories to 'poach' suppliers from each other thus duplicating transport routes at a hidden cost to suppliers and also to ratepayers of Shires through which the tankers ran.

The installation cost of facilities and plant necessary to treat whole milk in lieu of cream led to a spate of factory mergers. Directors of small companies realised they had not adequate financial reserves or sufficient throughput to

G and N cattle sale, Leongatha, 1981 (from P. Dwyer).

warrant the required expenditure. Following the merger of Korumburra and Kongwak factories in 1964, the Leongatha and Fish Creek factories merged in 1965 to form South Gippsland Dairy Products. The huge capital cost of building spray drying plants for the enlarged milk intake led to the further amalgamation of Korumburra Dairy Products Company and South Gippsland Dairy Products into South Gippsland Milk Industries in 1966 with a decision to erect a 100,000 gallon capacity spray drier at Leongatha. At the same time as this merger was being effected, suppliers and directors of Dumbalk and Mirboo North were canvassing a proposal to merge with northern co-operative Murray Goulburn instead of the Leongatha-Korumburra group. Following visits to the area by representatives of Murray Goulburn, suppliers at both Dumbalk and Mirboo North voted to merge with Murray Goulburn in July 1966. In speaking in favour of the merger, Mr Jack McGuire, Managing Director of Murray Goulburn, said 'it was too ridiculous for words that Dumbalk would ever close down'.[4]

The disposal of effluent from the increased intake at the Korumburra and Leongatha factories led to a joint venture in 1967 of an ocean outfall pipeline. In conjunction with Korumburra and Leongatha Sewerage Authorities, a 20.3 cm PVC pipeline was laid from Korumburra to Leongatha, where it was joined on the western side of the town by a 22.9 cm pipeline from the Yarragon Road pumping station. A 30.5 cm line with a capacity of almost 5,000,000 litres per day then carried the effluent to an outfall point at Venus Bay 7.2 kilometres south of Tarwin Lower and 2.4 kilometres from the nearest house. Opened on 3

April 1969 with a total length of 53 kilometres at a cost of $1,269,000, few people realised the tremendous advantage this project would give Leongatha during the next decade.[5] All dairy factories had the same problem with effluent disposal, and within eighteen months of acceptance of the merger with Dumbalk and Mirboo North, Murray Goulburn announced the impending closure of the Dumbalk factory and centralising of production facilities at Mirboo North.[6] The deciding factors in favour of Mirboo North were the cost of effluent disposal and also that Mirboo Council had offered the company freedom from rates for three years and half rates for a further three if production was centralised in that Shire.[7]

With the benefit of its ocean outfall pipeline and new centralised production facilities at Leongatha, South Gippsland Milk Industries quickly became one of the largest co-operative dairy companies in Victoria with a turnover in 1970-1 of over $17,000,000.[8] Murray Goulburn company was loath to commence large-scale expenditure at Mirboo North when such a first rate dairy complex was already in existence at Leongatha. After further talks between directors, an amicable merger of both companies took place in 1973, with the shareholders of South Gippsland Milk Industries receiving seven Murray Goulburn $1 shares for four South Gippsland Milk Industries $1 shares. Production was then centralised at the Yarragon Road complex with the Mirboo North and Dumbalk factories being closed. Korumburra factory operated on a limited scale for a short time, but it too closed leaving only the Leongatha factory operating by 1978. Within the space of fifteen years, five of the six butter factories operating within a short radius of Leongatha had merged into the one vast complex on Yarragon Road with incalculable long-term benefit to the Leongatha township. Its geographical position undoubtedly played a major role in this decision, but there were other factors, not the least being Leongatha's good water supply.

Modern dairy factories use immense quantities of water daily, and the Murray Goulburn complex could not have been developed were it not for the foresight and enterprise of Leongatha's Water Commissioners. Since its formation in 1905, Leongatha Waterworks Trust had carried out an on-going program of capital expenditure in an endeavour to maintain a high quality water supply to the town. A three million gallon service reservoir had been constructed on Bowler's Hill in 1921 to provide for increased demand in peak periods. This was followed by the 40 million gallon No. 2 Reservoir on Ruby Creek upstream from No. 1 in 1927. A water purification plant on Harvey's Road was completed in 1960 with a third reservoir of 165 million gallons in 1962. This was named the 'Hyland Reservoir' after Sir Herbert Hyland, MLA, veteran Member of Parliament who had represented South Gippsland since 1929. Extensions to the filtration plant in 1970 were followed by commencement of the Western Reservoir at the headwaters of the Ruby Creek in 1979 with a further capacity of 270 million gallons.[9] Although minor shortages occurred at infrequent intervals, basically Leongatha was well served by its Water Commissioners.

The State-wide drought of 1967-68 led to requests from Woorayl Shire Council to the Mines Department to sink exploratory bores in the Leongatha area to avoid any future water shortage. These bores sunk south of the railway line yielded exceptionally well at minimal cost; that is,

Racecourse Road	482ft	15,000 gals per hour	cost $450
Simon's Lane	492ft	10,000 ,, ,, ,,	,, $1,250
Hillgrove's Road	380ft	17,000 ,, ,, ,,	,, $400[10]

The increased use of spray irrigation by farmers, particularly potato growers, led to restrictions being imposed on pumping from the Tarwin during the 1967-68 drought. Fortunately, such droughts occur most infrequently with Woorayl Shire being practically the last part of Victoria to be affected.

Prior to the formation of Meeniyan Water Trust, town water for Meeniyan was pumped direct from the Tarwin River with many complaints regarding quality. Drinking water was obtained from tanks or from a bore in the main street that was pumped into a holding tank. In 1956 the newly-formed trust opened a 0.25 million gallon service basin — a filtered scheme was adopted in 1973 followed by a larger storage basin of 1.3 million gallons in 1979.[11]

Following many years of agitation by residents, the Inverloch Water Trust was formed in 1947 and arranged for a permanent supply from the reservoir at Lance Creek. Sustained efforts to have a sewerage scheme implemented resulted in approval of plans by the State Rivers and Water Commission in 1973 for sixteen miles (25.76 kilometres) of gravity sewerage, four pumping stations and nearly four miles (6.44 kilometres) of rising mains. These would take the town sewage to an ocean outfall near Eagle's Nest. Construction of sewers and manholes commenced in 1976 and was generally finished in 1981 with first tenements connected in July 1978.[12] Objection by local residents and the South Gippsland Conservation Society led to a change in plans for treatment of the sewage. Instead of disposal into the sea, a property of 256 acres (102.4 hectares) on the west of the town was purchased for land disposal. The Sewerage Authority then obtained a licence from the Environment Protection Authority

Yarragon Road complex, Murray Goulburn, 1985.

A'Beckett Street, Inverloch, 1987 (from Woorayl Shire).

to treat effluent for either land disposal or discharge into Bass Strait in special circumstances.[13] Finalisation of this scheme signalled a further growth in Inverloch township with consequent demand for other civic amenities. The loss by fire of the Mechanics' Hall on 30 July 1978 led to the building of a comprehensive Community Centre that was officially opened by the Hon. Neil Trezise, Minister for Youth, Sport and Recreation, on 11 June 1983. This much desired amenity was a fitting climax for the seaside township in the Parish of Kirrak that was first proclaimed by Governor Loch on 8 February 1886.[14]

Alternatives to dairying, cattle and sheep production continued to be sought by enterprising farmers within Woorayl Shire. Although onion and potato production continued on a limited scale, some farmers undertook contract growing of canning peas during the 1960s. The first crop was grown and harvested in 1961 at Boorool on the property of Mr Bill McIndoe. Improved harvesting machinery enabled the crop to be cut and the peas podded in the one operation thus reducing cartage costs to the factory. Contract pea growing continued in Woorayl Shire during the 1960s principally on the red soils of Boorool and Koorooman districts with some successful crops also being grown on the peaty soils around Buffalo.

Dairying and stock-raising, however, remained pre-eminent as Woorayl Shire's main enterprises. An outbreak of pleuro-pneumonia in beef cattle in the Buffalo district in 1965 caused grave disquiet amongst farmers and Department

Tarwin Lower Christmas sale, 1981 (from P. Dwyer).

of Agriculture officials alike. Immediate action by Departmental officers led to the slaughter of over 300 head and quarantining of 80 adjoining properties. Blood testing of over 3,000 head of cattle on these farms revealed that only four farms were infected, and the outbreak was controlled without further serious harm to the cattle industry in the Shire.[15]

Animal health was always high on a farmer's priority list. In 1939 suppliers of Dumbalk and Leongatha factories had inaugurated animal health associations in which a small annual payment by members entitled them to treatment of stock by a qualified veterinarian at concessional rates. The first veterinarian was sent to the Association by Messrs Rudduck and Co., but after the 1939-45 War, private practitioners participated in the scheme with great benefit to livestock producers in the district. Artificial breeding societies were begun at Leongatha, Dumbalk and Archie's Creek in 1959. Growth was rapid in the 1960s, and after the three centres amalgamated in 1969-70, the name was changed to South Gippsland A.B. Co-operative Co. Ltd. With 747 members and a staff of 11 technicians, a decision was made in 1972 to erect a modern administration and service block in Leongatha at the corner of Bellingham Street and Michael Place.[16] Growth in this service continued during the 1970s with a temporary setback due to the collapse of the cattle market in 1975-6.

The autumn of 1976 was a low point for district dairy and beef farmers. Depressed returns for skimmed milk products and butter on the export market threatened the ability of factories to pay more than forty cents a pound for butterfat. The United Dairyfarmers of Victoria, under newly-elected President Bill Pyle, organised a series of protest marches throughout Victoria designed to attract nation-wide publicity to their plight. 'Operation Concern' held on the last Tuesday in May saw McCartin Street, Leongatha, thronged with over 5,000 South Gippslanders waving placards with television cameras relaying the scene to all parts of the Commonwealth. Federal Member for Gippsland, the Hon. P.J. Nixon, MHR, made a special trip from Canberra to attend, while Mr Peter Webster, Chairman of the Australian Dairy Corporation outlined the problems facing the dairy industry.[17]

Both dairy and beef farmers were severely affected by the slump in cattle prices of 1975-76. Unfinished and chopper cattle became practically valueless. Store steers that had been purchased for $200 were sold twelve months later for half this amount. Chopper dairy cows were sold for as low as 50 cents each. Bobby calves brought 18 cents — the price of a postage stamp! Many farmers did not even bother to bring calves to the market but simply disposed of them on the farm. In order to bring about a reasonable return to the producer, farmer organisations persuaded the Government to introduce a killing subsidy. Under this scheme poor quality cattle were brought to selected killing spots where they were shot and buried in communal pits. The Government subsidy of $5 per head was distributed $4.50 to the farmer and 50 cents to Shire Councils for burial costs. The worked out gravel pits at Koonwarra purchased to replace the Leongatha and Meeniyan tips in 1970 were used for a cattle burial pit. In June 1976 on a bleak Tuesday morning, 580 head of cattle were brought there by district farmers, and were then shot and buried with Council equipment. Engineer Ray Moody estimated the cost of the burial was $800 or approximately $1.50 per head.[18]

Farmers adopted different methods of coping with the economic downturn of the mid-1970s. Some like Herb Wildes of Brooklyn, Nerrena, introduced farm holidays for city families who were quite happy to pay for the privilege of rural living and partaking in farm activities. Many young farmers sought off-farm employment and travelled daily to construction works in the Latrobe Valley. Others worked on the fabrication of oil rigs on Barry Beach at Welshpool, while some worked five days a week at factories in the metropolitan area. By this means sufficient income was obtained to keep farm enterprises intact until better times arrived. Fortunately, by the end of the 1970s, cattle and butterfat prices had recovered to a reasonably profitable level, with great benefit to farmers, stock agents and town businessmen alike.

Although overseas demand for dairy products and meat languished in the 1970s, other markets expanded. The steadily increasing need of sawn scantling for building purposes and wood pulp for cardboard and paper manufacture led to greater interest in re-afforestation. By reason of the terrain, farmers in the steeper hill country of Woorayl Shire were unable to adopt new farming practices that enabled greater output per man in the dairying and livestock industries. Many of these farms were sold to outside interests for tree planting — mainly of pines but some of eucalyptus. Present market trends indicate that final monetary return per hectare from farm forestry may well be equivalent to or even better than from other forms of farming. Several schools within the Shire also began commercial tree planting schemes on small areas, while the Leongatha Waterworks Trust planted thousands of trees on land bordering their reservoirs.

Another alternative system of land use was developed on the coastal land between Tarwin Lower and Walkerville. Willow Ware Aust Pty Ltd set up a commercial deer farming enterprise modelled on similar schemes operating in New Zealand. The high cost of the requisite fencing, however, and difficulties in the handling of these animals inhibited the growth of this branch of farming in Woorayl Shire.

As a means of avoiding the fluctuating fortunes of primary industry, Woorayl Shire Council embarked on a policy of encouraging light industry to the area. Council was particularly keen to stem the outflow of young people from the Shire following completion of their secondary schooling. The conversion of manual telephone exchanges to automatic systems in the 1960s was an example of the removal of job opportunities for girls which Council was anxious to remedy. Through the provision of suitable land with adequate water and sewerage facilities, Council was able to assist industries in the initial stages of development. A three and a half acre (1.4 hectares) site on the corner of Yarragon Road and Horn Street was purchased by Council for this purpose and became known as the 'Industrial Estate'. Home Pride Bakery, built in 1969, with a capacity of producing 750,000 units per week and with a total peak employment of over thirty people, was the first factory to be opened on the estate.[19] Other firms were quick to follow the example of Home Pride. Leongatha Squash Courts and machinery agents B.T. and B. Cusack opened spacious premises on the Industrial Estate in 1971-72, to be soon followed by many more business enterprises in the next decade.

The old established firm of J. J. Cash and Co., textile manufacturers, was attracted to the Leongatha area by reason of its relatively close proximity to Melbourne with good lines of communication and adequate labour force. With help from Woorayl Shire Council in the provision of land and design of premises, J. J. Cash and Co. built a modern textile factory in Holt Street in 1971-72 at a cost of over $300,000, providing employment for a regular staff of thirty. The first commercial order undertaken by Cashs at Leongatha was the production of woven tags for the Northern Territory Girl Guides. Producing an article that was valuable for its weight, Cashs was the ideal industry for Leongatha with a minimal freight disadvantage. Under the managership of Richard Pegler, production quickly increased until by the mid-1970s there were sixty women and twelve men employed at the factory working three shifts on a five-day week basis.[20]

Increased employment opportunities for women brought the need for more child-minding facilities. The Leongatha Pre-school Centre opened in 1949 but changed its name to the Leongatha Kindergarten in 1958 to take advantage of a larger government subsidy. With an increasing enrolment its capacity was soon taxed to the utmost. It was then decided to divide the service between residents depending on whether they lived north or south of the railway line with a second centre being set up in Hassett Street. A Neighbourhood Centre at the corner of Young and Bruce Streets began in a large weatherboard house purchased and equipped with funding from the Federal Government. Opened in February 1977, it catered for twenty-five children in the up to six years of age group. With its permanent staff assisted by voluntary helpers, this centre was greatly appreciated by mothers working outside the home.[21]

The growing complexity of tasks undertaken by local government caused grave accommodation problems for Council staff. Following the resignation of Secretary Keith Brydon and Engineer Fred Stansfield in 1970, Council appointed two young men, Mr Ron Stanley and Mr Ray Moody, to these two senior administrative positions. Both men were to play important roles in the urgent problem of providing increased accommodation for Council staff. Councillors were forced to decide whether to renovate and extend existing Council offices or undertake erection of a new complex that would include other civic amenities. When finally Council decided to accept tenders for a completely new complex, Cr E.J. 'Ted' Fisher said they were 'considering a project that would never happen again. Not because of the size of the tender but because the complexity is something no other council will have to face'.[22] Councillors were rewarded for their efforts when State Cabinet met in the newly-completed Shire offices on 19 February 1973. Premier Rupert 'Dick' Hamer then formally opened the new offices with the Hon. J.F. Rossiter, MP, Minister of Health, opening the senior citizens' centre, the Hon. I.W. Smith, MP, Minister of Youth, Sport and Recreation, opening the youth club and the Hon. A.J. Hunt, MLC, Minister for Local Government, opening the sports stadium.

The Warrawee Senior Citizens' Club, formed at Inverloch in 1965, preceded

Inverloch Anglican Church of the Ascension.

Leongatha Senior Citizens' by two years. The first President, Mrs Russell Scott, said at the opening of their new clubrooms in 1968 that it 'was born in a car late in 1964, when with the late Mrs Haig she discussed the problems of the aged'.[23] Minister of Health, the Hon. Vance Dickie, opened Warrawee clubrooms in May 1968 in the presence of 300 guests from nearby towns. Leongatha Senior Citizens' Club was inaugurated at a meeting sponsored by the Rotary Club of Leongatha in the old Council chambers on 4 April 1967 under the Presidency of Reverend A. Dakers. Weekly meetings were held in St Andrew's Hall in Peart Street until the new clubrooms became available in 1973.[24]

Insufficient provision for aged and chronically ill patients led to the opening of the new geriatric wing at the Woorayl District Memorial Hospital with beds for eighteen patients in August 1971. This was done by Dr J. Lindell of the Hospitals and Charities Commission who was present at the first opening in

State Service Orchestra, sound shell, Moss Vale Park, 1982 (from G.S. Bruning).

1958. Chairman of the WDMH Committee to welcome Dr Lindell back in 1971 was Mr R.P. 'Bob' O'Malley, son of former chairman Peter O'Malley who welcomed Dr Lindell in 1958. The new wing, costing $224,000 with furnishings and equipment, was named after the first Matron, Sister Jean MacRae. It was opened free of debt through fund-raising activities of the hospital committee and substantial legacies from former district residents.[25]

A decade later the WDMH Committee, under the chairmanship of Mr R.S. 'Ray' Alford, embarked on the provision of a further twenty-bed wing to provide long-term nursing care and family relief for the aged and disabled of the community. Opened on 7 November 1982 by the Federal Member for Gippsland, the Hon. Peter J. Nixon, MHR, Koorooman House, by its very name, gave a sense of continuity to the efforts of the pioneers of the district.

The Leongatha District Ambulance Service grew from small beginnings in 1949-50. Following grants of £750 from Council and the Government, a Dodge ambulance was purchased and manned on a voluntary basis by loyal members of a team under the charge of local businesman, Mr A.E. 'Bert' Smith. A seventy-six square ambulance station costing £20,000 was opened in 1963, but by 1975 members' subscriptions were insufficient to cover increasing costs and the service was heavily in debt. As treasurer, Bert Smith said members were powerless to stop the huge increase as most of the additional expense was incurred by new wage awards and conditions granted to ambulance workers. Volunteer workers had been replaced by paid staff working award hours with a resulting vast upsurge in costs. In June 1975 membership fees were increased by sixty-six percent to compensate for these increases.[26]

Meals on Wheels began at Leongatha in 1973 as a result of a community meeting of seventy people in June 1972. Over twenty service organisations pledged their intention to assist in this worthy project. An organising committee under President Ted Rundell, with Laurie Trotman as Secretary, managed to get the scheme started in May 1973. Ten meals daily were delivered from the WDMH, but within twelve months, this number had grown to thirty.[27] A similar scheme was inaugurated at Inverloch in 1974 under a joint committee sponsored by the Apex and senior citizens' club. With Mr Doug Muir as President and Mrs J. Beggs as Secretary, this committee was soon delivering thirty meals obtained from the Wonthaggi Hospital daily.[28]

The range of services expected of Council by ratepayers increased yearly. In 1969 Council sponsored the first Concert for the People at Moss Vale Park. The State Service Orchestra, drawn from members of the State Public Service, began the first of their annual visits to Leongatha as part of their objective to provide quality musical entertainment for country people. Although their first visit was marred by the sudden downpour of almost two inches of rain, the second concert in February 1970 proved a wonderful success with over 2,000 people attending and fully justifying Council's decision to purchase this picturesque remnant of Francis Moss's nursery on the Tarwin. The completion of a sound shell in the park in 1981 provided an extra facility for concerts and other events held regularly over the summer months. The Music for the People concerts at Moss Vale were well patronised by the senior citizens of the Shire and adjoining towns. The bussing and seating of such large numbers was one of the numerous community service projects undertaken by Leongatha Lions Club. Formed at

Leongatha in October 1968, under foundation President Arthur Bentley, this annual operation at Moss Vale was typical of the many worthwhile tasks performed quickly and efficiently by these busy men.

Moss Vale Park was only one of several parks acquired and maintained by Woorayl Shire Council. A growing concern amongst ratepayers for conservation of natural bushland led to more emphasis being placed on the provision of this type of amenity within the State. At Fairbank the late Carl Hamann, member of an early pioneering family, donated ten acres (four hectares) of natural bushland to Council for preservation. This was augmented by Council purchase of a further adjoining forty acres (sixteen hectares) of similar bushland. At Koonwarra Mr and Mrs J. Bacon, well known as proprietors of the Koonwarra store, donated several acres of bushland as a flora and fauna reserve. In March 1966, under an agreement with Council, Mrs Ivee Strazzabosco made available Nirvana Park, overlooking the main South Gippsland Highway, for public use.[29] Following the death of her mother, Ivee Strazzabosco (nee Menthe) spent her younger years living with her father in a humble dwelling adjacent to the Railway Reserve at Koonwarra. It consisted of two tents joined together by a passage-way made from galvanised iron. Its chimney was made from bricks scavenged from the defunct Koonwarra brick kilns carried home by Mr Menthe in bags over his back. Money and work were scarce around Koonwarra in the 1930s with the result that Ivee and her father lived chiefly on rabbits with potatoes, onions and apples gleaned from nearby farms.[30]

Other parks and reserves acquired and developed by Council from time to time were named after notable citizens. McIndoe Park in Hassett Street, Leongatha, was named after the longest-serving councillor of Woorayl Shire, Cr R.E. 'Bob' McIndoe, MBE. Elected to Council in December 1925, Cr McIndoe served on Council for a record forty-seven years before retirement in 1973 after five terms as President. The R.V. Fisher Reserve at Tarwin Lower was named after a prominent member of the pioneering Fisher family, another of whom, Cr E.J. 'Ted' Fisher, JP, has represented the area since election in 1968 with four terms as President. The Tom Kindellan Reserve at Nerrena was named after the late President of the Nerrena Progress Association and son of former pioneer teamster and councillor, Jack Kindellan.

Other reserves for wildlife were set aside by private individuals and organisations. In 1976 at Koonwarra the South Gippsland Field and Game Club paid for earthworks to form a permanent lagoon in a backwater of the Tarwin as a breeding ground and haven for wildfowl. Set in ten acres of land made available by club member Leith Johnson, this lagoon of three acres of permanent water was one of several in the Shire reserved by club members who installed over 200 breeding boxes in them from 1966 onwards. Basic aims of the club were to awaken in field sportsmen a sense of responsibility for the part they could play in wildlife conservation and game management. A long-term plan was developed to provide for wildlife preservation and an increase in native bird and animal life.[31]

Interest in conservation of flora and fauna and increased danger arising from the use of pesticides led to the formation of the South Gippsland Conservation Society. Further publicity for these ideas was gained by the holding of the

St Peter's Anglican Church, Leongatha (from Woorayl Shire Historical Society).

Natural Resources Convention at Leongatha in 1968, at which the need for more parks and reserves was stressed by visiting speakers. This movement attempted to gradually influence people into a more enlightened sense of responsibility in preserving their heritage. Their activity in this matter resulted in many tree plantings of vacant land caused by realignment of roadways within the Shire. The society's success in the campaign to have the ocean outfall of the Inverloch sewerage scheme altered encouraged it to further protect the natural coastline of the area. The Waratah Bay lime kilns and the surrounding area were of particular interest to conservationists, with members lobbying for strict limitations on future sub-division in the area.

Shorter working hours for many people with longer award holidays led to a diversity of leisure occupations. Although television exposed young and old to new concepts of entertainment, music in its traditional form still flourished. While the younger generation was being weaned on rock bands and The Beatles, the Meeniyan-Dumbalk Music Lovers' Club, formed in 1946, continued to function. Regular meetings provided an opportunity for members to enjoy good music, either provided through the talents of members or by visiting artists. Under the guidance of Mrs Eleanor Downie, a concert party operated for many years with the role of Secretary and pianist being held by Mrs Estelle O'Neill. Improvements in the South Gippsland Highway enabled many music lovers to periodically attend concerts and opera performances in the metropolitan area.

In February 1964 Shire President, Cr John Meikle of Meeniyan, called a public meeting at Leongatha to discuss formation of a historical society within the Shire. Having migrated from England forty years earlier in 1924, he was conscious of the need to preserve intact the history of Woorayl Shire and its development in the same manner in which British history was retained and recorded. Office bearers elected at this first meeting were John Murphy, President, Mrs G. Roughead, Vice-president and Mr Charles Rogers, Secretary. Members then embarked on a systematic program of recording and collecting data, documents, photographs and artifacts relevant to the formative years of Woorayl Shire.

Government-funded activities, such as Leongatha's 3LC Leisure and Learning Centre in the old Council chambers building attracted many. Subjects such as calligraphy, embroidery, yoga, bee-keeping and pottery enabled many people to gainfully employ their leisure time. In 1982 the McMillan Rural Studies Centre adjacent to the Leongatha Technical School began conducting short courses on a variety of subjects applicable to different aspects of farming. Demand for these courses came not only from full-time farmers but also from an increased number of hobby farmers. The downturn of farmers' income in the mid-1970s led to the selling off of small acreages for residential purposes to people who preferred the attractions of rural to urban living.

Excessive sub-division in both rural and urban areas leads to wasteful provision of services with additional cost to the ratepayer. It is a problem not peculiar to Woorayl Shire but prevalent in most areas within commuting distances of large centres of population. In an attempt to retain the economic viability of its farming industries and not allow good farming land to be indiscriminately sub-divided, Woorayl Shire Council enforced strict guidelines

Opening sale, Koonwarra, 4 January 1982 (from P. Dwyer).

on sub-division. A balance had to be struck between the demand for allotments used for weekend or holiday purposes, rural residential living and the effects such allotments had on adjacent farm holdings. Councillors were of the opinion that specific areas of the Shire of only marginal value for farming purposes should be reserved for future sub-division into rural residential lots.

The reduced income derived from the cattle industry during the mid-1970s brought about several mergers between stock and station firms. As a means of containing costs and providing up-to-date marketing facilities, Gippsland and Northern Co. Ltd decided to close their selling yards at Leongatha, Meeniyan, Tarwin Lower, Mirboo North, Boolarra, Fish Creek and Toora and build central marketing facilities on the South Gippsland Highway at Koonwarra. Like the decision of Murray Goulburn to centralise production facilities at Leongatha, the availability of town water from the Leongatha Waterworks Trust at Koonwarra influenced the decision of Gippsland and Northern in their choice of site. Construction of the new selling complex, which included weighing facilities for stock, commenced in 1981 with the official opening of the J.F. Rourke Selling Ring at the yards being performed by the Federal Member for Gippsland, the Hon. P.J. Nixon, MHR, on 22 March 1982.[32] Under the capable management of Peter Dwyer, the Koonwarra selling complex of Gippsland and Northern quickly became established as one of the leading cattle selling centres in the State, attracting stock from all quarters of Central, South and East Gippsland.

More than half of the one-teacher schools operating in the Shire before the 1939-45 War closed as a result of the inauguration of bus services and declining enrolments. Many residents expressed regret at their closing because these small schools provided a focal point around which a sense of community evolved. But the availability of a school bus network generally outweighed this factor in the minds of most parents. The desire for an alternative to the State system of education led to the establishment of two more schools on the old Labour Colony site in Horn Street, Leongatha. The Christian School was established in 1980 to cater for primary and post-primary students, while the Catholic community began the formation of Mary McKillop College for secondary students in 1986.

S.S.3723 Wooreen closed temporarily on Monday, 14 February 1977 for a totally unforeseen reason. Teacher Robert David Hunter, twenty years of age, and his nine students aged six to eleven years were found to be missing when parents arrived at the school at 3.30 p.m. A note on the door said they had gone for a nature walk, but by 5 p.m. anxious parents called Police Sergeant Graeme Washfold for assistance. A massive search by police, assisted by aircraft, people on foot and horseback failed to find any trace of the missing persons. Next morning they were located safe and sound at Woodside where they had been forcibly taken by escaped prisoner and kidnapper, Edwin John Eastwood, who was later charged with abduction.[33]

The adoption of modern technology displaced labour in some fields and created work in others. At the Yarragon Road complex in 1980, Murray Goulburn opened a new ultra high temperature milk plant that enabled milk to be kept for several months without refrigeration. At a cost of almost $2,000,000, the plant could be used for the processing of fruit drinks in addition to different types of flavoured milk. It was part of a long-term plan by Murray Goulburn to diversify their product range from the export to the local market. Demand steadily increased for UHT products, and the plant was soon placed on a fixed production basis of three shifts daily for five days a week, with a resultant increase in the work-force.

One of the ironies of modern technological progress was that, apart from this UHT milk, Leongatha residents were no longer able to purchase milk produced from local farms. Prior to 1954 milk was purchased from nearby farms and dispensed by local dairymen to households in billies. A bottling plant was then installed at the Bridge Dairy by proprietors R.J. Murphy and J. Gunn which served until the advent of pasteurised milk in 1958. The relatively small quantity of milk consumed daily did not warrant establishment of a pasteurising plant at Leongatha, so the milk was then obtained from Moe Co-operative Dairy Co. for many years. Following closure of the Moe plant in 1986, Leongatha town milk was then obtained from Associated Dairies at Rowville near Dandenong.

Other social changes were occurring in the lives of district residents. On Sunday morning 26 June 1977 almost 500 Presbyterians and Methodists met in the Memorial Hall for the inaugural service of the Uniting Church. Thanksgiving services had been held earlier in their respective churches in Peart and Church Streets with the two congregations meeting near St Peter's and then proceeding down McCartin Street. Led by the Reverend Trevor Williams and Reverend Roy Bowen, the procession included children carrying banners that proudly proclaimed, 'We are uniting — now we are Congomethbyterians'.[34]

Fortunately for posterity, the shorter title of 'Uniting Church' was chosen to signify this memorable union of the Congregational, Methodist and Presbyterian Churches. Canon Gibson from St Peter's, in congratulating members on the formation of the new Church, said the Methodists would be remembered for their graciousness, Presbyterians for their perseverance and Congregationalists for their independence. 'If the new church can combine all these attributes it will become a wonderful power for good', said Canon Gibson.[35] Strangely enough at the same time that these three Churches were being welded into one Uniting Church, two minor fundamentalist Christian communities opened on the outskirts of Leongatha: the Kingdom Hall in Simon's Lane and the Christian Revival Centre in the Hughes Street extension.

The building boom of the sixties and seventies resulted in townships developing an urban sprawl. The drive-in theatre on Koonwarra Road opened in 1963 was followed by sub-division of the Tarwin Vale Estate on Horn Street and the Simon Estate on Nerrena Road. Inverloch, Meeniyan, Venus Bay, and to a lesser extent Dumbalk and Koonwarra, shared in the building boom of the 1960s and 1970s, but the census returns for Woorayl Shire revealed that almost one-third of all dwellings were unoccupied.[36]

Summary of Housing	1971	1981	Proportion percent (1981)
Occupied Pte Dwellings	2,633	3,235	67.4
Unoccupied Pte Dwellings	955	1,567	32.6

A different percentage would have resulted if the census had been taken at the end of the year. Inverloch with a permanent population of 1,600 swells to almost 10,000 during the summer holiday period.[37] Nevertheless, these figures illustrate the development of holiday homes and leisure activities within Woorayl Shire. With a total population of 9,854 in 1981, an increase of over 1,000 in the twenty year period since 1961, the former dominance of farming over urban interests has gradually changed. Although agriculture was still the largest grouping of the work-force, 31.7 percent, other sectors combined began to outweigh it in voting power at Council elections.

In 1974 the first woman candidate, Mrs Roma Shea, contested the Central Riding seat against former Councillor Arthur Bentley. After a hard fought campaign, Mrs Shea was defeated but far from disgraced in her first attempt, with the final result being Bentley 753, Shea 624.[38] Four years later Mrs Margaret Joyce Joyner from Inverloch was elected to represent the West Riding in August 1978 — the first woman councillor since its formation ninety years earlier. Mrs Joyner, after serving her three year term, did not renominate in 1981, but the following year, Mrs Mary Checkley and Mrs Joy Hoy were elected to represent Central and North Ridings respectively.

In 1981 Council completed the second stage of its building program with the opening of extended Council chambers and library. Shire President Cr Harold Vagg had the pleasure of asking the Hon. L. Lieberman, MP, Minister for Local Government, to perform the official opening of these sorely needed facilities on 4 August 1981. But no sooner was this section completed and councillors were

Woorayl Shire Council, 1987-8. Back row, left to right: Crs Ron Christoffersen, Rex Bowman, John Dunne, Kevin McMillan, Peter Western, Robin Moncur, Terry Hall and Harry Jackson. Front row: Crs Brian Cusack, Harold Vagg, Mr Ron Stanley (Shire Secretary), Cr E.J. 'Ted' Fisher (President), Mr Keith Godridge (Shire Engineer) and Cr Joy Hoy.

Memorial Hall, Leongatha, 1987 (from Woorayl Shire).

faced with a major problem in the Memorial Hall. Serious structural defects began to appear in the building in the 1970s, and several councillors were of the opinion it would be better to demolish rather than restore it. Fortunately from the aesthetic and historical viewpoint, a majority of councillors favoured restoration. The Leongatha branch of the RSL had vacated their rooms in the hall on completion of their own new clubrooms at the corner of Smith Street and Michael Place in 1952. Their numbers, augmented by veterans from the Korean and Vietnam Wars, the RSL, together with many other members of the community, wished to retain the Memorial Hall as a visible reminder of the role played by ex-servicemen and women in the defence of their country.

In 1985 Council remodelled and restored the hall and its associated chambers in a manner befitting its central position and the intentions of Woorayl Shire residents when it was first built. This was done under the capable direction of a sympathetic firm of architects, Brian O'Connor and Associates, and the careful supervision of Engineer Keith Godridge. The original facade was retained, the interior of the main hall completely renovated and painted, while the old Council chambers area was converted into a courtyard.

With Leongatha the commercial and administrative centre of the Shire, the Memorial Hall is now a pleasing architectural centrepiece. The Mechanics' Institute adjoining, re-furbished by Council in 1983, and now occupied by Woorayl Shire Historical Society, complements the appearance of the hall. However, the Commercial Hotel opposite, with its exterior festooned with advertisements, bears little resemblance to the former classical Australian hotel architecture so prized elsewhere. The post office and Court House remain basically unaltered, but the cattle and pig yards adjacent to the railway have now been demolished. It was through these yards that a great proportion of the district's wealth was gained and from which most of the business premises of Leongatha derived their income.

The goods yard at the railway station, once a hive of activity, is now strangely silent except for the intermittent train loads of superphosphate so necessary for the maintenance of soil fertility on surrounding farms. The Murray Goulburn complex on Yarragon Road, with a peak work-force of over 250 in the spring-time, is a constant and comforting reminder of the district's reliance on the dairy industry. The huge stacks of firewood necessary for its boilers have long since given way to Yallourn briquettes. Like the concrete cycle track on the adjacent Recreation Reserve, these are the outward signs of new concepts in industry and leisure affecting rural as well as urban communities.

The changes that have taken place during the past century in Woorayl Shire have been remarkable. Few remain to recall the early years of settlement. Those men and women who shared the privations and hardships of the first generation of settlers are in many respects akin to the odd remaining giants of the forest still standing. Gnarled and knotted, their frail limbs able only to withstand a few more winter storms, many view the panorama of ordered farms and lush pastures from the windows of Koorooman House on land once owned by Hugh McCartin. Living on memories of their childhood, they still recall details related to them by their parents who settled the district.

The 'howling wilderness' described by McCartin now reflects the vision, enterprise and labour of four generations of men and women who transformed it from primaeval forest into one of the most productive rural Shires in the Commonwealth. The first six councillors who made their way through pack-tracks knee deep in mud to the first Council meeting at Mirboo North on 29 August 1888 set a pattern of service to the community that has been faithfully carried on ever since. The celebration of the first centenary of Woorayl Shire should serve as a source of encouragement and pride to councillors and residents alike. One century has passed but another beckons with different tasks, different challenges, different methods but basically the same goals — the creation of a society of free men and women living in harmony with nature and at peace with their neighbours.

APPENDIX 1. PRESIDENTS OF THE SHIRE OF WOORAYL

1888-1889	Cr W. Scarlett	1938-1939	Cr W. Hughes
1889-1890	Cr R. Smith	1939-1940	Cr H. Williams
1890-1891	Cr C. Watt	1940-1941	Cr H. Williams
1891-1892	Cr J. Allen	1941-1942	Cr R. McIndoe
1892-1893	Cr W. Cashin	1942-1943	Cr A.C. Ashenden
1893-1894	Cr B. Benn	1943-1944	Cr H. Williams
1894-1895	Cr M. Allison	1944-1945	Cr C. Bond
1895-1896	Cr G. Henderson	1945-1946	Cr A. Sloan
1896-1897	Cr H. Crutchfield	1946-1947	Cr K. Macdonald
1897-1898	Cr A. Allan	1947-1948	Cr H. Holt
1898-1899	Cr W. Cashin	1948-1949	Cr A.C. Ashenden
1899-1900	Cr W. Hughes	1949-1950	Cr H. Williams
1900-1901	Cr H. McCartin	1950-1951	Cr R. McIndoe
1901-1902	Cr W. Tack	1951-1952	Cr A. Richards
1902-1903	Cr W. Geale	1952-1953	Cr J. McDonald
1903-1904	Cr H. McCartin	1953-1954	Cr C. Bond
1904-1905	Cr R. Smith	1954-1955	Cr A. Sloan
1905-1906	Cr T. Mummery	1955-1956	Cr H. Bird
1906-1907	Cr W. Livingston	1956-1957	Cr H. Holt
1907-1908	Cr L. Donald	1957-1958	Cr A.C. Ashenden
1908-1909	Cr J. Wills	1958-1959	Cr R. McIndoe
1909-1910	Cr P. Johnson	1959-1960	Cr J. McDonald
1910-1911	Cr G. Black	1960-1961	Cr H. Bird
1911-1912	Cr H. Pearson/Cr T. Mummery	1961-1962	Cr A. Bentley
1912-1913	Cr W. Coulter	1962-1963	Cr C. Rousseau
1913-1914	Cr L. Donald	1963-1964	Cr J. Meikle
1914-1915	Cr A. McDonald	1964-1965	Cr L. Cantwell
1915-1916	Cr P. Johnson	1965-1966	Cr J. Haw
1916-1917	Cr G. Black	1966-1967	Cr R. McIndoe
1917-1918	Cr T. Mummery	1967-1968	Cr W. Hinds
1918-1919	Cr A. Hall	1968-1969	Cr H. Kinnish
1919-1920	Cr A. Hall	1969-1970	Cr W. Tilson
1920-1921	Cr A. McDonald	1970-1971	Cr A.R. Ashenden
1921-1922	Cr K. Macdonald	1971-1972	Cr E.J. Fisher J.P.
1922-1923	Cr J. Eccles	1972-1973	Cr J. Stiff
1923-1924	Cr R. Inglis	1973-1974	Cr J. Haw
1924-1925	Cr J. Henderson	1974-1975	Cr A.R. Ashenden J.P.
1925-1926	Cr D. Gibson	1975-1976	Cr L.J. Taylor J.P.
1926-1927	Cr H. York	1976-1977	Cr H.A. Pearsall J.P.
1927-1928	Cr K. Macdonald	1977-1978	Cr J. Haw
1928-1929	Cr H. Hyland	1978-1979	Cr T.G. Morter
1929-1930	Cr G. Jones	1979-1980	Cr E.J. Fisher J.P.
1930-1931	Cr K. Macdonald	1980-1981	Cr H.G. Vagg
1931-1932	Cr R. McIndoe	1981-1982	Cr E.D. Hattam
1932-1933	Cr E. Opray	1982-1983	Cr L.J. Taylor J.P.
1933-1934	Cr G. Black	1983-1984	Cr E.J. Fisher J.P.
1934-1935	Cr C. Bond	1984-1985	Cr R.W. Bowman
1935-1936	Cr C. Bond	1985-1986	Cr B.T. Cusack J.P.
1936-1937	Cr G. Henderson	1986-1987	Cr Reverend T.G. Williams
1937-1938	Cr A. Gibson	1987-1988	Cr E.J. Fisher J.P.

SOURCES

1. MANUSCRIPT SOURCES
Woorayl Shire Council.
Minute Books, 1887-1987.
Rate Books, 1887-1987.

National Library of Australia
Rawson, Samuel, 'Journal', 9 February 1840.

University of Melbourne Archives.
Brinsmead, G.S.J., 'A Geographical Study of the Dairy Manufacturing Industry in Gippsland 1840-1910.'
Thesis submitted for Master of Science 1977.
Grainger, P., Letters, 1901-14.

Royal Historical Society of Victoria.
Black, Maud, 'Notes on Early Settlement of Tarwin Meadows'.
Lyall, Family, Diaries by B.I. Ricardo.

Public Record Office, Melbourne.
Anderson, Samuel, Letter to LaTrobe 1840, File 40/602.
Townsend, T.S., 'Journal of proceedings while surveying Anderson's Inlet 1840'.
Lands Dept., Selectors Files, Section 19/20.
Railways, Chief Engineers Dept., Correspondence Files, 1889-90.
Education Dept., School Building Files, Correspondence Registers.

Department of Crown Lands and Survey.
Pastoral Run Records.

Department of Conservation, Forests and Lands.
Records, Mechanics' Institutes — Leongatha, Tarwin Lower.

Woorayl Shire Historical Society.
Minute books, Mechanics' Institutes, Leongatha, 1890-1917;
Leongatha South, 1897-1932; Fairbank, 1904-1934.
Records, ANA Leongatha Branch.
Churches — Leongatha Anglican, Catholic, Methodist, Presbyterian, Reformed Church of South Gippsland, Inverloch Anglican.
Inverloch Waterworks Trust and Sewerage Authority. Leongatha Butter Factory, 1895-1964, South Gippsland Dairy Products 1964-6, South Gippsland Milk Industries, 1966-73, Murray Goulburn, 1973-1987.
Leongatha and District Caledonian Society, 1927-41. Leongatha Waterworks Trust and Sewerage Authority.
Mines Dept., Report on Berry's Creek Coal Seam, 1901-48. PMG Records, Koorooman-Leongatha area.
Tarwin Valley Water Board. Inc. Dumbalk and Meeniyan Waterworks Trust.

Diaries.
Griffin, Amy, 1894-5.
Spencer, Georgina, 1892 (courtesy Rodney Emmerson).
Spinks, B., 1909, Leongatha Labour Colony.

2. GOVERNMENTAL SOURCES — PRINTED MATERIAL
Great Britain, House of Lords, Sessional Papers, 1841 v. 5 papers respecting New South Wales, report in copy of a despatch from Sir G. Gipps, Governor of NSW by Count Streleski [sic], no 2 (London 1841) p16.
Victorian Govt. *Gazettes.*
Victorian Year Book.
Victorian Municipal Directory.
Census, 1891, 1901, 1961, 1981, Govt. Statist.
Parliamentary Papers: Report of Select Committee of Inquiry upon Leongatha Labour Colony, 1899-1900.
Royal Commission on Soldier Settlement, 1925.
Royal Commission on Migrant Land Settlement, 1931.
Police — *Victoria Police Gazette.*
Statistical Registers, 1899-96.
Victorian Dept. of Agriculture — Annual reports, 1901-48.

3. NEWSPAPERS
Age, Melbourne.
Argus, Melbourne.
The Foster Mirror.
The Great Southern Advocate (Korumburra).
The Great Southern Star, 1890-1986.
The Herald, Melbourne.
The Leader, Melbourne.
The Leongatha Echo, 1934-51.
The Leongatha Guardian, 1982.
The Leongatha Sun, 1901-29.
The Mirboo Herald, 1887-91.
The Sun, Melbourne.
The Weekly Times, Melbourne.

4. BOOKS
Ashenden, Arthur, *A History of Dollar*, Stony Creek Centenary Committee, 1985, *Second Wind — A Collection of Real Life Stories*, 1985.
Billis, R.V. and Kenyon, A.S., *Pastoral Pioneers of Port Phillip*, Melbourne, Macmillan, 1932; 2nd Edition, Stockland Press, 1974.
Blake, L.J. (ed), *Vision and Realisation*, Vol. 3. Education Department of Victoria, 1973.
Blundell, A.M., *Francis Moss and Moss Vale Park*, Leongatha, 1956.
Bourke, J.P. and Sonenberg, D.S., *Insanity and Injustice*, Melbourne, Jacaranda Press, 1969.
Bowden, Keith M. Dr, *Early Days of Korumburra*, Korumburra, 1969. *The Great Southern Railway*, Korumburra, 1970.
Boyd, P.M., *A History of Meeniyan*, Meeniyan Progress Association, 1981.
Brewster, E., *Inverloch — A Patchwork of Historical Studies*, 1980.
Bride, T.F. (ed)., *Letters from Victorian Pioneers*, Melbourne, 1898. Reprinted Currey O'Neil, 1983.
Brodribb, William Adams, *Brodribb and Bennett, Recollections of an Australian Squatter and Account of a Journey to Gippsland by Lavinia Hasell Bennett*, Queensberry Hill Press, Melbourne, 1976.
Buffalo, A Brief History of Buffalo and Its Residents, Buffalo Hall Committee, 1983.
Burchett, Franklin, *Memoirs of Poowong District*, Melbourne, Poowong Back-to Committee, 1947.
Carter, Benita, *Gunnersen in Australia*, Melbourne, Gunnersens Pty Ltd, 1986.
Centenary of Gippsland, Leongatha, Back-to Leongatha Booklet, 1940.
Charles, J.R., *A History of Tarwin Lower 1798-1974*, Tarwin Lower, 1974.
Clark, Rev. Albert E., *The Church of Our Fathers*, Sale, Diocese of Gippsland, 1947.
Clerk, Nellie E., *Songs from the Gippsland Forest*, Mirboo North, 1887.
Cook, P., *Hallston Through the Years 1878-1978*, Hallston Centenary Committee, 1984.
Crawford, Rosemary, *Yanakie — Station to Settlement 1850-1983*, Yanakie Hall Committee, 1984.
Curr, E.M., *The Australian Race*, Vols II and III, Melbourne, 1886-7.
Daley, C., *The Story of Gippsland*, Melbourne, Gippsland Municipalities Association, 1960.
Dumbalk Saga 1878-1970, Souvenir of Easter 1970 Back-to Dumbalk.
Dunderdale, G., *The Book of the Bush*, London, Ward Lock and Co., 1870.
Eunson, Warwick, *The Unfolding Hills*, Mirboo North, Mirboo Shire Council, 1978.
Ferres, Colin D., *Tuesday at Eight*, A History of the Victorian Young Farmers, Melbourne, R.L. Polk (Aust) Vic. n/d.
Fitzgerald, B., *A Tale of Two Towns*, Dumbalk and Fish Creek, n/d. *A Tale of the Lands which Embrace Famous 'Tullaree'*, 1980.
Fleming, P., *The Waratah Story*, n/d.
Haydon, G., *Five Years in Australia Felix*, London, 1846.
Henderson, Leslie M., *The Goldstein Story*, Melbourne, Stockland Press, 1973.

Horton, Thos. and Morris, Kenneth, *The Andersons of Western Port*, Bass Valley Historical Society, 1983.
Howitt, A.W., *The Native Tribes of South East Australia*, London Macmillan, 1904.
Kaluski, Marian, *Sir Paul E. Strzelecki. A Polish Count's Explorations in 19th Century Australia*, Melbourne, A.E. Press, 1985.
Kemp, D., *A History of Shire of Maffra*, Maffra, 1975.
Koonwarra. Early History of Koonwarra, Back-to Committee, 1965.
Loney, J.K., *Wrecks on the Gippsland Coast*, Third Edition, 1971.
Malone, H.J., *A Short History of Central South Gippsland*, Buffalo, 1932.
Medew, R.S., *The Days of Thy Youth*, Federal Press, Rockhampton, Qld, n/d.
Menadue, J.E., *A Centenary History of the ANA 1871-1971*, Melbourne, Horticultural Press, n/d.
Meyrick, F.H., *Life in the Bush*, London, Nelson, 1939.
Mitchell, S.R., *Stone Age Craftsmen*, Melbourne, Tait Book Co., 1949.
Murphy, J., *Leongatha Labour Colony 1893-1919*, Woorayl Shire Historical Society, 1983.
Neilson, J.S., *John Shaw Neilson, Autobiography*, Canberra, National Library of Australia, 1978.
Noonan, J. and Fraser, A., *Of Wamman and Yanakie*, 1969.
Peck, Harry H., *Memoirs of a Stockman*, Melbourne, Third Edition, Stockland Press, 1946.
Rawson, G.A., *A Life of Sir Paul Edmund Strzelecki*, Melbourne, Heinemann, 1953.
Reichl, P., *Mountain Forests of Gippsland*, Melbourne, Nelson, 1968.
Shears, Richard, *The Lady of the Swamp*, Melbourne, Nelson, 1981.
Sillcock, K.M., *Three Generations of Dairying in Victoria*, Melbourne, Hawthorn Press, 1972.
Smith, James, (ed)., *Cyclopedia of Victoria*, Melbourne, Cyclopedia Co., 1903.
Smyth, R. Brough, *The Aborigines of Victoria*, Vol I and II, London, 1878.
South Gippsland Pioneers' Association, *The Land of the Lyre Bird*, Korumburra, Shire of Korumburra, 1920, (reprinted 1967).
Spreadborough, R. and Anderson, H., *Victorian Squatters*, Melbourne, Red Rooster Press, 1983.
Stony Creek, A History 1885-1985, Stony Creek Back-to Committee, 1985.
Strzelecki, Paul, E. de., *Physical Description of New South Wales and Van Diemen's Land*, London, 1845.
Tarwin, A Brief History of Middle Tarwin, 1855-1979, Back-to Committee, 1981.
White, Joseph, *They Called it Arawata*, Arawata Centenary Committee, 1982. *The Town Called Outtrim*, 1976.
Young, Lynette, *The Melody Lingers On — Biography of Tarlton Rayment*, Melbourne, Hawthorn Press, 1967.

5. ARTICLES AND PAMPHLETS

Beaumont, B., 'Development of SEC in Leongatha District', Leongatha Jaycee's *Phoenix*, July 1972.
Bennett, Lavinia Hasell, 'Diaries', *Morwell Historical Society News*, Vol. IV (1965) Chp. 10.
Church of England Messenger, Melbourne, Church of England Diocese of Melbourne, 1890-5.
Cuthill, W.J., 'The Gippsland Road, 1836-48', *RHSV Magazine* Vol. 29, No. 1, February 1959.
Footprints, Quarterly Journal of Melbourne, Catholic Historical Commission, 1971-87.
Kelly, M., 'A Great Doctor: Horace Pern of Leongatha 1872-1936', *RHSV Magazine*, Vol. XXXIV, No. 1, August 1963.
Massola, A., 'Aboriginal Journeys', *Victorian Naturalist*, Vol. 91, No. 2, February 1974.
Morgan, P., 'Forgotten in the Fertile Crescent, The Settling of Gippsland', *Quadrant*, November 1983.
Murray Goulburn Co-operative Co. Ltd., *Supplier Newsletters*, 1973-87.
O'Donnell, P.M. Rev. Fr., 'History of Catholic Church in Gippsland', unpublished m/s, Sale, 1937.

REFERENCES

Abbreviations

The Great Southern Star GSS
Public Records Office PRO
Royal Historical Society of Victoria RHSV
Woorayl Shire Historical Society WSHS

Chapter One

1. Rawson, S., 'Journal of Samuel Rawson', 9 February 1840, National Library of Aust.
2. Supt. Pt. Phillip Correspondence, File 40/62, PRO, Laverton.
3. Blake, L., *Place Names of Victoria*, Melbourne, Rigby, 1977, p253.
4. Townsend, T.S., Report to Melbourne Survey Office, 21 December 1840, PRO, Laverton.
5. Surveyor-General's Outward Correspondence, 1841-3, PRO, Laverton.
6. Daley, C., *The Story of Gippsland*, Gippsland Municipalities Association, 1960, p18.
7. *Letters from Victorian Pioneers*, edited by T.F. Bride, 1898-1983, p243.
8. ibid., p244.
9. Haydon, G., *Five Years in Australia Felix*, London, 1846, p134-5.
10. 'Bennett Diaries', *Morwell Historical Society News*, Vol. IV (1965), Chp 10, *Brodribb and Bennett, Account of a Journey to Gipps Land by Lavinia Hasell Bennett*, Melbourne, Queensberry Hill Press, 1976.
11. Gellion, J., letter to partner Rickards, 1 August 1844. Reprinted *Gippsland Mercury*, 19 May 1911.
12. Map 1, *Victorian Naturalist*, Vol 91, 1974, p46.
13. Haydon, G., op.cit., p130-152.
14. Mitchell, S.R., *Stone Age Craftsmen*, Melbourne, Tait Book Co., 1949, p125.
15. Smyth, R. Brough, *The Aborigines of Victoria*, 1878, Vol. 1, p32.
16. Dunderdale, G., *The Book of the Bush*, London, Ward Lock and Co., 1870, p269.
17. Black, Maud, Notes on Early Settlement of Tarwin Meadows, RHSV.
18. Curr, E.M., *The Australian Race*, 1886, Vol III, p543.
19. Smyth, R. Brough., op.cit., Vol. II, p133-51.

Chapter Two

1. *Government Gazette*, 4 October 1848.
2. GSS, 12 January 1923.
3. Black, Maud, Notes on Early Settlement of Tarwin Meadows, RHSV.
4. ibid.
5. ibid., and Loney, J.K., *Wrecks on the Gippsland Coast*, 1968, p17.
6. Black, Maud, op.cit.
7. Kaluski, M., *Sir Paul E. Strzelecki*, Melbourne, A.E. Press, 1985, p62.
8. Daley, C., *The Story of Gippsland*, Melbourne, Whitcombe and Tombs, 1960, p66.
9. Lands Department File, PRO, Laverton, Henderson, G., 4733/19.20.
10. 'Musgrave Memoirs', GSS, 14 November 1944.
11. ibid.
12. Fleming, P., 'The Waratah Story', *The Foster Mirror*, 28 May 1964.
13. ibid., interview by author, 1986.

14. *GSS*, 10 August 1894.
15. Fleming, P., op.cit.
16. Victorian Education Dept. Records, *Vision and Realisation*, p1231.
17. Lands Dept. File, PRO, Laverton. M. Wiberg, 7902/19.20.
18. Melbourne, *Age*, 24 December 1878.
19. South Gippsland Pioneers' Association, *The Land of the Lyre Bird*, Korumburra, 2nd Edition, 1966, p131.
20. *GSS*, 4 June 1897, 28 January 1938.

Chapter Three

1. Lands Dept. file, PRO, Laverton, Wm. Millar, 5190/19.20.
2. 'Musgrave Memoirs', *GSS*, 6 April 1937.
3. Lands Dept. File, PRO, Laverton, J. Nation, 13438/19.20.
4. 'Cross Memoirs', *GSS*, 28 September 1934.
5. Musgrave, loc.cit.
6. ibid., 17 April 1942.
7. South Gippsland Pioneers' Association, *The Land of the Lyre Bird*, Korumburra, 2nd Edition, 1966, p202.
8. ibid., p132.
9. Cook, P.G., *Hallston Through the Years 1878-1978*, Hallston Centenary Committee 1978.
10. 'Hamann Memoirs', *GSS*, 31 August 1934.
11. Cross, op.cit., 28 September 1934.
12. Johnson, E., 'Memoirs', WSHS, 1956.
13. *Victoria and Riverina*, edited biographical sketches, Melbourne, 1933, Pt 1, p87.
14. Johnson, E., op.cit.
15. Information supplied by Wm Ryan, Fairbank, 1960.
16. *Land Selector's Guide*, 2nd Edition, Melbourne, G.A. Goodwin, 1873.
17. Johnson, E., op.cit.
18. Horn, W., Coalition Creek. Interview by author, 1935.
19. South Gippsland Pioneers' Association, op.cit., p300.
20. PMG Records, WSHS.
21. Lands Dept. File, PRO, Laverton, J.N. Horn, 12782/19.20.
22. ibid., Wm Russell, 13651/19.20.
23. *GSS*, 10 February 1933.
24. ibid., 16 March 1894.
25. *Mirboo Herald*, 2 November 1888.
26. Bowden, K.M., *The Great Southern Railway*, Australian Railway Historical Society (Vic. Division), 1970, p26.
27. *Koonwarra*, Back-to Committee Booklet, 1965.
28. Leongatha Cemetery Records.
29. Bowden, K.M., *Early Days of Korumburra*, Korumburra, 1969, p41.
30. *Mirboo Herald*, 20 September 1889; Johnson, E., op.cit.
31. Johnson, E., op.cit.
32. Cross, G., op.cit.
33. Medew, R.S., *The Days of Thy Youth*, Rockhampton, Federal Press, n/d, p14.
34. Shingler, P., Letters, WSHS.

Chapter Four

1. South Gippsland Pioneers' Association, *The Land of the Lyre Bird*, 2nd Edition, Korumburra, 1966, p203.
2. ibid., p401.
3. Victorian Education Dept., File S.S. 2964.
4. Johnson, E., 'Memoirs', WSHS.
5. ibid.
6. Victorian Education Dept. Records, *Vision and Realisation*, p1243.
7. ibid., p1254.
8. Victorian Education Dept., File S.S.2981.
9. ibid.
10. ibid.
11. ibid.
12. ibid.
13. *GSS*, 5 February 1952.
14. *Centenary of Gippsland*, Back-to-Leongatha Booklet, Leongatha, 1940.
15. Clark, A.E., *Church of Our Fathers, History of Church of England in Gippsland 1847-1947*, Sale, Diocese of Gippsland, p252.
16. ibid.

17. Lands Dept. Survey Maps, La Trobe Library.
18. *Mirboo Herald*, 15 October 1887.
19. *Victorian Government Gazette*, 25 May 1888.
20. *Municipal Directory*, 1889.
21. Minute Book, Woorayl Shire Council, 16 October 1888.
22. GSS, 26 November 1890.
23. PMG Records, V368/3/1344, WSHS.
24. Minute Book, Woorayl Shire Council, 23 September 1890.

Chapter Five

1. GSS, 30 August 1890.
2. Lands Dept. File, PRO, Laverton, J.P. Gwyther, 6685/19.20.
3. *Municipal Directory*, 1890.
4. GSS, 16 August 1890.
5. GSS, 29 May 1923.
6. 'Musgrave Memoirs', GSS, 9 June 1942.
7. GSS, 20 January 1891.
8. GSS, 16 August 1890.
9. Information supplied by Bair family, 1975.
10. GSS, 13 March 1891.
11. ibid.
12. ibid.
13. GSS, 19 December 1890.
14. GSS, 3 January 1896.
15. ibid.
16. ibid.
17. ibid.
18. *Koonwarra. Early History of Koonwarra*, Back-to Committee Booklet, 1965.
19. *Stony Creek: A History 1885-1985*, Back-to Committee Booklet, 1985, p90.
20. Wesson, A., 'Mechanics' Institutes in Victoria', *RHSV Mag*, Vol. 42, No2, p609.
21. ibid., p613.
22. Minute Book, Leongatha Mechanics' Institute, 29 July 1890.
23. GSS, 16 August 1890.
24. Minute Book, Leongatha Mechanics' Institute, 1 May 1891.
25. GSS, 9 March 1891.
26. Minute Book, Leongatha Mechanics' Institute, 23 February 1891.
27. ibid., 15 September 1891.
28. ibid., 11 June 1891.
29. GSS, 22 May 1896.
30. GSS, 19 June 1891.
31. GSS, 28 August 1891.
32. Blythe, Ronald, *Akenfield. Portrait of an English Village*, Penguin Books, Harmondsworth, England, 1977, p80-7.
33. GSS, 12 September 1890.
34. GSS, 24 April 1891.
35. GSS, 12 February 1892.
36. Menadue, J.E., *A Centenary History of the A.N.A. 1871-1971*, Melbourne, Horticultural Press, n/d, p292.
37. Minute Book, Leongatha Mechanics' Institute, 1 May 1903.
38. Victorian Education Dept., *Vision and Realisation*, p.1271.
39. La Trobe's Journeys, 1839-54, No. 32 La Trobe Library.
40. *Stony Creek: A History 1885-1985*, Back-to Committee Booklet, 1985, p79.
41. Leishman, J., Records, WSHS.
42. Malone, H.J., *A Short History of South Gippsland*, 1932.
43. Victorian Education Dept., *Vision and Realisation*, p1275, *Buffalo 1894-1983*, Buffalo Hall Committee 1983, p89.
44. Tarwin Lower Mechanics' Institute File, Lands Dept.
45. Brewster, E., *Inverloch, A Patchwork of Historical Studies*, WSHS, 1980.

Chapter Six

1. GSS, 31 January 1891.
2. Minute Book, Woorayl Shire Council, 23 September 1890.
3. ibid., 12 February 1889.
4. Johnson, G., interview by author, 1985.

5. Minute Book, Woorayl Shire Council, 5 May 1896.
6. Johnson, E., 'Memoirs', WSHS.
7. Burchett, Franklin, *Memoirs of Poowong District*, Melbourne, Poowong Back-to Committee, 1947.
8. Johnson, E., op.cit.
9. ibid.
10. Lands Dept. File, PRO, Laverton, Wm. Begg, 12077/19.20.
11. ibid.
12. GSS, 9 January 1891.
13. Wilson, D., Evidence Royal Commission Vegetable Products, *Weekly Times*, 7 July 1886.
14. GSS, 12 February 1892.
15. Statistical Register, 1891, 1901.
16. *Victorian Government Gazette*, 25 October 1889, 25 November 1889, GSS, 20 December 1895.
17. Annual Report, Dept. of Agriculture, 1900-01, p221.
18. GSS, 21 November 1892.
19. GSS, 13 March 1896.
20. ibid.
21. ibid.
22. ibid.
23. GSS, 16 February 1894.
24. GSS, 6 July 1894.
25. GSS, 4 August 1894.
26. GSS, 21 September 1894.
27. GSS, 28 December 1894.
28. GSS, 12 April 1895.
29. *Centenary of Gippsland*, Back-to Leongatha Booklet, Leongatha, 1940.
30. GSS, 14 October 1895.
31. ibid.
32. GSS, 27 August 1897.
33. GSS, 15 November 1901.
34. *The Cyclopedia of Victoria 1905*, Vol. III, p609; *Leongatha Sun*, 20 September 1905.
35. *Stony Creek: A History 1885-1985*, Back-to Committee Booklet, p61.
36. ibid., p62.
37. Johnson, E., op.cit.
38. GSS, 20 July 1894.
39. Peck, Harry H., *Memoirs of a Stockman*, Melbourne, Stockland Press, 1942. p210.
40. ibid., p22.
41. Trotman, L., WSHS. 1985.
42. Peck, H., op.cit., p217.
43. ibid., p218.
44. GSS, 6 March 1896.
45. South Gippsland Pioneers' Association, *The Land of the Lyre Bird*, Korumburra, 2nd Edition, 1966, p432.
46. *Dumbalk Saga 1878-1970*, Back-to Committee Booklet, p15.
47. Lands Dept. File, PRO, Laverton, H. Borrow, 12084/19.20.
48. Blundell, A.M., *Francis Moss and Moss Vale Park*, 1956, p14. Lands Dept. File PRO, Laverton, W.E. Moss, 051/50.51.
49. Victorian Dept. of Agriculture, 'Annual Report', 1912.
50. *Leongatha Sun*, 21 January 1903.
51. GSS, 19 June 1896.
52. Victorian Dept. of Agriculture, 'Annual Report', 1912.
53. GSS, 10 December 1893.
54. Minute Book, Leongatha Mechanics' Institute, 5 August 1893.

Chapter Seven

1. Census of Victoria 1891, Pt 1, p21.
2. Knight, Mrs U.V. (nee Bellingham), interview by author, 1986.
3. 'Musgrave Memoirs', GSS, 27 October 1942.
4. Clerk, N.S., *Songs from the Gippsland Forest*, Mirboo North, Booklet, 1887.
5. *Mirboo Herald*, 22 June 1888.
6. Spencer, Georgina, 1892, Diary lent by R. Emmerson, WSHS.
7. Griffin, Amy, 1894-5, Diary donated to WSHS by Dorothy Shingler.
8. GSS, 17 January 1956.
9. 'Cross Memoirs', GSS, 23 September 1934.
10. Davis, Les, interview by author, 1980.
11. GSS, 27 November 1934.

12. *GSS*, 30 June 1899.
13. ibid., 3 December 1893.
14. Spencer, Mrs L. (nee Blackmore), interview by author, 1940.
15. Roughead, Mrs J. (nee O'Reilly), interview by author, 1970.
16. Lyall, Family, Diaries by B.I. Ricardo, RHSV.
17. Blundell, A.M., *Francis Moss and Moss Vale Park*, 1956, p7.
18. *GSS*, 3 January 1896.
19. ibid., 17 January 1896.
20. ibid., 21 February 1896.
21. Watson, G., interview by author, 1985.
22. *GSS*, 10 July 1891.
23. ibid., 5 February 1952, author not stated.
24. *Weekly Times*, 12, 19 October 1929, 'Early Leongatha' by F. Whitcombe.
25. Shingler, D., interview by author, 1985.
26. *GSS*, 15 July 1898.
27. ibid., 29 September 1911.

Chapter Eight

1. 'Musgrave Memoirs', *GSS*, 18 January 1944.
2. *GSS*, 2 November 1943.
3. ibid., 10 July 1896.
4. Minute Book, Woorayl Shire Council, 3 December 1899.
5. ibid., 12 April 1892.
6. ibid., 24 November 1896.
7. ibid.
8. ibid., 15 December 1896.
9. *GSS*, 1 October 1896.
10. Records, Leongatha District Methodist Church, WSHS.
11. Clark, A.E., *Church of Our Fathers, History of Church of England in Gippsland 1847-1947*, Sale, Diocese of Gippsland, p252.
12. Records, Leongatha District Methodist Church, WSHS.
13. *GSS*, 20 September 1895.
14. *GSS*, 5 July 1895.
15. Records, Leongatha District Presbyterian Church, WSHS.
16. *GSS*, 15 April 1892.
17. *GSS*, 2 December 1898.
18. *Leongatha Sun*, 12 March 1902.
19. ibid., 7 January 1903.
20. *GSS*, 19 April 1912.
21. Minute Book, Leongatha Mechanics' Institute, 16 August 1890.
22. ibid., 28 July 1893.
23. *GSS*, 31 August 1900.
24. *Leongatha Sun*, 4 February 1903.
25. *GSS*, 16 May 1919.
26. ibid., 1 July 1911.
27. *Leongatha Sun*, 19 August 1903.
28. ibid., 17 March 1909.
29. Minute Book, Woorayl Shire Council, 28 January 1902.
30. *Leongatha Sun*, 22 March 1905.
31. *GSS*, 1 September 1906.
32. Dannock, V., 'Memoirs', WSHS.
33. *Leongatha Sun*, 19 June 1907.
34. ibid., 2 October 1907.
35. ibid., 16 January 1907.
36. ibid., 10 March 1909.
37. ibid., 24 March 1909.
38. ibid., 2 April 1902.
39. Minute Book, Woorayl Shire Council, 26 July 1904.
40. *GSS*, 4 September 1907.
41. Dannock, V., 'Memoirs', WSHS.
42. *GSS*, 6 September 1908.
43. ibid., 20 January 1899.
44. Brewster, E., *Inverloch-Patchwork of Historical Studies*, WSHS, 1980.
45. Minute Book, Woorayl Shire Council, 28 January 1902.

46. *Leongatha Sun*, 1 December 1909.
47. O'Donnell, P.M. Rev. Fr., 'History of Catholic Church in Gippsland', Unpublished M/S, Sale, 1937.
48. GSS, 30 December 1910.
49. O'Donnell, loc.cit.
50. *Leongatha Sun*, 7 October 1903.
51. ibid., 13 July 1904.
52. ibid., 23 January 1907.
53. Minute Book, Leongatha Mechanics' Institute, 8 July 1904.
54. *Leongatha Sun*, 17 November 1909.
55. ibid.

Chapter Nine

1. Lands Dept. Correspondence, WSHS.
2. GSS, 4 December 1896.
3. ibid., 12 March 1897.
4. Dannock, V., 'Memoirs', WSHS.
5. GSS, 15 December 1893.
6. ibid., 16 February 1900.
7. *Leongatha Sun*, 22 March 1905.
8. ibid., 25 June 1902, 'Drag', a light wagonette used for carrying passengers.
9. GSS, 12 June 1896.
10. ibid., 22 May 1896.
11. *Leongatha Sun*, 9 July 1902.
12. Howard, Jas., GSS, 4 June 1957.
13. GSS, 20 December 1901.
14. *Leongatha Sun*, 5 March 1902.
15. 'Shingler Memoirs', WSHS.
16. GSS, 29 July 1892.
17. ibid., 12 August 1898, 21 September 1948.
18. ibid., 9 March 1900.
19. ibid.
20. ibid., 1 June 1900.
21. *Dumbalk Saga 1878-1970*, Back-to Committee Booklet, p46.
22. GSS, 20 July 1900.
23. ibid., 9 February 1900.
24. ibid., 23 February 1900.
25. ibid., 27 December 1895.
26. Information supplied by C.R. Carmichael, South Gippsland Racing Club, 1987.
27. GSS, 29 March 1899.
28. ibid., 23 March 1900.
29. ibid., 5 January 1894.
30. ibid., 23 March 1900.
31. ibid., 6 November 1896.
32. ibid., 29 September 1899.
33. ibid., 25 May 1900.
34. ibid., 19 February 1892.
35. *Leongatha Sun*, 18 June 1902.
36. GSS, 10 April 1896.
37. ibid., 1 May 1896.
38. Information supplied by York family, 1985.
39. GSS, 25 May 1896.
40. Ashenden, A., interview by author, 1987.
41. GSS, 8 March 1912.
42. GSS, 28 October 1908.
43. Grainger, P., Letters 1901-14, University of Melbourne, Archives.
44. GSS, 30 June 1906.
45. ibid., 25 July 1906.
46. ibid., 1 September 1906.
47. ibid., 13 November 1907.
48. ibid.
49. *Centenary of Gippsland*, Back-to Leongatha Booklet, Leongatha, 1940.
50. GSS, 21 May 1910.
51. ibid., 29 May 1896.
52. ibid., 19 March 1897.

53. *Leongatha Sun*, 6 August 1902.
54. ibid., 18 February 1903.
55. ibid., 25 March 1903.
56. Lands Dept. File, WSHS.
57. *Leongatha Sun*, 15 February 1905.
58. ibid., 1 March 1905.
59. ibid., 10 November 1909.
60. GSS, 5 June 1896.
61. Minute Book, Leongatha Mechanics' Institute, 5 August 1901.
62. ibid., 8 July 1904.
63. GSS, 13 January 1899.
64. GSS, 21 September 1900.
65. *Leongatha Sun*, 22 April 1903.
66. GSS, 20 February 1912.
67. GSS, 12, 29 March 1912.
68. ibid.
69. Minute Book, Leongatha Mechanics' Institute, 8 July 1912.
70. GSS, 12 April 1912.

Chapter Ten

1. GSS, 26 July 1895.
2. ibid., 30 January 1912.
3. Information supplied by Wm Ryan, Wooreen, 1960.
4. GSS, 21 April 1916.
5. ibid., 21 August 1891.
6. *Leongatha Sun*, 22 July 1903.
7. ibid., 8 February 1905.
8. ibid., 6 February 1907.
9. ibid., 13 March 1907.
10. ibid.
11. ibid., 5 June 1907.
12. ibid., 6 October 1911.
13. ibid., 24 October 1911.
14. ibid., 23 February 1912.
15. *Settlement on Lands Act*, 1893.
16. GSS, 8 March 1912.
17. ibid., 2 May 1913.
18. ibid., 18 August 1914.
19. ibid., 20 January 1914.
20. Victorian Parliamentary Select Committee of Inquiry, 1899-1900.
21. ibid.
22. Annual Report, Leongatha Labour Colony, *Journal of Agriculture*, 1912.
23. GSS, 11 March 1913.
24. ibid., 6 October 1914.
25. ibid., 22 July 1913.
26. ibid., 12 June 1914.
27. *Leongatha Sun*, 31 May 1905.
28. ibid., 13 January 1910.
29. GSS, 13 February 1912.
30. O'Donnell, P.M. Rev. Fr., 'History of Catholic Church in Gippsland', Unpublished M/S, Sale, 1937.
31. GSS, 27 January 1914.
32. ibid.
33. GSS, 29 April 1908.
34. ibid., 17 July 1908.
35. ibid., 19 November 1912.
36. GSS, 31 August 1908.
37. ibid., 20 November 1908.
38. *Leongatha Sun*, 20 April 1904.
39. ibid., 17 March 1910.
40. Le Maitre File, WSHS.
41. GSS, 20 October 1906.
42. ibid., 24 October 1911.
43. ibid.
44. ibid., 3 August 1915.

45. ibid., 27 August 1912.
46. *Leongatha Sun*, 3 March 1910.
47. GSS, 20 September 1915.
48. ibid., 7 January 1913.
49. *Leongatha Sun*, 5 May 1909.
50. GSS, 22 March 1912.
51. ibid., 18 November 1913; O'Donnell, P.M., op.cit.

Chapter Eleven

1. GSS, 1 July 1913.
2. ibid., 22 January 1915.
3. ibid., 10 February 1914.
4. Williams, S.J., Interview by author, 1986.
5. GSS, 9 October 1914.
6. ibid., 30 October 1914.
7. ibid., 19 July 1914.
8. ibid., 6 July 1915.
9. ibid., 31 August 1900.
10. Minute Book, Leongatha Mechanics' Institute, 28 April 1913.
11. GSS, 24 November 1914.
12. ibid., 17 November 1914.
13. ibid., 15 March 1915.
14. ibid., 16 February 1915.
15. ibid., 6 August 1915.
16. ibid.
17. ibid., 20 July 1915.
18. *The Leader*, 6 April 1912; Charles, J.R., *History of Tarwin Lower 1798-1974*, Tarwin Lower School Committee, 1974, p36.
19. GSS, 24 August 1915.
20. GSS, 15 September 1915.
21. GSS, 21 September 1915.
22. Minute Book, Woorayl Shire Council, 22 December 1909. Financial Statement Woorayl Shire Council, 1910.
23. GSS, 29 October 1915.
24. ibid., 9 January 1914.
25. Minute Book, Woorayl Shire Council, 20 June 1918.
26. GSS, 26 August 1913.
27. ibid., 30 September 1913.
28. Minute Book, Leongatha Mechanics' Institute, 2 November 1915.
29. Tattersall, J., *History of Leongatha Bowling Club*, 1987.
30. GSS, 26 March 1915.
31. Young, Lynette, *The Melody Lingers On*, Hawthorn Press, Melbourne, 1967.
32. GSS, 16 July 1916.
33. ibid., 8 August 1916.
34. ibid., 18 July 1916.
35. ibid., 18 January 1916.
36. ibid., 4 April 1916.
37. GSS, 3 August 1917.
38. ibid., 16 November 1915.
39. ibid., 13 October 1916.
40. ibid.
41. ibid., 27 October 1916.
42. Statistical Returns, Commonwealth Electoral Office, 1916.
43. Minute Book, Leongatha Mechanics' Institute, 12 August 1916.
44. GSS, 22 August 1916.
45. ibid., 24 April 1917.
46. Minute Book, Woorayl Shire Council, 1 September 1916.
47. GSS, 30 August 1918.
48. ibid., 27 October 1916.
49. ibid., 15 December 1916.
50. ibid., 6 March 1917.
51. Statistical Returns, Commonwealth Electoral Office, 1917.
52. GSS, 25 June 1918.
53. ibid., 13 August 1918.

54. ibid., 4 October 1918.
55. ibid.
56. ibid., 15 November 1918.
57. ibid.
58. Le Maitre File, WSHS.

Chapter Twelve

1. GSS, 10 September 1918.
2. ibid., 4 February 1919.
3. ibid., 7 March 1919.
4. ibid., 11 July 1919.
5. ibid., 23 July 1919.
6. ibid., 6 June 1924; 26 May 1925.
7. ibid., 15 September 1922.
8. ibid., 20 January 1927.
9. ibid., 22 May 1931.
10. ibid.
11. ibid., 17 April 1931.
12. ibid., 4, 18, 25 November 1921, 2 February, 13 April 1923.
13. ibid., 17 January 1922, *Koonwarra*, Back-to Committee Booklet, March 1965.
14. ibid., 18 February 1921.
15. ibid., 24 May 1921.
16. ibid., 15 June 1926.
17. Crombie, Alex, interview by Alan Box, WSHS, 1984.
18. GSS, 14 October 1924.
19. ibid., 18 March 1924.
20. Minute Book, Woorayl Shire Council, 10 February 1921.
21. *Leongatha Sun*, 8 April 1925.
22. GSS, 25 May 1926.
23. Burchell, I., interview by author, 1986.
24. GSS, 21 May 1926.
25. Bair, A.C., interview by author, 1970.
26. *Leongatha Sun*, 3 September 1925.
27. GSS, 1 March 1929.
28. Beaumont, B., Notes on development of SEC in Leongatha District, July 1972, WSHS.
29. Minute Book, Woorayl Shire Council, 19 February 1925, GSS, 25 February 1925.
30. GSS, 16 December 1930.
31. Lands Dept. File, WSHS.
32. GSS, 11 March 1924.
33. ibid., 16 March 1926.
34. ibid., 26 February 1929.
35. ibid., 27 September 1929.
36. Kelly, M., *Victorian Historical Magazine*, Vol. XXXIV, No 1, August 1963, p15.
37. GSS, 24 April 1936.
38. Neilson, John Shaw, *The Autobiography of John Shaw Neilson*, National Library of Australia, Canberra, 1978 p26. Leongatha Cemetery Records.
39. GSS, 14 June 1921.
40. Kemp, D., *History of the Maffra Shire*, Maffra, 1975, p92.
41. GSS, 15 March 1928; Loney, J.K., *Wrecks on the Victorian Coast*, p96.
42. GSS, 30 October 1928.
43. Minute Book, Woorayl Shire Council, 28 July 1926.
44. ibid., 14 March 1930.
45. ibid., 11 April 1930.

Chapter Thirteen

1. GSS, 19 May 1936.
2. Minute Book, Leongatha Caledonian Society, 1933.
3. Davis, F., interview by author, 1970.
4. GSS, 14 June 1932.
5. ibid., 6 May 1932.
6. ibid., 20 January 1927.
7. ibid., 27 March 1936.
8. Bacon, D. (nee McKinnon), interview by author, 1975.

9. Brewster, E., *History of Leongatha Guide Movement*, WSHS.
10. GSS, 1 November 1932.
11. Bowden, K.M., *Early Days of Korumburra*, Korumburra, 1969. p41.
12. Land, Vic., address to WSHS, December 1977.
13. Findlay, D.W. 'Jock', interview by author, 1980.
14. GSS, 18 December 1934.
15. Minute Book, Woorayl Shire Council, 14 December 1934.
16. GSS, 3 December 1935, 2 June 1936, Melbourne *Sun*, 6 December 1935. Bourke, J.P. and Sonenberg, D.S., *Insanity and Injustice*, Melbourne, Jacaranda Press, 1969.
17. GSS, 17 May 1935.
18. ibid., 10 May 1935.
19. Minute Book, Woorayl Shire Council, 9 October 1936.
20. Trotman, L., address to WSHS, 1987.
21. GSS, 3 November 1933.
22. ibid., 25 August 1936.
23. ibid.
24. Trotman, L., op.cit.
25. GSS, 13 June 1933.
26. Smith, Jean, interview by author, 1980.
27. GSS, 16 February 1943.
28. ibid., 19 March 1937.
29. ibid., 19 February 1937.
30. ibid., 28 April 1936.
31. ibid., 24 March 1934.
32. ibid., 12 January 1937, 17 December 1937.
33. ibid., 18 February 1936.
34. Trotman, L., op.cit.
35. GSS, 5 June 1936.
36. ibid., 1 June 1937.
37. ibid., 14 January 1938.
38. ibid., 9 September 1938.
39. ibid., 8 February 1938.
40. ibid., 17 June 1938, 20 September 1938.
41. Minute Book, Leongatha Waterworks Trust, 11 March 1939.
42. GSS, 23 May 1939, 14 July 1939.
43. ibid., 31 January 1939.
44. Boyd, P.M., *A History of Meeniyan 1881-1891*, 1981, p26.
45. GSS, 20 September 1938.
46. ibid., 19 January 1940.

Chapter Fourteen

1. GSS, 25 July 1939.
2. ibid., 21 June 1940.
3. ibid., 4 February 1941.
4. ibid., 2 December 1941.
5. ibid., 6 May 1941.
6. ibid., 9 May 1941.
7. ibid., 16 December 1941.
8. Smith, Jean, interview by author, December 1986.
9. Smith, Clarrie, interview by author, November 1985.
10. GSS, 5 August 1941.
11. Minute Book, Leongatha Sewerage Authority, 29 March 1941.
12. ibid., 18 December 1940.
13. GSS, 16 December 1941.
14. ibid., 24 February 1942.
15. ibid., 30 January 1942.
16. ibid., 17 March, 24 April 1942.
17. ibid., 6 March 1942; Charles, J.R., *A History of Tarwin Lower 1798-1974*, Tarwin Lower School Committee, 1974, p57.
18. GSS, 26 May 1942.
19. ibid., 21 April 1942.
20. ibid., 23 June 1942, 31 July 1942.
21. ibid., 22 September 1942.
22. Lyndon, Ellen, records held by WSHS, 1982.

23. GSS, 25 August 1942.
24. ibid., 6 August 1943.
25. Wisdom, Adeline, interview by author, 1972.
26. GSS, 24 September 1940.
27. Hopkins, Joy, member of Revue Co., interview by author, September 1987.
28. GSS, 1 October 1943, History of CWA, Leongatha Branch, 1931-81.
29. ibid., 24 August 1943.
30. ibid., 16 January 1945.
31. ibid., 28 October 1941.
32. ibid., 6 January 1944.
33. ibid., 6 June 1944.
34. ibid.
35. ibid., 30 July 1940.
36. ibid., 15 June 1943.
37. GSS, 18 February 1944.
38. ibid., 27 October 1944.
39. ibid., 14 March 1944.
40. ibid., 18 August 1944.
41. ibid., 8 December 1942.
42. ibid., 14 November 1944.
43. Records, ANA Leongatha Branch, 1935.
44. GSS, 29 December 1933.
45. Minute Book, Woorayl Shire Council, 10 May 1946.
46. GSS, 21 August 1945.
47. ibid., 3 October 1945.
48. ibid., 16 April 1946.
49. ibid., 12 February 1946.
50. ibid., 12 March 1946.
51. ibid., 19 November 1946.
52. ibid., 23 April 1947.
53. ibid., 1 June 1948.
54. ibid., 13 June 1947.
55. Minute Book, Woorayl Shire Council, 11 February 1949.
56. GSS, 2 February 1951.
57. ibid., 6 August 1946, 24 June 1952.
58. ibid., 4 February 1949.
59. ibid., 10 May 1946.
60. *Leongatha Echo*, 21 May 1947.
61. ibid., 19 March 1947.
62. GSS, 7 November 1947.
63. ibid., 18 February 1947.
64. ibid., 18 October 1946.
65. ibid., 4 November 1949.
66. ibid., 5 May 1944.

Chapter Fifteen

1. GSS, 14 April 1964.
2. Personal recollections of author, 1936.
3. GSS, 13 March 1956.
4. ibid., 15 September 1959.
5. Records, Leongatha Housing Society.
6. GSS, 13 July 1954.
7. ibid., 11 August 1959.
8. ibid., 16 December 1952.
9. ibid., 1 July 1958.
10. Minute Book, Leongatha Sewerage Authority, 25 November 1955.
11. GSS, 6 October 1959.
12. GSS, 29 July 1958.
13. *Victorian Municipal Directory*, 1896.
14. GSS, 14 November 1950.
15. ibid.
16. ibid., 2 September 1952.
17. Minute Book, Woorayl Shire Council, 5 January 1944.
18. ibid., 1 September 1958.

19. GSS, 15 March 1955.
20. ibid., 15 September 1954.
21. ibid., 15 March 1955.
22. ibid., 27 January 1953; Lands Department File, J.S. Clement, 0772/54, 98.56; Shears, Richard, *The Lady of the Swamp*, Melbourne, Nelson, 1981.
23. Records, Leongatha Apex.
24. GSS, 18 December 1962.
25. GSS, 16 February 1954.
26. Records, Woorayl Lodge.
27. ibid.
28. Minute Book, Leongatha Swimming Pool Committee.
29. GSS, 20 December 1960.
30. ibid., 18 February 1958.
31. ibid., 3 March 1953.
32. Records, Leongatha Methodist Church.
33. GSS, 16 December 1958.
34. ibid.
35. Records, Lord Brassey Lodge.
36. Records, Leongatha Presbyterian Church.
37. GSS, 4 November 1969.
38. Records, Leongatha Reformed Church.
39. GSS, 6 September 1955.
40. ibid., 15 November 1955.
41. *Leongatha Echo*, 18 June 1947; Tattersall, J., *History of Leongatha Bowling Club*, 1987.
42. Records, Meeniyan Bowling Club.
43. GSS, 14 November 1961.
44. Records, South Gippsland Racing Club; GSS, 6 October 1964.
45. GSS, 5 April 1960.
46. ibid., 23 March 1965, 19 February 1970.
47. ibid., 6 July 1965.
48. ibid., 23 November 1965.
49. ibid., 14 October 1969.
50. Records, Leongatha Horticultural Society.
51. GSS, 30 June 1970.
52. Personal attendance by author.
53. GSS, 5 October 1954.
54. ibid., 15 November 1966.
55. Records, Leongatha Guides, WSHS.
56. GSS, 15 July 1958.
57. ibid., 31 January 1961.
58. ibid., 11 June 1963.
59. Census figures, Government Statistician.
60. GSS, 16 December 1969; interview by author, 1987.
61. Minute Book, Woorayl Shire Council, 1969-70.
62. GSS, 3 May 1955.
63. ibid., 21 March 1961.
64. ibid., 31 October 1961.
65. Minute Book, Woorayl Shire Council, 9 June 1961.
66. ibid., 13 May 1960.
67. ibid., 20 October 1967.
68. Leongatha Municipal Library Records, WSHS.
69. ibid.
70. GSS, 25 March 1969.

Chapter Sixteen

1. GSS, 13 October 1959.
2. ibid., 18 April 1961.
3. ibid., 13 October 1964.
4. ibid., 12 July 1966.
5. Records, Leongatha Sewerage Authority.
6. GSS, 31 October 1967.
7. ibid., 31 October 1967.
8. ibid., 5 October 1971.
9. Records, Leongatha Waterworks Trust.

10. GSS, 19 September 1967.
11. Records, Tarwin Valley Water Board. Boyd, P., *A History of Meeniyan 1881-1981*, 1981, p27.
12. Records, Wonthaggi-Inverloch Water Board.
13. ibid.
14. *Victorian Government Gazette*, 12 February 1886.
15. GSS, 28 September, 19 October, 26 October 1965.
16. ibid., 13 June 1972.
17. ibid., 1 June 1976.
18. ibid., 8 June, 22 June 1976.
19. ibid., 17 February 1970.
20. ibid., 2 December 1975; Pegler, R., interview by author, June 1987.
21. ibid., 27 May 1958, 15 February 1977.
22. ibid., 9 May 1972.
23. ibid., 21 May 1968.
24. Records, Leongatha Senior Citizens' Centre.
25. GSS, 19 August 1971; Records, WDMH.
26. ibid., 4 March 1975, 3 June 1975.
27. Records, Meals-on-wheels Committee, March 1973, GSS, 9 July 1974.
28. GSS, 2 April 1974.
29. ibid., 29 March 1966.
30. Strazzabosco, I., interview by author, May 1987
31. GSS, 22 March 1966, 27 January 1976.
32. Records, Gippsland and Northern Co.
33. GSS, 15 February 1977.
34. ibid., 28 June 1977.
35. ibid.
36. Census figures, Government Statistician.
37. Records, Wonthaggi-Inverloch Water Board, 1987.
38. GSS, 27 August 1974.

INDEX

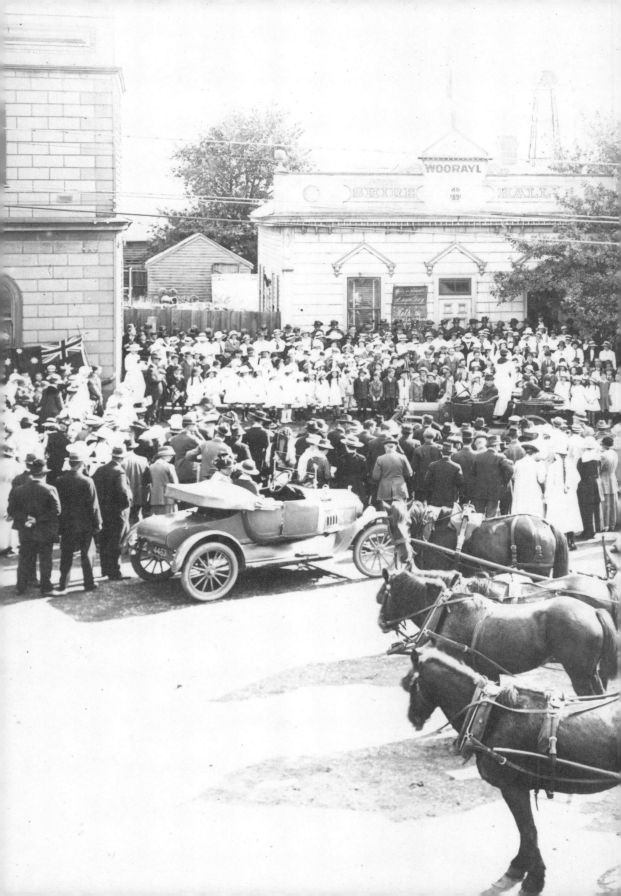